MIDNIGHT IN BROAD DAYLIGHT

A Japanese American Family

Caught Between Two Worlds

D0359315

Pamela Rotner Sakamoto

HARPER PERENNIAL

NEW YORK • LONDON • TORONTO • SYDNEY • NEW DELHI • AUCKLAND

A hardcover edition of this book was published in 2016 by Harper, an imprint of HarperCollins Publishers.

MIDNIGHT IN BROAD DAYLIGHT. Copyright © 2016 by Pamela Rotner Sakamoto. All rights reserved. Printed in the United States of America. No part of this book may be used or reproduced in any manner whatsoever without written permission except in the case of brief quotations embodied in critical articles and reviews. For information, address HarperCollins Publishers, 195 Broadway, New York, NY 10007.

HarperCollins books may be purchased for educational, business, or sales promotional use. For information, please e-mail the Special Markets Department at SPsales@harpercollins.com.

FIRST HARPER PERENNIAL EDITION PUBLISHED 2017.

Designed by Michael Correy

The Library of Congress has catalogued the hardcover edition as follows:

Sakamoto, Pamela Rotner
  Midnight in broad daylight : a Japanese American family caught between two worlds / Pamela Rotner Sakamoto. — First edition.
    pages cm
  Includes bibliographical references and index.
 1. Fukuhara, Harry K., 1920–2015. 2. Fukuhara, Pierce, 1922–2008. 3. Fukuhara, Frank, 1924–2015. 4. World War, 1939–1945—Japanese Americans. 5. Japanese American families—Washington—Seattle. 6. World War, 1939–1945—Japan—Hiroshima-shi. 7. Translators—United States—Biography. 8. Soldiers—Japan—Biography. 9. Japan—Relations—United States. 10. United States—Relations—Japan. I. Title.
  D753.8.S24 2016
  940.53092'356073—dc23

2015017943

ISBN 978-0-06-235194-4 (pbk.)

19 20 21 LSC 10 9 8 7 6 5

FOR MY PARENTS,
SANDRA AND HOWARD ROTNER

Day of spacious dreams!
I sailed for America,
Overblown with hope.

—HAIKU BY ICHIYO,
   from *Issei: A History of Japanese Immigrants
   in North America* by Kazuo Ito,
   translated by Shinichiro Nakamura and Jean S. Gerard

War forced us from California
No ripples this day on desert lake

Cactus field
local train
huffing and puffing

At daybreak
stars disappear
where do I discard my dreams?

—THREE HAIKU BY NEIJI OZAWA, a poet interned at Gila River,
   from *May Sky: There Is Always Tomorrow,*
   compiled by Violet Kazue de Cristoforo

August 6, 1945
midnight in broad daylight
people inflicted on God
a punishment of fire
this one evening
the fires of Hiroshima
are reflected in the beds of humankind
and, before long, history
will lie in ambush
for all those who imitate God.

—EXCERPT FROM SANKICHI TŌGE'S poem "Flames"
   in *Poems of the Atomic Bomb,*
   translation by Karen Thornber

CONTENTS

CONTENTS

CONTENTS

AUTHOR'S NOTE

The true story of a Japanese American family engulfed by war on both sides of the Pacific came to me by serendipity one summer day in 1994. I had recently moved to Tokyo and was attending a press conference for former Jewish refugees who had survived the Holocaust thanks to a Japanese diplomat. The diplomat was the subject of my dissertation. Harry Fukuhara, a retired American colonel with decades of experience in Japan, was accompanying the group as a favor for his travel agent friend. I saw Harry navigate the crowd at the Miyako Hotel, managing American journalists and Japanese diplomats with crystalline Japanese and English. When I remarked to a filmmaker that the refugees had amazing stories, she replied, "If you think their stories are incredible, you should talk to Harry."

Harry and I introduced ourselves but didn't talk further. But when he came back to Tokyo from his home in California a few months later, he invited me to lunch. An extrovert and frequent mentor, Harry met with many on his trips. Over the next few years on his occasional visits, we chatted over cheeseburgers and iced tea. Harry confided his family's story. I realized that there was far more to his account than what the odd newspaper feature had captured.

In late 1998, I asked Harry whether he had ever considered a book as a legacy of U.S.-Japan relations, the Japanese experience in America, and the *nisei* second-generation Japanese American story. His story was remarkable, rare, and unknown. Harry soon arrived in Tokyo and introduced me to his brothers. So began my journey of research and interviews in two countries.

I would comb archives, museums, and libraries across Japan and the United States and interview more than seventy-five people in Japanese or English in both countries. In Tokyo, I discovered Harry's parents' passport applications for the United States and evidence that his father had attended college, an uncommon feat for a poor immigrant. Harry, his younger brother Frank, and I talked over the course of a decade—in coffee shops, restaurants, ferries, and taxis. Most interviews were formal, with my notebook and tape recorder on hand. Others were impromptu conversations. Frank, who was based in Japan, became my travel partner. Harry never wanted to go to Hiroshima, but Frank did not hesitate. When the bullet train from Tokyo whooshed into Nagoya Station, he hopped on, sat beside me, and handed me a homemade lunch. We met relatives on the sacred island of Miyajima, attended his elementary school reunion, and spoke with the man who had once bullied Harry. One autumn afternoon in Hiroshima, we were walking to the family's former home when a woman came running. "*Fu-ra-n-ku*," she called in her singsong voice. It was Masako, a neighbor who had been with Harry and Frank's mother on the day that the atomic bomb exploded; Frank had not seen her for more than half a century. She was bursting with memories.

The home in Hiroshima that Frank and I entered with Masako by our side? The present owners had bought it with its American furniture and fixtures from Harry and Frank's mother; it was a preserved time capsule of the 1930s and 1940s. I was stunned that there were also shards of glass embedded in the stairwell, debris from the atomic bomb blast. Harry and I flew to Los Angeles, where he had lived before he was interned in 1942. At the house where he had worked and been treated as a surrogate son, the subsequent owner still displayed the service flag that Harry's employers had hung in their window when Harry enlisted in the U.S. Army and went to war in 1943. I could not be more grateful that Harry was a packrat. From his disorderly den in San Jose emerged his teenage Japanese diaries, ribbon-tied packets of 1930s letters from friends in the United States, and his Japanese military-training text. He also had a small trove of American and Japanese propaganda and captured letters.

I had first been drawn to this story because I knew little about the internment. When Harry and I visited Seattle and Los Angeles, fellow Japanese Americans at coffee shops would casually ask him, "Which camp were you in?" This was an immediate, indelible bond that few outside this group were aware of. I had wondered how Harry could enlist in a military that had imprisoned him and would then send him into possible combat against his brothers. I had never learned about the tremendous Japanese American contribution to the American war effort. These were compelling reasons to delve into research, but, over time, the story revealed new significance. Above all, it was a tale of tragedy luminous with hope and resilience, a story of abiding love for family. My belief in the power and dimensions of this project sustained me on the lengthy, uncertain path to publication.

As amazing as many of the events may seem, please note that this is a work of nonfiction. No names have been altered, characters created, or events distorted. If a comment appears in quotation marks, it is verbatim from an interview, oral history, letter, or other primary source. I corroborated each vignette with repeat interviews with the source, multiple interviews with others, and historical research. In re-creating scenes of those who were not alive at the time of writing this book, I used a combination of primary and secondary sources. In recollections that have been told before, I went back to the original source, whether in Japanese or English.

Please note that Japanese names are written with the first name followed by the surname. Although the convention is to record Japanese names with the last name preceding the first name, there are so many Japanese American names in this book that I chose consistency to avoid confusion.

There are stories we stumble upon in life that are so rich with delicious details, imbued with meaning, and resonant with epic events that they can consume a writer. I have been entranced by this looking glass into the past. I wish the same for intrigued readers.

Pamela Rotner Sakamoto
Honolulu

PROLOGUE: SHOCKWAVE

山雨きたらんと欲して風楼に満つ

San-u kitaran to hosshite kaze rō ni mitsu

When strong winds begin to blow, showers cannot be far behind.

Nothing seemed amiss that first Sunday in December 1941. Ponytailed beauties strolled the boardwalk, bodybuilders paraded for show at Muscle Beach, and children shrieked aboard the Whirling Dipper coaster as it clattered over the metal track at the Santa Monica Pier. The day was young, the nation placid, and Christmas was just a few weeks away. No one could have guessed that at that moment, 2,500 miles across the Pacific, Japanese planes were zeroing in on military installations throughout the island of Oahu.

So it was that sometime before noon, a twenty-one-year-old gardener working in the scorching sun had no cause for alarm when his employer emerged from the shade of her house. He stopped the mower to catch her words. "Harry," she said, "Japan has attacked Pearl Harbor."

"Oh, is that so?" The news meant little to him. He nodded and the woman returned inside.

When she reappeared a short time later, he was puzzled. She said, "Japan has invaded Pearl Harbor."

"That's terrible." Harry didn't know what else to say. He had never heard of Pearl Harbor. Was it a bay fed by the Pearl River in China, where Japan had long been at war? He vaguely remembered a headline about an American ship sunk by the Japanese there a few years earlier.

The woman paused. "I think maybe you should go home."

"Why?" Harry asked and added without thinking, "I had nothing to do with it."

She stiffened. "Japan has invaded the United States." When Harry hesitated because he hadn't finished the job, she fired him. Stunned, he loaded his mower into his Model A Ford and drove home to Glendale fourteen miles away.

Harry had been let go before—at the end of a harvest picking peas and strawberries in Washington State. But this departure, from a normally friendly employer for whom he worked regularly, had struck out of the blue. Much later, he would recall feeling "wounded," as if a knife had drawn beads of blood without warning.

ON THAT SAME MORNING, FOUR THOUSAND MILES from Pearl Harbor, a seventeen-year-old high school student named Katsutoshi walked from his house to the local train station in Takasu, an affluent district of country homes in greater Hiroshima. He passed wooden and ceramic-roof-tiled homes set back from the street, the post office staffed by a newlywed woman who loved to gossip, and the police kiosk manned by officers intent on prowling the neighborhood. In the haze of sunrise, Katsutoshi, blurry with sleep, saw the station platform awash in khaki and indigo. Soldiers, shouldering rucksacks, paced back and forth, and housewives, dressed in bloomers, huddled, clutching empty duffels.

Katsutoshi did not blink at the scene. Soldiers were always coming and going in Hiroshima, a major port of departure for the war in China. Women, too, were on the move daily, but they were traveling to black markets in rural areas, where they hoped to scrabble up radishes, pumpkins, and sweet potatoes for dinner. His mother often made this trek as well.

Nothing seemed amiss. The day was young, the nation long at war, and New Year's a few weeks away. Katsutoshi was conscious only of his extravagance. He wasn't supposed to take the train to school, but he had a track meet that morning and didn't want to tire himself out before his twelve-mile race. He patted his calves, stretched his hamstrings, and stood on his tiptoes to limber up.

As the train rumbled into the station, Katsutoshi moved toward the edge of the platform, peering for a spot inside the crammed coach. Above the din of the screeching wheels, he heard someone yell from behind. Before he could look for the source, the train doors opened. He jumped on, and the train rattled toward the city. The coach was quiet. All the way to school and during his race, lap after lap, he kept turning over in his mind the phrase that he had caught in passing. It had to have been garbled, or had he really heard "our victorious assault on Hawaii"?

A FEW HOURS LATER, HARRY AND KATSUTOSHI returned to their respective homes, in Glendale and Hiroshima, still thinking about how little they understood about the day's events. Harry, in a grass-stained T-shirt and jeans, joined his employers, Clyde and Flossie Mount, for whom he worked as a live-in houseboy. The sun poured through a leaded glass window in the living room. Outside billowed an American flag.

Katsutoshi, in his sweat-stained uniform, folded his legs beneath him at the low table in his mother's *tatami*-matted sitting room, where a hibachi brazier offered scant heat and the paper window screens flattened the pallid sunlight. Kinu had left a few panels open, through which he caught a glimpse of the garden with its spinney of persimmon, loquat, pomegranate, and fig trees. A crimson camellia blossom hugged the side of a weathered stone basin.

ON THIS DAY THE RADIOS, CRACKLING WITH static, consumed each household's attention.

After Katsutoshi had left the house early that morning, Kinu had been puttering in the kitchen when a naval hymn blared forth from loudspeakers positioned throughout the neighborhood. "Defend and attack for our country," roared a soldier. Kinu, chills coursing down her back, had turned on her radio.

The Mounts, too, had their first heart-clenching moment when they heard Stephen Early, the White House press secretary, step to the microphone for a live broadcast. In a clinical tone, he had said, "A Japanese attack upon Pearl Harbor naturally would mean war. Such an attack would naturally bring a counterattack, and hostilities of this kind would naturally mean that the President would ask Congress for a declaration of war."

By the time Harry took a seat at their table, they had begun digesting the news and considering the consequences. The white-haired, middle-aged couple, longtime teachers, looked at Harry, whom they regarded as a son. "This is going to bring up all kinds of problems," Mrs. Mount said even before Harry shared the news of his abrupt job dismissal.

A LOW-GRADE SENSE OF DREAD DESCENDED OVER Kinu and Katsutoshi in their corner of Hiroshima. Nothing unsettling had yet occurred, but the future held little promise. There would be more fresh-faced recruits marching to the port to be dispatched to the front, greater rationing of essentials, and more mass funerals for the soldiers who would return in a year's time as cremated bone and ashes. Kinu thought of her four sons, who were draft age, and Katsutoshi of his brothers.

The next morning, Kinu opened her local *Chūgoku Shimbun* newspaper to a stream of jubilant headlines from official Japanese news sources throughout the Pacific. "Surprise attacks" had stunned "every direction," including the "first air raids on Honolulu"; Singapore was "under bombardment," as well as foreign military bases at Davao, Wake, and Guam. In Shanghai, the British fleet had been "sunk," while the American one had "surrendered." Japanese raids were pummeling Hong Kong and the Malay Peninsula. Kinu, trembling, put the newspaper down and waited to confide in her son.

The Japanese headlines were accurate; Allied forces were struggling to repel Japan's lightning attacks and stunning advances. In Washington, President Franklin Delano Roosevelt was wheeled into Congress, where he invoked in his inimitable baritone, "a date which will live in infamy." His entire speech lasted little more than seven minutes. Within an hour, Congress passed a declaration of war, with all but one dissenting vote. On Oahu, where the battleships moored at Pearl Harbor listed, smoldered, and burned, the tally of sailors, soldiers, and civilian deaths would soon surpass 2,400.

IN THE AFTERMATH OF PEARL HARBOR, A location of which he now had no doubt, Harry took a fountain pen to paper. Back in Hiroshima, Kinu dipped her horsehair brush in *sumi* (ink). Both wrote urgent letters to the other in vertical lines of intricate, cursive Japanese characters. Harry rushed to the post office en route to his part-time job and college courses. Kinu handed her envelope with its tissue-thin contents to Katsutoshi, who had, at an earlier age in a world apart, gone by the name of Frank. He ran to the Japan Red Cross, a concrete monolith near the copper-domed Industrial Promotion Hall close to the T-shaped Aioi Bridge downtown and the only place now accepting enemy-nation mail. Kinu prayed that her instructions to Harry, the only one of her sons still in America and Katsutoshi's dearest brother, would be delivered.

PART ONE

AMERICAN BORN, BICULTURAL BRED

昔の剣今の菜刀
Mukashi no tsurugi ima no na-gatana
Fortune is made of glass.

1

At Home in Auburn

O nce Harry made a decision, he rarely looked back. The injustice was minor, but it scratched the eight-year-old boy's pride that afternoon in 1928. Dashing from his house in Auburn, Washington, he pedaled his bicycle over the backyard grass, crunching onto the gravel lane. He raced to West Main Street and, three blocks later, clattered over the Interurban railroad tracks, avoiding the live third rail. When he reached the West Valley Freeway, he sped toward Seattle. The metropolis lay a formidable twenty-two miles away.

Harry bumped over the two-lane highway, where dense evergreens cast shadows over his path. Occasionally, a roadster rumbled by, splattering mud. Harry pedaled harder.

The road, offset by a leaden sky, rose and fell before him. When the waning sun broke through the White River Valley's cumulus clouds, shafts of light lightened his journey. As he coasted down inclines, he caught the scent of cedar and a whiff of rain, never more than a cloudburst away.

The farther he traveled, the more convinced he became that his impromptu plan would succeed. He was certain he could hide out at his friends' house. After that, he didn't know what would happen. When he began to recognize the rolling farmland outside Seattle, his spirits soared.

By the time Harry reached the Bitows' house, it was long after dark. As soon as he ground to a dirt-spewing halt, Mr. and Mrs. Bitow ushered him inside and dialed his father, their close friend. Harry had an inkling that they had been alerted in advance and were waiting by the window all along.

A short time later, Katsuji Fukuhara stood holding his bowler hat and bowing before the Bitows, apologizing for Harry's insolence in showing up uninvited. His father's humility was practiced etiquette but Harry couldn't dismiss how grim his father looked. He roped his bicycle to his dad's Buick and slumped into the backseat. The rush of adrenaline was long gone; his legs and shoulders were beginning to throb. Yet he felt buoyed by his daring jaunt. His parents now understood the strength of his resolve.

Secretly, he was relieved to return home. His mother wouldn't greet him with open arms and tears of relief; Japanese parents were not demonstrative. But the corners of her mouth might crinkle when she filled his rice bowl, set his favorite *takuan* pickled radishes on the table, and ladled him a generous helping of *miso* soup. His kid brother Frank would sit wide-eyed by his side, while Harry sank his chopsticks into his dinner.

Katsuji did not lecture or punish Harry that night. Perhaps, he concluded, miles of bumping over brick pavement was agony enough. Surely he breathed easily that Harry, who had once walked in circles for hours until he found his way home from school after dark, had not become lost on unfamiliar roads. But if Katsuji reckoned that Harry would regret his impulsive behavior, he was underestimating his son's optimism, resilience, and penchant for adventure. Harry's bicycle sprint to imagined freedom would not be the last time that he escaped in order to come home.

.   .   .

HOME WAS AUBURN, A TOWN LATTICED WITH railroad tracks and berry and vegetable farms, a pocket of the White River Valley at the foot of glacial, snow-capped Mount Rainier. Japanese farmers were drawn to the valley, in part because it reminded them of the landscape of Japan, and cloud-swathed, volcanic Rainier of Japan's most sacred peak, Mount Fuji. The immigrants called Rainier "Tacoma's Fuji" and lovingly translated the valley's name into Japanese. *Shirakawa.* The soft syllables rolled off their tongues, like a whisper with a finger to the lips, for someplace intimate and empyreal.

Auburn itself, population five thousand, was a young town, born the same month and year as Katsuji, in February 1886. It soon shed its original name Slaughter, in memory of a Lieutenant William Slaughter killed in an Indian uprising, when the unwelcoming moniker became the butt of local jokes. The name Auburn, a nod to a stately New York cousin, gave a gloss of worldliness. As the western frontier was settled at a furious pace, Auburn hitched itself to progress, vying for railroad routes. By 1020 steam whistles punctuated the air as up to 180 trains—from the Seattle-Tacoma Interurban Railway, the Northern Pacific Railway, and the Milwaukee Road—hustled through town each day.

Katsuji, who had been at one point Katsuji Fukumoto, had also shed his name. By the time he reached Auburn, he was, to Americans, Harry K. Fukuhara—Harry because it was accessible and easy to pronounce, K for Katsuji, and Fukuhara his rightful surname. Katsuji's father in Japan had loaned out the once-noble name in return for funds to defray a debt. When the duration of the loan was up, the name reverted to the family. Both Katsuji and Auburn aspired to a prosperous future.

Yet, in 1926, the same year that the Fukuharas moved to town, the Northern Pacific pulled out of its Auburn terminus.

Meanwhile, Japanese dairy farmers, with whom Katsuji had recently opened a creamery, were abandoning their plots due to plunging milk prices. Katsuji held his ground as the local economy slowly soured.

Nothing struck Harry as amiss. He loved Auburn. Chilled bottles of fresh milk topped with cream left outside the front door before dawn. The crunch of a tart Gravenstein apple plucked from the Fergusons' tree next door. Salmon flopping on the front lawn when the White River flooded. An inner-tube ride down Easy Canyon Stream, the sockeyes' coral scales shimmering in the sunlight. The perfume of ripe strawberries wafting from the loamy soil on Japanese farms. The gentle touch and steady beat of cool drizzle. Harry's images were as collectible as snapshots from the new, pocket-sized Kodak Vanity camera taking the nation by storm.

Harry was an American citizen by birth, born in Seattle on January 1, 1920. His mother, Kinu, had left the pristine island of Miyajima, outside Hiroshima, at eighteen to wed Katsuji in 1911. For a picture bride—her marriage was arranged in Japan, her knowledge of her husband limited to a photograph—learning English was an afterthought and never came easy. She could not quite master her r's, rolling them in her mouth like marbles. "Harry" sounded a lot like "Hurry."

"Hu-ri!" Kinu called from her kitchen perch, glimpsing her son, as skinny as a somen noodle, loop out the front door to meet his friends waiting outside. Catching her voice before the door banged shut, he replied, "Itte kimasu," "I'm going but will come back," a proper goodbye before leaving Japanese courtesy behind.

As tall as his Caucasian friends, Harry had straight bangs, a direct gaze, and oversize ears with elongated lobes. In Japan, this size and shape were esteemed: fukumimi (ears of happiness) augured prosperity and good fortune. At least, Harry's parents assumed that he would be able to hear well, and, maybe, when he was older, would listen. Harry disregarded the lore but his mighty ears did come in handy when he twitched them to his friends.

The boys took a hard right on to Main Street, with its packed-dirt thoroughfare, brick and shingled storefronts, open lots, and the guarantee—not necessarily available elsewhere—of the glories of electricity. They were headed to the Mission Theater, the local nickelodeon. Harry, who had a penchant for serial westerns with the lone cowboy pulling the trigger on Indians in a saguaro-spiked desert, didn't care what was playing. What mattered was that he was with friends. Neither he nor his pals jingled much change, but, even if they had, they would have pulled their regular stunt.

One boy purchased a ticket and entered the theater legally, walking upstairs to the men's room and opening the window, ostensibly for fresh air. The rest of the group headed to the back of the building, where a metal pole rose from the ground to the roof. One at a time, they shinnied up, crossed the roof, and dropped to the men's room via the open window. There was one hitch: the roof turned slick in the rain. One slip and a boy would crash to the solid earth two stories down.

The risk, Harry had decided, was worth the reward. He sank into a plush seat, the warmth of the dark theater washed over him, and he surrendered to a double feature. Sometimes Charlie Chaplin bumbled across the screen in loose shoes, baggy pants, cane, and derby hat. In Hollywood, the actor was tearing up the Great White Way, cofounding United Artists, and producing and directing popular films in which he starred. But what Harry savored most was the idea that Charlie Chaplin was his father's friend.

Katsuji had first met Chaplin through the actor's longtime Japanese aide, Totaichi Kono, who hailed from the same rural Hiroshima district. Every time he visited Los Angeles, Katsuji saw the actor, who, he told his rapt children, kept his iconic costume in a glass case. In a photograph, Katsuji and Charlie, roughly the same age and height, in their early forties and about five feet five inches, stood wearing wool blazers accented by silk handkerchiefs, and knife-creased, light trousers. In front of the camera they appeared as equals. But they were not remotely equal before the law.

Though they were both immigrants, Katsuji—who had a head start on Chaplin, having arrived in the States a decade before, in 1900—didn't land far from the bottom of the immigrant heap, inflating to more than 14 million between 1850 and 1930. America was changing rapidly, xenophobia flared, and the issue of citizenship turned on color. It always had.

In 1790, Congress had restricted naturalization to an alien who was a "free white person," thereby excluding slaves. Almost a century later, in 1870, five years after the Civil War, former slaves became eligible for citizenship. But Japanese nationals, who had first legally immigrated to Hawaii in 1868, were, like the Chinese, excluded. By the early 1920s, more than twenty-five thousand legal immigrants from Hiroshima lived in the United States, more than from any other area in Japan. Yamaguchi and Kumamoto prefectures sent many immigrants, too. They were all aliens in a foreign land.

Although *nisei* (second-generation) children like Harry and his siblings were citizens because they were born in the United States, their immigrant *issei* (first-generation) parents continued to be rebuffed. In 1922, the Supreme Court, in *Ozawa v. U.S.*, stated that *issei* were "aliens ineligible to citizenship."

Harry sat entranced by the comedian on the silver screen.

Just as his dad and the dashing Chaplin shared a friendship, so did he with his buddy Elgin, a rugged blond football player. When it came to best friends, nothing, he figured, would ever come between them.

DURING THE WEEK, HARRY AND HIS BROTHERS attended the Washington Elementary School, a short walk off East Main Street. Harry, though he preferred play to study, skipped two grades. He developed an enduring crush on Helen Hall, a lithesome blonde who sat in front of him in the back of the room. When he tugged her long, wavy hair, Helen giggled, all the more reason to pull it again.

Harry cast a wide berth around the stern principal, Flora Holt. Mrs. Holt was not receptive toward Japanese American students, who comprised 20 percent of the school's population. Her attitude set the tone at a time when teachers wielded fierce authority, often rapping their charges with rulers. Katsuji, the rare *issei* influential in community affairs, took note.

Generally, Harry blew into the house late, calling out breezily, "*Tadaima!*" "I'm home!" He ran by the formal living room with its Japanese ceramic figurines, the love seat with the kimono-silk pillow, and his mother's mahogany Monarch piano. He had forgotten to remove his metal-soled shoes and, despite Kinu's reproof in Japanese—"*Hu-ri!*"—he clanged up the stairs.

In the attic bedroom where the bedposts touched, Harry confided to his brothers Pierce and Frank about sneaking into the Mountain View Cemetery at night to gape at Auburn twinkling below. Cautious like his mother, Pierce was awed by Harry's exploits but had no desire to partake. Frank, the baby, four years younger, who looked up to his big brother, couldn't wait to take the exhilarating journey with him. He never wanted to be left out.

Frank couldn't imagine a better brother. He called Harry by his first name in English and switched to the honorific "*Onisan*" ("elder brother") when he spoke in Japanese. He felt especially fortunate to have Harry as his eldest brother since, in the sibling hierarchy, oldest brothers were generally serious, responsible, and dull. Not Harry, who dragged Frank in a red Radio Flyer wagon up and down the street and balanced him on the edge of his bike seat for heart-thumping rides down steep hills. Harry agreed that Frank and Pierce were lucky to have him. The three boys, it seemed, had forgotten about their other two siblings Mary and Victor who had been absent from family life for their seminal early childhood years, having been sent to live with their wealthy maternal aunt in Hiroshima. Victor, the eldest, was brought to Japan at age five in 1919, before Harry, Pierce, and Frank were born. In 1923, Katsuji deposited a baffled seven-year-old Mary, too.

Kinu believed the time abroad was for the good of their eldest children. She stressed to Katsuji how important it was to start them early so they could attain native fluency in Japanese. Otherwise, it would be impossible to catch up with the three written alphabets, including the two thousand *kanji* (Chinese characters) required to be functionally literate. Kinu was too busy to instruct Victor and Mary herself. Katsuji grudgingly admitted that even paying room and board would be cheaper than providing for the children in the United States—so favorable was the exchange rate and low the cost of living in Japan.

Kinu dreamed of the day Mary, draped in a heavy ivory silk kimono embroidered with golden cranes, would follow her groom with mincing steps. After the ceremony, the young bride would don a lace wedding gown, its gauzy veil trailing on the floor, and stand next to her tuxedoed mate. She would lead a gratifying life as a *yoki tsuma, tsuyoi haha,* or good wife and wise mother, in the United States. A Hiroshima girls' school diploma would bolster her chances of finding a suitable mate—of Japanese descent, of course.

Kinu and Katsuji could not envision Victor's future unless he obtained a proper Japanese education. Racial discrimination toward Americans of Japanese descent was so pervasive that even a *nisei* who graduated summa cum laude from a university could not find a job. At the time a Stanford representative remarked, "Many firms have general regulations against employing them; others object to them on the ground that the other men employed by the firms do not care to work with them." A representative at the University of California, Berkeley agreed: "It seems a tragedy that these intelligent men should spend four years in college to find there is no market for their qualifications. Isn't there some channel through which they could be informed?"

But if Victor were truly bilingual—literate, polite, and adept in calibrated cross-cultural situations—he might secure a post with a Japanese trading company or consulate. Katsuji hoped that all his sons would graduate from college, ascend the professional ranks, and purchase their own homes. He had attained white-collar status and attended some college, but a sheepskin diploma and a land deed remained beyond reach; he had run out of money to complete school, and *issei* were prohibited by law from buying land. When Katsuji and Kinu sent their firstborn youngsters five thousand miles from American shores to be immersed in all things Japanese, they were thinking ahead.

Nor were they alone. In 1929, almost four thousand *nisei* Japanese Americans attended elementary and middle schools in Hiroshima prefecture. So common was the practice that the Nippon Yusen Kaisha (NYK) Japan Mail shipping line printed farewell postcards with steamship photographs for passengers to fill in their departures. Unlike a daily trek to school, the two-week-long Pacific commute involved homestays with relatives that stretched into years.

Harry, Pierce, and Frank saw a few photos of Victor and Mary, but the association did not register. The nearly toothless toddler wearing a jaunty conductor's cap and striped knickers on their Seattle front stoop? The girl with a giant bow in her bobbed hair and a beaded necklace standing with Harry, Pierce, and their parents? Those children must have been distant relatives from Japan. The younger boys' photos multiplied over time, displacing the few photos of their siblings, who slipped unnoticed between the album pages.

The boys continued to stand for formal portraits, Frank always maneuvering to end up next to Harry. To the photographer's consternation, Harry couldn't keep a straight face, the accepted Japanese pose. The older he got, the wider he grinned. When Kinu and Katsuji examined the studio shots—taken at some expense with the intention of sending to relatives in Japan—they winced at the irrefutable proof that their middle son, in particular, was turning one hundred percent American.

They agreed that Harry must embrace not only his American birthright, but also his Japanese heritage. At an age when he could have been boarding a ship for a lengthy stay in Japan, his parents considered his defiant nature and penchant for running away. They sent him to a local Japanese school instead.

After school and on Saturdays, for five years straight, Harry climbed the eighteen steep steps of the Auburn Buddhist Church, a shingled, pitch-roofed box with an ornate lacquered portal. Deaf to the dreams of the *issei* who had scrimped and saved to construct this building, Harry hesitated at the entrance.

At the last minute, he sauntered into the classroom and bowed to the *sensei* (teacher), who nodded perfunctorily and filled the blackboard vertically right to left with rows of multistroke characters. Harry watched everyone copy the letters in their Japanese composition notebooks, the strike of pencils punctuating the silence. He followed in due time, pausing to stretch his legs, daydream, and stare out the window.

The *sensei* drilled his wards in reading, composition, penmanship, dictation, and, above all, grammar. The children were expected to master three alphabets, including the *kanji* ideographs. The Auburn Buddhist Church, like other schools dotting the West Coast and Hawaii, had undertaken an ambitious program to incorporate American courses under the auspices of the Japanese Education Association of America: "The goal to be attained in our education is to bring up children who will live and die in America, and as such, the whole education system must be founded upon the spirit of the public instruction of America." To this end, Harry was subject not only to Japanese geography but also American history. Everything, of course, in Japanese, including singing "Auld Lang Syne."

Harry found the spartan emphasis on Japanese discipline alienating. Monica Sone, who attended Japanese school in Seattle, recalled the rigid expectations. "We must talk and walk and sit and bow in the best Japanese tradition." Having to address the *sensei* in honorific language, use the humble form of verbs for himself, march in unison, sit straight-backed, and bow at a precise forty-five-degree angle felt stultifying to this buoyant young man.

He rebelled from the start. "With no amount of persuasion did I want to have anything to do with the school or the language." Harry was not the only student among 150 strong who disliked Japanese school, but he was the most determined to reject it. Allergic to authority, he held his nose and swallowed, despite his distaste. He didn't play hooky, protest, or disrupt class. He staged a passive rebellion. "I made no attempt to learn." It wasn't easy to avoid comprehending what he could intuitively absorb. But, gradually, Harry fulfilled his own exquisitely low expectations. "My Japanese," he said smugly, "was zero."

Harry knew more than he was willing to admit. He spoke Japanese with his mother and her friends, greeted Japanese dignitaries who paid courtesy calls on Katsuji, and jumped between English and Japanese without a glitch. He tripped over some words when reading and skipped some strokes when writing, but he flung spoken Japanese like a native speaker.

Harry's parents did not call attention to his abominable academic performance. The *sensei*, though, placed responsibility for Harry's poor performance squarely on his shoulders and failed him every single year. Harry repeated second grade annually, developing into the biggest, tallest, and most notorious student in the class. He took sheepish pride in this distinction.

Katsuji kept a bemused distance, leaving most family matters to Kinu. In the mornings, Kinu rose in the pitch dark, stoked the wood-burning stove, and cooked by kerosene lamp. The boys awakened to a warm house and the aroma of baking bread. When they stumbled downstairs, their mother called out, *"Ohayō Gozaimasu!"* "Good morning!" She was making peanut butter sandwiches for lunch and planning a Japanese menu—grilled fish, steamed rice, and stewed vegetables—for dinner. On special occasions, the rich scent of roasting Cornish hens and syrupy apple pies with butter crusts perfumed the air. In her spare afternoon hours, Kinu taught *nisei* girls *ikebana* (flower arrangement), the *koto* (zither), and *shamisen* (lute). She took piano lessons on her polished Monarch. In the evening, Kinu set Katsuji's place at the head of the table with a fork and chopsticks, but his seat usually remained empty. Scraping her pots and pans in the dark, Kinu, as vital as oxygen to her household's harmony, was the last to sleep.

The children would rarely remember their father at home. He was constantly working. Katsuji had risen from hard-bitten railroad worker to houseboy to co-owner of an employment agency to a self-employed entrepreneur with his own shingle, "H. K. Fukuhara Co.," and offices in Seattle and Auburn. He sold fertilizer, insecticide, and life insurance, largely to Japanese farmers. He also worked with them to decipher the byzantine legalities of real estate and mortgage loans.

Katsuji never ceased to be active in community affairs. He had served for close to two decades on the board of Seattle's Hiroshima *kenjinkai* (prefectural association), a support group for Hiroshima immigrants to share experiences and advice, and financially support one another to surmount the ever-lurking catastrophes of illness, death, or economic ruin. In his few short years in Auburn, he had galvanized the town's Japanese Association. He would soon become the first Japanese selected as a trustee of the Auburn Chamber of Commerce, taking a seat alongside his established neighbors J. W. Meade and I. B. Knickerbocker. "When will your father become the mayor of Auburn?" Harry's friends would tease.

Harry could have interpreted the comment as a cruel joke. An elected position was out of the question for those who could not vote. Forever a legal alien, Katsuji still believed in setting an example for his children: a Japanese could succeed in a white man's land, and all Japanese should bear their ethnicity with pride. One day when Harry blurted out, "I wanted to get a different name, not Fukuhara," Katsuji reddened at his son's shame. In truth, Harry said, "the last thing I wanted to be was a Nisei." Katsuji stiffened and clenched. Harry thought that his father might strike him. Katsuji stormed from the room instead.

Perhaps the gap between any immigrant and his American children is, at some point, inevitable. Katsuji never spoke of

Harry's affront. He redoubled his focus to provide for his family. Across the West Coast, many an *issei* couple lived by the mantra, *"kodomo no tame ni,"* for the sake of the children. This drive to diligence was powered by the hope that the *nisei* second generation, accorded the privileges of citizenship, would succeed where the parents could not.

The summer of 1929 found nine-year-old Harry ebullient, rooted, and happy in Auburn. Under clear skies, the sun sparkled, the salmon spawned, and Mount Rainier's wildflowers bloomed in vivid profusion. In the morning, he played with his friends; in the afternoon, he attended Japanese school, his requisite dose of cod liver oil. In the evening, he bid his parents good night—*"Oyasuminasai"*—only to form a tipi with blankets and regale his brothers with ghost stories in English about the Muckleshoot Indians who speared salmon from their canoes on the Green River.

Auburn Day, an annual two-day festival, began on August 9 that year. Harry didn't take into account that his father had labored for months after work, coordinating several Japanese groups' efforts to contribute to the state's oldest holiday and the town's most important civic event. Hearing Katsuji cough into the night, Kinu fretted that he was becoming exhausted, but he persisted, telling an *Auburn Globe-Republican* reporter, "There will be many surprises," adding, "The Japanese are anxious to do their bit in making the celebration a success and the parade will be interesting."

The festivities began with fireworks, organized by the Japanese Association of Auburn, followed by a lengthy parade. A float of a majestic ship, with the Stars and Stripes fluttering on its bow and a Rising Sun rippling on its stern, sailed down Main Street. Fourteen Japanese girls dressed in kimonos sat on deck beneath a wisteria-draped arbor; paper lanterns swayed above.

One of many displays sponsored by the local Japanese community, this extravaganza won first prize.

Harry and his brothers, dressed in formal black silk kimonos embossed with the Fukuhara triple-clover crest, marched behind the floats. Katsuji followed, dignified at the wheel of his waxed Buick festooned with ribbons running from roof to radiator. He smiled and waved to the crowd. Harry, clopping down Main Street in *geta* (clogs) with Frank scrambling to keep by his side, relished the audience, even though he would rather have been casting a fishing line in shorts than sweating in a kimono.

The next night, Harry and his brothers gathered at the Interurban train depot, where two thousand paper lanterns, the cost defrayed by Japanese organizations, were distributed to the town's children. As many as ten thousand people, more than double the town's population, waited along Main Street for the spectacle to begin. Holding their candlelit lanterns, Harry, Pierce, and Frank made their way with friends into the velvety night.

The boys, who were thrilled by the crowd's awed hush and the lanterns' flickering lights, didn't recognize how reminiscent the event was of a Japanese military procession or a ceremony paying homage to the emperor.

All Harry knew was that Auburn glittered as his Ptolemaic universe. He was certain that his future held many more Auburn Day celebrations—shining with amusements, chock full of friends, and sustained by his parents and brothers, especially little Frank. His future was American, albeit with a Japanese twist, in the adored town he called home.

2

Hiroshima Sojourn

ater that summer, five-year-old Frank and his mother boarded an NYK steamer at Smith Cove in Seattle, bound for Japan. As Frank leaned over the promenade railing and reached for the streamers, his father watched from the pier three stories below. The ship horn bellowed, the funnel coughed black smoke, and the steamship pulled away from the pier. Frank was taking his first, but not last, trip across the Pacific.

After two weeks on heavy seas and travel by train across western Honshū, the main island of Japan, Kinu and Frank reached Hiroshima, renowned for its five-story white castle surrounded by a moat clotted with lotus blossoms. Once a sleepy castle town, Hiroshima had burgeoned into a modern city during the Sino-Japanese War, when it had served as an embarkation point for China-bound troops in 1894. By 1929, it was the seventh-largest city in Japan, with a population of more than 270,000. Frank leaned into his mother's side, astonished by the press of people rushing through Hiroshima Station.

A driver roped their steamer trunks to the car while Frank peered through the window at kimono-clad shoppers emerging from the cluttered storefronts of two-story wooden buildings. There were no sidewalks along the narrow streets. Pedestrians picked their way among soldiers, for, even in peacetime,

Hiroshima was a military center. Bicyclists competed for space with rickshaws, pulled by lean men in *fundoshi* (loincloths), and oxcarts, tugged to market by farmhands in coarse *aizome* (indigo-dyed) shirts and loose trousers. Squat buses with blunt hoods muscled aside smaller vehicles. The noise from truck horns, bicycle bells, and slamming brakes overwhelmed the boy. He leaned closer to his mother.

This sense of barely controlled chaos, of a mass of people moving within a constricted space, arose from Japan's mountainous geography, in which most of its population settled along the coasts. Hiroshima was no exception—bounded by the Seto Inland Sea and bordered by the Chūgoku Mountains. The car passed through the city center, crisscrossed by catenary wires spitting electric-blue sparks. Streetcars, a technology for which Hiroshima was famous, clanged inches from Frank's hand.

The car turned on a quiet residential street near a river and groaned to a halt before a long, low-lying, dark wooden house. They had reached their destination, the home of Kiyo Nishimura, Kinu's sister and the undisputed family matriarch. For the next few months, Kiyo, a bold woman for any age and culture, would play hostess to the Fukuharas.

At first glance, Kiyo looked prim. Puffy cheeks and a weak chin highlighted her plain features; her narrow, hooded eyes gave her a skeptical air. But the moment she spoke, Kiyo attracted attention, her speech bursting with exclamation points. Proper Japanese women lowered their heads, averted their eyes, and brought a lily hand to the mouth when they murmured. Not Kiyo, unless it served her purpose.

Seven years senior to Kinu, Kiyo was the fourth of eight siblings; her middle-child birth order did not constrain her. At age forty-four, Kiyo didn't have many soft spots, but one was reserved for her self-effacing, modest, and deferential sister Kinu.

Opposites in personality, the sisters were bound to one another at heart.

Kiyo ushered her tired travelers inside and directed maids in starched aprons to serve tea and bean sweets. While his mother and aunt gushed in Japanese, catching up where their letters had left off, Frank wandered out back. He passed beneath bamboo bird cages of chirping canaries in the outer hall and came upon an expansive, manicured garden, where a swept path led to a pond teeming with crimson, alabaster, and golden carp.

After Frank had returned to the grand *tatami* hall where his mother and aunt sat, Kiyo called for two people named Katsumi and Hisae. Two teenagers appeared. Frank looked up at a boy with a shaved head and glasses, wearing a dark, high-necked, brass-buttoned, military-style uniform, and a girl, her hair in pigtails, in a navy-and-white sailor dress. Frank had no idea why these strangers, with their scrubbed faces, broad cheekbones, and gentle eyes, peered at him with interest. He struggled to understand what his aunt was saying in her staccato Japanese. The solemn teenagers bowed, and then it dawned on Frank. These students had American names, too: Victor and Mary. They were his brother and sister, whom he was meeting for the first time.

FRANK MAY HAVE BEEN SURPRISED, BUT NO one was more incredulous than Mary. She had been waiting for this moment for so long—six years to be exact—that she could not actually believe it. Mary had thought that her family was moving back to Japan, and she had been sent ahead to avoid falling behind in her education. When no one arrived and the years stretched on, her anxiety had heightened. "My parents fooled me," she concluded. But as her mother bowed and gazed at her daughter, Mary shelved her resentment. She rejoiced: "When mother came back, we were so happy to see each other."

No one else in the extended Fukuhara family had ever mentioned moving back to Japan; why Mary believed so is unclear. By all accounts, Kinu never intended to deceive, mislead, or disappoint her only daughter. At every stage she had considered what was best for Mary, though Kinu and Kiyo were at odds over that very matter.

KIYO POSSESSED A SINGLE OBSESSION: HER BUSINESS, Meijidō, one of the largest and most venerable traditional sweet shops in western Japan. She had started it alone in the early 1900s out of her home. A few years later during the Russo-Japanese War, Kiyo was hired by city hall to prepare *manjū* (cakes filled with bean-paste jam) for the emperor's visit to Hiroshima Castle. She rolled up her kimono sleeves, dipped her hands in rice flour, and molded rounded pastries. Emperor Meiji deemed them ethereal. Praying for generous compensation, Kiyo settled for ten vertical wooden tablets that recorded the honor that the emperor had bestowed upon her.

Kiyo hung those panels outside her door, and they proved more valuable than bullion. The imperial seal of approval lured more customers than she could have imagined. Kiyo assiduously cultivated every one. She opened a shop and extended its premises. By 1927, Kiyo was one of the first merchants in the exclusive Hondōri Street shopping district to incorporate her company. Her three-story Western-style building dwarfed most of the other two-story storefronts on the street. Kiyo opened a branch in the nearby entertainment quarter; depending upon the season, she employed anywhere from forty to a hundred in staff.

Every morning, Kiyo pulled her hair into a tidy chignon,

dressed in a lustrous silk kimono with the help of her maids, and stood inside the entrance of her Hondōri headquarters. "*Irasshaimase*," she welcomed her customers in a lilting voice. Bowing deeply, Kiyo guided them over the earthen entryway. In the dark, cool display space, for there was no refrigeration, the sweet fragrance of boiled *azuki* (red beans) mingled with the bitter aroma of unsweetened chocolate. On any given day, Kiyo offered custard-filled cream puffs; meltaway chocolates; chewy caramels; whipped-cream layer cakes; golden *castella* (sponge cake), which had come to Japan by way of Portuguese merchants several hundred years earlier; and seasonal desserts made from sweetened sticky rice and bean paste. Like fruit flies hovering over sugar, clients placed their orders, to be delivered fresh in *furoshiki* (cloth-wrapped) bundles on the appointed day by Mei-jidō's army of uniformed bicycle couriers.

Kiyo reveled in her confectionary empire. Several years earlier, in 1925, the Hondōri merchants had commissioned their first light fixture to illuminate the district at a time when electricity was a curiosity. Ninety-eight electric light-bulbs were welded to cast-iron poles to form elegant arches of *suzuran* (lily-of-the-valley) flowers. When the switch was pulled, Hondōri was transformed into a garden of incandescence. The district expanded shopping hours until eleven at night, customers flocked to the stylish kimono and clothing shops, and couples strolled to restaurants on romantic dates. Meijidō's sales soared. The luminous crystal blooms cast Kiyo at the center of what was regarded as the largest and brightest venue in western Japan.

Kiyo had only one problem: she was childless and in need of an heir. Her first husband, it was whispered, had infected her with a sexually transmitted disease, perhaps syphilis. Kiyo had survived the illness but been left barren. The family was scandalized, and her marriage ended in divorce after less than a year. That she could never have children was her great personal tragedy.

By the time Kiyo married her second husband, Tokichi, in 1910, she was an elderly twenty-four. All her relatives in Hiroshima knew about her search for a successor. At one time or another, there had been many contenders. She was seeking someone with culinary skills, accounting acuity, marketing genius, boundless energy, and superior salesmanship. As picky as she was imperious, she had steadily eliminated all the candidates. As they came of age, Mary and Victor had caught her eye. The children were sensitive, intelligent, and honest. They seemed to expect little of Meijidō, whereas Kiyo's other nieces and nephews craved her sweets and riches. That her sister Kinu's children may have longed for America, Kiyo did not consider.

Victor and Mary were also popular with their Hiroshima relatives. Cousin Takehiko, one year older than Victor, had spent five years on and off at Meijidō, attending school nearby, and eating sweets in the restaurant on the second floor. Victor was usually by his side. When the cooks wouldn't let them pounce on what was cooling on the trays in the kitchen, they headed for the tins of leftovers. The boys were, Takehiko recalled, as close as brothers though polar opposites. Victor was "very kind," "excessively diligent," and "passive," Takehiko remembered. "He was the type who would make a mistake, become very quiet, and lower his head."

By contrast, Mary chose to confront situations that she should have let pass. After all, a girl raised in Japan was supposed to be reserved and submissive. But Mary felt sorry for Victor, alone in Japan before she arrived. He was too docile for his own good. "People would pick on him, and I used to fight for him," she said. Whether he wanted her to or not. Her outspokenness extended to school, where she gained a reputation as a brash "Yankee" and a bully. She was so different from Victor, who seemed to have lost his English, turned Japanese, and fled from his American past.

Standing beneath her *noren* (shop curtain), Kiyo coolly observed Mary and saw something of herself. Although most of Meijidō's delectable perishables were prepared in-house to her exacting standards, she ordered some name-brand items, like Morinaga candy bars and Meiji Seika milk caramels, directly from the national candy makers. Kiyo constantly had to negotiate contract terms with hard-bargaining salesmen. Mary's forthright attitude would be an advantage in a male-dominated business.

Kiyo also concluded that Mary appeared *modan* (modern) or chic. When she wasn't wearing her school uniform, Mary walked tall and dressed stylishly. In a nod to the Art Deco rage, kimono makers were producing bold designs with geometric patterns dyed in primary colors. The fashionable women who bought them wore their hair short and coiffed, not in a bun. Mary wouldn't need to wear pigtails, in accordance with school regulations, much longer. When she graduated in a year, Mary could have her hair permed in a soft wave and dress in a dazzling contemporary kimono.

If Mary's spoken Japanese was just a bit off-kilter, Kiyo thought, well, Japan was changing. Etiquette was no longer as formal and rigid. When Kiyo crossed the street, she caught snatches of conversation—children calling their parents a casual "Mama" and "Papa," instead of the distant honorific *Okāsan* "Mother" and *Otōsan* "Father." Mary's occasional sprinkling of English when she couldn't come up with the appropriate Japanese words might pass as exotic, even au courant.

Victor would be the man behind the scenes much like Kiyo's

husband, Tokichi. Tokichi had lost an eye to an enemy bullet during the Russo-Japanese War in 1905 and was grateful to Kiyo, for Meijidō provided him a livelihood and a glass-eye replacement, which he partially hid behind wire-frame glasses. Their arranged marriage was not a love match. Bald with a rotund face, Tokichi may not have been dashing but he proved to be smart, dependable, and hardworking.

Every morning before six, Tokichi roused a dozen or more workers who boarded upstairs at Meijidō, with his booming baritone. "Let's wake up, let's wake up," he called, pacing the first floor. Cousins Takehiko and Victor, snoozing on futons on the second floor, hurried to get ready for school. Takehiko found his uncle's good cheer at that ungodly hour unwarranted, even "strange." How was it that during the course of a long day, Takehiko wondered, the man rarely tired? While Kiyo occasionally vanished to supervise the second homes she was building, Tokichi toiled in the industrial-sized kitchen, managing the growing staff.

When Tokichi did leave the premises, he loaded his Harley-Davidson sidecar with wrapped boxes and delivered Kiyo's best-selling *senbei* (rice crackers) and *kaki yōkan* (persimmon-flavored bean jelly). Rumbling down the dirt lanes of Hiroshima, the motorcycle created a racket. Startled residents slid back their *shōji* (latticed paper window screens) and glimpsed the portly master of Meijidō, riding his imported mechanical wonder. As the mistress of Meijidō, Kiyo never deigned to appear at her customers' doors, but Tokichi considered his personal service a marketing event. Regardless of the occasional theatrics, Tokichi was essentially a gentle soul, much like his nephew Victor.

In 1929, when Victor was fifteen and Mary thirteen, Kiyo hatched her plan to adopt them. She trusted that her sister would agree. As long as they worked hard, Mary and Victor were assured a life of servants, fine homes, and bulging profits stored in the sturdy safe of a venerable bank down the street—a more prosperous existence than most Japanese in America.

For the first time, the worlds of urban Meijidō and rural Auburn threatened to collide. A short walk north from Hondōri Street, the grounds of Hiroshima Castle bustled with carpenters hammering barracks, trucks unloading weapons, and recruits in training. Five thousand–plus miles away, Kinu and Katsuji, consumed by the demands of making ends meet and raising a young family, didn't have the leisure to ponder corporate heirs or evolving global politics. That is, until they caught wind of Kiyo's project. Kinu had hurried to Hiroshima expressly to retrieve their children. She loved them no less for having lived with them so little. "No, I didn't give you my girl," Mary remembered her mother saying in defiance of Aunt Kiyo. "She's the only girl I have."

Kiyo could not reply. Kinu had every right to take her children. Instead of arguing, the women made plans for Kinu's visit. Any tension between them evaporated as frost under the morning sun. Kiyo would seek other heirs.

In the coming weeks, Kinu made the rounds of relatives, taking the thirty-minute ferry ride to the island of Miyajima, where most of her family still lived. In Miyajima, the mountains dropped to a bay. The Itsukushima Shrine, one of the nation's most ancient, stood on pillars; its towering vermilion *torii* (gate), with its base partly submerged by the sea, was lapped by waves when the tide rolled in. Kinu walked among the tame deer loitering on the sandy grounds near the ferry entrance, dug for clams at the beach, watched from afar the classical dancing in the shrine's gilded open chambers, and listened to the twang of her favorite *shamisen* and *koto* performed by court musicians. Returning along cobblestone paths to her family's homestead, she feasted on oysters grilled over hibachi braziers and gathered strength for her return voyage.

Kinu would need every ounce of fortitude she could summon. After waiting so long for her parents to rescue her, Mary was torn about leaving Hiroshima. It was the only place she knew well, and she had grown accustomed to her aunt doling out affection with shiny coins and frosted sweets. She was distraught at the idea of separating from her cousin Tazuko, her loyal confidant. She was unsure of what lay in store. Most of all, Mary had yet to come to grips with how to forgive her mother for sending her to Hiroshima in the first place.

Kiyo, who thought now only of pleasing Kinu, was determined that Mary leave Japan with proof of the proper Japanese education that she had come such a distance to obtain. She bribed Mary's principal to let her graduate early. Merely a small gift to the *sensei*, Kiyo told her niece in a conspiratorial whisper. When Kiyo handed Mary the certificate with the official seal, she blanched with shame. "I bought my graduation diploma by money." The counterfeit certificate would haunt her forever.

THE DAYS ON THE CALENDAR FLUTTERED BY with gatherings and farewells. On the date of their autumn departure, Mary and Victor boarded the steamship tense with excitement and trepidation. Like their parents decades before, they were leaving from Yokohama, where the briny breeze augured a fresh start. Their knowledge of life across the Pacific was limited: they recalled Seattle's Japantown, where they once had lived, but Auburn was nothing more than a foreign word. Their recollections of their father were faint and they didn't really know their brothers at all. Victor and Mary did, however, know something about Japanese superstition. Legend had it that if, at the time of one's departure, snow-wreathed Mount Fuji were visible, the passengers would someday return to Japan. Frank, who was watching the steamship streamers snap in the wind, was too young to be aware of the significance of the shifting weather. Mary, who was the only one in a position to remember later, did not note the occasion. When the mist swathing Fuji cleared, her mind was too clouded to care.

3

Growing Pains

The ship docked at Smith Cove in Seattle in early November 1929. Kinu and Frank plus two filled Katsuji's Buick. There wasn't enough room for Harry and Pierce, who had been left at home.

The family headed south, passing Japantown, with its signs in both Japanese and English, and the immigrant neighborhood of Beacon Hill, where Kinu had delivered her children at home with the aid of a Japanese midwife. They entered the countryside, bouncing on the brick West Valley Highway, fragrant with the scent of pine, fir, and spruce that brought back *natsukashii* (nostalgic) memories of their mother's and Aunt Kiyo's Miyajima.

Berry and pea fields unfolded before Mary, but she did not see many people. When they entered Main Street in Auburn, she felt disappointed. No *suzuran* lily-of-the-valley lights brightened the dingy November sky. No women in brilliant kimonos rushed from doors decorated with swaying blue-and-white *noren* curtains. No streetcars announced stops with bells and a clamor. Auburn didn't glitter; nor did it beckon.

When her father turned the car down East Street Southwest, Mary's interest was piqued. Victorian homes, adorned by frilly porches, sat back on spacious lawns. Katsuji rolled to a stop across the street from the Knickerbocker mansion. He

pointed to a one-story, maroon-and-cream bungalow with a cement front stoop. A bay window covered by a matching striped
canopy was its nod to extravagance. Over the years in Japan
Mary imagined her father as an up-and-coming mogul. But this
functional A-frame on a pocket-square lawn made a mockery of
that fantasy.

Harry and Pierce rushed to the car to greet everyone. Fifteen-
year-old Victor bowed to nine-year-old Harry and seven-year-
old Pierce, brothers he was meeting for the first time. They
didn't remember Mary even though they once knew her. The
introductions were stiff. The siblings were strangers.

Mary watched Harry, Pierce, and Frank charge up the front
steps and disappear inside, the screen door banging behind
them. She was appalled by their coarse behavior. The boys had
not removed their shoes. For all her sassiness, Mary had spent
six years in a rarefied Japanese household. The boys should
have placed their shoes neatly by the front door, toes pointing
outward for stepping into with graceful ease later. Clearly, she
would be living with barbarians. And Harry was the ringleader.

Meanwhile, Harry and Pierce were miffed. Sent to stay with
their family friends the Bitows and enrolled in a different school
while their mother was away, they had been waiting for three
months for her to return. "It seemed like a long time," Harry
said. He did not grasp that his experience paled in comparison
to what his elder brother and sister had endured for years. Although the Bitows were his runaway refuge, once he had been
forced to stay with them, all he had wanted to do was "get out
of there."

If the two sets of siblings had been able to communicate, they
might have bonded at their shared experience. But the teenage
pair spoke mostly Japanese and the younger trio largely English.
Mary and Victor were now *kibei—nisei* educated in Japan who

had returned to America. *Kibei* often seemed, by dint of their years abroad, more Japanese than American. So different in mien and perspective, the two sets of siblings appeared to have little in common.

Mary was given her own room on the first floor, prime real estate, while the four boys, including Victor, slept cramped in the attic. After having enjoyed her pick of quarters in Aunt Kiyo's three homes, Mary couldn't suppress her disappointment with her room. "I was a spoiled brat," she admitted.

Kinu struggled to keep up with the cooking, laundering, and housekeeping in a snug house with five children. Harry was satisfied simply to have her back, but Mary was dismayed that their mother seemed distracted. She had hoped to make up for their lost years together. "I was hungry for my mother's love."

Mary, who had never lifted a finger in Hiroshima, was deaf to Kinu's pleas to help in the house. When she complained about her chores, her parents scolded her. "They used to tell me that I was born mouth first, then head." Kinu and Katsuji had assumed that Mary would grow—under Japan's civilizing influence—into a compliant young lady. They were mistaken. The difficulties of merging the two sets of siblings into one harmonious family were complicated at best.

Yet by the end of the month the family rejoiced. Katsuji had again helped pull off a civic triumph. The Japanese Association of Auburn was donating six custom light fixtures, featuring an iron eagle perched atop a crystal globe, for the joint elementary, junior high, and high school campus. At the dedication ceremony in the high school auditorium, the school superintendent, C. E. Beach, compared the lights to the Statue of Liberty. The *Auburn Globe-Republican* newspaper reported that each lamp was "a tribute to the friendship of foreign citizens for American people."

Katsuji took to the lectern. He did not point out that many immigrants wanted to become naturalized Americans but could not. According to the newspaper, Katsuji explained that the lamps were given in "gratitude for what Auburn schools were doing for the American-born Japanese in the community." The school board president formally accepted the lights, and another Japanese speaker stepped to the podium: Henry Tatsumi, a local Japanese teacher who had fought for the United States during the Great War. The veteran urged young *nisei*, wrote the reporter, "to be ready to serve when called upon in wartime or peace."

Harry, sitting with friends in the auditorium, was proud of his father's prominent role and fluent English. Mr. Tatsumi's sentiment seemed inappropriate to the occasion; the man's earnest words fell on deaf ears.

THANKSGIVING ARRIVED IN THE AFTERGLOW OF THIS fund-raising success. Kinu rose early to roast a turkey and bake an apple pie, the aromas wafting through the house. Katsuji took his seat at the head of the table, and Kinu served him first, followed by Harry. When everyone had a full plate, the family blessed the meal in the secular Japanese fashion. "*Itadakimasu.*" "I humbly accept."

The boys began to eat with gusto, but Mary sat stunned. Their mother should have served Victor, her eldest child, first after her husband. They had been away too long, Mary concluded. She and Victor often felt excluded, as though they were on the outside looking in. Harry, ravenous and oblivious, ate with abandon, while Mary seethed on Victor's behalf.

Mary still wanted to be part of her family and presumed her rightful place in the hierarchical order so instinctive in Japan. As the eldest sister, she had the right to discipline her younger brothers. Frank became her most frequent target. Mary ordered him around, but he rarely obliged, mostly because he couldn't understand her Japanese. Besides, as the youngest in the family, he exploited his pampered position. "Everything I say, I get," he remembered thinking. Mary tried to baby him, again her prerogative. In the morning, she marched up to the attic to carry him downstairs. He recoiled when he heard her coming. Frank had no desire to cuddle when he could run, preferably after Harry.

Mary was less enamored with Harry. She had spent more than enough time around him already. Every morning, she and Victor walked to school with Pierce and Harry. But instead of parting at the campus entrance, with Victor and Mary heading to the junior high for ninth grade and seventh grade respectively, they followed their younger siblings into the Washington Elementary School. In the middle of the term, they had been assigned to Pierce's class, owing to their broken English. Victor, Mary, and Pierce were all second-grade students.

By default, Harry became his siblings' *senpai* (superior)—two years ahead, frolicking through fourth grade, running by them at recess, playing with his white friends. Mary and Victor brooded alone. For their homeroom picture, they stood in the back row, towering over their classmates, conspicuous and glum.

Mary detested school. At the time, knowing another language was not considered an advantage. Her hesitant English further undermined her fragile confidence. Overnight, the thirteen-year-old had gone from writing essays in two phonetic syllabaries and one complex ideographic system to poring over the challenges posed by a mere twenty-six-letter alphabet. Writing, erasing, and rewriting, Mary struggled with the mysteries of English grammar. Recovering her latent English and bringing it up to speed was as slow and clumsy as performing ballet in a sandbox.

Spelling was one problem, pronunciation another. Tsuyoshi Horike, another *kibei* from the Seattle area, recalled how difficult it was to mouth basic combinations. "The f in food, the r in rice, the th in mouth, and the difference between u and a in bug and bag, were impossible for me to pronounce." Mary and Victor had to train their tongues to move differently, without, of course, the benefit of speech therapy. Even when they answered questions correctly, they were not sure whether they were understood.

The curriculum, too, confounded. The Pilgrims, the founding fathers, the first president of the United States. American history was unfamiliar. Cultural anecdotes like George Washington and the cherry tree were hard to believe, although they had been fed a diet of equally questionable myths in Japan, such as Momotarō, the tiny boy who emerged from a peach pit so strong and fearless that he ventured to an island of demons and single-handedly squashed them. Mary carried a load of books home, intent on learning the new information by heart, without questioning its veracity. At least memorization was a skill that she had mastered in Hiroshima.

Mary knew that her parents, while overjoyed to have her back, regarded her as a "rebellious tomboy." Indeed, Kinu was determined to reform her only daughter. The Japanese word for wife—Mary's expected future—was *kanai*, meaning, literally, in the home. Kinu purposely kept her there. "If you are a Japanese lady," Mary remembered her mother repeating, "a woman has to stay in the house."

Mary hated mending clothes with the tiny, precise stitches her mother required. Seeking a diversion, she asked if she could go to the Methodist church where the boys attended Sunday services. Kinu said no. Mary couldn't understand why *Okāsan* didn't let her walk to Main Street. "I felt like a bird in a cage," Mary remembered.

She began to long for the freedom she enjoyed in Hiroshima. She had become accustomed to making small decisions herself—whether to catch a streetcar from school with Tazuko, how long she could wander Hondōri Street at dusk, and how much pocket money she could spend on treats. Aunt Kiyo had not showered Mary with affection, but she was generous. Stopping on occasion to purchase a soy-soaked, grilled *senbei* cracker from a street vendor, Mary relished reaching for change without hesitation.

Mary compared her mother and aunt. She had never forgotten watching her aunt cross the street one day and pause when a woman, dressed in clothes too shabby to withstand the winter, struggled against the blustery wind. Kiyo removed her fur coat and placed it on the woman's shoulders. Yet her own mother was always pinching pennies to save for the boys' college tuitions, leaving nothing for her only daughter, let alone a stranger. "My mother was so tight, you know. My aunt was big-hearted."

If her parents perceived her as "spoiled," as Mary suspected, they had only to blame themselves. Childless, career-driven Auntie Kiyo had no idea how to raise children. "Why did you take me to Japan?" Mary cried in anguish. "Why did you leave me at Meijidō?"

In the throes of adolescence and culture shock, Mary tried to sort out her feelings. Lately, she had overheard that she had been born earlier than expected when her mother had been visiting Japan, and her father had paid off an American lawyer to draw up a birth certificate. American immigration officials could have regarded Mary as a foreigner since she was born on Japanese soil and prevented her from entering the United States at a time of stringent quotas. Where did she belong?

And, if she seemed confused and petulant in Auburn, it was partly because she had not been nurtured in Hiroshima. At her proper girls' school, Mary had been chosen the chief cheerleader at the *undōkai* (track meet), an annual school-wide celebration of physical fitness. This honor attested to her vocal gifts and leadership potential and gave her a chance to shine in front of Aunt Kiyo. Students prepared for months, running practice races on the school grounds, forming teetering human pyramids, and performing synchronized dances. As the anticipated day grew closer, they decorated the campus with strings of national flags, staked bold striped canopies for protection from the sun, and placed high-backed chairs for VIP visitors in prominent locations.

On the appointed morning, students leaned out of the classroom windows, and parents and friends stood around the track. Mary strode to the center of the school grounds in a *montsuki* (formal-crested kimono). Dozens of girls dressed as samurai turned in unison to face her. In a loud, clear voice, Mary initiated the proceedings. The band struck up its music, and the samurai clapped, stepped, and swayed to flutes, cymbals, and drums. The event was off to an auspicious start. Mary scanned the crowd in vain for Aunt Kiyo. Finally, she spied one of the maids, who had been sent to cheer instead. By the time that everyone broke for lunch, the maid was gone. While her classmates picnicked with their families, Mary ate alone.

This lapse in her aunt's attention was hardly an isolated occasion. Later in the year, Mary took the stage as a lead in the school play. In the dark, she searched the audience for Kiyo, who once again was absent. The audience's applause was not enough; Mary craved her aunt's interest and approval. For all those years abroad, she gulped back her disappointment, but when she got back to Auburn, she directed her pain toward her mother. Kinu was blindsided.

The steady drone of Mary and Kinu bickering resounded through the house, competing with the boys' banter. Kinu, regarded as calm and caring by almost everyone who knew her, rose to Mary's bait and redoubled her efforts to tame her impetuous child who was born, not surprisingly, in the Year of the Dragon.

All across the West Coast and Hawaii, similar scenes were playing out in homes where thousands of *kibei* struggled to re-acquaint themselves with their families. There was no name for this dysfunction, no support group, no prognosis. Families muddled through the misunderstandings, the frustrated *kibei* feeling alienated, the baffled *nisei* siblings discomfited, and the chagrined parents praying that time would heal the heartache.

The demands of the holiday season were a welcome dis-traction. After Christmas, Kinu began pounding and molding glutinous *mochi* (rice cakes), symbolizing strength and purity. She set aside most of the cakes for meals, but stacked two large round ones, topping them with a tangerine, to form a *kagami mochi* decoration, which represented the family's hope for a fruitful new year. Cutting pine branches and bamboo, Kinu set a *shōchikubai* (pine-bamboo-plum blossom) arrangement, embodying discipline and endurance, on the front stoop. She placed a small dish of salt at the entrance to symbolize purity, imbuing every tradition with hope.

On New Year's Eve, Kinu served a late supper of boiled *soba* (buckwheat) noodles to dip in a soy broth. As the family slurped the salty noodles, Kinu stood satisfied: the noodles' length sig-nified longevity, an appropriate ritual for crossing over into a new year. Surely, she had covered every base, ensuring her fam-ily's safety, prosperity, and welfare.

Yet for all the wishful activity, faithful traditions, and ap-peased superstitions, the Fukuharas would soon be engulfed by a storm. On October 28, 1929, forever known as Black Monday, the Dow Jones Industrial Average plummeted 13 percent in one day after dropping all autumn. Over the next three years, the stock market crash destroyed the domestic economy, upending lives and obliterating good fortune. The tempest traveled westward. The Great Depression would darken the White River Valley, Auburn, and East Street Southwest, too. Like millions of American households, the Fukuharas would struggle to hold on.

4

The Great Depression

Striking at the worst possible time with the onset of winter, the economic downturn added greater uncertainty to *issei* farmers' already precarious existence. Farming had always been a risky business: weather wreaked havoc, crops failed, market demand fluctuated, and prices vacillated wildly. Perennially short of cash, the farmers generally borrowed money in the winter to pay back after the harvest when their crops went to market. Now the banks had stopped lending.

The *issei* farmers had worked incessantly to attain a semblance of economic stability. They had transformed ragged stump-lands, which had been denuded for lumber, into fertile fields that counted among the state's most productive farms, growing 75 percent of the area's vegetables. They cultivated a cornucopia of cauliflower, cabbage, carrots, radishes, lettuce, and berries, in addition to producing half of the region's milk at well-tended dairy farms. Yet highly discriminatory state laws permanently circumscribed their opportunities.

The Washington Alien Land Law, enacted in 1921 with the *issei* in mind, prohibited those ineligible for citizenship from buying or leasing land. Aspiring landowners were reduced to being tenant farmers, tilling for whites. "*Shikata ga nai.*" "It cannot be helped," they said as they continued to toil from dawn to midnight while quietly purchasing land in the names of their American children, who would legally cultivate the plots upon turning twenty-one. But in 1923 an amendment passed, in the wake of the devastating 1922 Supreme Court decision denying *issei* citizenship, which eliminated this loophole. Malcolm Douglas, the prosecuting attorney for King County, encompassing the White River Valley, vowed to pursue violators with zeal. If he proved successful, he proclaimed in the *Auburn Globe-Republican*, he would drive Japanese from the county.

Douglas's anti-Japanese sentiments echoed local history, dating as far back as 1893, four years after Washington became a state. When *issei* first appeared in the White River Valley to labor on white-owned farms, the *White River Journal* had proclaimed, "STOP THE JAPS." A year later, it sounded the same note with "THE JAPS MUST GO."

The recurring scourge of sensationalistic yellow journalism aside, over time no form of discrimination would prove more fatal than government-mandated legislation. By 1925, the number of Japanese farms in the state fell to 246, from 699 five years earlier; total acreage dropped almost two-thirds, from 25,340 to 7,030 acres. Farmers hung up their shovels and trudged back to the railroads and logging mills, relegated to rock bottom pay. Shoved off the ladder of American upward mobility, heartbroken farmers, one *issei* lamented, were "swallowing their tears."

By the time Katsuji moved to Auburn in 1926, his largely *issei* clientele represented a shrinking market. Their only weapon against anti-Japanese legislation and an unpredictable economy was renewed diligence. Every day after school, the farmers' denim-clad children crouched and labored in the fields. So industrious were the families that Rev. Daisuke Kitagawa, an Episcopal minister in the White River Valley, commented, "I used to make all my pastoral calls right in the fields." Although he had *hakujin* (white) clients to whom he sold New York and Northwestern Mutual life insurance, Katsuji's future was chained to these indefatigable immigrant families. If they stumbled, he too would fall.

Unable to afford electricity, the farmers hunched over their kitchen tables at night, balancing their books by the light of kerosene lamps. As long as they could, they would truck their produce to Seattle's Pike Place Market, where they commanded 70 percent of the stalls. Katsuji helped clients translate contracts from English into Japanese and extended credit at 8 percent annual interest so that they could purchase life insurance.

Keeping track of accounts largely in his head, Katsuji penned loose notes as personal reminders, not bothering with specific dates, counting on goodwill more than a firm contract. An anxious winter melted into a promising spring, pink apple blossoms fluttering across the fields carried by a sweet-scented wind. The mild weather, however, did little to mitigate the economic tailspin. In 1930, more than 4.5 million Americans stood out of work, and the number would continue to swell to 8 million by the end of the year.

Some bright spots appeared that tremulous new decade. Katsuji became the first Japanese trustee to serve on the Auburn Chamber of Commerce, joining nine white trustees at a polished boardroom table. His neighbor I. B. Knickerbocker presided as president; another neighbor, J. W. Meade, also held a seat. Katsuji was proving a valued bridge between the working-class *issei* community and the middle-class white establishment.

That summer, he succeeded in dispatching Flora Holt, the elementary school principal, to Japan to tame her ill humor. Summer days in Japan ran thickly humid; in minutes, even the most starched cotton looked like rumpled linen. But Katsuji would prevail because he had Kiyo to play his cupid. The mistress of

Meijidō whisked the irascible educator to her country estate and ferried her to her sisters' homes in Miyajima. If Flora Holt had ever doubted that Japan was an ancient and refined civilization, her disdain evaporated on the moss-carpeted paths of the island village. By the time school resumed, the spell had set. Students noticed the difference. Harry was astonished by Mrs. Holt's transformation. "She went out of her way to be accommodating to the Japanese community."

THAT YEAR, KATSUJI SENT HARRY AND PIERCE to the Salvation Army Fresh Air Camp for *nisei* boys on the banks of the Green River for two weeks. At the rustic camp, the boys built a shack devoted to a traditional Japanese bath, which they made out of a fifty-gallon metal drum. They planned their meals around rice. Most of the campers came from Seattle's Japantown and lived above their parents' storefronts in tenement-style wood or brick dwellings; their parents saved all year long for these summer sessions. The children of White River Valley farmers did not go to camp because their parents needed extra hands in the fields. Coming from Auburn, Harry and Pierce were an anomaly. Their friend Ray Obazawa, who hailed from Seattle, was amazed when Katsuji and Kinu roared up in Katsuji's gleaming Buick for a visit. "Their wallet folds had money."

Up until this point, Harry had socialized mostly with his white peers, avoiding fellow *nisei*. At Fresh Air Camp, he discovered how comfortable he was with others who also juggled two cultures. Whether it was plucking the jaw harp, his new-found hobby, or steaming rice for his tent mates, this sense of ease within his community would never leave him.

BY 1931, THE DEVASTATING IMPACT OF THE state's anti-Japanese legislation, passed in 1921 and 1923, hit hard. Almost all the valid leases that had been concluded before the legislation was enacted were due to expire that year, leaving only 927 and a half acres belonging to *nisei* children. Some of this paltry acreage was already escheated, while other portions were litigated. No more than 10 percent of *issei* farmers were expected to continue to farm the land they had nurtured for decades.

Katsuji was affected, too. Stricken farmers weren't buying insurance policies, though he continued to fund his own. Struggling to hold on, many men became tenant farmers in order to stay with and provide for their families. They needed fertilizer, which Katsuji supplied as well. He took his clients' word that they would pay him a percentage of profits when their crops came in, adding their names to his growing list of outstanding receipts.

Early that year, the Chamber of Commerce and the Auburn Japanese Association hosted two Japanese teachers. Katsuji must have been heartened by the bicultural support, but when he went to pick them up, he found the burgeoning shantytown near the Port of Seattle disturbing. Homeless men were living on vacant, rubble-ridden, swampy grounds in one-room shacks hammered together with whatever they could get their hands on—nail-pocked plywood, musty corrugated cardboard, and splintered fruit crates. Even if the teachers and their host turned their heads away to avoid looking at the shantytown, they could not escape the smell of sewage.

There were growing numbers of homeless in Japan, too. The nation had descended into what officials called the "dark valley" of a gripping depression. The overall mood was grim, and the government was beginning to mobilize resources in a lockstep march toward war. The window for hopeful trans-Pacific understanding was closing.

By the time a new school year was under way, war would erupt in distant Manchuria. On the evening of September 18,

1931, a group of restive Japanese Imperial Army officers, with the tacit knowledge of their superiors, staged an explosion on the tracks of the South Manchurian Railroad near Mukden, the capital. The railroad was administered by the Japanese government, and the incident provided an excuse for the army to invade Manchuria. The bogus provocation commenced Japan's "fifteen-year war." Hiroshima, with its instrumental logistical port, took on a war footing. Katsuji's deft international exchanges ended abruptly.

Japan's bellicose behavior did not register with Harry, who was eleven, thoroughly confident of his American identity, and too young to be interested in foreign affairs. The Great Depression, however, resonated. It was spreading beyond his school desk and outside his front door. On the first day of school, Harry made it a habit to check who had new shoes. Some of his classmates were placing cardboard inside their shoes to cover the holes. Another girl had stopped attending school because she had no clothes other than her mother's single baggy dress. School began providing milk and three-cent "potato blanket" lunches to indigent students.

And then the Pacific Commercial Bank, the biggest Japanese bank in Seattle, went bankrupt. One *issei* recalled that "for several days afterward you could not hear the 'ching' of the cash registers in Japanese stores. It was as if the fire had all gone out, and some people couldn't make their living anymore." Vacancies followed, said another, "one by one, like teeth dropping off a comb, and gradually the district went into decline."

Without money to pay the loans on their flatbed trucks, purchase fuel, or buy seeds and fertilizer, the farmers' straits tightened. Some gave up, letting vegetables rot in the fields. Others who were more enterprising collected the salvageable crops, then pickled and conserved them. Katsuji and his clients conferred by back doors. The intimacy and trust remained. A handshake or bow, a promissory note, and a bushel of radishes later, Katsuji returned to his trusty Buick. The tubers wouldn't pay the rent, but Kinu would boil and simmer them. Increasingly, Harry, rushing out of the house to see friends, noticed burlap sacks of produce by the stairwell in partial payment.

By 1932, Auburn was reeling from the Depression. Many residents were out of work. Moreover, the freight trains that rumbled to and from Seattle overflowed with hundreds of hoboes and the unemployed, toting bedrolls, seeking work wherever word of mouth and a hop on a train took them. Some in search of odd jobs disembarked in Auburn.

HARRY BECAME INCREASINGLY ABSORBED IN HIS OWN world. He would leave the house without saying where he was going and head toward Soos Creek. Hiding among the conifers, he waited for the telltale rhythmic rumble of a Northern Pacific freight train. When the locomotive shimmered into view, he timed the precise moment to leap for the hatch.

Climbing down the roof while the train barreled forward, Harry reached for the outstretched hands of hoboes who helped him board the boxcar. They made room for him amid the sooty cargo and taught him their shorthand lingo. Harry was enthralled with their tales. He was taken by the unwritten law that hoboes helped each other and intrigued that they did not appear imperiled by their kingdom of hardship. Sometimes he sought out the men at their campfire on the outskirts of town, where he accepted a helping of mulligan stew.

Harry was living on the edge, pursuing what few conscientious, obedient *nisei* dared experience. Confined by Auburn and at some level craving his father's attention, he felt compelled to pursue these adventures. Wrestling with his identity and forging independence, he was a young American boy on the cusp of adolescence.

Had Katsuji known, he might have berated him, and Harry might have run away again. Yet Katsuji understood his son's wanderlust. In 1900, he had been a tad older than Harry, only fourteen, and a railway job was his sole track out of a poor, dead-end life in rural Gion, Hiroshima prefecture. On his application for his first passport, he had written that he intended to labor on the railroads. Later, he learned how tough it was to be a menial worker and saw the spirit drained from too many *issei* men. It was the last life he wanted for his sons.

In 1932 Katsuji was too distracted to talk to Harry about his experiences. He was preoccupied with the decimated economy. That year unemployment stood at a whopping 25 percent, and the GDP dropped a stunning 13 percent. A quarter of all banks would shut their doors and nine million people would lose their savings. Hardworking Americans became chronically unemployed and, increasingly, homeless. Hundreds of shantytowns—Hoovervilles—popped up throughout the country. The ramshackle huts on the Port of Seattle property were multiplying into the hundreds. Twice police had burned the premises to eradicate the settlement, but the residents reconvened and rebuilt. The new mayor accepted that Seattle's Hooverville was semipermanent.

Katsuji watched the real estate industry spiral downward. His interest, helping *issei* buy property or lease land, was virtually obsolete. Yet in Auburn he had been selected the "district chair for real estate brokers supporting President Hoover's reelection." Perhaps Katsuji liked the leadership role. Or Hoover appealed to Katsuji because he had signed an immigration bill in 1929 that allotted a maximum one hundred immigrants from Japan annually. It was a paltry number, but still, it was better than nothing, which had been Japan's humiliating status since Congress passed the Japanese Exclusion Act of 1924, which abruptly ended Japanese immigration; in the United States then, there had been no ripple of mass reaction, but in Tokyo massive anti-American riots had erupted.

The Depression would drive the presidential election. On November 8, Katsuji and young Frank pinned badges bearing the president's face to their wool coats and stood at the polls in Seattle. At 48 degrees Fahrenheit, the day was overcast and raw. Katsuji was chilled and coughed a lot but said nothing to concern his young son, who, sensing the honor of the occasion, held his hand.

When the votes were tallied, Franklin Delano Roosevelt had won by a landslide, taking forty-two states, including over 57 percent of the votes in Washington State. Given what Roosevelt would later do to the nation's ethnic Japanese, including tens of thousands of native-born citizens, Katsuji's choice may have been prescient. The course of history lay, as yet, unrevealed.

Fifty-eight-year-old Herbert C. Hoover had been trounced and forty-six-year-old Katsuji Harry Fukuhara was about to falter. Hoover would continue to garner authority and wealth over the course of his lengthy life. For Katsuji Fukuhara there would be no second chance.

5

Ivory Bones and Leaden Ashes

f Katsuji was upset by Roosevelt's election, he did not express it. But then, he was conversing less with each passing day. Pale and drawn, he had caught a cold that developed into pneumonia. "He was never in robust health," Harry recalled; his father had moved to Auburn in part for its clean air. But a civic-minded workaholic with five children and limited opportunities didn't have time to be sick, not during the Depression.

Instead, he went about business as usual, commuting between his H. K. Fukuhara Co. office on Main Street in Seattle and another in Auburn. By December he was suffering from a persistent fever and dry cough. When he hacked, he winced.

Three days before the family's anticipated New Year's Eve celebration, Katsuji was admitted to the Owen Taylor Hospital in Auburn. The physician tapped his stethoscope on Katsuji's chest and picked up a rough, scratching sound that was a telltale sign of pleurisy, an inflammation of the tissues lining the lungs and chest wall. A common illness, pleurisy sometimes arose from pneumonia. Fortunately, many patients recovered with sufficient rest. In the future, it would be best treated by penicillin, recently discovered in a British lab and a decade away from mass global production. At the time, doctors could drain the fluid, mucus, and pus if necessary. But if treatment failed, pleurisy could kill.

By the end of the month, bed rest had done little to alleviate Katsuji's symptoms. While the Green River flooded to historic levels, Katsuji foundered, his lungs awash in fluid. On January 26, doctors operated to relieve the buildup. The procedure failed, and Katsuji was transferred to the respected Swedish Hospital in Seattle. In his hushed hospital room, his body grew frail and his pallor waxy. His racking cough worsened.

March would prove challenging. As Katsuji labored to breathe, the world was gradually falling toward a cataclysmic confrontation. On March 4, a dismal, snowy day, Franklin Delano Roosevelt was sworn in as president of the United States for the first of four historic terms. At the end of the month, Japan would withdraw from the League of Nations in protest over censure of its incursion into Manchuria and creation of the puppet state Manchukuo. In between, surgeons would remove part of Katsuji's rib to relieve the pressure on his swollen lungs. His second surgery in three months was a disappointing failure.

Immersed in his teenage world, Harry thought he had bigger problems. The police chief had caught him breaking into a factory with friends. Chief Ludwig released the delinquents to their parents, but not Harry. He sat him in his police car and lectured him for several hours. Harry feared that Chief Ludwig would tell his mother, but she did not let on that she knew, and Harry didn't broach the subject.

Chief Ludwig's handling of the matter was an act of kindness. Aware of Katsuji's crisis, he and his wife did not want to trouble Kinu. Mrs. Ludwig made chicken soup for Katsuji, hoping the old wives' remedy would do the trick.

On April 4, physicians performed another rib resection. It

was their last hope. Katsuji was placed under an oxygen tent and tended by a private nurse. He did not respond, his health rapidly deteriorating as his lungs began to collapse.

Kinu did not tell her children that their father was gravely ill. She held out hope that he would rally; she did not want to worry them and felt that they were too young to understand. She contacted her friends the Bitows, who came running. The children were aware that their mother was often absent, but little more.

In early April, Harry tried to visit his father for the first time in weeks but was not allowed in the room. From the door, he could see his father's chest heaving under the canopy shrouding the bed. The oxygen pump whirred as his father rasped for breath.

The next day, April 8, Katsuji lay comatose. That Saturday morning, Harry, Pierce, and Frank were attending Japanese class at the Auburn Buddhist Church. Mrs. Ludwig marched upstairs and asked the principal to call the boys. No one ever interrupted class, certainly not a *hakujin* lady. She brought the boys to their father's hospital room, where the lights were turned low and an odor of mucus mixed with ammonia. Around their father's tented space stood Kinu, Victor, Mary, and the Bitows. Katsuji was unconscious and breathed raggedly, his blanket rising and falling on his withered frame.

Kinu had not prepared the children for this moment. But a family friend did not mince words. "Stay in the hospital," she whispered to Harry. "It is a matter of time before your father passes away."

Harry could not bear to be there. "I just took off." He ran into one of the Bitow boys in the hall, and they dashed outside. Harry lost track of time. When the pallid warmth of the midafternoon sun waned, the boys returned chilled to the ward. By that time, Katsuji was dead.

Harry understood immediately that he had messed up. He was the only family member not present when his father died. He had neither an excuse nor a reason. He looked at his mother, who appeared grave, cold, and distant——so unlike her. "If my mother had scolded me, it would have been okay," he said. Kinu was silent. Ashamed, Harry didn't want to draw attention to himself. Isolated by guilt and grief-stricken, he stood alone.

On April 13, the day of the funeral, spring graced the White River Valley, where the apple orchards were in bloom. The mood, however, at the White River Buddhist Church was somber. Inside the meeting hall, decorated with screen paintings and a black lacquer platform housing a golden altar, smoky plumes of incense scented the air with sandalwood and camphor. What looked from the outside like any modest Protestant house of worship, with its clapboard façade and small belfry, was on the inside virtually identical to a Japanese Buddhist temple. For the *hakujin* mourners, the church was exotic. For the *issei*, it was welcoming and familiar.

Priest Aoki chanted three sutras in Japanese. Four *issei*, all community leaders and Katsuji's friends, gave eulogies in their native tongue. Harry Leslie, the owner of the *Auburn Globe-Republican* newspaper and a Chamber of Commerce trustee, made the final address in English. Although most of the mourners were unable to fully follow his eulogy, his respect for a Japanese peer who had surmounted the racial divide spoke volumes. Following the funeral, the newspaper reported, "A wide circle alike among the Americans and Japanese feel the loss of a true and sincere friend."

After the ceremony, more than two hundred mourners stood for a photograph, barely fitting in the photographer's panorama frame. *Issei*—in some places six rows deep—stood behind several dozen standing floral wreaths. One group of *hakujin* mourners, including Flora Holt, gathered at the side. Wearing black armbands, Pierce and Frank flanked the front of Katsuji's casket, cascading with lilies and roses. Harry, Mary, Kinu, and Victor lined up behind. The children stared grimly. Kinu tilted her partially veiled face toward the casket, deep shadows darkening her eyes.

At the crematorium, flames consumed Katsuji's body, reducing it to ivory bones and leaden ashes. Kinu carried home his remains in a porcelain urn. At forty-one, she walked alone, a resident alien and the sole guardian of five American children during the Great Depression.

MONEY LOOMED AS AN IMMEDIATE CONCERN. THE funeral costs were most likely covered by *kōden* condolence money given by the mourners, especially those from the *kenjinkai* association, of which Katsuji was president. But Katsuji had not earned any income for months while hospitalized. Kinu didn't know where to begin. She and her husband, like most Japanese couples, had kept their spheres strictly separate.

Kinu turned to her middle son. Together, she and Harry walked to Katsuji's Auburn office, turning it upside down, rummaging through his books. Katsuji, a consummate salesperson for New York Life and Northwestern Mutual Life Insurance, was not an accountant. He had trusted the details to his head, relying on the acuity of his memory. His memos were disorganized, cursory, and in two languages. Kinu and Harry couldn't make head or tail of them, discarding papers as they sifted. They left with a stack of outstanding promissory notes, which may only have represented part of the whole.

The family's financial condition was dire. Since 1926 Katsuji had been extending loans that had not been paid. His savings account held a mere $65.74, and the monthly rent on the bungalow was twenty-five dollars. Kinu had little time or financial leeway before she would need to tap other sources.

She did stand to benefit from Katsuji's life insurance policies, but he had reduced his insurance by half when he became ill and could no longer pay the premiums. There was not a single breadwinner among the six surviving Fukuharas, as eighteen-year-old Victor still struggled in high school, and the chances of securing a lucrative job as a *nisei* when as many as 15 million people were out of work nationwide seemed slim, at best. Moreover, Katsuji's estate was intestate.

Three weeks after Katsuji died, the law firm of I. B. Knickerbocker, the Auburn Chamber of Commerce president, submitted Katsuji's estate to probate court. The banker W. A. McLean, who had become close to Katsuji while they both served on the Chamber of Commerce, served as an appraiser. Out of necessity, he began nosing around the house, evaluating the household belongings as those "frequently kept in the home of a family of moderate means and living simple."

While McLean practiced what had to strike Kinu as an invasion of privacy, she grappled with overwhelming responsibilities. She began to consider returning to Japan, where the cost of living was far lower and her family would provide emotional support. Harry and Mary adamantly refused; for the time being, Kinu didn't push. She tried to keep life as normal as possible, sending Harry, Pierce, as well as Frank to the Fresh Air Camp for two weeks. As her husband had splurged during the beginning of the Depression, so did Kinu in the depths of the downturn and at the height of her sorrow.

But after camp was over, Harry noticed that his mother had changed. The summer still stretched lazily, but Kinu, who was normally serene—with the exception of her sharp exchanges with Mary—seemed tense. One day she suggested an outing in the country, a picnic for two. On the way, she needed to see some farmers who owed the family money. Since she didn't drive, would Harry take her?

Harry jumped at the suggestion, honored that his mother had turned to him, not Victor. Harry would prove that he was worthy. After his disappearance on the day his father died, this opportunity was a second chance.

Kinu did not ask Harry because she thought he was more responsible than Victor but because he spoke the best English. There was one small hitch in her ingenious plan. Harry did not know how to drive. Nor did Kinu. Katsuji's beloved 1927 Buick had always been off-limits.

Kinu asked Chief Ludwig to overlook Harry's driving as a favor to the family. Ludwig, who was also the pastor at the First Methodist Church, served both Uncle Sam and the Almighty. Bearing responsibility for Harry's safety and his soul, he was predisposed to decline Kinu's request. Nevertheless, he acceded. "That's not right but there's nothing else you can do," he admonished Harry, "so just go ahead. Be careful!"

Harry was delighted to flout the law that summer of "no lessons and no license." He lurched along Main Street toward the outskirts of Auburn and nearby Kent. He had never experienced such control and power. The six-seater sedan accelerated, bounced in and out of potholes, and chugged on open thoroughfares. If Kinu appeared rattled when she adjusted her cloche hat and wobbled on the sideboard upon exiting, Harry did not notice. He relished the journey. As a bonus, they made it to their destination.

Kinu faced the next task alone. Harry's rudimentary Japanese was inadequate. She summoned her strength as she walked to the farmhouse front doors. If Kinu had known these families, she would have knocked on the back door, as her husband had, but they were strangers. Some may have been friends of Katsuji and attended his funeral, but they had no money to spare. If she asked for just half of the outstanding funds, she reasoned, that would be more than fair.

Often, Kinu did not have a chance to press her case, as few were home during the harvest season. Sometimes, Harry and Kinu would stop by a farm three times before Kinu could speak with the head of household.

Harry took in the conversation from the driver's seat, peering over the dashboard. The men, their faces tanned and deeply creased, took off their faded caps and bowed low in their sunbleached overalls. His mother bowed back. The farmers shifted their weight, digging their scuffed boots into the ground. They avoided direct eye contact. His mother, too, stared at the ground. Like a seesaw rocking in the wind, one person bowed and the other bowed back.

After a morning of excruciating cold calls, Harry drove to a shady spot. Kinu spread a blanket and handed Harry a peanut butter sandwich and a bottle of home-brewed root beer from her picnic basket. It was agonizing to approach strangers for money. Harry listened, but he did not sense the gravity of the situation. After a short break, Kinu flecked the crumbs off her lap, and they resumed their round of visits.

Impressed that his big brother could drive, Frank hankered to join them. Content just to be with Harry in the car, he pestered Kinu until she relented. The boys sat and waited for their mother to make her calls. On these sun-kissed days, cozy in the backseat, "I didn't miss my father much," Frank admitted. Their mother rarely returned empty-handed. Often she carried a bunch of carrots, a bushel of peas, or a couple of heads of lettuce as a token of the farmers' appreciation; the loans, principal and interest, remained outstanding.

On the few occasions that Kinu walked back to the car with money, even 10 percent of the total, her step was buoyant. Smiling with relief, she grasped the side of the seat and readied for the ride. Frank held the produce to make sure that it didn't roll when they careened around curves. Harry grinned and turned on the ignition. The engine purred.

THE FAMILY'S CLOSEST FRIENDS SOON CONVERGED ON the house. "*Ojama shimasu.*" "Sorry to interrupt you!" Kinu's wan smile was authentic; she welcomed their presence. Her women friends commandeered the kitchen, replicating her mild Hiroshima dishes, while she huddled with her husband's confidants. Kinu did not stand on ceremony now. She placed piles of thumb-worn invoices on her dining table for the men to evaluate her situation.

Moving back to Hiroshima increasingly struck Kinu as a solution to her money problems. Harry could not have been more opposed to this line of thought. He wasn't nervous about the family's financial prospects. "When you're thirteen years old, you don't worry about those things." His mother could still buy a sack of rice, jugs of milk, and a tank of gas. Holes in his jeans didn't bother him.

Mary agreed with Harry. She had grown fond of Auburn and progressed in school, from second to eleventh grade within four years. Just as important, women in America—with their flapper dresses, lipstick, rouge, and perms—were kicking up their heels, far more liberated than their *geta*-clopping counterparts in Japan. Having won suffrage in 1920, American women voiced their opinions. Japanese women may have been wearing bolder kimonos, but they were still denied the vote and prevented from living full lives. By now Mary knew enough of both cultures to recognize where she belonged. She felt as if she had just returned from Japan. How could her mother make her go back again?

Harry blamed himself for complicating his mother's evolving plans. "The only problem she had was me." But Harry wasn't holding Kinu back. It would take until fall for Mr. McLean and two other appraisers to submit the estate paperwork to the court. By that time, she needed to pay her debts in full. McLean devalued the initial estate estimate from $5,500 to $2,216.74. Given that the entire Fukuhara estate included everything, even pots and pans, Kinu could not afford to stay long.

By summer's end, Kinu had given up on outstanding receipts but settled her own accounts. The lawyers would handle the rest. However complicated her feelings were about leaving her adopted country after twenty-two years, she was going home. No one in the family knew that on August 9, Tokyo had conducted its first major air-raid drill in preparation for a future war.

Kinu began to pack and Harry threw his wild card on the table. "She couldn't leave without me," he declared. Kinu, ground down by her children's demands and preoccupied with her preparations, softened her stand. "If I didn't like it, I could go back," Harry insisted that his mother promise. The same went for Mary. Temporarily appeased, they began saying goodbye to their friends and teachers. Harry promised them that his trip was just a visit, not a stay; he would be back before long.

On the afternoon of November 15, 1933, Kinu, Mary, Harry, Pierce, and Frank walked the ramp at Smith Cove to board the *Hikawa Maru*, one of NYK Japan Mail's flagship luxury liners. Kinu had purchased third-class tickets for sixty dollars each; Pierce and Frank received the children's rate of thirty dollars a head. Victor would stay behind with one of Katsuji's relatives and make his way in Seattle or follow later. Although Victor was the least comfortable in the United States, as a dual citizen he faced the almost certain prospect of being drafted into the Japanese army. Like his father three decades before him, staying abroad kept a mandatory sentence at bay.

Already loaded in cargo were Kinu's Monarch piano, her *koto* zither from Miyajima, Katsuji's accumulated Victorian furniture, assorted steamer trunks, Frank's red Radio Flyer wagon, and crates of fresh-picked celery, gifts from farmers that Japanese relatives would find odd, malodorous, and unpleasant. A priest from the Buddhist church and close *issei* friends clustered at the pier. While the crowds jostled to lean over the railing for a final view, Kinu kept her balance, clutching an ivory urn wrapped in a dark *furoshiki* cloth, protecting her husband's crispened bones and ashes.

Only Harry and Pierce had never been to Japan. Two years younger than Harry, Pierce was still a child, content to follow his mother's directions. But for Harry, being torn at this moment from his carefree boyhood, still unblemished by the scars of adolescence and the disappointments of adulthood, struck him as cruel, arbitrary, and unjust. Harry held Auburn sacred. Turning over incidents in his mind, the most mundane already shimmered in pristine memory. Any sense of having rebelled against the narrow confines of small-town life, or of unease with being treated less than equally, were fast forgotten.

Lost in their thoughts, the Fukuharas stood on deck as the ship's horn blasted, its red-and-white striped smokestack belched, and the turbine screws turned. The *Hikawa Maru* set sail for Japan, the flag of the Rising Sun whipping wildly at its stern.

PART TWO

ADRIFT IN TWO COUNTRIES

酸いも甘いも知りぬく

Sui mo amai mo shirinuku

To know thoroughly the sweet and the sour.

6

Land of the Rising Sun

The voyage from Seattle to Yokohama took two weeks. The ship stopped in Vancouver, crossed the International Date Line, and covered 4,200 nautical miles, steaming across the Pacific at twenty-one miles per hour. It cruised far above Midway and well below the Aleutians, leaving passengers nothing to ponder but the hazy horizon. In November, a gray sea rocked the 11,000-ton luxury liner.

Whenever they could, Harry and Frank escaped from third-class steerage below deck to the separate third-class promenade above—for fresh air, open space, and a less vertiginous ride. Hunching in their jackets, the boys pulled up their wool collars.

When they descended to their room, they felt the pitch and roll. Sleeping quarters, with eight people and four bunk beds, were tight. The stale air smelled musty. A porthole, revealing a sliver of racked sea, didn't help. When the boys became seasick, there wasn't much space to escape. Turning green, bile rising, Harry decided that he was a landlubber.

First-class passengers called the *Hikawa Maru* the "Queen of the Pacific," given her elegant Art Deco appointments designed by a Parisian interior designer, and her ten-course French cuisine prepared by European chefs. Just a year and a half earlier,

Charlie Chaplin, in his silk smoking jacket, had walked up the wrought-iron central staircase and strolled to the dining room with its arched, stained-glass ceiling.

But the Fukuharas ate in steerage. The cost of the trip for the entire family was less than one first-class accommodation, which ran at $250 a head. Kinu had also selected the least expensive option of Japanese cuisine, though no one was disappointed. The food was authentic, abundant, and delicious. Rather than compare her family's circumstances to those of Mr. Chaplin, Kinu's baseline was an average Japanese lifestyle. At the time, it cost 1,000 yen to build a house in Japan, and Kinu had spent 936 yen on tickets. Their single trip was virtually one house, but her remaining funds would go far in Hiroshima. Kinu's anxious days of feeling nearly broke in Auburn faded with each nautical mile.

The more Harry explored the cramped third-class quarters that the *issei* generation called "a rackful of silkworms," the more intrigued he became. The cabins were climbing with *nisei* boys en route to Japan for their schooling, planning to stay with relatives, as Mary and Victor had in Hiroshima. "Just kids, a whole mess in the same room," he marveled. They were boisterous and fun. Like Harry, they called the Pacific Northwest home. Harry began to relax as he discovered that he just might not be alone.

On November 28, word spread that the *Hikawa Maru* would anchor on schedule in the port of Yokohama at 7 a.m. the following day. But that afternoon, the ship was unexpectedly delayed. Gale-force winds picked up, and the port became too treacherous to enter. After a hailstorm, the *Hikawa Maru* circled miles away, waiting for an all-clear. Longing for land, the passengers endured a turbulent night at sea. Howling winds ripped along deck, waves tossed the ship, and those in third class bore the brunt of upheaval. If ever there was a time to be seasick, it was that pitch-black, starless night.

But in the wee hours of a new day, the ocean calmed. Shortly before dawn at 6:30 a.m., as the *Hikawa Maru* was sailing toward Yokohama, the groggy passengers were called to a wondrous sight. The sun's spreading rays bathed the swirling nimbus behind snow-capped Mount Fuji in a brilliant, crimson light. For Kinu, catching a glimpse of Fuji in its morning splendor was auspicious. And even as a cynical teenager, Harry could not deny that Fuji, so soulful for Japanese and *issei*, was more beautiful than he could have imagined.

The *Hikawa Maru* anchored at the port's major pier, Osanbashi. The moment they descended the stairs, the Fukuharas were officially *Amerika-gaeri* (returnees from America) who were often perceived, correctly or not, as wealthy and ostentatious. What was certain was that *Amerika-gaeri* were ethnically Japanese, but different in mien, style, habits, and thinking. For starters, neither Mary nor Kinu wore kimonos; Mary rarely would.

The Fukuharas saw Japan through the eyes of foreigners. People everywhere, pressing upon them. Men walking the docks incongruously dressed in dark kimonos with felt or straw cowboy hats; women bound in pastel kimonos with strawberry-cheeked babies strapped to their backs; male students in Western-style military uniforms with high collars and brass buttons, sporting black capes. Since the weather had turned from unseasonably warm to brisk and wintry, many wore black or white gauze masks to protect themselves and others from the spread of viruses.

There was little opportunity to gawk. Porters honked their horns, maneuvering in miniature trucks. Bicycles tottered, rickshaws went this way and that, the sensory overload punctuated by rata-tat talk. Harry brightened at the sight of Yamashita Park with its bubbling circular fountain and the Western-style Hotel

New Grand across the street, landscapes with which he could connect. But, above all, at this moment, he needed to see a bathroom, in particular a flush toilet.

One of Kinu's brothers stood waiting to guide them to the train for the hour-long trip to Tokyo. Pressing their faces to the window, the boys watched the international district's stately brick buildings recede, replaced by one block after another of one- or two-story wooden buildings with corrugated-tin and iron roofs. Only Kinu and Mary could read the signs in *kanji* characters. The metropolis appeared poor, sprawling, and dreary, revealing little that suggested its place as one of the world's most important cities. The next morning the family left for Hiroshima.

AUNT KIYO HAD RENTED THEM A HOUSE near Meijidō, where they could stay until they settled on something more permanent. The building was wooden and adorned in the traditional fashion with *shōji* screens and *tatami* mats. Pleased with her surroundings, Kinu visibly relaxed.

It was Harry—usually a quick study—who kept making foolish mistakes. As soon as he entered the *genkan* (vestibule), Kinu scolded. *"Kutsu o nuginasai."* "Take off your shoes!" Harry smarted. In the short time since he had set foot in Japan, he had felt that he had no one with whom to share his discomfort. Frank and Pierce clung to their mother; Mary moved confidently, although her expression was sour. Harry was seized by an unfamiliar loneliness. He didn't have to look closely to notice the stark differences. This house did not have a telephone: only one or two families in a neighborhood were affluent enough to afford one. Calls took as long as twenty minutes to connect, and the devices were frowned upon as an expensive indulgence.

Harry felt chilled to the core whether he was inside or out. Winter was finger-clenching cold, exacerbated by a moldy dampness. In Auburn, the boys had awakened to a warm house, thanks to their mother's early firing up of the wood-and-coal-burning oven. The round ceramic *hibachi* charcoal brazier in Hiroshima didn't disperse heat much beyond its circumference. The *tatami* chilled his toes and the futons made him clench from the draft. Harry shivered on the toilet, its narrow basin set over a dark, deep, stinking hole.

For the first time in his life, Harry was out of his element. He hadn't liked Japan even before he arrived and nothing he saw now compelled him to change his mind. He started writing to friends in Auburn and Seattle. Little more than two weeks after he reached Hiroshima a reply came from Nobufusa Bitow, who reported that the Green River had flooded, the season's first snowfall had already melted, and the basketball team was drawing a crowd.

At a time when Auburn's Main Street would be strung with holiday lights and tinsel, Hiroshima glowed with *chōchin* (paper lanterns). Crown Prince Akihito, the first son and fifth child of Emperor Hirohito and Empress Nagako, was born in late December. Celebrations of his birth, the heir to the Chrysanthemum Throne, occurred throughout Japan. In Hiroshima, the Fukuharas watched the night procession of marching soldiers, flickering lanterns, and Rising Sun flags. The present emperor represented the 124th in an unbroken imperial line dating from 660 BCE. Frank, who knew how fleeting a presidency could be, was curious. "The Emperor and prince system was new to me."

The celebration may have been unusual for the Fukuharas, but veneration of the emperor came naturally to a city embroiled in global conflict. Japan had been at war in Manchuria since it manufactured the Mukden Incident in 1931 and established the puppet state of Manchukuo. Ujina, Hiroshima's port, was a major logistics and embarkation center for troops bound for the region. Hiroshima's economy, once devoted to producing lacquered umbrellas and farming seaweed, oysters, lemons, and persimmons, now depended more and more on army and navy expenditures. Troops lodged in and around Hiroshima Castle. Whenever longtime residents heard the sounds of vehicles rumbling down the city's thoroughfares in the middle of the night, they understood that tanks and artillery were being dispatched to distant conflicts.

The Fukuharas tried to adjust. Christmas arrived, but it was tinged with loss and disappointment. Even in the merriest of years, celebrating the holiday in Shintō and Buddhist Japan would never compare with the unbridled delight of the twinkling American version. One of Harry's *nisei* friends from Hiroshima would later write: "Don't you long for those good holidays the way they used to celebrate it back home? You never could find such gaiety anywhere in this land of the rising sun. In Tokyo, they do seem to celebrate Christmas, but all I can say is that It's Dead. Give me the good old American Xmas."

And, before the year had ended, Frank developed pleurisy. In the gloom of a dank winter, he lay coughing on his futon, watching his mother fret. Kinu fed Frank rice gruel and diluted barley tea, hovering by his side. "She was scared that maybe I might die." If so, before he perished, he wanted only to bite into a hot dog and sip Coca-Cola.

Kinu matriculated Harry and Pierce at the local elementary school. They would have to stay back, she explained, until their Japanese improved. Harry fell from the ninth grade and Pierce from the sixth. Both—like Mary and Victor in Auburn—landed in second.

Harry rebelled from his very first day. The rules required that he wear a uniform and shave his head. Harry refused. He wore a wool three-piece suit instead. When the second graders saw the tall newcomer, they assumed that he was a substitute *sensei* and bowed. Harry bowed in return and slunk to a seat in the back of the class. "I couldn't speak their language," he recalled.

Kinu was eager to hear about his day. "What did you learn today?" "Nothing," he replied. "I'm really mad and I'm having no fun." Harking back to his spectacularly unsuccessful Japanese career in Auburn, Kinu threw up her arms without a fight. "It's no use," she said and promptly found an English-speaking tutor who would teach Harry Japanese at home. His brief Japanese elementary school career had ended.

Mary was struggling, too. Though she had officially graduated, owing to Aunt Kiyo's bribing the principal four years earlier, the seventeen-year-old had to resume where she left off. Her former classmates were long gone, and her written Japanese had deteriorated. Mary despaired, crying later, "I was all mixed up."

SITTING AT THE *KOTATSU* (TABLE COVERED WITH a quilt), the damp draft sneaking through the *shōji* screens, Harry lost himself in pen and paper, writing to friends, classmates, and teachers in Auburn. His mother had prepared return address labels in Japanese so that his American contacts wouldn't be troubled. His friends applied the addresses upside down. Still, the envelopes were full of pages and pages of letters, sometimes sticky with photographs. The exuberant exchange of mail sustained Harry, confirming that his authentic place in the universe was far from Hiroshima.

The family soon moved to another house in the Hakushima district, a quiet, residential area of upper-middle-class homes for the families of high-level bureaucrats and military officers. Aunt Kiyo lived nearby. The Ōta River, forking through the city into Hiroshima Bay, flowed immediately to the west. Hiroshima Castle dominated the skyline a short walk to the south.

Here Harry discovered *nisei* neighbors. A Japanese family, named the Matsumotos, lived around the corner and were the guardians for a trio of *nisei* boy relatives from Los Angeles. Kaz Nagata and his cousins Mitsu and Mas Matsumoto had been sent, like Mary and Victor and several thousand others, to study in Hiroshima. Harry loitered at their *genkan*, a dragonfly drawn to water. The boys became fast, inseparable, lifelong friends. The Matsumoto home was more like a boarding school dormitory without a proctor than a private residence. "When you went into that house, it was all English," said the boys' cousin Chieko, who marveled at their chatter and laughter. For the rest of his life, Harry would recall the Matsumoto home as one of the few places in Hiroshima where he could walk down the hall with his shoes on.

By the spring of 1934, Harry and his pals were wearing the uniform of the Sanyō Commercial School, a large high school where Harry's tutor had used his influence to have Harry admitted. Since Sanyō was private, Kinu didn't have to register Harry at the local ward office, which would have required him to take Japanese citizenship in order to enroll in a public school. Over time, she would end up filing paperwork for all her other children.

Sanyō had as many as ten to fifteen *nisei* in each class, and they were often several years older than their Japanese peers since some had already graduated from high school in the States. Japanese teachers of English taught Japanese to the *nisei*. To compensate for their academic deficits, the students were given oral exams at first, not written. So steady was the demand for an accessible *nisei* education that the school expanded over time, charging a pricey tuition. Despite his tutoring, Harry "really didn't understand what was going on" at first. But, over time, he would perform well. He was growing accustomed to Hiroshima, but resigned to living there permanently? Never.

Even at a school as cosmopolitan as Sanyō, the students were immersed in an ideology of emperor worship. When they entered and left the school grounds, Harry and Pierce bowed to a portrait of the emperor and empress housed in a small *hōanden* (shrine) for this purpose. The austere auditorium also held *goshin'ei* (portraits of the emperor and empress) to which they bowed upon filing in and out. On national holidays, the principal read aloud the Imperial Rescript on Education. Holding the book aloft and bowing to it, he intoned the principle that subjects should be prepared to die for their emperor. Heads bowed low, the students listened reverently. Mary experienced the same rituals at her girls' school, as would Frank at the public elementary school.

Neither the military nor the emperor held much sway over Harry. He did not mind if people stared and raised their eyebrows when he and his pals horsed around, speaking English. He was not bothered if people misconstrued their expansive gestures and emphatic expressions as disrespectful and unseemly. He did not care if *nisei* aroused suspicion. Brought up in a culture passionately devoted to individualism, Harry thumbed his nose at formality and convention.

One balmy summer evening, Harry and his pals strolled the night stalls down the street behind the elementary school, where festival vendors gathered to sell small treats. The aroma of *yakitori* chicken skewers and charcoal-fired sweet potatoes drew crowds. Scarlet goldfish swam in buckets to be scooped for a coin or two, colorful water balloons bobbed in wading pool containers, and a shooting gallery of revolving tin ducks dared players to take their best shot. If not for the eerie beating of a *taiko* (drum), Harry might have been at the canopied Redondo Beach stalls outside Seattle.

The boys chewed *yakitori* and swigged *ramune* (carbonated lemonade). At some point, they noticed a local gang headed by a bully named Shigeru Matsuura, who lived near the Fukuharas. The boys eyed one another and kept their distance when out of nowhere, Matsuura rushed at Harry, throwing a punch. Harry hit him back. There were a few more furious exchanges before the fight sputtered out. Matsuura swaggered off, disappearing into the shadow-cast crowd with his friends. Embarrassed, Harry waved off his pals and limped home alone to nurse his bruises.

He had no idea what had happened. Had Matsuura picked a fight because Harry was *nisei*? So was Matsuura's father, although he was much older and originally from Hawaii. Matsuura had been born and raised in Japan, but Harry thought that he would identify with their shared roots. Was he projecting his anger onto Harry because his own father had returned bitter and poor from the pineapple and sugar plantations? Did Harry strike him as a stereotypical, nouveau riche *Amerika-gaeri* returnee? Or did Matsuura simply resent what he perceived as a *nisei* invasion of his turf?

Harry was shaken up. Over time, this incident stung less, but Harry would never forget the burst of violence. He looked to America for solace. "For the first year in Japan, that's all I thought about—going back."

With each passing month, the Matsumoto enclave became a refuge from the intensity of Japan—its crowds, confined spaces, enforced unity, and stringent expectations. Until eight or nine at night, the boys played gin rummy, trump, and bridge. Harry spun 78 rpm records on his portable phonograph and listened to "Home on the Range."

Before long, Kinu moved the family to another rental. Although they could live comfortably on the proceeds of Katsuji's life insurance policy, she wanted to save funds to build a house. With each displacement, Harry felt more and more removed from Auburn. When one of his former teachers sent him a letter, the distance felt insurmountable. In her breezy update, Ruth Woods wrote, "The O'Neill's (he's a barber) bought the house where you folks used to live."

Meanwhile, Victor, who had returned from the United States shortly after his family, had graduated from Sanyō and completed a two-year accounting course in record time and at the top of his class. Just when Victor was finally regaining his stride after interrupted lives in two countries, he was drafted. In November 1935, he was officially assigned to the First Reserves and ordered to report to duty on December 1. He was twenty-one.

Victor's assignment alarmed Harry. On November 26, the fifteen-year-old stretched his legs under the *kotatsu* and wrote a letter to the American consulate in Kobe. The day after Thanksgiving, Consul Kenneth C. Krentz answered.

He couldn't advise Harry how someone might lose his Japanese citizenship, Krentz wrote, but the law on American citizens was clear. "A native American citizen serving in the Japanese army would lose his citizenship if he took an oath of allegiance to the Emperor of Japan, or renounced his American citizenship by specific act." An American would not be stripped of his citizenship, he verified, simply by living in Japan.

For these words, Harry could be grateful. Victor's American citizenship was certainly at risk, but Harry still had time. Placing the letter back in the envelope, he kept the information to himself, seeing no reason to worry his mother or warn his younger brothers.

This letter provided peace of mind, for Harry's schooling was predicated on service in the Japanese Imperial Army. "Unique" among nations, diplomat historian Ulrich Straus would write, Japan had instituted requisite military training in secondary school that was led by active-duty officers. Harry served under a lieutenant colonel, warrant officer, and master sergeant. Harry, an avowed American citizen, would undergo four years of Japanese-style ROTC training, but this was not the same as serving in the Japanese army.

He donned a military uniform and wrapped his shins in *gētoru* (puttees). Depending on what was available at the time, he drilled with an old rifle, a discarded bayonet, or a model light machine gun several times a week, virtually all year long. Among other skills, Harry learned to load and clean a rifle, march in strict formation, decipher a map, and bivouac. He learned to obey orders, at once. When the drills ended, he gathered the shells scattered on the school's dirt grounds. Like other *nisei*, though, Harry employed the American penchant for efficiency and convenience, scooping up the errant shells with a handy net. The Japanese students picked them up methodically one at a time.

Although Japan was already at war with China, the intended target of the drills was the United States, viewed as the greatest threat to Japanese expansionist goals. The instructors ranked America as the Empire's "number one enemy." Vaguely aware of global politics, Harry could only hope that circumstances would change. He shrugged. "It was kind of awkward."

Not for the first time, Harry toed the line while staying loyal to the United States. In his diary, he betrayed no sense of being torn by the conflict of being an American in arms in Japan, partly because he did not commit psychologically to training. "Got pretty tired carrying the guns all day," he wrote. On Saturdays when school attendance was compulsory, he had four periods of class "and then marched around." The mindless drills, he figured, were simply "part of the curriculum." The officers' furious exhortations did not make an impression. Harry looked beyond the drills. He planned on returning to the States, and life outside school was still bearable. Indeed, he followed up one dusty morning of drills with a Thanksgiving party for ten. It was probably a Hiroshima Nikkei Club dinner, a coed group to which Harry gravitated.

He began organizing dances at his house, which Kinu supervised, and at a room at the girls' Catholic school, where there was an American advisor. Harry supplied a phonograph, vinyl records, and Frank—his deejay by default. At first shy, soon smiling, the students formed couples. When Frank wound the phonograph and the music spilled forth, they waltzed and foxtrotted in their bobby socks across the straw *tatami* floor. Outside they kept their distance as formal Japanese youth should, barely making eye contact. Inside, they held hands, pulled close, and swayed to "Blue Moon."

Harry thought he had a handle on maintaining his equilibrium, but life became more challenging and fraught from 1936, with a failed coup d'état by young army officers directed toward senior government officials. The cabinet was in turmoil, the army's heavy hand stretching more deeply into the government and society each year. Regimentation and intolerance increased.

One day, Harry was on a streetcar with a few Sanyō pals, in uniform, speaking English so that the other riders would not eavesdrop. They had been told at school not to speak English in public, but it hadn't posed a problem thus far. Out of the blue, a *kempeitai* (military police) officer in uniform, who was also a passenger, yelled to the conductor to stop. The *kempeitai*, regarded as thought police, generally terrified the public. The streetcar screeched to a halt and the officer ordered Harry and his friends off at once. "Are you Japanese?" he screamed after they had lined up, standing at attention.

"*Hai*, yes, we are Japanese," the boys answered.

"What language were you speaking?" he bellowed.

"English."

"Were you practicing in English?"

"Yes."

"*Bakayarō.*" "You fools," he shouted, slapping each one in turn. "That's not so, you are Nisei." After berating them further, the officer reported their infraction to their school. "To the Japanese," Harry reflected later, "the antagonist was the United States and we represented America." From that day on, he never again spoke English in public.

Harry's determination to return to the States remained as vigorous as ever. Nor had Mary wavered. Her anger toward her mother hadn't softened with time; she was unable to relinquish her sense of abandonment. "Mary and my mother argued all the time," said Harry. "I don't think my mother or older sister were close at all," Frank agreed. Harry called Kinu the honorific "*Okāsan*" in public and referred to her lovingly in his diary as "Mom." But Mary was so tightly wrought that she could not say either. "I couldn't, there was something between us." Mary addressed her mother by nothing at all.

Kinu was at a loss over her only daughter's resentment. Why did she bring out the worst in Mary? She didn't have that effect on others. When she used "Chi-chan," an endearing nickname for her neighbor Chieko, the girl lit up. Didn't Mary understand how much Kinu loved her?

Mary knew only that she yearned for independence, away

from Hiroshima, far from Kinu. She graduated from high school at last in March 1936, and her campaign to flee began. Equally as tenacious, Kinu had other plans.

Kinu and Kiyo had already scheduled Mary's *gyōgi minarai* (bridal training). In an age when a woman was considered a *hatachi baba* (old maid at twenty), Mary had reached a ripe nineteen. With a proper girls' school certificate, her alluring "*moga*" ("modern girl") glamour, her family's relative wealth, and Aunt Kiyo's ample connections, Mary would be a catch. Kinu and Kiyo planned to find the perfect groom immediately after her training.

Less than six months before Mary's twentieth birthday, Kinu arranged for Mary to go to the nearby city of Kure, one of Japan's most important naval bases, where the great battleship *Yamato* would soon be built. Like the naval cadets streaming into the city, Mary would be put through boot camp: her rigorous education would occur at no less than the house of the sitting mayor, related to Kinu's elder sister through marriage.

Mary railed against the plan but Kinu insisted. It was time for Mary to learn social graces: traditional dance, flower arrangement, tea ceremony, and other fine arts. It was common for mothers to send their daughters elsewhere to learn these skills; otherwise, they might argue. There was nothing, Kinu assured Mary, to become alarmed over. The training would last as long as it took to turn Mary into a promising matron.

In Mary's case, the training might require double the usual duration, a year or longer. Mary knew she had no choice. Still, she did her best to defy her mother. Instead of changing into a demure kimono and *geta*, Mary stormed out in a dress with bare legs to greet the mayor's wife, the equivalent as far as Kinu was concerned of wearing a bathing suit to a black-tie reception.

Kinu promptly purchased Mary a formal silk kimono, at

considerable cost, for her new situation. When Frank delivered it, Mary vented. She resented being awakened at 5 a.m., corseting herself in a cotton kimono, and scrubbing the premises, but that wasn't as bad as her night duty as a waitress. The mayor entertained almost every other evening. Mary may have appeared subdued, submissive, and gracious in her new kimono, but she bristled under the household's stern expectations. She had to open and close sliding doors with one hand and on her knees, bow a precise number of degrees, set down lacquer trays just so, and remove the covers of *miso* soup bowls with the other maids in unison. Worst of all, everyone watched her hands shake when she poured chilled *sake* into tiny porcelain cups.

"I didn't want to stand for it," Mary said of the drudgery, pressure, and humiliation. Within two weeks, she quit. Borrowing money from an aunt, Mary purchased a train ticket home from Kure.

"You ran away?" Kinu and Kiyo asked in horror. "Sure, I ran away," Mary answered, now more than ever resolved to return to the States. During the torrid heat of summer, as the crickets whined incessantly, mother and daughter were at loggerheads. Kinu refused to let Mary sail for Washington; she worried about a young woman alone. Mary accused Kinu of breaking the promise that had helped her survive the past three years in Japan.

By autumn, as her twentieth birthday neared, Mary grew desperate. One night, she swallowed sleeping pills to frighten her mother. "I just couldn't take it anymore," she explained. Kinu called a physician, who examined Mary and determined that she would make a complete recovery. Relieved but overwhelmed, Kinu relented at last. "I'll let you go," she said, giving Mary two conditions. "You marry somebody and we choose your husband." That was it.

On the spot, at 1 a.m., Mary called four or five close relatives, including her cousin Tazuko and another cousin in Kure, where the naval yard was abuzz day and night with workers constructing warships. "Oh, this is Hisae," Mary said, using her Japanese name. "I called to say goodbye because I'm going to America." "What, what?" came one drowsy reply after another. Most didn't know what else to say, but Tazuko understood clearly that the time for her strong-willed cousin to leave had come.

Mary and Kinu took a train to Hiroshima Station. Seven hours later, they reached Kobe, where Mary boarded a steamship for Seattle. Amid the crush of excited passengers, Kinu sobbed and begged Mary not to leave. Mary insisted. On deck she gathered streamers in her hands and flung them into the air. She had long pictured this moment, expecting to feel victorious and elated. But when she looked at her mother on the dock below, Kinu's face tear-stained and forlorn, Mary felt nothing but melancholy.

BACK AT HOME, KINU DISCOVERED THAT MARY had left behind her kimonos. Kinu clutched the *furisode* (long-sleeved kimono) commonly worn by young, unmarried women. "Auntie still had a dream for her daughter," said Masako Kaneishi, a young neighbor. Kinu folded the bright silk between thick layers of rice paper and placed it in a paulownia chest for safekeeping. In time, she would treat Chieko and Masako, both motherless, like daughters.

The demands of her boys kept her busy. The next autumn, Kinu was cheered when Harry joined a largely all-*nisei* powerhouse basketball team as a second-string guard. The *nisei* were, on average, a few years older, given that they lagged behind academically because of their time abroad. They towered by as much as six inches over the Japanese players, who were only about 5'3", on account of diet and age. At 5'7", Harry was among the tallest. The *nisei* team played a fast-break game, running more than their Japanese counterparts and dominating the court. Wherever they played, they were the talk of the town. They looked Japanese but spoke something else, shouting loudly and gesturing while running the length of the court, so different from the quiet, composed Japanese players. They ultimately competed against college teams, won the Hiroshima prefectural tournament, traveled to the neighboring island of Shikoku, and advanced to the Meiji Shrine in Tokyo, where they represented southern Japan. There the spectacular winning streak came to an end.

Even though the Saturday games softened the edge of the dreaded military drills, Harry set his course. After he graduated from Sanyō in 1938, he would follow in Mary's footsteps and return to Auburn. He could not wait to see his friends. As willful as his sister, Harry began to prepare one year in advance.

He wrote one of his former teachers, now married to the Auburn junior high school principal. Mrs. Rutherford tried to help Harry sort out his feelings. "Yes, I realize how difficult it would be to break away from one's family," she wrote. "Yet, one has to realize that each has his own life to live." The exchange continued. In May 1937, when Harry's Auburn classmates Elgin and Fergy and Helen were donning their graduation gowns, Mrs. Rutherford again encouraged him. "You are torn between the wishes and desires of your Japanese family and people, and your own desires. But Harry, try to do what you really want because you have to live your own life, no one can live it for you. I do so want you to be happy."

In Japan, the pursuit of happiness was subordinated to wartime readiness. On the night of July 7, 1937, Japanese and Chinese forces near the Marco Polo Bridge near Beijing clashed, the two sides firing on one another. War between China and Japan, simmering since Japan's 1931 incursion into Manchuria, erupted.

So many soldiers were assembling in Hiroshima to depart for the fronts in China that the military lacked enough barracks to house them. The extra soldiers were assigned to stay for several days to a week with families in the neighborhood. Kinu was forced to volunteer because her house was spacious. She was offered a small food allowance to defray her costs and was expected to comply.

So it was that the widow and mother of five American children became hostess to soldiers in the Imperial Army and Navy. Kinu cooked for three to five additional, hungry young men on the days she had boarders, filled their baths, and jammed her own family on the second floor. There they huddled, sharing futons so that the strangers could luxuriate below. No one complained. Citizens were expected to do their part. Kinu did worry, though, about the ships of returning soldiers, many prostrate with contagious dysentery from China's putrefying trenches.

Frank was enrolled at Hakushima Primary School just north of Hiroshima Castle. Once a week he and his classmates marched to Ujina and lined up to send off troops bound for the China front. As the soldiers approached, all lockstep and bristle, Frank and his friends wildly waved their red and white *hinomaru* (Rising Sun flags) and shouted *"Banzai!"* with hundreds of other well-wishers.

Among the soldiers sailing for China was Shigeru Matsuura, Harry's nemesis, whose father had tired of his troubled teen and made him enlist at eighteen, a year before he graduated from high school. Harry and Matsuura had eyed each other warily since their tussle at the crowded night festival. When Harry heard that the bully had left, he sighed with relief, certain that he would never cross paths with him again.

WHEN BEIJING FELL TO JAPAN IN AUGUST 1937, a parallel exodus out of Hiroshima was taking place. While Japanese men were boarding Imperial Navy ships for China, *nisei* were clambering on Japan Mail steamers for the United States. A Nikkei Club member Ruth Yamada wrote, "It was just a short while since I got acquainted with you but I think I have found a friend in you." By the time that Harry received her post, she was en route home. These friendships forged in a foreign culture at war were affectionate and intense, tinged by the knowledge that they would be short-lived.

Harry's *nisei* friends in the States worried for him. Writing from Oregon, Mary Okino, a former Nikkei Club pal, asked, "Oh yes, I have heard that a couple of Hiroshima Ken Nisei boys are at war in China, is it true?" Two pages later, she added, "I heard that nobody can come from Japan now, is it true? Especially the men and boys." These words could have made Harry tremble had he not held tangible proof, via the United States consul, of his inalienable rights as an American.

The war in China and the growing friction with the United States over its aggression lent urgency to Harry's quest to return as soon as he graduated. He did not want to be drafted into the Imperial Army, which would conscript more men if the conflict widened. Besides, he belonged in the States. Yet one letter after another warned that anti-Japanese sentiment there was rising. When the Japanese navy sunk the USS *Panay* gunboat, moored on the Yangtze River outside Nanking, in December 1937, American and Japanese relations deteriorated. Kaz Kojo, Harry's *nisei* friend in Auburn, wrote, "Everybody over here reads the paper and talk about war all the time. You go to a show and you'll see newsreels of the war. The people in U.S. are sure against Japan though. After the 'Panay' incident, white people think 'those dirty Japs' and all kinds of things like that."

IN EARLY 1938, KINU AT LAST MOVED the family to a house she had built to her specifications in Takasu, two and a half miles from the center of Hiroshima. Takasu, a newly developed suburb where wealthy Hiroshima residents had once built their country homes, still bore a sleepy, rural air. Graced by a large front yard, backed by persimmon, loquat, pomegranate, and fig trees, the house was designed to accommodate Katsuji's Victorian furnishings, Kinu's wood-and-coal-burning cast-iron stove, and the flush toilet Harry had always wanted. It was rumored that the toilet accounted for one-third of the cost of the house. While the rest of the neighborhood listened for the familiar clop of horse-drawn carts collecting night soil before dawn, Kinu had a septic tank placed behind a wall in the backyard.

As Kinu planted roots in Hiroshima, Harry prepared to leave. He wanted to look like his American pals, not a close-cropped Japanese soldier, so he began growing his hair. He asked his mother to petition the school for permission to deviate from its regulations on hair length. He wrote friends about his imminent departure, including the trustee of his father's estate, W. A. McLean. He attended rousing farewell parties. And, on March 3, 1938, he strode across the auditorium, bowed to the principal, and accepted his high school diploma. Harry was among the youngest *nisei* in Sanyō's graduating class. Harry had kept his end of the bargain. Now his mother was obligated to keep hers.

Kinu struggled to keep her sadness at bay. Not only would she lose Harry but also Victor, who had been drafted into the regular army. He was bound for China in six months. When

Kinu peered at the dense crowds lining the streets to bid farewell to soldiers, she couldn't help but notice that the patriotic audience was hardly jubilant. The schoolchildren assigned to wave flags had no choice. Mothers were admonished not to cry. They bowed to convention. It was, the government repeated, an honor to be called to military service.

Kinu feared the day when she would be watching a procession with her heart in her throat as one of her sons marched toward Ujina and the violent unknown. *Tatemae seikatsu* (a life of appearances) had nothing to do with real emotions. The battle cry "Die for your country" uttered in public did not begin to address a parent's haunting fear of heartbreak.

Determined to see Victor as often as possible before he left, Kinu and Kiyo went to see him at his base during visiting hours on Sundays. They packed his favorite *makizushi* sushi roll with marinated eel and vegetables, passing it secretly to him as a treat. Kinu suspected that Victor, quieter than ever, was being bullied. When Harry accompanied his mother one day, Victor was abruptly called to duty. He returned an hour later, his face bruised. Victor wouldn't say what happened, but the family later learned that he was regularly beaten because he was *nisei*. The abuse became more brazen. "They hit him right in front of the family," Harry recalled. In a military notorious for brutality toward its own for the sake of training, being *nisei* invited punches.

THE WORLD APPEARED TO BE GROWING MORE belligerent by the month. On March 12, 1938, German troops marched into Austria, annexing it one day later. Japan, too, embroiled in China and governed at home by the military, girded for war. On April 1, the government enacted the National Mobilization Act, taking control of industry, capital, labor, goods, and materials.

Over time, this law would permit the tentacles of government to invade almost every aspect of people's lives.

Attuned to the excitement of his voyage, Harry noticed little of these developments. In early April, when falling cherry blossoms tinted Hiroshima's rivers pink, Harry packed a steamer trunk. He added his father's postcard collection, including an auspicious card of Mount Rainier, his own diaries, and his math assignments, perhaps for good measure. With red grosgrain ribbons, he tied together stacks of letters from his Auburn teachers and friends, warm and familiar voices calling him home.

On the day of his departure, his family accompanied him to Hiroshima Station, where they posed for a photograph in the glare of the midday sun. Aunt Kiyo had brought Harry's young cousins Toshinao and Kimiko. Everyone was dressed Japanese-style, except for Harry. The boys wore their military-style school uniforms, the women classic striped kimonos; five-year-old Kimiko a smock. Harry, dapper in a three-piece suit, held a fedora and smiled. Kinu appeared drawn; a lock of hair escaped her bun. Frank, who had undergone a growth spurt and reached his big brother's shoulders, stood close to Harry. Their sleeves touched. Normally buoyed by his big brother, Frank appeared solemn. Each person, caught up in the moment, had no inkling that this was the last time this group would ever be together.

When eighteen-year-old Harry climbed the steps to the coach and disappeared inside, Frank blinked back tears. At thirteen, he was the same age Harry had been when they had moved to Hiroshima. For five years, since their father's death, Frank had viewed Harry as both a father and brother. Never more so than now.

A Sorrowful Homecoming

Harry relished the trip, making fast friends with a group of *nisei* boys traveling in steerage. One looked familiar. In the course of conversation, they discovered that they had traveled the first leg together on the *Hikawa Maru* five years earlier. Taking a break from playing poker and horsing around, Harry met an older *issei* woman, a natural raconteur traveling to Vancouver. In Japanese, she reminisced about journeying to the United States two decades earlier as a picture bride, clutching a photograph of the groom she had married in absentia in Japan. These couples would search for one another at the port, she said, matching their *shirokuro* (black-and-white) photographs to faces in the crowd. Lest she become hopelessly lost, she had tied a string around her neck with a card listing her particulars in English.

This story reminded Harry of his own nineteen-year-old mother venturing overseas for the first time in the summer of 1911. She was a lovely girl with raven hair pulled into a full bouffant, her slim frame corseted in an indigo cotton kimono, her lily hand safeguarding a frayed photo. Leaving everyone she loved in Miyajima, his mother had packed her best silk kimono in a willow trunk and wrapped her *koto* zither.

Harry could imagine his father pacing below the ship,

dashing in his derby hat and light wool suit, glancing back and forth at his wife's formal bridal portrait. Kinu was the second-youngest daughter in a formerly prosperous, lately impoverished family that had lost its ancient pawnshop business to a devastating fire in which the only heirlooms spared were the samurai swords flung into a well. This was a family whose eldest son had ventured to America first because there was little to inherit at home, a family willing to later dispatch a beloved younger daughter who would never protest her filial obligation.

Katsuji, too, had strong but muddied roots. His father was steadily selling the land owned by the family for seventeen generations, only to throw away his wad of wrinkled yen on rickshaw rides and sumo tournaments. Ignored by his stepmother, Katsuji—a mere second son in a land of primogeniture—was reduced to occasionally accepting charity from friends. When the tofu vendor bicycled through Gion, tinkling his bell, a neighbor slipped Katsuji a block. The protein staved off his hunger but did not pacify his dread, and at age fourteen, weeks shy of his primary school graduation, he saw no future. But beyond the undulating Ōta River, past the Seto Inland Sea, across the vast Pacific, America beckoned.

HARRY HAD ALWAYS REGARDED HIS MOTHER AS a typical Japanese housewife and his father as an ambitious community leader. Looking back, he realized that Kinu and Katsuji had been young and unsure once, too. But their marriage as strangers, common at the time, had proved resilient. They had met countless challenges in a foreign land. As his respect for his parents grew, Harry felt less alone.

When he stepped off the ship at Smith Cove, Mary stood waiting. She looked older but elegant and at ease. She had permed her hair and tweezed her eyebrows. But something beyond the crisp air of America contributed to Mary's regal bearing: a gleaming gold band on her ring finger. In Japanese, she spilled her exciting news. While Harry was sailing across the Pacific, Mary had married. She was officially Mrs. Jerry Oshimo, her husband an *issei* eighteen years older than her kid brother.

In the year and a half since her dramatic departure from Hiroshima, Mary had matured, fending financially for herself. Initially, life had been fraught. Her first job as a live-in maid paid only seven dollars a month. She was expected to clean the house, wash the dishes, scrub laundry, and prepare meals. Mary was shocked by the menial labor. Even during her truncated bridal training, she had "never done that kind of work." She soon found a better job arranging flowers. Her *ikebana* skills, repugnant during her bridal training, had "come in handy"; Mary earned more than double her first salary.

In a hotel lobby that she was decorating, Mary met Jerry, a chauffeur for the president of Boeing. He whisked her off to luxurious restaurants and pampered her with shows and shopping sprees. Although he was only half an inch taller than Mary at five foot three and had a receding hairline, Jerry made Mary feel protected. "He was my watchdog." His family hailed from Gion, her father's hometown, where the Oshimos were farmers; the local connection would please her mother, who promptly conducted a customary background check, found the family satisfactory, and approved the match.

When Mary and Jerry visited a photography studio to commemorate their wedding, Mary changed into a traditional *uchikake* (wedding kimono) adorned with an auspicious flower-cart motif, sprouting chrysanthemums and peonies. She held a closed fan. Then, like the sophisticated American bride that she was, she switched into a white wedding sheath with a long train, put on a lace veil and gloves, and held a bouquet of cascading roses. Next to her tuxedoed groom, Mary looked stunning.

During the sweet early days of their union, Mary and Jerry lived in the carriage house on the boss's sprawling estate in Edmonds, occupying the generous space above the four-car garage. They had ample room to host Harry, who joined the newlyweds for a few days. Mary was working as a housekeeper for the Johnsons, cooking and cleaning, while Jerry held a responsible and lucrative post as Mr. P. G. Johnson's driver. True to form, Mary expressed no regret for her abandoned kimonos. She had not, however, escaped serving others.

Despite her fierce independence, Mary was—not for the first time—buffeted by circumstances beyond her control. A domestic was one of the few occupations open to *nisei* women, who were perceived as hardworking, gossip-averse, and compliant. At the Johnson home, Mary cooked for nine, cleaned the first floor, ironed, and served at dinner parties. Despite the pert perm and shiny ring, her life appeared no more liberated than the one she had abandoned in Hiroshima.

Harry was eager to make up for lost time. Racing to Auburn, he caught up with Helen Hall, his high school crush, who was now a statuesque University of Washington coed. The boy in Hiroshima to whom she had signed letters as "Your old pal" was just that. Helen was friendly but her special connection with Harry was nothing more than sweet nostalgia.

Harry knocked on the door of his best buddy, Elgin Biddle. Upon seeing Harry after five years, Mrs. Biddle invited Harry in for a chat. Elgin was away, she explained, completing his freshman year at college. Mrs. Biddle had once gushed in a letter, "OH Harry I wish you were back with us again. Be a good Boy so you can come back again soon." As dusk settled, Harry lingered, anticipating the usual invitation to stay for dinner, even without Elgin. To his consternation, Mrs. Biddle never offered.

Life in Auburn, Harry sensed, had danced along at a merry clip, leaving him on the sidelines. He had missed five autumns of football games, especially those when quarterback Elgin sprinted to victory, and five winters of the Green River's salmon-gushing floods, when he and his neighbor Fergy would have gathered the flapping fish. He had missed three springs of high school Barn Dances, one April boutonnièred Senior Ball, and what should have been his own June commencement. The people Harry cherished had grown up, graduated, and left town. They regarded Harry with fondness, but comfortable at home, they had not longed for him as he had them from such a distance.

There was something else lurking in the shadows—the specter of discrimination. Harry had downplayed the facts that he was not welcome at the homes of some *hakujin* friends because their parents were uneasy and that his flirtation with pretty *hakujin* girls had no future. Owing to his close friendships with *hakujin*, he had overlooked that which most other *nisei* readily acknowledged.

His friend Amy Kusumi was close to the Halls. "They were really nice girls from a very religious family," Amy recalled. "They always encouraged us to go to church, and we started going to their church, the Free Methodist church with some other Japanese friends. I was like three years old. We walked over a mile. They never offered to take us. That was kind of cold." Amy's family prayed to the same God at the same house of worship but suspected that their ethnicity prevented them from being offered a ride to church.

Walt Tanaka, another *kibei* who would become Harry's friend, experienced a mortifying incident in junior high school in California when his teacher took his class on a field trip by bus to a swimming pool. Walt purchased a towel for a quarter along with his white classmates before entering the premises. "Step aside," the attendant told him. Walt obeyed, only to wait three hours for the group to return, all the time listening to the squeals of laughter and the whoosh of splashing. Walt only then realized why his *nisei* classmates had opted out of the excursion from the start.

"Do you think I'm dirty?" he wanted to rail at the attendant. His own teacher stepped aboard the bus at the end of the outing and never said a word.

It wasn't that Harry didn't detect the discomfort woven into everyday conversations. He did. But he preferred to focus on the genuine friendships he had experienced. He assumed all the letters he got while he was away were tangible proof that he was immune to discrimination and would be insulated from hurt. He did not realize that his disheartening reunions were following a predictable course. *Nisei* friendships with *hakujin* peers tended to weaken after high school graduation, as white students advanced to university and *nisei* groped to find their place. Yet at this point, he refused to give up on Auburn.

The Great Depression further winnowed opportunities. In 1938, the sputtering recovery and visionary New Deal faltered. That year more than four million lost their jobs, and the stock market slumped. The *nisei* were considered less desirable than ever. They beat a retreat to West Coast Japantowns, bustling working-class districts bursting with underemployed over-achievers. There, too, trudged Harry.

He moved into the Northern Pacific (NP) Hotel, managed by his father's old friend Mr. Shitamae, in the heart of Seattle's Japantown. The NP was considered one of the finer hotels catering to the Japanese community. In exchange for meals, Harry worked as a waiter and dishwasher at the nearby Jackson Cafe, piling Western food high on heaping servings of rice. In between, he slipped into darkened movie theaters, catching a reel and extra winks. Yet, despite his frugality, he was still running short on money.

Unable to afford his hotel room, Harry sublet it to migrant workers, designing a schedule for sleeping shifts. In addition to cinema seats, he discovered other spaces for catnaps—cars, hotel lobbies, buses, and train stations. He was not above requesting a booking in jail, where he was locked in a cell until the considerate police chief released him in the morning. Within eight weeks of his return, Harry hankered to leave Japantown—the press of close quarters; the stale odors of day-old broth and thrice-used cooking oil; the tongue-rolling slurs slobbered among drunken workers. Harry still kept his eye on the American dream—college, a white-collar job, a home of his own. Leaving his treasured black steamer trunk—including his stacks of letters from Auburn—in the custody of the Shitamaes, Harry set off again for Auburn.

Harry called on W. A. McLean, his father's old Auburn Chamber of Commerce friend. The McLeans welcomed Harry overnight, and Mr. McLean drove him to the College of Puget Sound. If Harry could make the tuition, he could stay with them and realize his father's dream of college. Harry appreciated the McLeans' generous offer, but it was out of reach. A kid who sought shelter in jail did not possess cash for tuition.

By the time of the harvest, Harry's course was clear: college would have to wait. For the next three months, from June through August, Harry picked strawberries and peas at farms in the White River Valley and Bellevue. His day began at 7 a.m. and ended twelve hours later, when the sun began to set. Harry barely noticed. He didn't break, except to chew peas and snack on strawberries, which stained his fingertips. But by the end of the day, he couldn't stand up straight. Long past dark, sweaty, dirty, and exhausted, Harry collapsed on a straw mattress in a farmer's shed, reeking like his roommates—crammed-in, used-up *issei*. Harry grasped what his father had never said. The allure of the hobo was only romantic when one slept in soft sheets on a sturdy bed. Falling into a heavy slumber, he awakened to the cloying fragrance of overripe fruit. Another day of dogged labor had begun.

On Sundays, Harry rested, visiting his parents' friends in Seattle, devouring their Japanese food, on the lookout for sour *takuan* pickled radishes. Skinnier than ever, Harry had the insatiable appetite of most eighteen-year-old young men.

When these jobs dried up, he hitchhiked to other dusty farms, where he cut flowers, harvested cucumbers, and tugged greenhouse tomatoes from their vines—whatever was needed. All for a dollar a day and—if he was lucky with steady work—a whopping thirty dollars a month. His fellow pickers were wizened *issei*, bronzed Filipinos, and pale *nisei*, the latter tasting hard work for the first time before returning to school. Like the older men who had forsaken their dreams, his American adventure was, in a single Depression summer, shriveling under the mounting weight of plywood produce crates.

At the end of his first summer back in Auburn, Harry had nowhere to live and nowhere to go. He looked into an Alaskan cannery job, but the union was on strike, and there was no work to be had. Summer ended early in the Pacific Northwest, and he decided to "drift" south, where the citrus fields might need a hand. Better yet, Los Angeles. Before the Gravenstein apples turned golden and crimson, Harry headed to the City of Angels, leaving behind his sister, his steamer trunk, and his faith in once-halcyon Auburn.

PACIFIC NORTHWEST CLOUD COVER AND THE DAMP chill gave way the farther south Harry traveled. In September 1938 he disembarked to brilliant sunshine and T-shirt temperatures. Los Angeles hummed with people, activity, and ambition. Its population, surpassing more than a million, made it the fifth-largest metropolis in the United States. Priding itself in innovation, Los Angeles had hosted a summer Olympiad at its recently enlarged Coliseum, introduced traffic lights along its handsome boulevards, opened an experimental television station, and converted a bean field into its first drive-in movie theater. While Harry, initially befuddled by his reliably poor sense of direction, was getting the lay of the land, Charlie Chaplin was at home in Beverly Hills, penning his satirical screenplay for *The Great Dictator.*

Crooner Bing Crosby's hit "I've Got a Pocketful of Dreams" was soaring at the top of the *Billboard* charts. It could have been Harry's theme song. Harry wasn't the only one. Thirty-five thousand Japanese Americans lived in Los Angeles, most in Little Tokyo. Harry knew a few very well. His Hiroshima pals Kaz Nagata and the Matsumoto brothers had resettled with their families. They knew Harry wasn't a migrant worker. They knew him for who he truly was, an American like them from a good family, a *kibei* by default, a boy lately of Hiroshima. Harry stayed with Kaz at first, finding his bearings.

The Nagatas and, later, the Matsumotos hosted Harry with affection. But he discovered what he hadn't realized before—most *kibei* needed the support of their families to resume their lives in the United States. As genuine as his friends were, other than the newly married Mary, Harry had no immediate family in the States. His ties were more tenuous than he had thought.

Although Kaz and the Matsumotos had been considered wealthy in Hiroshima, their family's thriving market was a first-generation business, owing its success to hard work, long hours, and tight margins. There was no room for another employee. Harry scrambled on his own, cobbling together two eight-hour • jobs. He worked one shift at a produce market and the other as a night watchman, with just one hour in between. Totaichi Kono, his father's friend and Charlie Chaplin's assistant, had introduced him to the market's owner, also from Hiroshima. Harry settled into a boardinghouse for *issei* and *nisei* gardeners and greengrocers, taking one day off a week.

Neither job lasted long. Finally, before Thanksgiving, he found a job at the Three Star Produce Market, located on Hyperion Avenue at the border of Glendale and Hollywood. The owner hailed from Gion and the manager was a *kibei* who lived in the same boardinghouse as Harry. Although he worked long hours, like his generation and the generation before him, Harry wasn't disappointed. At last, he held a job without a harvest end date; it might become permanent.

Across the street from Three Star Produce sat Walt Disney Studios. Animators working on *Bambi* required live animals to serve as models for their drawings, and the lot took on the appearance of a zoo. Every day Harry carried over buckets of trimmings—discarded leaves, vegetable skins, and bruised chunks—for the critters, about to be immortalized as Disney's eternal and irreverent cartoon characters. The Disney Studios sent him a Christmas card signed by Walt Disney in his tidy, looping hand. It was one of the few personal greetings that Harry would receive in Los Angeles.

But just after Christmas, Harry was fired. It wasn't personal: business was slow and he wasn't needed. If he continued at this pace, "I would just go from job to job." He couldn't shake the words of an old *issei* he had met in his travels who had once dreamed of earning enough gold in three years to return to Japan a rich man. "Don't end up like me," he warned. Harry was sobered by the thought. There was only one solution. He needed to go to school.

Paying for tuition was not a problem that Harry could easily resolve. The instability was eating at him, and he sometimes displayed a short fuse. A relative on his father's side, whom Harry came to know in Los Angeles, remembered running into Harry at a dance. Harry got into a fight and was beaten up. There were *nisei* gangs in Los Angeles, but Harry did not belong to one of those. Still, Harry's cousin Bob, who hadn't known Harry as a gregarious and freewheeling young man, regarded him as a "tough guy." Harry was developing an edge.

Harry soon placed an ad in the newspaper offering his services as a "house boy" or "domestic servant," who would serve as a housekeeper and babysitter in exchange for room, board, and nominal pay. In January Harry received a response. A family in nearby Glendale, named the Mitchums, needed someone to look after their two boys for fifteen dollars a month. Harry grabbed the opportunity. If the thought crossed his mind that he was converging on the same path his father had taken as a fourteen-year-old immigrant in 1900, he buried it. Harry's dreams of college and success flickered again.

The Mitchums, Harry recalled, were "sympathetic" to his circumstances, giving him two Sundays off a month and allowing him to attend night school. He enrolled part-time in Glendale Junior College, where he studied business. Hitchhiking to school proved impractical, so Harry persuaded Mr. Mitchum to loan him ten dollars a month to pay off the $135 cost of a used Model A Ford.

It didn't matter that Harry's salary barely covered his loan.

Nor did it faze him that he still had to hitchhike on occasion when he couldn't afford gas, or that he could only purchase three gallons at a time for fifty cents a pop. Sometimes, he ran the car on flat tires; when he had no choice, he drove on bent rims, clattering all the way. Harry loved his jalopy as much as his father had adored his shiny Buick sedan. He just couldn't afford to maintain it.

Since Harry's arrival in the City of Angels just six months earlier, Japan had continued to pursue its dangerous military conflict in China. The world was taking notice. In September, the same month that Harry set foot in Los Angeles, the League of Nations officially termed Japan an aggressor and recommended support of the Chinese government. Ignoring the international rebuke, the Imperial Army dispatched more soldiers to China. Japan's euphemistically labeled China Incident was expanding into a quagmire. The situation hit home when Harry's mother wrote him that among the soldiers to leave the port of Ujina for China was his gentle brother Victor.

Harry stayed with the Mitchums for six months, until Flossie and Clyde Mount, who had observed Harry from their house on the hill above, offered him a job. The Mounts promised thirty-five dollars a month, an increase of twenty dollars. He could supplement his salary with odd jobs on the side, and the Mounts approved of Harry's plans for higher education. Harry couldn't refuse and the Mitchums understood. In the summer of 1940, Harry bumped up the short ridge in his rusty Ford, parked in the Mounts' shady driveway, and entered their warm embrace.

He would stay with them for a year and a half. When he left, it would not be by choice. Few Japanese Americans left Los Angeles, or for that matter, the West Coast by choice in 1942. Not after Pearl Harbor.

8

Hazing in Hiroshima

In autumn 1938, when eighteen-year-old Harry was hauling trimmings to the Disney menagerie, fourteen-year-old Frank was finishing his final year of elementary school in Hiroshima. His Japanese was virtually flawless. Proud of Frank's prowess, Kinu encouraged him to take the rigorous exam for the Hiroshima First Middle School, one of the most prestigious all-boy middle and high schools in the city. When Frank passed the test, Kinu rejoiced.

The news spread through the neighborhood and among the network of relatives. In a culture accustomed to numbered ranks, *Icchū*, or First Middle, carried weight. Students all over the city vied for coveted spots, and the school was so renowned that the Meiji emperor had deigned to visit. "Everyone who went there was smart," said Masako. Everyone recognized an *Icchū* boy by his brown shoes and the distinctive white *gētoru* cotton strips wrapped around his shins. People accorded *Icchū* boys—often the valedictorians and salutatorians of their primary schools—respect.

In early April 1939, Frank was officially inducted into *Icchū*. The portrait of the serious, mustached, spectacled emperor consecrated the auditorium, supervising his faithful subjects. Regarded as a living god descended from the sun goddess, the ruler was never referred to by his name, Hirohito, but rather as

"His Majesty the Emperor." It didn't matter that he was a small, homely man with a weak chin and questionable political authority; to even privately entertain such thoughts was high treason. No citizen outside the cabinet had ever heard the god called the "Sacred Crane" speak.

Upon the principal's command *"Kiritsu,"* Frank Katsutoshi Fukuhara stood up, his head closely shaved, his expression earnest. At *"Rei,"* Frank bowed in unison with the incoming students. When the principal intoned *"Chakuseki,"* Frank sat down bolt straight, alert as to what would follow.

At the podium, the principal commenced his speech, reminding students and their families of *Icchū's* venerable history. Students should aspire to the school motto of "simple and sturdy" and "polite and distinguished." Frank found the Confucian concepts reasonable, harmless, and imbued with humility.

In the audience, Kinu beamed. The future of her youngest child appeared the most assured. Pierce was enrolled in Harry's alma mater, Sanyō Commercial School, which was more than adequate. But *Icchū* was elite. Kinu worried about her eldest three—Victor overseas in the army, Mary married in Seattle, and Harry teetering on the economic brink in Los Angeles. But Frank flourished at her side. He was, she thought, at home in Japan. He was, she knew, intellectually and physically blessed. On this celebratory day, charged with purpose and promise, Frank might have solemnly agreed.

Kinu wanted Frank to become a doctor; he liked that idea too. *Icchū* would prepare him for the next step of applying to a prestigious medical faculty of a premier national university. When Kinu had been Frank's age, she had hoped to enter the First Hiroshima Prefectural Girls' High School, situated near *Icchū,* but her family could not afford tuition for a daughter. At forty-six, she was content to live through her son.

. . .

BY MAY, WHEN THE PEONIES BLOOMED, FRANK began to gain his footing. His initial anxiety was fading and he believed he could handle *Icchū*'s rigorous academic and competitive sports program. Then one day the fifth-year seniors called all the freshmen to an after-school meeting in the auditorium where a *sekkyō* (sermon) would be delivered.

The freshmen trembled, struggling to stand still in perfect rows in the vast room. Beyond the closed doors, faculty occasionally padded by in the corridor. Confident and contemptuous, a group of seniors faced the freshmen and stared them down. The freshmen looked at the floor. One upperclassman stepped forward, took a deep breath, and began to lecture. He and a couple of others selected ten or fifteen first-year students, including Frank, to stand apart. A senior began to rant and yell with a rage so heated that it would lodge in Frank's memory forever.

"You didn't salute me!" he screamed. *Slap*—the sound of a hand hitting flesh reverberated in the open space. An unprepared freshman reddened, the mark temporarily branding his cheek.

One after another, the freshmen were hit, slapped, and punched. When Frank's turn came, the upperclassman screamed *"Namaikiya!"* "Spoiled brat!" Frank watched him throw back his arm as if in slow motion to wind up for a punch. When the fist came, hard on his jaw, Frank tried not to flinch and stumble. He resisted bringing his hand to his mouth; he tasted blood. The men took another round. When he wasn't being slapped a good dozen times in succession, Frank was punched, five to ten times for good measure. The upperclassmen rarely paused, debasing and abusing the younger boys for two hours straight.

The seniors were irate. Hadn't the school rules been posted and announced? Hadn't they been made perfectly clear? An *Icchū* student should never be out of uniform. An *Icchū* student should wear only white T-shirts. An *Icchū* student should not use a wristwatch. He should not carry a fountain pen or gloves. He should not don an overcoat. An *Icchū* student should not frequent restaurants or movie theaters. Indulging in frivolous habits, bellowed the upperclassmen, revealed sloth, a penchant for luxury, and inadequate self-discipline. These weaknesses, they warned, cried for punishment, which they were obliged to deliver.

Where were the teachers? Frank wondered. Didn't they hear the commotion through the open windows or from the hall? Why didn't someone open the door, poke his head in, ask whether anything was wrong, and halt the violence?

The beatings were a ritual that took place once or twice a month, often on Mondays, a bruising start to the week. Sometimes, twenty or thirty upperclassmen surrounded one freshman. On the days a whole group was selected, Frank was inevitably among them. *"Oi Fukuhara!"* "Hey Fukuhara!" Frank stepped forward. The upperclassmen expected absolute, automatic, and utterly silent submission. They largely succeeded. At each interminable session, Frank inhaled, braced himself, and waited to be pummeled into weary compliance, for whatever he may or may not have done.

After school, Frank retreated to his mother's home, a soothing hybrid of East and West. Occasionally, he invited over a few friends, including an *Icchū* classmate named Hiroshi Ogura. The moment Hiroshi walked into the house, past the Edwardian coat-and-hat stand and into the living room with its Monarch piano, he felt his suspicions confirmed. Some people tried to imitate Western design, decorating with whatever struck them as exotic—a hodgepodge of wicker tables, crochet-draped chairs, and inlaid-pearl divans—the jarring effect more furniture showroom than sophisticated salon. The Fukuhara house artfully intermingled Japanese and American pieces. Mrs. Fukuhara greeted the boys warmly. She was wearing a dress, not a kimono. At that moment, Hiroshi recognized why the Fukuhara boy had struck him as different. Mrs. Fukuhara was a refined woman, he thought, but both she and her son were "*batakusai.*" They stank of butter.

Batakusai was a figurative description for Westerners, who, stereotypically, relished butter and a dairy-rich cuisine. As a pejorative, it carried an unctuous connotation, as if foreigners oozed grease from their pores. Hiroshi intended no harm. After all, he was *nisei*, too. He hailed from Portland, Oregon, and his preferred name was Henry though he couldn't use it at *Icchū*. The Fukuhara boy and he made two; there were a few other *nisei* at school but no one willingly divulged such information. Indeed, Frank was destined to graduate never knowing that some of his classmates shared this common bond.

Hiroshi revealed his past, to Frank's delight. From that point on, they called each other Frank and Henry in private. Over Kinu's savory curry rice, dealing cards for gin rummy, they laughed and unwound. Henry sensed that Frank's mother was happy he had found a kindred spirit.

Frank gradually grew more cautious about his habits, dressing carefully, speaking only Japanese in public, and forgoing his given American name, even in Takasu. But one day Frank was wearing a blue T-shirt, a hand-me-down from Harry, and sitting in the living room near the window when an *Icchū* senior whom he hadn't known lived nearby walked by the house. "You don't wear that blue thing in Japan!" the upperclassman yelled. Frank froze. "I knew that I had been watched."

Frank would be punished. The next time he had to attend the

sermon ritual, his neighbor took the lead and singled out Frank. "He gave me a really rough time," Frank said of the dressing-down and physical attack. The psychological effects would long outlast the shiners.

Frank was shocked that the trigger for his latest beating had come from his own neighborhood, where everyone seemed so friendly. The landscape was a luxuriant world apart from *Icchū's* urban locale. Flowering lotus fields and verdant rice paddies hugged the residential blocks. A shrine overlooked the area surrounded by an orchard of fig trees and a gurgling stream. Takasu was Frank's beloved backyard, where he had felt secure.

His *nisei* status was an open secret in Takasu, and there were other families with American roots, as well. But Toshiko Fukuda, the post office lady, who often visited Kinu, would later remark, "The older brothers seemed different. I almost wondered if they spoke Japanese. They were more Americanized than Frank." Frank may have appeared less American than his brothers, but he was clearly not Japanese enough. In Mrs. Fukuda's eyes, the Fukuharas were ethnic Japanese fundamentally altered by their American experience. She was intrigued. But in a wartime xenophobic culture, this subtle difference made the family appear almost foreign, less legitimate than born-and-bred citizens.

Creeping militarism or not, Kinu had always known that in the tight quarters of overpopulated Japan, walls had ears. "*Hitori ieba sannin kiku.*" "If someone says something, there are three people listening." In general, Kinu kept her own counsel. But at night, when her chores were finished, she sat with Frank on her American couch in her moss-colored living room, poured them barley tea, and let her guard slip. She yearned to see Harry. She was shocked and disappointed when Harry left but now she was worried. She had been concerned about

Harry venturing to the United States alone, but he had worn her down over time with *"Wakai toki no kurō wa katte demo seyo."* "Buy suffering when young." But Harry was suffering too much. He had submitted his father's outstanding promissory notes to a collection agency. The Fukuharas received 50 percent of what the agency collected and Harry refused to touch a penny. His life had turned hard-bitten. Kinu wished he had kept the cash.

Frank nodded. He was his mother's confidant now, as Harry had once been over their sun-dappled picnic lunches in Auburn. Kinu did not ask Frank much about *Icchū*, where she believed that he was being impeccably educated. Frank didn't have the heart to contradict her; he kept his school-day agony to himself. Yes, he agreed while listening to Kinu reminisce about Harry, he was lonely for him, too.

SOME CLASSMATES WHO WENT FROM *ICCHŪ* TO military academies were astonished by how little Frank comprehended about the zeitgeist. Of course, the sermons were official bullying and common at such an elevated institution, where half the graduates advanced to service academies, becoming officers. They didn't find anything wrong with this approach. After all, was not the school motto, "simple and sturdy," consistent with accepted military values? *Icchū* emphasized the philosophy of *bushidō* (the way of the warrior), critical to the molding of the Japanese military. The sermons would, presumably, develop physical and moral strength, rectitude, devotion, and valor, all *bushidō* values. *Icchū* was a superior institution, in part, because nothing was left to chance, not even the sermons, tacitly endorsed by the staff. To see it any other way was naïve.

If *nisei* thought they could mask their identity and fool their Japanese classmates, they were mistaken. Frank stood out from the beginning. Frank may have looked Japanese, but he did not act it. Most Japanese expressed themselves with ambiguity; Frank said exactly what he thought. Most students listened to their teachers without comment; Frank argued back. There was something rough and rebellious about him that raised eyebrows and probably irritated upperclassmen who demanded respect.

Frank's undoing came in English class. "Spell *tulip*," the teacher directed. Japanese students stumbled on the "t-u" combination and rolled the "l," garbling the word as "tsu-ri-pu." But Frank pronounced it fluently, as any native speaker would. "Where did you learn?" the teacher asked. Down the hall, Henry Ogura was purposely mispronouncing his English vocabulary and faking a British accent to blend in and deflect doubts about his origins. Frank could have used Henry as his tutor.

On the days that Frank came home with a black eye and swollen cheek, he rushed upstairs to his bedroom to avoid his mother. At dinner, Kinu's normally cheerful youngest son kept his face averted. When she questioned how he was feeling, he mumbled about a headache. Frank downplayed his latest ordeal, and chewing with difficulty, made light of his lack of appetite. He was usually hungry, he assured his mother, just not tonight. Determined not to show his face and see her blanch with concern, Frank excused himself early. "*Gochisōsama deshita*." "Thank you for the feast," a polite finish to dinner. Kinu bit her lip but did not push Frank to say more.

As a housewife, Kinu saw providing for her family as her duty. But the wartime economy was faltering. With so many materials diverted for munitions and supplies, the home front was forced to reduce expenditures, become accustomed to bare shelves at home and in stores, and be content with less. Around the time Frank entered *Icchū*, people began greeting one another with a sigh, "Not enough, not enough." *"Tarin, tarin."* No sooner had this phrase caught the public's imagination than it gave way to *"Zeitaku wa teki da,"* "Extravagance is the enemy," a command on what to think and how to act. The government plastered posters and hung banners to this effect, and people took the phrase to heart.

Kinu folded her kimono and put away her silk dresses. Increasingly, neighbors, heeding government recommendations, wore simple blouses and cotton *monpe* bloomerlike pants, gathered at the ankles. All the better to cultivate rice paddies, plant vegetables, and tend fruit trees. Young male farmers, leaving their fields fallow, were marching to war.

Frank summoned the strength to persevere. Yet, the more he advanced at *Icchū*, the more immersed he became in a vast military apparatus. Frank and Kinu had missed the mark when Frank had applied there. Japan had gone to war in China while Kinu was in America, and *Icchū*'s mission had gradually altered. After two decades away, Kinu may no longer have possessed the keen sense of what was understood without being articulated. Frank's vantage point was decidedly American. While he perceived the teachers as bystanders, they may have viewed themselves as instilling responsibility in the upperclassmen by having them train younger students. Out of step with other Hiroshima citizens, the Fukuharas were ill-equipped for the militaristic lifestyle that others accepted.

Now that Frank was enrolled in what he called a "high school that was a preschool to the military," he had to endure its martial program. Since the early 1920s, Japanese army officers had been attached to the Empire's middle schools as staff. Standing on a dais in the middle of the grounds, they oversaw drills conducted by the thousand-plus-strong student body. *Icchū* boasted no less than an active warrant officer and full colonel on staff. Whatever reservations career educators felt toward the incursion of the military on campus, many were products of military-style training themselves. Even those studying to be elementary school teachers had been required to conduct training drills, live in spartan barracks, and conform to stiff discipline in their Normal Schools.

Students proved receptive to military ideals. Reared on a diet of fables elevating the martial as supreme, they no longer dreamed of becoming physicians or professors. Instead, they saw themselves as helmeted tank drivers and scarf-draped pilots. Practical considerations came into play. Masako knew *Icchū* well. "If you were a soldier," she said, "it was cheaper to send a child there. After that he could go to a military college, too."

Frank's hazing would continue for three excruciating years, followed by a one-year break. Then, in his fifth and last year of *Icchū*, he would be expected to turn into an abuser too. After he and his classmates advanced to a service academy, the cycle would commence again. Ultimately, obedient *Icchū* graduates would transform their bullying into blunt brutality directed at the enemy.

The violence shook Frank to his core. "*Sekkyō* had changed my life entirely," he said later. From that moment on he "hated school," so much so that "I was ready to leave but I didn't want to worry Mother." Every additional sermon took a toll. Undone by the "emotional shock," Frank became taciturn, angry with himself for being "passive," "cowardly," and for mutely accepting the punches. Initially excited about *Icchū* and a motivated student, outside the oppressive auditorium he became, by his own account "wild" and cantankerous. He blamed himself, in part, for calling attention to his blatant individualism. Frank hated the hazing and cursed who he had become.

Frank suspected that his mother and Pierce both knew something was wrong. "But nobody asked me, so I never told anybody." When Kinu lamented to Frank again how Harry was suffering in the States, she had no idea that her saying, "Buy suffering when young," also applied to Frank.

All Frank could think about was what it would be like back in Auburn biting into a grilled hot dog on a buttered bun, chugging a Coke, devouring a handful of Bing cherries, and spitting out the pits in the backyard. He imagined the fragrance of evergreens after a rain shower. Suddenly, Frank urgently wanted to go back. There would be no hazing in Auburn. Driven by desperation, he vowed to find a way.

If Frank left school in Japan, he had no choice but to return to America. The alternative was an immediate draft. He had waved too many flags at too many send-off parades in elementary school not to know what followed. One year after departing for the front, soldiers often returned as fallen heroes, their cremated remains carried in a memorial procession on the same route they had once marched. Everyone, even primary school students, knew soldiers were destined to die. Japanese education prepared citizens to sacrifice themselves for the emperor and the nation, in victory or defeat. To do otherwise was unthinkable. Surrender was never an option. It was better to die with honor than live with shame.

FOR THE TIME BEING, FRANK NEEDED TO stay at *Icchū*, but he could not attract too much attention. If he excelled, he would be recommended for officer-candidate school, an honor he could not refuse. Watching his classmates graduate to a military academy was sobering. He resolved to transform himself, chameleon-like, into an average Japanese recruit-in-training at school and preserve his American exuberance at home. The delicate balance induced vertigo. At *Icchū*, Frank shrank, keeping his head down, his expression blank, his gestures restrained, his gait clipped, and his lips sealed. A mighty challenge for a boy whose country of birth was imprinted on his soul.

An unexpected opportunity arose when Frank ran in a track meet during his freshman year. He had always been athletic. In America, he had climbed fog-washed Mount Rainier with his father and chased Harry along the banks of the Green River. In Japan, he had taken to hours-long martial-art practices and competitions in austere *dōjōs*. He was swift and well coordinated. Flying around the dirt track, Frank soared to first in the prefecture in both the 100-meter and 200-meter dash events. He had discovered a latent talent that invigorated him.

A few years earlier, Frank had listened to the breathless radio coverage of Jesse Owens sprinting to victory at the Olympic Games in Berlin in 1936, winning four gold medals, among them the 100- and 200-meter dashes. Frank had cheered for his fellow American. Perhaps Frank could be a runner, too. *Icchū* boasted a venerable tradition in track and field. Alumnus Mikio Oda had won a gold medal in the triple jump at the Amsterdam Olympics in 1928. Coach Takanari Yoshioka was a famous 100-meter runner and former Olympian. Frank envisioned an escape route: If he excelled in athletics, he could delay his draft. With practice and determination, he could, literally, outrun it.

By the beginning of his second *Icchū* year, in April 1940, Frank focused on his mission. *Icchū* mandated that students walk to school if they lived within three miles; otherwise, they could take the train to the three-mile point. Takasu lay slightly farther away, but Frank traveled entirely by foot anyway. He ran each way six days a week. *"Ame ni mo makezu, kaze ni mo makezu.*" "Not losing to the rain, not losing to the wind . . ." So went the beloved poem by poet Kenji Miyazawa.

He left Takasu slowly, weaving past horse-and-carts, then picked up steam before crossing the wooden Koi Bridge. Entering the city proper, Frank traversed four more bridges, trying to avoid bicyclists and charcoal-powered buses—gas was siphoned to the war effort. North across the small stretch of the Motoyasu River, Frank glimpsed the green-copper, domed Industrial Promotion Hall, Hiroshima's architectural gem, and, beyond, the distinctive T-shaped Aioi Bridge. He headed south, skirting the streetcar tracks. *Icchū* lay directly behind City Hall, which was decked out in banners with wartime slogans the length of four floors. Farther south, at the city's edge, lay Ujina, bulging with naval transports ready to embark fresh-faced soldiers and disgorge sick and broken veterans.

Entering *Icchū*'s main gate, Frank straightened up. He could not afford to be careless from this point on. No hands unconsciously thrust in pockets: the penalty would be taking off his clothes in front of his classmates. No thoughtless loping. Frank marched across the grounds, stopping to bow at the waist to the miniature *hōanden* shrine housing the imperial portraits.

Icchū emphasized emperor-centered worship. If Frank intended to perform adequately, he had to immerse himself in a curriculum of ethics, Japanese history, martial arts, physical education, mathematics, and science. The ethics teacher chalked the Imperial Precepts of 1882 on the blackboard for the students to learn by heart. Military men should never forget, explained one of the crucial passages, that "duty is weightier than a mountain, while death is lighter than a feather."

At the end of the day, Frank ran home in the soupy dusk; the government had outlawed the use of neon lights. By the time he reached Takasu, his stomach growled with hunger. His mother's marinade would not be sweetened with much sugar, rationed by December 1940. The restrictions especially impacted Meijidō, though Kiyo had troop contracts to sustain her. Kinu increased the soy in her sauce to season the root vegetables. Shopping was becoming increasingly arduous as more shops were permanently closed. Fortunately, Kinu sensed that healthy hunger and normal fatigue propelled her youngest son. Whatever else had once troubled him appeared to have diminished.

Although the sermons continued unmitigated, Frank had adjusted. He grasped *Icchū's* priorities, accepted the group-mentality ethos behind hazing, didn't take the pummeling personally, and put the stress behind him more quickly. The blisters, bruises, and cuts would heal. Still, Frank despised the seniors who believed that they were inculcating the freshmen with a noble spirit.

Channeling his fury, Frank ran the 100- and 200-meter dashes his second year of school. He was growing, though still a few inches shorter than Harry. Frank ran barefoot. In time, he ran as fast as Coach Yoshioka, but, of course, the coach was past his prime at thirty-five. Frank redoubled his efforts. The coach noticed.

One day, Coach Yoshioka pulled him aside. He knew his athlete was training hard and *Icchū* didn't have many sprinters. The team needed Fukuhara. But the coach couldn't let him participate if he failed a course and was expelled from school. Given the political climate, the subject in question wasn't highly valued and had less class time allocated than before, but it was still part of the curriculum. Fukuhara had best bone up quickly on English grammar.

Frank was shocked. So intent had he been to disguise his

nisei identity that he had succeeded too well, forgetting much of what he had learned in Auburn. Frank had to retrieve his English without exposing his past. He hunkered down with his dry Japanese textbook of English grammar, stored his American English in the recesses of his mind, and kept on running.

ON THE MORNING OF MONDAY, DECEMBER 8, 1941, Frank rose early to attend a track meet. At 7 a.m., he was standing on the platform at Takasu Station, having decided to catch a train to conserve his energy before the race. Housewives were heading to market despite the latest government slogan chiding them, *"Kawanu kesshin, kachinuku ketsui."* "Decide not to buy, resolve to triumph!" Frank focused on staying warm. He limbered up, jumping on tiptoe until the train rolled into the station. Above the clamor of the screeching wheels, a man behind him yelled—something about a victorious assault on Hawaii. Frank hopped on the train. Bewildered, he grasped that the news was important. "I was excited and didn't know what was going to happen."

After the meet, he ran home to find that his mother had already heard about Japan's attack on Pearl Harbor. Everyone had. A Japanese naval hymn had trumpeted forth from strategically positioned loudspeakers, jarring citizens before they sipped their first cup of green tea that morning. "Defend and attack for our country," the announcement blared. No one knew what would happen next.

The next day, Kinu opened her local *Chūgoku Shimbun* newspaper to martial headlines from official Japanese news sources throughout the Pacific. The titles were so bold, they roared. "Surprise attacks" in "every direction"—"first air raids on Honolulu"; Singapore "under bombardment," too; Davao, Wake, Guam, as well. In Shanghai, the British fleet "sunk," the American one "surrendered." "The commencement of attacks on Hong Kong." "The arrival of a surprise attack on the Malay Peninsula." Stunning developments that were all accurate.

On the surface, nothing changed terribly at first. In Takasu, neighbors gathered around radios, anxious for breaking news. At the market in Koi, housewives traded shopping tips. Was there a sugar substitute to sweeten homemade fig jam? Prices were climbing as swiftly as a kite in a typhoon. What to do? The New Year holiday was coming.

A new name for all-out war came first. Since 1931, the start of Japan's aggression in Manchuria, the government had portrayed skirmishes and battles in Manchuria and China as separate incidents. On December 12, 1941, the government announced that the war against the United States and Great Britain, as well as the Sino-Japanese conflict, would be called the Great East Asia War, a title imbued with a sense of holy mission.

Regardless of nomenclature, Japan had been at war for one agonizing decade. Those *Amerika-gaeri* returnees who had once lived in the States were pessimistic about Japan's prospects. "Japan shouldn't fight the United States," said Masako's father, who had labored in Hawaii for three years when he was younger. Even in that sleepy island outpost, he had seen industrial resources—mammoth tractors, plows, and trucks—that dwarfed the Japanese versions. "You don't go to war against a country like that!" But now that Japan had attacked, he was resigned to an uncertain future.

Gofuyo Yempuku, a *nisei* who had relocated from Oahu to an island near Hiroshima in 1933, would recollect, "We knew it would be a tough, tough struggle for Japan. But we couldn't talk about this with others because we feared possible police action."

At seventeen, Frank foresaw that the military would require more soldiers and the draft would cast a wider, swifter net. He renewed his personal mission. "I decided to behave." He would excel in track, earn adequate grades, and strive to be a nondescript student.

Kinu was patriotic, but she couldn't allow herself to become overwrought. She did not say what she sensed, did not divulge what awakened her with terror in the deep of night. The military would seize her sons. Victor, having survived a tour in China and Indochina, would be called up again. Wounded once and recovered, would his luck hold? Pierce, a college student in Yokohama, would be drafted next. Susceptible to sickness, would he cope? In their boot-thumping footsteps, little Frank would follow. And, far away in the States, what would happen to her second son, her irrepressible American, her Harry? Kinu ached for each one.

9

Panic in Los Angeles

"JAPS OPEN WAR ON U.S. WITH BOMBING OF HAWAII," "Japan's Daring Attack on Hawaii Designed to Cripple U.S. Fleet," "Attacks Climax Ten-Year Crisis," and "Bombers Roar Out of Manila." The news mirrored what Kinu was reading almost six thousand miles away.

Harry discovered for the first time that the front-page news related to him. Several articles concerned ethnic Japanese, the *issei* first-generation legal aliens and the *nisei* second-generation citizens. Altogether, the community on the West Coast was 120,000 strong; two-thirds were American citizens by birth.

Within hours of the attack on Pearl Harbor, FBI agents in fedoras embarked on a "man hunt" for alleged ethnic Japanese subversives. Immediately, they barricaded three hundred *issei* fishermen on Terminal Island twenty-five miles south of Los Angeles and labeled them "classified for internment." Two hundred more Japanese—it was unclear whether *issei* or *nisei*—were rounded up in Los Angeles that afternoon. By evening, Harry read, the agents were fanning out through Southern California, bearing a list of three hundred suspects. Within a day, they anticipated arresting an additional three thousand.

The FBI sweep paralleled deteriorating attitudes toward Japan. Although all eyes had faced eastward toward Europe since Nazi Germany had attacked Poland in September 1939, tensions with Japan had taken an alarming turn in the latter half of 1941. In July, Japan had occupied French Indochina to strengthen its Southeast Asian presence and plumb the region's natural resources. The United States immediately froze Japanese assets in the States and implemented a full oil embargo to curb Japan's expansionist ambitions in Asia. Harry, who could not afford to subscribe to a newspaper and did not have enough savings to merit opening a bank account, registered the global chaos as a distant din.

In retrospect, perhaps he should have paid more attention that last placid summer before the world plunged into its second world war in little more than two decades. Perhaps he should have reflected more on the troubling way his Auburn friends responded to him on his return. But he was only twenty-one and eager to look forward, ready to act, not contemplate failure.

That summer of 1941, Harry had rattled up the coast in his Model-A Ford, taking a well-deserved vacation. Summer in Seattle, the perfect season to reunite with his Auburn buddies who had been away at college when he had last visited in the spring three years before. Harry had just completed his two-year associate of arts degree at Glendale Junior College and would begin Woodbury College in September. Halfway to his goal, Harry would not feel embarrassed in front of friends, some now University of Washington seniors deciding on careers.

HARRY STOOD AT THE ENTRANCE TO THE Biddles', anticipating a hearty welcome. He knocked and Mrs. Biddle opened the door. She barely said hello before blurting out that Elgin was out, working at a summer job. Harry sensed a marked difference in her chilly response, even by comparison to his last visit. They were strangers now. Chastened, he quickly said goodbye and retreated to his trusty Ford. "They were like my own family, but she didn't even tell me to come in."

Harry would later learn that Elgin's older brother Bill had enlisted in the navy, and Mrs. Biddle feared he was bound for the Pacific. French by birth, Mrs. Biddle was more attuned to the war in Europe than most Americans. On June 14, 1940, Nazi German troops had goose-stepped down the Champs-Élysées and through the Arc de Triomphe, parading their occupation of France. Two months later, on September 27, 1940, Japan concluded the belligerent Tripartite Pact with Germany and Italy in Berlin. Mrs. Biddle reviled the Axis powers and worried about her son. On edge, she perceived Harry as the enemy.

Stunned, Harry cut short his trip after one day, returning to Los Angeles, to the safety of the Mounts, to the comfort of Hiroshima friends like Kaz Nagata and Mitsu and Mas Matsumoto. It was the last time he would venture to his beloved hometown for more than twenty-five years.

NOW, IN THE WAKE OF PEARL HARBOR, Harry determinedly maintained his sangfroid. Shortly after the rash of arrests in the Japanese community, he sent a telegram to his mother via the International Committee of the Red Cross: he and Mary were fine. It was strange when his mother did not reply.

Life's obligations continued. Driving through Little Tokyo between gardening jobs, Harry was struck by how swiftly the neighborhood was losing its sparkle. Christmas and the New Year normally attracted shoppers, but they had fled the enclave. Once-packed eateries looked forlorn with empty tables; going-out-of-business sales proliferated overnight as owners sought to move deeper within California or to the heartland, where they could evade exclusion, already a burning topic in the press. Americans were shunning commerce with "enemy aliens," the new term for Japanese legal immigrants, which would soon also include *nisei*. Ethnic Japanese bank accounts had been frozen; *nisei* had to show birth certificates to release their funds and *issei* accounts remained untouchable. Business was drying up. Little Tokyo, having survived and prospered for half a century, bore the dingy air of a neighborhood in distress.

Behind the shuttering storefronts lay, Harry suspected, disrupted lives. Many of his *nisei* friends were anxious; their fathers and brothers had been picked up, for no clear reason, by the FBI and incarcerated. No one knew where they were or when they would return. Any leadership affiliation in the Japanese community—church, school, or a prefectural association board—led to their downfall. Family businesses faltered. Deprived of citizenship, the *issei* had no political clout to protest their plight. The Japanese American Citizens League's avowals of loyalty fell on deaf ears. Perhaps, it was best that his father had not lived to experience this turmoil. With his résumé of leadership positions, he would have been one of the first arrested. His mother, Harry knew, would have been frantic.

That New Year's Eve in Los Angeles, thousands of revelers stayed away from the downtown district, where the annual festivities had been canceled owing to the threat of an air raid. Nor did Little Tokyo residents wander down East First Street warbling "Auld Lang Syne" in Japanese. Instead, behind blackout curtains in light-dimmed apartments they raised thimble-sized *sake* cups, whispered a prayer for peace, and sipped in silence. A short trolley ride away at elegant hotels, white partygoers raised champagne flutes to a midnight toast, clinking expressly for the demise of the Imperial Japanese Navy, yelling "Bottoms up!"

ON JANUARY 1, 1942, HARRY TURNED TWENTY-TWO. Soon after, he visited the local army recruiting office. Harry wanted to join the throngs of men signing up, but he failed the physical because of his eyesight, poor since grade school, and a bad back he had developed after falling off a neighbor's roof while cleaning gutters. The year was off to a disappointing start.

Although Harry knew that he was a patriotic American, he was conscious that his *kibei* status made him suspicious. He gathered his photos from his Sanyō high school days, showing him in his military uniform, and threw them in the brick trash incinerator in the backyard. The flames crackled; the photos curled and blackened.

Harry tried to resist dwelling on the brewing enmity toward those of Japanese descent, but he was constantly reminded. When other drivers caught sight of him at stop signs, they yelled racist slurs. One evening in class, he approached a classmate, whom he viewed as a fellow Asian American. "I thought she would have some empathy." But when Harry tried to engage the young woman in conversation, her eyes narrowed. The Japanese were terrible to have attacked Pearl Harbor, she said. She was Korean, and her father and brothers did not want her talking to a Japanese. It was true that Japan had annexed Korea in 1910 and was treating it harshly. Koreans had been assigned to forced labor in abysmal conditions in Japan and other areas. But this encounter was personal, between two Americans. Harry smarted from his classmate's derision.

The atmosphere in the City of Angels was degenerating. Dining establishments placed signs in their windows banning ethnic Japanese patrons. "This Restaurant Poisons Both Rats and Japs." Right-wing extremists stuck stickers saying, "Remember a Jap is a Jap," depicting a rat with a Japanese face, on their windshields. The words and images translated into action. Harry heard from friends that their parked cars were rear-ended and the windows of their homes shattered in what he would later call a "climate of harassment." Chinese residents took to wearing badges, "I am a Chinese," lest they be mistreated.

Continuing to commute to Woodbury College at night was becoming dangerous. Even imbued with a healthy sense of youthful immortality, Harry couldn't help but hesitate. Nor could he dismiss a nagging urgency to save money. In such unstable times, school seemed frivolous, a self-indulgent luxury with an uncertain payoff. When he withdrew, he told himself that he was postponing his dream. Someday soon, he would be back.

Meanwhile, yellow journalism inflamed passions by legitimizing rumors of espionage inflicted by maniacal fifth columnists. It was said that enemy pilots shot dead in the Pacific were found wearing beveled American college rings. That informants guided Japanese submarines close to the West Coast. Off Laguna Beach, a Japanese fishing boat was seen flashing messages to shore. In Los Angeles, Japanese were sighted holding binoculars and maps. At a *kenjinkai* picnic, attendees allegedly placed signs with arrows telling Japanese forces where to shoot. *Nisei* were blocking traffic, creating logjams for soldiers heading to base. The enemy was everywhere; the enemy was close; the enemy was homegrown. Although every case of alleged sabotage would prove unfounded, the list of accusations became too prolific to refute.

Rational thinkers, Harry figured, would discount these ridiculous stories. Certainly, the idea of *nisei* impeding military traffic was preposterous. After all, thousands of *nisei* boys were lining up at recruiting stations in their eagerness to serve in the armed services, answering the call of Uncle Sam's finger-pointing exclamation: "I WANT YOU!"

Yet the press's jingoistic campaign only heightened over time. On December 8, the *Los Angeles Times* had published the front-page "Death Sentence of a Mad Dog." Harking back to "Yellow

Peril" fears dating from the turn of the century, in which the perceived threat of economic competition from Japanese immigrants morphed into an imminent Japanese invasion, the editors warned that the Pacific Coast, "from the Aleutians to the Canal," represented a "zone of danger" for sabotage. Of the *nisei*, the newspaper hadn't yet cast its verdict. "Some perhaps many, are loyal Nisei, or good Americans, born and educated as such."

Less than two months later, the benefit of the doubt had vanished. On February 2, columnist W. H. Anderson wrote in the *Los Angeles Times*, "A viper is nonetheless a viper wherever the egg is hatched—so a Japanese American, born of Japanese parents—grows up to be a Japanese, not an American." He proposed to "limit and control their activities." Harry cringed at the rhetoric.

The developments in Asia exacerbated anti-Japanese tensions. The Japanese navy and army had seized British, French, Dutch, and American colonial outposts. They had occupied Manila and Hong Kong and driven the British to the southern tip of the Malay Peninsula, to Singapore, "the Gibraltar of the East." This bastion, too, would fall before long.

At the Presidio of San Francisco, Lieutenant General John L. DeWitt, the commander of the army's Western Defense Command, responsible for protecting the Pacific Coast, was galvanized by the "Yellow Peril" conspiracy theory, raw panic over Japan's string of military successes, and simmering distrust of the ethnic-Japanese concentration on the West Coast. DeWitt would soon demonstrate that the heartless efficiency of an empowered bureaucrat could be perilously productive. Harry's days as a free citizen in pursuit of the American dream were numbered.

Although they tried to objectively parse the truth and fiction from articles and editorials, even the Mounts were not immune to the deleterious effect of Japan's mounting victories. "What's wrong with Japan?" they asked Harry. "I don't know," he replied, smarting at the assumption that he would know any more than they did about Japanese objectives.

On Valentine's Day, DeWitt—demonstrating a marked absence of affection for fellow Americans—wrote Secretary of War Henry Stimson, "The Japanese race is an enemy race and while many second and third generation Japanese born on United States soil, possessed of United States citizenship, have become 'Americanized,' the racial strains are undiluted." He added, in a feat of paranoia and contorted logic: "The very fact that no sabotage has taken place to date is a disturbing and confirming indication that such action will be taken."

Five days later, on February 19, 1942, President Franklin D. Roosevelt signed Executive Order 9066, according military commanders the authority to remove suspect populations—alien and citizen alike—from any area. The decree would ultimately be regarded as one of the most shameful moves of his presidency, but at the time, Attorney General Francis Biddle, who opposed it, noted of the president, "I do not think he was much concerned with the gravity or implications of this step." Given carte blanche, in less than two weeks DeWitt would begin carving exclusion zones from Arizona, California, Oregon, and Washington, the first step to a massive evacuation effort and long-term internment.

NOT A MOMENT TOO SOON, IT SEEMED at first. In the wee hours between 2 a.m. and dawn on February 25, DeWitt's worst nightmare struck with an alleged Japanese attack on Los Angeles. Air-raid sirens whined, searchlights beamed, and antiaircraft guns pummeled the night. In a stunning display of firepower, the booming barrage of almost fifteen hundred antiaircraft shells smoked the land and damaged houses and cars, but, curiously, downed not a single enemy plane. There were casualties, however: two residents died of heart attacks and three in car accidents.

Within hours, Secretary of the Navy Frank Knox admitted that the raid was, in fact, a "false alarm." The trigger for what would subsequently be called the "Battle of Los Angeles" was a single wayward weather balloon whipping across the sky in haphazard flight.

Regardless, the next day, all residents of Japanese descent on Terminal Island were given forty-eight hours to evacuate. Earlier in the month, the *issei* fishermen had been sent to internment camps run by the Justice Department. Now the hasty transfer of their families to churches and community centers, with eventual internment, marked the first wholesale evacuation of an ethnic population since the Indian Removal Act of 1830 resulted in the Trail of Tears, the devastating trek of Native Americans from their land to desolate reservations.

Harry drove to take a look at Terminal Island, where until now three thousand ethnic Japanese had lived and toiled. Seagulls squawked over dirt roads lined with one-story clapboard houses built by the fish canneries. There was commotion inside one of the houses; Harry heard furniture being dragged across wooden floors, dishes clattering, and shouts in Japanese. People were rushing to settle their affairs. A man emerged from one house, lugging furniture. Harry lent him a hand, and they began to speak in Japanese. It dawned on Harry that he could take the furniture, sell it, divide the proceeds, and send the money later. The suggestion struck the man as more profitable than practically giving away his hard-earned items to scavengers. He handed Harry his goods and trusted him to keep his word.

Safely ensconced in their hacienda on the hill, the Mounts were incensed by the prospect of internment. It was unconstitutional, they asserted, denying citizens the writ of habeas corpus, the right to seek release from unlawful incarceration. "Stand up for your rights," they told Harry. They tossed around possible solutions to address his narrowing circumstances. Perhaps it all came down to a name, they suggested. If Harry changed his surname to an Anglo one like theirs, he might escape suspicion. Their feelings for Harry did not waver; he was more a son than an employee. Clyde and Flossie Mount offered to legally adopt him.

Touched and intrigued, Harry considered the idea, but he had to run it by his mother. Names were linked to ancient bloodlines in Japan. Adoption was employed to perpetuate a name, not disguise it; a prosperous family without an heir might adopt a son or son-in-law to prolong the line. Forfeiting Fukuhara for expedience could estrange Harry from his family; masquerading as a Mount would hurt and disappoint them. Harry sat down in his bedroom and composed a cable to his mother. Oddly enough, for the second time, he did not receive a reply.

But a change in name wouldn't have mattered. The issue of race concerned blood. Inquiring at a local government office, Harry was told that anyone who was at least half Japanese might be evacuated from the West Coast in the future. "I said that I was 100% American." There were all kinds of Americans; he just happened to be Japanese American. The staff person replied that the United States was at war with Japan. "So what?" Harry asked. He mentioned the prospect of adoption. It didn't make any difference. Harry recalled that he was told, "You could change your name to Hitler but you still have to go."

Harry still wanted to enlist in the army. With his back healed, he was ready to try again. He didn't think about where he might be sent, only that it felt right to serve. This move, too, he knew, had to be run by his mother. For the third time, he cabled her and waited for a reply. Again, none came.

Meanwhile, Mr. and Mrs. Mount put their heads together, seeking an answer to Harry's predicament. "Have you ever considered Columbus, Ohio?" they asked. Mrs. Mount's sister lived in the Buckeye State, where few Japanese immigrants and their children had settled. Harry could live with her family, continue his education, and retain his rights as an American. It was imperative, the Mounts plead, for Harry to move to the interior of the country.

For the fourth time, Harry cabled his mother. Again, no reply. By now he assumed the war had severed communication. He had to imagine what his mother would say. She probably would have frowned on his adoption and sighed over him enlisting, but Ohio would pass muster, even if she had to look up the Midwest region on a *katakana*-marked map.

But just as Harry was considering moving to the heartland, Mary phoned, frantic. The press was as fanatical in Seattle as in Los Angeles and talk of evacuation prevailed, but Mary had a more pressing problem. She had held out for several weeks and feared for her safety. Harry immediately sent money for her trip to Los Angeles. Toting her toddler daughter Jeanie and one suitcase, Mary landed on the Mounts' doorstep.

After having been married almost four years, Mary wanted a divorce. Her husband, Jerry, gambled, drank to excess, beat her and two-year-old Jeanie, and had lost his job as a chauffeur. On a wager he had pawned her engagement ring for four hundred dollars, the equivalent of more than six thousand dollars today. The Johnsons allowed Mary to stay in the carriage house after Jerry left, but Mary knew they would find another chauffeur soon. She couldn't continue to work for them and care for Jeanie at the same time. At twenty-six, Mary was missing several teeth, owing to Jerry's drunken rages.

The Mounts welcomed Mary and she relaxed under their kindness, but Harry was concerned that he was imposing on them. Staying with the Mounts, he decided, could only be temporary, little more than a month, at best. With Mary in town, he shelved plans for Ohio.

As *nisei* friends prepared to move inland to evade evacuation, Harry rushed to purchase their gardening routes. In mid-March, he learned that a large group of ethnic Japanese would be removed from Los Angeles to a temporary detention center. "We knew that we were going to be interned; it was a matter of time."

Harry needed to make as much money as possible, which was a challenge. One day while he was mowing a lawn in Santa Monica, a police car pulled up to investigate a reported "Japanese invasion." Harry looked around. He hadn't noticed anyone; the only person who appeared Japanese was him. Had he seen an enemy tank? the police asked. In her panic, the woman who had called the police had mentioned that possibility. No, Harry couldn't help on that matter, either, although a street-cleaner machine had just swept the pavement.

On March 24, the Western Defense Command imposed a 9 p.m.–6 a.m. curfew and five-mile travel restriction on ethnic Japanese, hobbling Harry's ability to reach his far-flung jobs and return to Glendale on time. To add insult to injury, these security measures incited the fervor of some twelve thousand volunteer air-raid wardens.

People for whom Harry had done yard work and babysitting abruptly stopped talking to him. He was, he felt, becoming persona non grata. When he rumbled back to Glendale, racing against the curfew, night weighed heavily. One evening a neighbor cum air-raid warden was standing outside, wearing his white helmet and an armband with its triangular red-and-white striped insignia. Someone must have tipped him off, for he was waiting for Harry. Motioning Harry over, he called, "Harry, you shouldn't be out after 9 o'clock." "I just couldn't get back in time," Harry answered. He had no excuse, the man snapped, and this had better be the last time.

Harry got off without having to report to the local police station, but he knew his luck wouldn't hold. His friend Sho Nomura had been indicted over an accidental oversight. When the temperature in the family's walk-in refrigerator dropped and the inside light automatically turned on, the bulb cast a small shadow on a wall outside his house. Sho, his brother, and father were hauled to the local police station for questioning. Told to empty their pockets and remove their belts, the three men were confined to a cell, where they sat and waited. It was only when Quaker friends interceded that they were released. Charged with violating a blackout edict, Sho confidently entered a "not guilty" plea at court. "Hold your tongue," the judge censured, only to drop the suit because the men were due to be evacuated within the week anyway.

Most days, Harry unwound with the Mounts when he returned home. They sat in the library by the fireplace, digesting the day's events. Although the Mounts did not minimize Harry's troubles, they often tried to make light of his distressing encounters in order to soothe him. When the event only had dark sides and sharp angles, they cautioned Harry against losing his temper. "Count to ten or count to twenty and don't do anything about it until the next day."

The Mounts' calming presence heartened him, but they could not completely dispel his distress. Enlistment in the army was still tantalizing, but this option evaporated on March 30 when the War Department declared that all *nisei* would be classified as IV-C, or "enemy aliens," and were, therefore, ineligible to serve their country. "It was just the indignity heaped upon the indignity," he recalled.

Perhaps Harry was fortunate. Many *nisei* friends already in the army were discharged after Pearl Harbor. Those who remained were largely removed from combat duty and stripped of their guns. "To take a gun away from a soldier is like taking chopsticks away from someone who is real hungry," Harry said later.

Walt Tanaka had been inducted into the army six months before Pearl Harbor, with a "royal sendoff" by his family. After completing basic training, he was assigned to a combat division at Fort Ord in California, but about a week after Pearl Harbor, his assignment was abruptly changed to a work detail. He spent his days shoveling asphalt, digging trenches, wading into rivers to cut willow trees for coverings, and pouring concrete pillboxes. Roy Uyehata, living in the same barrack as Walt and inducted in early 1941, had handed in his weapon after Pearl Harbor, blinking at the "cruel blow because I swore to defend the United States." Exacerbating his shame, Roy was ordered to haul heavy, often wet garbage and break boulders with sledgehammers. Through no fault of performance, but fear of sabotage, the *nisei* soldiers had plunged to the bottom of the army pecking order.

LOS ANGELES COUNTY WAS SYSTEMATICALLY LOSING ITS ethnic Japanese population. From early April on, Civil Exclusion Orders, promulgated by the headquarters of the Western Defense Command and the Fourth Army, were hard to miss. These bold-faced announcements were hammered on telephone poles, stapled to post office bulletin boards, and taped on brick courthouses, clapboard Buddhist churches, and government office windows. The evacuees were given anywhere from a few days to a few weeks to register at a Civil Control Station; days later, they would be transported to an assembly center. People tried to maintain a stoic front, but the printed commands elicited a silent panic. As long as possible, Harry looked the other way, doggedly pursuing a living.

In Little Tokyo, the liquidation sales turned legion. At Asahi Dye Works, where old clothes could be dyed a vibrant hue, the owners had penned, "CLOSING We won't take it to OWENS VALLEY for U." Owens Valley, the location of the Manzanar War Relocation Center, would hold ten thousand *issei* and *nisei*. At the Iseri Pharmacy, the taped sign over satin-swathed shelves of Japanese and American cosmetics read, "Many thanks for your Patronage. Hope to Serve you in Near future God be with you till we meet again. Mr. and Mrs. K. Iseri." Even the 10 Cent Store had a "CLOSING OUT EVACUATION SALE," reducing prices from dimes to pennies. White bargain-hunters jammed the sidewalks, departing with arms full. At night the wind tossed tumbleweeds of trash through the emptying blocks.

The five-mile travel restriction and the daily expansion of evacuated areas were rapidly closing in on Harry and Mary. Harry could no longer reach his gardening jobs. They weren't certain what would come first: running out of low-rent neighborhoods to obtain a short-term lease or confronting head-on their own internment. To avoid evacuation, Harry, Mary, and Jeanie moved in with Kaz Nagata, who had married Harry's Auburn friend Amy Kusumi. Then they switched to Kaz's cousins, the Matsumotos, until the Matsumotos closed their store in an evacuated area and had to leave. Harry found another spot nearby, a temporary solution.

As evacuees organized, stored, and discarded a lifetime

of personal belongings, they also sought to sell some. Harry needed more work. Again, he offered to take the personal effects on consignment and share the proceeds. Continuing his Miyajima relatives' pawnshop tradition, he set up space on the curb of an empty lot. His odd jobs and ingenuity lent him an air of experience and confidence. Harry hawked his wares in both Japanese and English, demonstrating a facile ease with people that he hoped might be applied in another setting at another time.

Having exchanged his jalopy for a small truck, he collected a motley array of used goods—aged refrigerators, faded gardening hoses, flat tires rummaged from the dusty recesses of garages, dented cars, and rusted trucks. The Japanese army had seized rubber plantations in the Dutch East Indies upon which the United States depended. Scarce rubber was rationed by the end of April. By recycling rubber goods, Harry was doing his civic duty and earning a small profit. When he was shooed from one spot, he set up shop in another. These days, he was never sleepy, only famished. The money would only flow as long as he had a supply of goods to sell; his supply sources diminished with each evacuation. Harry was holding on. "It wasn't that much, but we still had to live, my sister and the baby."

Resigned to his own evacuation, he was adamant that he did not want to enter camp with Mary and Jeanie alone. He turned to Kaz and the Matsumoto brothers. Harry instinctively understood that these friends—thick as family—would give him a sense of context in a place where he did not belong. He would do everything possible to make sure these Hiroshima neighbors, bonded over their shared American identity and no small amount of fun, would be incarcerated together in the country they called home.

•   •   •

ON APRIL 30, 1942, CIVIL EXCLUSION ORDER No. 30 appeared in southwest Los Angeles on doors, posts, and windows in a fury of hammering and taping between noon and midnight. Harry, Kaz, and the Matsumotos were living in Compton, falling under the order's jurisdiction. They had until noon, the latest, on Thursday, May 7 to evacuate.

On Wednesday, May 6, 1942, the same day when General Jonathan Wainwright surrendered all American and Filipino forces to the Japanese in the Philippines, Harry pulled up to the curb at the Firestone Park train station with Mary and Jeanie. Only permitted to bring what they could carry, they had packed the requisite bedrolls and linens, clothing, toiletries, dishware, glassware, and utensils, as well as a few personal effects. On the curb lay mountains of bamboo trunks, wicker cases, leather suitcases, and twine-bound, paper packages.

Crowds of evacuees milled in their Sunday best, while armed military police towered over and supervised their charges. Some women and children had layered their clothing so heavily that they were more prepared for an Arctic dog sled excursion than a day trip aboard an ancient locomotive. Even before leaving, they looked like displaced persons.

Unloading the bags, Harry turned to face a young Mexican in search of a last-minute fire sale. He peered hungrily at Harry's truck. Harry handed him the keys and told him that he could have it. The man asked for his name and address and promised to send money later. Harry gave him the Mounts' information but assumed he would never hear from him again.

Several days earlier, Harry had registered at the Civil Control Station. The federal government would store some larger items for each family. Harry deposited eleven bamboo ropes, one grass cutter, one grass roller, and one lawn mower. He wanted to believe—as did the Little Tokyo shopkeepers—that soon he would be back in business.

Harry and Mary attached oversize white cardboard tags with the number 10464 to their and Jeanie's coat buttons. The same tags labeled their luggage. Their last names didn't matter now; this five-digit number would identify them from this point on. As the sun began to warm the crowd, they—together with the Nagatas and Matsumotos—boarded the train, bound for an unknown destination.

At 8:15 a.m., the whistle blew and the locomotive trembled, steel wheels grating, sparks hissing. Jeanie gazed at her normally playful uncle, whom she adored, expecting him to catch her eyes and smile. He was pensive. The months since the Pearl Harbor attack had been the most demoralizing of Harry's life. He reminded himself what the Mounts had taught him. Now was not the time to explode. The locomotive rumbled, belching acrid smoke. Beyond the window, a tangle of magenta bougainvillea glowed. Harry began the slow count to twenty, dreading wherever they were ending up tomorrow.

10

Silence from Glendale to Hiroshima

rank knew the necessity of counting to twenty. This skill was called *gaman* (self-restraint). In Japan, where it was essential for a pressed population living in limited space, *gaman* had been elevated to an art. Since Frank had entered *Icchū* in April 1939, he had been learning how painstaking it was to master.

At last, his efforts at *gaman* were paying off. Frank was excelling in *kendō*, the ancient art of swordsmanship similar to fencing. It was promoted by the wartime regime because of its emphasis on physical and mental discipline. Frank had demonstrated an early aptitude in elementary school when he won a citywide tournament. If he practiced and persevered, he knew he could succeed.

On weekends at home, Frank charged down the hall in his padded helmet and uniform, a quilted kimono-style jacket, and wide *hakama* (pleated culotte-like trousers). He relished the rapid strikes and thrusts of his bamboo sword, which if handled properly, would not injure an opponent. The point of the sport was to advance to *mushin*, a state of grace that enabled one to be fully in the moment.

But at this particular moment he was preoccupied. Shortly after war broke out with the United States, all *nisei* residents of Hiroshima had been summoned, some via *nisei* clubs, to gather at a local high school and register. Filling out his name and address, Frank wondered what more the prefectural government needed to know about this group of people. Almost everyone had been a dual citizen of the United States and Japan since 1940, when rationing began and registration of all foreign-born Japanese was required. Anyone who was not a Japanese citizen did not receive coupons, making a life of growing shortages arduous at best. Besides, the information was already on hand. Whenever births, deaths, and marriages occurred—domestically or abroad—heads of household updated their family registers at city hall. In addition, anyone who attended a public school had to record his particulars at city hall. The only person Frank had met who had evaded taking Japanese citizenship was Harry.

Harry had arrived in Japan at age thirteen listed on his mother's passport. In a paperwork oversight, his parents hadn't edited their family register upon Harry's 1920 birth in Seattle. Because he had never attended a Hiroshima public school and had left before rationing was introduced, Harry had slipped through a crack in Japan's cement bureaucracy. Frank wasn't as fortunate. The idea that the government was separating dual nationals from the general Japanese population scared him. Nothing, he hoped, would come of it.

DESPITE JAPANESE PROPAGANDA ABOUT UNITY—"100 MILLION HEARTS beating as one"—the *nisei* in their midst were isolated. Frank had heard a joke that Japanese men departed for military training carrying a stack of towels; a single toothbrush; one bar of soap; some cash; their *Senjinkun* (Field Service Code) manual exhorting "death before dishonor"; and a *senninbari* (thousand-stitch stomach warmer) that was an amulet for battlefield success. More concerned with grooming than combat, *nisei* soldiers, people sneered, packed a Dopp kit with aftershave.

Frank bristled at the implication. *"Nisei* were sissies, sort of."

Anti-American sentiment abounded, even among the most innocent. Two decades earlier, American schools had donated 12,700 dolls to Japanese schools in a gesture of goodwill. Shortly after Pearl Harbor, elementary schools nationwide were ordered to immolate them, the dolls' glassy blue eyes melting in crackling bonfires. Some dolls were impaled with bamboo spears. Only two hundred would survive. In the neighborhoods Frank ran through, young children played war, complete with backpacks, helmets, and bayonets. Instead of playing house, the girls acted as nurses at the front. The enemy was always America.

Frank was glad to learn, though, that Harry and Mary were well. A cable from Harry had arrived promptly after the hostilities between the United States and Japan erupted. Their mother had brightened with relief. Kinu was increasingly occupied with plotting her daily errands, necessitating energy, pluck, and *gaman.* Gradually, more items were rationed; shortages were mounting. That autumn alone, eggs, fish, and sweet potatoes had been rationed. In the pallid light of dawn, Kinu dressed in *monpe* for a day of hunting—rushing from shop to shop, standing in line for vegetables, paltry specimens that had never looked less appetizing but seemed more desirable. People were suffering from vitamin deficiencies and catching colds that turned into pneumonia.

Seeing his mother pressed, Frank did not share the whispered rumors he was hearing about *nisei* and the draft. *Nisei* who served in the Japanese army could never return to the United States. Even someone who only took a physical, without beginning training, would forfeit his American citizenship. What if this were true? Frank worried.

Frank, now seventeen, had been only eleven when Harry had written the American consulate in Kobe about his own citizenship concerns in 1935. Harry could have told Frank that even taking a military oath at the time of induction would lead to loss of American citizenship, but he had squirreled away the information, never imagining that the plight might not apply to him, but to his little brother. The rumors that Frank heard were true.

THE NEW YEAR BROUGHT LITTLE RESPITE. IN school, children practiced their calligraphy in the 2,602nd year of unbroken imperial reign, brushing slashes of ebony ink across ecru rice paper. "The Great East Asia War," "Good Fortune in War," "One Hundred Million, One Heart." The year ahead augured nothing but war. The stridency of the slogans marched in lockstep with the ratcheting of rationed foodstuffs, as if vehement words would mitigate growing hunger.

On January 1 ration booklets were issued for salt, without which the delicately seasoned Japanese cuisine was disappointingly bland. Women would find it more difficult to conserve without pickles, essential to the Japanese diet. In February, ration tickets were distributed for *miso* (soybean paste) and soy sauce, as well as clothing. The tickets guaranteed only a portion of what was necessary to maintain basic food needs, a measurement that vacillated according to government inventory. In the past eighteen months, all the major staples—including fish, sugar, and rice—had fallen under bureaucratic control. Kinu's bloomers and Frank's trousers sagged at the waist.

Kinu did her best. At a time when white rice was scarce and the populace was expected to demonstrate its patriotism, Kinu prepared Frank a *hinomaru bentō* (boxed lunch), named after the *hinomaru* flag, with its rectangle of white rice and a red *umeboshi* (pickled plum) in the center. The lunch symbolized the home front's solidarity with its troops, who were probably eating much the same. If this humble fare were enough for the troops, the conventional wisdom went, so too for civilians. Everyone knew that this austere *bentō* arose from expedient bravado: no one had the ingredients for the fish, vegetable, and savory side dishes.

Kinu began to seek other sources to augment rations. She rose earlier—in the black of night—to catch a train before dawn and carried a large satchel on her back for a foray into the countryside, where she frequented the *yami* (black markets). Some called these makeshift areas "*aozora*" ("blue skies") since the farmers displayed their wares on blankets outside, all the easier for packing up and disappearing as soon as they earned a profit. Kinu bought the little that she could afford.

She could still turn to her older sister Kiyo, who in her inimitable way, kept Meijidō open while one after another of her competitors closed, victims to rising rations and government-decreed low prices to prevent skyrocketing inflation. Kiyo negotiated a government contract for caramels that could be purchased with ration tickets, receiving a prized allotment of eggs and sugar. She secured large military contracts for troops overseas, accepting a requisition of flour, too. Her pantry brimmed with bags of rice, wheat flour, and powdered milk.

If Kiyo had her way, the war would never invade Meijidō's kitchen. Her business sustained and propelled her. When an extra contract came, she contacted Frank, who rushed to help amid the vats of steaming *mochigome* (sticky sweet rice) and boiling sugar coloring to caramel. Kiyo's slippers slapped the floor as she patrolled the kitchen, barking commands. "*Hai!*" "Yes!" the cooks replied, stirring the sugar with vigor.

They were preparing *senbei* and *konpeitō* (star-shaped sweets) that melted in the mouth like rock candy. Both had a shelf life of months, enough time to reach soldiers throughout

Asia. Frank packed tins of candy and crackers, welded the lids to prevent moisture from seeping in, and placed them in crates to be delivered to Ujina, where they were deposited in the cavernous cargo holds of hulking troop transports.

Meijidō rescued Frank from gnawing hunger. On rare occasions when the cooks were occupied making cakes and buns and Kiyo was nowhere to be found, he helped himself to a handful of eggs and moved to a different section of the kitchen. He scrambled the eggs and devoured them directly from the skillet. "No one knew," he confessed of his guilty pleasure.

Despite the semblance of normalcy, beyond Meijidō's kitchen the grip of war tightened. Meijidō's storefront had closed, as had many establishments on once booming Hondōri Street. The blocks looked bare, bereft of *noren* curtains, advertisement banners and sandwich-board signs. Soldiers marched by a decimated produce stall in front of the grand Mitsui Bank. Female shoppers surveyed piles of sprout-eyed potatoes as if they were Kiyo's imperial buns. Kiyo knew it would be inappropriate to don one of her favorite kimonos so she wore her homely *monpe*. Yet, as long as the landmark *suzuran* lights rose over Hondōri Street, Kiyo was certain the district would endure. After all, she had seen the district rise from its dirt-lane beginnings.

Engrossed in her work, Kiyo did not dwell on the falling standard of living and the decreasing quality of life for most Hiroshima residents. But even as resilient a spirit as Kiyo Nishimura had to escape Meijidō sometimes. She cut freshly baked *castella* cakes into bite-size pieces, stacked them in Meijidō tins, and wrapped them in her best cotton *furoshiki* wrapping cloth, a gift for her sister.

Kinu was overjoyed to see Kiyo. In Kinu's American living room, the women avoided news accounts of the Great East Asia War and the American enemy. Instead, over Kinu's pale green tea and Kiyo's golden *castella*, they chatted and laughed and lamented. Since the government had prohibited gasoline for the general population, Tokichi could no longer drive his beloved Harley-Davidson. Although some desperate drivers were digging pine tree roots and steaming them to produce oil that could be used in place of gas, he thought the rough substitute would harm the Harley's delicate engine. For Kiyo, the man was underfoot too much and too often. She was happy to be away visiting her sister.

When Masako popped in to visit, the older women played the *shamisen* and *koto* and instructed Masako on how to perform *nihon buyō* (classical dance) with slow, pronounced, elongated movements that they had learned during their childhood in Miyajima. Kinu and Kiyo were exquisite dancers who had been exposed to master performers at Itsukushima Shrine, where the immense vermilion *torii* gate rose from the shallow sea in another time and in some ways, another place.

IN MARCH AS THE CHERRY TREE BOUGHS thickened with tight buds, Frank anticipated his fourth year of *Icchū* and his break from hazing. Kinu, who at fifty was no longer young, trusted that the spring would lighten her daily burdens—the sun rising earlier, the morning chill receding, the miles walking to market less demanding.

It was at this moment of relative calm that Kinu received a letter from Harry's employers, the Mounts, whom she knew he liked. Frank helped her understand the English. The couple wanted to know whether they could adopt Harry. What could they be thinking, she thought, seizing her son as their own?

Kinu knew all about adoption. Kiyo and Tokichi had adopted Tokichi's nephew, who had married their niece. Together the young couple had four children; two were Toshinao and Kimiko.

This adoption assured two generations of Meijidō successors. But the practice was serious, undertaken when there was no other choice. When her husband Katsuji's family had briefly loaned out their surname and adopted the name Fukumoto to defray a debt, Katsuji had been ashamed by his father's humiliating circumstances.

To forgo the name Fukuhara made no sense to Kinu; she could not grasp the prospect of Harry's internment. She was insulted by the Mounts' proposal. Yet she knew that Harry was not a heartless, ungrateful child. For him to cast aside his family was out of character. Perplexed, Kinu promptly replied to the Mounts in Japanese, counting on Harry to translate. The soft-spoken woman did not swathe her sentiment in a veil of ambiguity. She rejected their offer.

To post the reply, Frank ran downtown to the Japan Red Cross, a large concrete building near the domed Industrial Promotion Hall at the corner of the T-shaped Aioi Bridge. Frank and Kinu waited several weeks for Harry's response. None arrived.

MEANWHILE, UNSETTLING NEWS ABOUT *NISEI* IN AMERICA rippled across Japanese airwaves. Early in March, the government-controlled radio broadcast the impending evacuation of "70,000 American-born Japanese" as a case of "'diabolic savagery.'" The newscaster editorialized further, "The viciousness of the American government in persecuting a helpless, strictly civilian and manifestly innocent minority will remain in history as one of the blackest crimes ever committed by the so-called great powers." If Kinu had been listening, the inflammatory statements—the facts of which were true—would have shed light on Harry's rationale for adoption. She missed the announcement.

In the throes of black nights, Kinu groped for an explanation, trying to understand why Harry had not yet written back. It was not his fault. War was, needless to say, an interruption. Surely he would read her words and comply. Finally, after several weeks of agitated sleep, a letter arrived.

Kinu was thrilled to recognize Harry's spare handwriting, but her joy almost immediately gave way. Harry did not address the burning issue of adoption; rather, he mentioned a state called Ohio, somewhere she had never heard of. She couldn't stomach the idea of Harry moving to a place without a supportive Japanese community. Although this was precisely Harry's point, Kinu couldn't help but think of what her husband used to say: it is easier to break a single chopstick than a bundle. Kinu wrote back, expressing dismay.

Shortly after, Hiroshima's *Chūgoku Shimbun* newspaper reported information communicated to Japan's Ministry of Foreign Affairs by the International Committee of the Red Cross. Forty-four Japanese citizens in Oregon and California had been arrested and dispersed to prisons across the United States. The small article on page two hinted of a gathering dragnet. Kinu did not notice.

Nor did she know that on March 18, 1942, the War Relocation Authority (WRA) was created by executive order to manage the detention of all ethnic Japanese on the West Coast. Within a few short months, the agency would supervise the construction and administration of ten concentration camps scattered in remote areas across the United States.

Kinu knew only that Harry did not reply as quickly as she hoped. It was unlike him, she thought, not to answer. Once he and his Auburn friends had been voracious pen pals. Now when Harry's own situation was far more uncertain, he was keeping his mother in the dark. The wait was excruciating. Kinu had gleaned from earlier letters that it was tough to be Japanese in

America. Since Harry neither elaborated nor complained, she hadn't questioned him further.

The third letter from her middle son landed in the mailbox sometime in April. "I might join the Army," was the gist. Kinu was shocked. Normally unflappable, she dipped her brush in ink and responded with a rapid flow of elongated *kanji*. On behalf of his late father and herself, Kinu expressed exactly what she felt. "No, don't join the military!"

By May, the letters from Harry ceased. Kinu had no idea that Harry could no longer enlist because of his ethnicity. She had no idea that he could no longer reside in California. Her daughter, granddaughter, and son were transient and trapped in Los Angeles, on the verge of being interned. Although some divided families learned during the war of their loved ones' incarceration, Kinu and Frank never did.

Their letters were censored. From December 19, 1941, on, every letter that crossed borders was slit open by government employees and perused for problematic details. By September 1942, almost one million envelopes and packages were investigated each week, including the correspondence to and from 3113 Sparr Boulevard in Glendale and 244-7 Furue in Takasu, Hiroshima. Censors blackened the objectionable portions of letters with markers or excised areas with a blade, carving the sheets into puzzles of ragged pieces. In a worst-case scenario, an entire letter could be condemned.

Kinu's three messages would have, at the very least, raised eyebrows. In rejecting adoption, she most likely alluded to the importance of filial piety to one's Japanese parents. Adoption in the States was controversial, as well; for Harry to be adopted by a Caucasian family could have been rightly viewed by the censor as a ruse to avoid internment. Kinu's second message about Ohio again concerned a strategy to evade incarceration. Her third thoroughly rejected her son's desire to enlist, a demonstration of his loyalty to the United States. Her letters wrestled with fundamental issues of loyalty to one's family and country. In theory, Kinu's charged correspondence should have been returned to sender. In reality, her letters were probably disposed of at the overworked censor station in Los Angeles.

IN THE GENTLE SUNSHINE OF EARLY MAY, Kinu focused on her relentless routine to obtain nutritious foodstuffs; to some degree, making the rounds of shops lent a reassuring rhythm to her days. She believed that her family—at home and in America—was safe, for now. She refused to let her thoughts run amok. Even the most manic mind could not have conceived that, already, 120,000 ethnic Japanese in America were incarcerated or that the citizens of Japan would seriously consider consuming common weeds, even thistle, as part of their diets.

In time, the consequences of the fractured communication would rattle Harry and Kinu. But not yet. Perhaps it was best that in early 1942 Kinu did not reach her son and he did not respond. The silence shielded them from the heartbreak to come.

PART THREE

THE WAR ON THE HOME FRONTS

踏んだり蹴ったり
Fundari kettari
To add insult to injury.

11

Incarcerated in California

The train lumbered into Tulare Assembly Center on Wednesday evening, May 6, 1942. It had taken eleven hours to journey north through the Mojave Desert. But Tulare seemed far more distant than a day trip.

They disembarked from the train in the gray wash of dusk. The Assembly Center, situated in central California's San Joaquin Valley, was a county fairground leased by the army. They crossed the road, lined by guards, and approached the grandstand around the racetrack, where they would be processed. In less than one month, Tulare—one of fifteen assembly centers in California and the West Coast—had been transformed into a temporary detention center for approximately five thousand ethnic Japanese from Los Angeles and central Californian coastal communities, as well as the Southern California coast. Already 2,400 had arrived, 680 on May 6 alone. With 171 barracks, a barbed-wire fence around the perimeter, watchtowers, and armed guards, there was no mistaking Tulare's latest incarnation.

The detention center, in its haste to prepare for its "volunteers," hadn't completed its transformation. Assigned to J-6-10—another dehumanizing bureaucratic detail like their family number 10464—Harry, Mary, and Jeanie trudged along a dirt path. Although contractors had raced to fill the fairgrounds with new barracks at an astonishing rate of one every forty-five minutes, the family's assignment was in an older section, where the buildings had been judged solid. Without street names, it wasn't easy to find theirs. Moreover, each wooden barrack looked identical to the others, with the familiar Z-brace pattern of barn doors. Indeed, that is exactly what the buildings were.

When they stood before Barrack 10, Harry opened the door, assuming that the inside had been refurbished. Squinting in the murky gloom, he searched for the family "apartment." What he found instead was a horse stall, a single lightbulb flickering overhead, throwing shadows on the rough plank walls.

Only by lining up the army-issue steel cots could Harry cram in eight people, let alone their baggage. The Matsumotos had been assigned to the stall next door. Harry, Mary, and Jeanie would share the allotted space with Kaz and Amy, Kaz's brother and sister, and their mother. It wasn't even a stall, Harry would later say. "It was a chicken coop."

It was up to the residents, weary after their journey and check-in, to fill the mattress sacks with straw. At least, pillows and khaki blankets were provided. "New!" Mary would recall with overwrought cheer. The latrines, as well as the showers, were housed separately, but even in these buildings privacy and space did not exist. Partitions, not walls, divided each unit, for which there were no doors. The lights-out curfew was at 11 p.m. and Harry hurried to stuff the mattresses that first night. In the suffocating heat, he finally drifted off to the labored breathing of his stable-mates.

The next morning, everyone got up early. Breakfast began at 7 a.m. A line of as many as five hundred snaked in front of the mess halls that could only accommodate one-third as many at a time. The Western-style breakfast of eggs, toast, coffee, and milk was served cafeteria style. Harry devoured his fare.

Although he was disturbed by the surroundings, people were sociable. The immigrant farmers and small merchants, who had toiled for years without a break, were giddy with fatigue and unaccustomed to idleness. On one level, too, Harry acknowledged, "our financial situation was so bad it was almost a relief to go to camp and let the government take care of us for awhile."

As the mercury rose, his sense of relief evaporated. Tulare was scalding: temperatures routinely soared above 90 degrees. Within weeks, the hospital and mess halls would dispense sodium chloride tablets gratis in order to thwart heat exhaustion. Just outside the detention center sat a grove of trees. "Their boughs are so interlocked that it appears as though this camp were surrounded by a cool woodland," wrote Tulare internee Hatsuye Egami in her diary. But evacuees were warned to stay five feet from the perimeter fence and abstain from talking to the armed guards on duty twenty-four hours a day. Inside the fence, where the vegetation had been bulldozed for buildings, the sun baked the barracks. The heat raised the stale stench of the horses that had once stood in the stalls. Harry spent most of his time outdoors with a crowd under the shelter of a large tree, the only one in the area.

Tulare was a town-in-progress, and the bustle fueled an ambient energy. Staff was needed to operate 11 mess halls, 3 hospitals, 5 laundries, 21 baths, and 30 latrines. Within weeks, the center would have a church, school, library, post office, and fire brigade. Although the civil administration was white, the residents, who would be represented by an elected council, would keep the facility humming. Camp manager Nils Aanonsen hoped that it would sing. "Like the early American pioneers," he wrote, "you have left your homes and have started a new life in a strange place. Like them you have adjustments to make and hardships to endure." Aanonsen, who would be moved by the evacuees' wholehearted response, recognized that this "move was not of your own choosing."

Crouching in the heat, Harry, at twenty-two, considered his options. The assembly-center setting and lifestyle were "a heck of a way to live." Loitering daily with the crowd was out of the question. He needed a job. Pay ranged from six dollars a month for unskilled labor to sixteen a month for professional and technical workers. By June 1, Harry was employed as a clerk in the accounting office, where he made eight dollars a month. He would parlay it into a small managerial job, hiring three or four cobblers to repair shoes, a service in high demand since residents could not leave the premises and, using their cramped "apartments" only to sleep, were often on their feet. His salary rose to twelve dollars a month as a "skilled" worker.

With three meals a day at the mess hall, Harry now had access to more food than he had had since leaving the Mounts several months earlier. At the camp stores, he bought briefs and pajamas for himself and a slip and pink dress for Mary. Yet, even with an in-house swing band, jitterbug dances—which Harry could not resist—and an outdoor movie screen at the grandstand showing dated Hollywood "flickers," Tulare beat the life out of its residents.

It wasn't the threat of violence that enervated them. It was captivity under a relentless sun with no end in sight. This harsh sentence was particularly disheartening because 70 percent of Tulare's interned population, or 3,440 persons out of a total 4,893, were *nisei* native-born citizens of the United States; the remaining were *issei* first-generation legal aliens. When the *Tulare News* published its second issue in early May, it called itself "A newspaper for better Americans in a greater America."

The newspaper journalists were evacuees, too. Everyone was

doing the best they could to persevere. Most people stifled their frustrations, but young, ambitious people couldn't be satisfied for long. Thirty percent of Tulare's citizen population ranged between ages eighteen and thirty. Sho Nomura, who had laughed at being arrested with his law-abiding father for leaving a refrigerator light on during curfew in California, felt "cheated out of living a normal life."

"Normal" wasn't an option, even in the workplace. Those who were employed had little prospect of a promotion and a raise. The army had determined that evacuee wages should not exceed those of its newly enlisted, who earned twenty-one dollars a month for their first four months of service. All assembly center wages were kept deliberately low to deflect criticism of pampering. Even if Harry had been a highly trained physician—and there were a number—he would always earn less than a green private.

Nor did the mess hall menu escape vigilant government discussion. At a time when the ration allowance for an army soldier was fifty cents per day, Tulare kept its cost below, at thirty-nine cents per day per person. Accepting what they could not change, people threw their energies into the tasks at hand. As the immigrant generation knew by background and experience, trials necessitated *gaman*. The *issei*—whose advanced age reduced their resilience and heightened their physical and emotional vulnerability—braced themselves, chewing on hard-earned wisdom: "*Fukō wa kasanatte kuru.*" "Hardships seldom come alone."

IN A SITUATION WHERE THE RESIDENTS HAD little control, the rumor mill provided steady grist, in the mess halls during the thirty-minute cafeteria shifts; at the library, where all Japanese language books, except for dictionaries, were banned; at the laundry, where women washed their families' sweat-darkened clothing in aluminum tubs. As spring turned into summer, the whispers became louder and more frequent, reaching Nils Aanonsen, who felt compelled to address the residents.

Aanonsen acknowledged that the evacuees were becoming "restless and upset" and revealed that his office had recently received instructions regarding another relocation. He had, however, no idea when it would begin or where everyone would go. Aanonsen intended to quell fears among the populace, but his candor inadvertently put them in a panic.

At the end of June and the onset of Tulare's broiling summer, Harry and Kaz fell ill and were admitted to the infirmary, where they were diagnosed with valley fever, or coccidioidomycosis, a fungal pulmonary infection brought about by the soil. Endemic to San Joaquin Valley, the illness was the second leading cause of hospital admission at Tulare. If valley fever worsened, it could behave much like pleurisy, with a similarly dire prognosis.

Harry refused to succumb. He rallied and escaped to a dance only to be bawled out by the nurses who accused him of being irresponsible. One day, a check for seventy-five dollars arrived from the Mexican man to whom Harry had sold his truck before boarding the train for Tulare. Harry was elated: not only was the money considerable—worth more than a thousand dollars today—but he was thrilled that a stranger had kept his word. And, despite how dispiriting Tulare was, Harry was making friends. These connections, forged under stress, would endure, some for a lifetime. But nothing cheered Harry more than the prospect of a visit from the Mounts.

They had been writing back and forth to arrange the details in advance. Harry had to request permission from the administration and mail an official permit to the Mounts, who were saving gas-ration coupons to make the journey. When the time came, they drove 170 miles over the Tehachapi Mountains at a "victory speed" of 35 miles an hour on rationed gas and tires.

But when they arrived, they were not allowed to enter the premises. Instead, they waited at a "visiting house" near the gate for Harry to be called. To his great delight, the Mounts had brought him a crate of grapes. Though their time together was fleeting and awkward under the circumstances, Harry found the Mounts' effort to cheer him up moving. They "were defying public sentiment," he said. "Mr. and Mrs. Mount were like parents to me."

WITH EACH PASSING WEEK, HARRY AND MARY grew more accustomed to Tulare, where the monotonous routine of endless lines, undulating heat, and stultifying boredom either dulled their spirits or enraged them. The administration worked to improve the center, and the residents tried to create more hospitable surroundings. Yet for every improvement, a harsher truth revealed itself.

Telephones were installed in boxes outside the mess halls, and those outside Tulare were welcome to call anytime. For the internees, however, only emergency calls within the complex were possible. The morning and evening roll call was scaled back to mornings only at six, but the 11 p.m.–6 a.m. curfew stood. A five-man council was elected in early June, but the Western Defense Command and Fourth Army office decreed a reelection one month later, after ordering that aliens could neither vote, hold office, nor be appointed to any self-governing committee at any assembly center. When the election of three *issei* was summarily overturned, Harry lost hope.

While the evacuees wondered how much longer they would be at Tulare before being transferred to a permanent facility, the Pacific War turned. On June 6, 1942, the United States Navy routed the Japanese Combined Fleet near the islands of Midway, placing the Japanese forces on the defensive. If there were ever a rationale for removing an allegedly suspicious population from the West Coast, it was lost in the churning waters of the Central Pacific. Nothing changed at Tulare, however, or at the other fourteen assembly centers. The internees languished, misjudged and forgotten.

A note of anxiety crept into conversations. "We had no idea what would happen next," said Harry. Hatsuye Egami—indefatigable in raising four children, teaching piano and voice, and greeting each day with hope—wrote in her diary. "My sadness becomes more pronounced because this life we lead has no goal and this mode of living seems without promise of change. The Army determines our fate and we do not know how many years this pattern must continue."

Yet, as the Fourth of July approached, the Tulare residents welcomed the distraction and took to their beloved holiday with gusto. They organized a full schedule of events, including a three-quarter-mile-long parade, sumo and judo contests, relays, and a tug-of-war. From early morning, the parade groups lined up at the racetrack. The Boy Scout Drum and Bugle Corps warmed up for their opening number, and the swing band practiced a tune inspired by "Swing and Sway with Sammy Kaye." The center vibrated with excitement.

The audience in the grandstand whooped with laughter as the costumed marchers tapped to the beat of a kitchen orchestra of spud peelers, carrot scrapers, and cabbage shredders, clanging paring knives. The elected council appeared, and in a role reversal, was dressed as a "happy family" while the police paraded as jailbirds in striped uniforms, dragging a ball and chain. World War I veterans marched with pride. A parade official read the Declaration of Independence and the audience sang "America."

In the grandstand, some saw goodwill, others humor, and a few irony. Harry, in particular, was troubled by what others may have missed. Among the Boy Scout and veteran marchers were several *nisei* who were neither. They were young men who had received discharges from the army in the wake of Pearl Harbor when they were classified as IV-C, or "enemy aliens." They carried American flags and wore their uniforms, but their trim appearance belied their humiliating status. Harry knew one of them personally. Although the man was not bitter, as a group the soldiers were upset at "being kicked out for no particular reason." Harry, too, was disturbed by their dismissal. "Where was the justice in all that?"

For all the drum rolls, applause, and patriotism, nightfall brought anxiety to Tulare that Fourth. While residents had savored the merry break in routine and a rare menu of strawberries and watermelon, it was difficult to reconcile the celebration with reality. The back pages of that day's issue of the *Tulare News*—filled with articles touting American independence and freedom—bore the dreaded announcement: "11 CENTERS PLANNED FOR EVACUEES."

THE DAYS GREW LONGER AND THE TEMPERATURE soared that July, Tulare's hottest month. The smell of horses and manure permeated the former fairgrounds, and the San Joaquin dust invaded. Harry faltered again with valley fever, and even though a cooling system had been installed in the infirmary, it did not lessen his symptoms. Finally, when painters finished whitewashing the perimeter fence in an effort to beautify the complex, residents learned that they were Arizona-bound within a month. They would be resettled in a camp at Gila River, outside Phoenix. Reassurances began immediately. "According to advance reports," wrote the *Tulare News*, "it has a very healthy climate, and is hot for only a few months out of the year." Residents could expect to tan to a "rich nut-brown color" in the "soft and balmy" air, blowing in "gentle zephyrs."

On the night of August 2, the cherished tradition of *obon* dance, an annual Buddhist festival honoring ancestors, took place. More than seven hundred dancers, clad in kimonos, danced in a sinuous line to the plaintive beat of *taiko* drums under lanterns lacing the racetrack. The magic, however, evaporated in the brash slant of sunlight. People balked at the second evacuation in four months. The immigrant population— largely stoic, numbed by their ordeal, and resigned to forbear— practiced "*shikata ga nai.*" "It cannot be helped." But anger among the young *nisei*, who had been raised at school and home to aspire to the highest rung of American upward mobility, was building.

The date for evacuation was ever subject to fluctuation. It would be complete by August 11; no, it would probably begin August 20; actually, it would commence August 26. Internees would learn their specific date only four or five days before. Harry and Mary did not need much time to pack, but their turbulent emotions required care. No matter how much Harry tried to stay occupied with work and an occasional dose of fun, he was, to his horror, "hardened," his "resentment for authority" fomenting.

In preparation to leave, some evacuees wrote their families in Japan to alert them of their impending move. Each family was allowed one free cablegram written in English—presumably for the benefit of government censors—that the International Red Cross would transmit. Owing to the war, they were warned, it could take months for the messages to reach their destinations.

Mary, still angry at her mother over her childhood tribulations, did not write. Harry, unsure of whether his mother had ever received any of his correspondence post–Pearl Harbor, did not bother, either.

ON AUGUST 31, 1942, HARRY, MARY, AND Jeanie, along with the Nagatas and Matsumotos, walked through the Tulare Assembly Center gate past rifle-toting sentries to an idling, soot-stained locomotive. Gray plumes of smoke curled over the 516 people assembled for the trek. On their twenty-eight-hour trip, they would cross their second desert in four months, the Gila, moving farther inland to another dust-clogged basin.

Harry, Mary, and Jeanie took their seats. The soldiers pulled down the shades, allegedly for the evacuees' own safety from belligerent mobs. Harry and Mary knew better. They were being kept invisible, lest the unexpected flash of their faces pressed against the coach windows disturb the citizens of the towns they passed through. Harry, Mary, and Jeanie settled in for the journey away from the West Coast, the repository of their family's collective dreams, the site of their individual sorrows. This time they knew where they were going.

12

The Empire's Home Front

I n early June, while Harry and Mary steamed under the Tulare sun, their mother endured the rainy season in Takasu. Dense clouds leached the light from her garden, humidity seeped through the windows, pearls of moisture pooling at the sills. The futons and laundry soured, blackening with mildew. Kinu turned on her Victorian ceiling light and Art Deco lamp from Seattle often, using more bulbs than the government's conservation efforts allotted.

She stayed inside more during this soggy spell and tried to read the newspaper between the lines. Most remarkable were the omissions. The military's General Staff Office (GSO), which controlled all war-related news, had decided to shield the citizenry from the navy's decisive defeat at Midway. One week after this turn of events, the Imperial Headquarters claimed victory: Japan had lost only one carrier and the United States two. The staggering truth: Japan had lost four carriers, one cruiser, 322 planes, and 3,500 men. From this point on, Kinu's *Chūgoku Shimbun*, recently reduced in length to save paper, would prove an even less reliable source of information. The only way that she and Frank could assess what was really happening was to note the deterioration in their daily life.

Frank's dream of becoming a doctor no longer seemed possible. Student mobilization, in which students were requisitioned for community projects, had begun early that year, though many Hiroshima schools did not yet take part. That was not the case for *Icchū*, which cooperated fully. So it was that seventeen-year-old Frank helped construct athletic grounds for training drills, spending more and more days away from the classroom. Hoisting sacks of sand on his shoulders, he sweated under the Sisyphean task. His trials had just begun.

Yet this mandatory service provided Frank a rest from *Icchū*'s intensified military drills. Instead of entering and exiting via the school's main gate, students now had to climb over walls erected to strengthen them for combat. Upping the ante, the training increased from once to several times each week. Students lined up with their rifles before the *hōanden* building housing the imperial portraits to pay their respects to the emperor for whom they would be fighting. Outside, they sat *seiza* (folding their legs underneath) while the head teacher bellowed instructions, including the admonition that any infraction would be disciplined. Frank knew that meant the sort of corporal punishment with which he was intimately familiar.

Punches hurt more on bare flesh. Upon command students had to undress to their underwear—always white, never blue—and go bare-chested, no matter the weather. The officers in charge believed that this would not only allow them to better gauge the physical shape of their subordinates but also strengthen the unity and emotional stamina of the group as a whole. Any notion of a carefree childhood receded as fleetingly as Japan's naval victories.

Frank shinnied up and down bamboo poles, swung from wooden bars, and ran distances that qualified as marathons. He learned to take apart his rifle and quickly reassemble it, inserting a dull, but still lethal, bayonet at the tip, all the better to kill the enemy at close range. Frank and his classmates doubted the efficacy of these drills. The army and navy were counting on weapons from two previous wars and a sense of victory. What had succeeded during the Russo-Japanese and Sino-Japanese wars, apparently, was powerful enough for the Great East Asia War. Where technology fell short, patriotic fervor would compensate. Swallowing their doubts, they placed dummy bullets in their rifle chambers and soldiered on.

The drill leaders overlooked archaic equipment because emotional fortitude, essential to the philosophy of *bushidō*, was paramount. Almost twenty-five years earlier, the government had proclaimed, "In future combat we shall not be able to surpass our enemy in military forces. Neither can we expect to excel the enemy in weapons and materials for arms. On any battlefield we should steel ourselves to winning glorious victory despite military forces and weapons inferior to the enemy's. Since we must be prepared for such a situation, it is self-evident that more spiritual education is necessary." Drills at *Icchū*, and other schools nationwide, continued unrevised, unaddressed, unabated with this viewpoint in mind.

FORTUNATELY, BY THE FALL OF 1942, FRANK caught a break when his hazing trials diminished in rancor. He remained haunted, though, by his thinly veiled secret, his *nisei* status. Frank's class staged an anti-American play in which General Douglas MacArthur and Admiral Chester Nimitz were portrayed as *Kichiku Bei-Ei* (devilish Americans and British), their bloated heads crowned with small devil horns. The depiction, building on historical stereotypes equating foreigners or outsiders with demon spirits, energized the rapt audience. Frank tried not to squirm and bit his tongue. "If you said anything, you could get into trouble."

In truth, he should have been accustomed to the *Kichiku*

Bei-Ei caricature: it proliferated throughout Japan. The demonic imagery appeared in political cartoons printed in every medium. It was widely discussed in general conversation. On elementary school grounds, ten-year-olds bayoneted straw bags with *Kichiku Bei-Ei* labels, attacked paper targets of President Roosevelt and British prime minister Winston Churchill, and tacked posters on their school walls, urging "Kill the American Devils!"

Increasingly estranged from his immediate culture, Frank watched Hiroshima evolve. Once an abundant landscape of clanging streetcars, incandescent lights, and crowded shops, the city had lost its stardust. Groceries and teahouses had closed since they were ordered not to use rice, commanded to lock in their prices, and required to augment the number of days off per month. On the block where Meijidō's headquarters stood, both the most practical and the most enchanting stores were failing. The purveyors of dry goods, stationery, and hardware bowed farewell to their neighbors—toy, eyeglass, and dress shop owners—who were also going out of business. Kiyo strained to convince herself that her beloved shopping district was simply suffering a slump. She looked up at the *suzuran* lights. They were no longer illuminated but no one had removed them.

Ultimately Kiyo had no choice but to shutter Meijidō's branch in the nearby entertainment district when sweets were strictly rationed. There weren't many customers anyway. The cinemas had stopped running American and European films, except for those from Axis ally Germany. And despite the Japanese love affair with Charlie Chaplin, *The Great Dictator*—his satire of Adolf Hitler and critique of fascism—was pointedly prohibited. Japanese actors had already abandoned stage names written in *katakana*, the syllabary for foreign words, which had once lent them an exotic cachet. The theaters played only patriotic sagas.

Masako had long avoided the movie theater anyway because she could not read the English subtitles in silent movies. Frank had avoided these films precisely because he read the subtitles and reacted without thinking, drawing angry stares. When Masako and Frank heard that someone had painted a mural of Churchill and Roosevelt on the ground in front of the theater— all the better to stomp on—they deliberately stayed away until rain showers washed away the belligerence.

Yet Frank could not evade the unpleasant rumors spiking the air with vitriol. "*Hakujin* eat meat," people scoffed, "which is why they are so severe relative to the Japanese." This stereotype, a variation on the *batakusai* stinking-butter prejudice, reminded Frank that he must continue to keep his head down, and he did.

Meanwhile, his mother was interacting more than ever with her neighbors. The government would not have it any other way. Kinu was an active member in her *tonarigumi* (neighbor association), which began nationwide in 1940 as a tool for the government to control the flow of goods and the emotional tenor of communities. By April 1941, seven months after the system was created, there were already more than a million associations nationwide, each one consisting of ten households and accounting for much of the population, given that families were often large and multigenerational. The Furue neighborhood of the Takasu district consisted of 425 households and 1,812 people. The associations participated in everything from soldier send-off parades, to air-defense drills, bond drives, and ration distributions. Masako's father, approaching seventy and one of the few men left in the neighborhood, headed Kinu's. She was fortunate. He was a good man who appreciated Kinu's kindness toward his beloved only daughter. Owing to his own three-year sojourn in Hawaii many years earlier, he didn't doubt Kinu because of her decades-long ties to the United States. In time, Kinu would need every bit of his goodwill.

"During the war, people had to cooperate," Masako remembered. The ten families met once a month to discuss hypothetical problems. "What should we do if there is an air raid?" "Where should we dig trenches?" As the summer heat condensed into the autumn typhoon season, rations were distributed via the neighborhood associations. Masako did the neighborhood's shopping on behalf of her father. She bought fish once a month and vegetables daily. One whiff of the fish and a glance at its glassy eyes suggested that it was rotten. Upon receiving the meager goods, Kinu and her neighbors had no choice but to smile. *"Itadakimasu."* "I humbly accept," they said, withdrawing to their respective kitchens to count their cabbage leaves and potatoes.

In the autumn of 1942, Kinu and Frank understood, after four years of mounting restrictions, exactly what to expect of their days—less of what they needed and more unappealing substitutes. Emergency flashlights, presumably for use while fleeing incendiary nighttime raids, were made of wooden, not metal, cylinders, highly flammable, defeating their purpose. If Kinu wanted another bucket for a drill, she could purchase a flimsy fabric one with bamboo handles; precious metal was commandeered by the military. Frank's thin socks were synthetic, popping holes every time he wore them; cotton was claimed for military uniforms. If he needed his shoes resoled, he could use sharkskin or discarded rubber. For every nagging problem, there was an ingenious solution. One simply had to mouth the latest slogan reverberating from loudspeakers, and displayed on huge posters and white banners. *"Hoshigarimasen katsu made,"* "I don't want any until victory."

Kinu and Frank trusted that what they read and heard was

true. They would endure until Japan emerged victorious. Yet in quiet moments Kinu caught her youngest son unaware. With his shaved head, flat expression, and *kokuminfuku* (national uniform), Frank looked like a pure Japanese boy, a budding soldier. No one would have guessed his American background. At eighteen, he was the same age as Harry when he had left for America. In little more than a year, Frank would graduate *Icchū*, and most likely be bound for the army base at Hiroshima Castle. What, Kinu wondered, was he thinking?

Trained to be stoic, Frank kept his feelings to himself. His mother's life was fraught. He didn't want to upset her by discussing how intensely he wanted to delay his draft. The more pressed his days became, the more he dreamed of the person who had always protected him. More than ever, Frank thought about his brother Harry.

13

Arizona Sandstorms

n autumn 1942, Harry had endured almost three months at Butte Camp, one of two internee settlements at the Gila River Relocation Center in Arizona. He had adequate food at the mess hall for Block 49, rudimentary shelter in apartment B in Barrack Seven, and basic clothing purchased from the Sears, Roebuck catalog with income from his nineteen-dollars-a-month auditor job. Otherwise, he was miserable.

Wherever he looked, he saw rows of low-slung, white-sided, red-roofed barracks that lay in a grid, fading flat into a horizon broken by only an occasional butte. Camp construction had begun in May but was not yet complete. Stacked lumber still cluttered vacant lots and construction equipment littered the ground. Gila was lackluster and nondescript, except for the air, a bracing mix of fresh wood, raw sewage, pungent sage, and wild mesquite.

It was the air that left the greatest impression. Not just the dramatic shifts in desert temperatures from blistering days to freezing nights—as much as a fifty-degree difference—but the fury of a wind foreign to Gila's residents from the West Coast. Harry, Mary, and Jeanie met it within moments of their arrival.

Stepping from the army truck to the ground after two days and eight hundred miles of travel, they had just enough time to glance at the camp before they heard the storm coming. A granular rattle rising in volume, hissing and roaring as it approached. The gale—gusting at forty or fifty miles an hour—darkened the sky and assaulted those in its wake. They shut their eyes and covered their mouths, stung by the wind clotted with dust, sand, silt, and clay. They dared not move until it passed. The dust storms recurred daily. So much for the "gentle zephyrs" the internees had been promised before leaving Tulare.

Harry and Mary's "family apartment" offered little respite. Although the single room was double the size of their Tulare horse stall, the accommodations were hardly inviting. The barrack walls were single-ply beaverboard, less substantial than particleboard. The floor was raised off the ground and full of gaps, exposing the soil beneath.

Harry and Mary were not alone in their dismay. Milton S. Eisenhower, the youngest brother of Lieutenant General Dwight D. Eisenhower and the first director of the War Relocation Authority (WRA), the federal agency that administered the ten concentration camps, had found the overall camp construction "so very cheap that, frankly, if it stands up for the duration, we are going to be lucky." He called the camps "sand and cactus" centers. By the time Harry and Mary moved into 49-7-B, Milton Eisenhower had resigned in protest over the anti-Japanese prejudice he had encountered in trying to institute a benevolent resettlement.

Harry and Mary chased sleep. Stunned by their internment, they had, by necessity, come to accept it. It was Gila's unearthly nights that kept them tossing on their straw mattresses. Long after sunset, the desert glowed with natural light edging the horizon, outlining the hills, mountains, and plateaus cloaked in darkness. The temperature plunged and the wind shrieked. Somewhere a coyote howled. In the morning, pallid sunlight revealed dust motes suspended in the air and a thick layer of sand littering the room's surfaces. It had poured between the slender window frame and the thin wall, churned from the ground below, and flown through the gaps in the floor. While Jeanie still drowsed, Mary noticed grains clinging to her daughter's lashes. Not wanting to awaken her, she knelt and blew softly on her daughter's eyelids, scattering the powder aloft.

Cleaning the room was Sisyphean drudgery. No sooner would Mary dust and sweep than the wind would pick up again. Harry spent as little time there as possible; he preferred to work. Before taking the auditing job, he had been employed as an interpreter arranging menial jobs for single *issei* men, who were inept in English, confounded by their internment, and largely depleted. They had led lives of hourly wages at stoop labor, accompanied by payday binges on gambling and booze, mingled with sour, lingering disappointment, exactly the lifestyle his father had warned Harry to avoid. Harry was certain of one point: when a less depressing job opened, he would take it.

Both Mary and Harry were struggling with their health. Harry's valley fever threatened to turn chronic, scarring and weakening his lungs. Little more than a week after his arrival, he came down with diarrhea, a common problem at Gila, where ingredients spoiled in unfinished, unsanitary kitchens. The novelty of the government taking care of him had worn off. Harry hated the food, especially the canned fruit cocktail with its cloying syrup, too often frosted with sand.

No sooner had Harry recovered than ten days later, Mary arrived at the Butte Camp hospital doubled over with abdominal cramps. She had not urinated for forty-eight hours. The doctors admitted her and prescribed rest, fluids, and an enema. No one figured out that Mary might have been anxious over her new living situation and too uptight to withstand the latrines, mortified by the lack of privacy. The hospital doctors and nurses were also internees, suffering under the same communal conditions. All they could do was treat and release.

Jeanie lent purpose to Mary's days. Mary knew people were wondering what a married woman from Seattle was doing in camp with her brother from Los Angeles. The situation was highly irregular. Why wasn't she—if she were a devoted wife—at Tule Lake in California instead, with her husband and others evacuated from Washington State?

Mary tried to ignore the gossip, busying herself by stitching muslin curtains with Sears, Roebuck fabric and hanging a cheery room divider. Their roommate Haruko was straining her nerves. Single women had been assigned to live with small families in the overcrowded barracks. Harry and Mary had no choice when Haruko suddenly showed up. "Haruko was cuckoo," said Mary. Harry, wary of the women's personality clash, cringed at the lack of privacy. "That made it kind of awkward there," he said. Mary's divider did little to mitigate the tension.

Harry jumped when an audit job became available. Preparing payment vouchers and tabulating data held little appeal, but the opportunity to hire twenty young women as clerks sounded fun. "That was the reason I took the job." Among Harry's congenial office mates, his heart lightened. The job came with the added benefit of access to information. Ensconced in an administration building, Butte Camp's nerve center, Harry kept his ear pressed to the ground, listening for a murmur of hope.

IN THE THIRTY-SIX RESIDENTIAL BLOCKS, THE MOOD was bleak. So overt and troubling was the general attitude that the inaugural issue of the *Gila News-Courier* camp newspaper addressed the matter. In its article "Issei Father," an imaginary immigrant watching children at play lamented: "What would become of them? Could they live a normal life in a place where people of only one race lived?" he asked. "Would they grow narrow and bitter and prejudiced?" The piece ended on a positive note affirming the greatness of America, but it had touched on a nerve animating the alleys, barracks, and communal areas.

Internees at other concentration camps also fumed with discontent, expressed, at first, through civil disobedience. At Tule Lake, farm laborers held a strike in August, protesting the lack of goods and low salaries. Packing shed workers followed one month later, and the mess hall staff struck in October. The prospect of more violence simmered.

The *kibei* were among the most disillusioned. They felt as if the *nisei* blamed them with their fluent Japanese and broken English for having attracted undue negative attention to the entire ethnic group. In Japan, the *kibei* had been scorned as children of emigrants, suspect for their fluent English. Nowhere did they belong.

Harry was a *kibei*, too, though he perceived himself as a *nisei* first, more at ease with English and the States. Working both sides of the aisle, he was privy to information from both. One tantalizing rumor ran that someone had snuck a contraband shortwave radio into camp and listened to an unnamed broadcast in Japanese reporting that the Imperial Army would enter Mexico, drive north into Arizona, and head for the concentration camps at Gila and Poston. The Japanese mission: to release their ethnic brethren from detention.

Harry decided that the rumor carried no weight; only imagination and desperation kept it burning. Gila lay approximately 150 miles from the Mexican border. But the closest that the Imperial Navy had come to successfully breaching the American mainland was an attack by a lone submarine on an oil refinery near Santa Barbara that February. Every shell missed and the sub had retreated after fifteen disastrous minutes. Given their indefinite incarceration, it was no wonder that some looked to the Empire for rescue. Another rumor circulated that Congress was about to abolish citizenship for *nisei*, many of whom were dual citizens of Japan and the United States. Although a related bill was introduced in the Senate, it had not advanced. The WRA reassured internees that passage required a two-thirds vote in the House and Senate plus ratification by the states before it could become a constitutional amendment. Passage was a long shot.

Amid the daily stress of lines, dust-ridden heat, and listless uncertainty, tension swelled. Some of Harry's acquaintances, whom he had first met in Hiroshima, had despised Japan when they lived there. Now they were seething at the States with a vehemence that Harry understood but did not share. A few would eventually be repatriated on exchange ships, renouncing the land of their birth, only to be embattled by dire conditions in Japan.

Other *nisei* friends had never set foot in Japan. They were also resentful but defended the American government on national security grounds. Some cast doubt on Harry's loyalty to the United States because he had family in Japan. Under the dangling lightbulb in the room where the young men talked, Harry felt besieged, as if he were "constantly questioned, suspected, and branded a Japanese sympathizer." Didn't they understand how often he had defended the United States while in Hiroshima, where Sanyō, his requisite military training, and the anti-American atmosphere had posed such hostile challenges? Rather than dilute his affection for America, those experiences bolstered it.

Slipping toward despair, Harry began to break rules. At night, he stole plywood from the open lots to build a table and chairs for the apartment. Sometimes he tramped past the mesquite and the saguaro, head down on the lookout for scorpions, rattlesnakes, and tarantulas, to the edge of camp, where he bargained with the Pima Indians. Passing wrinkled dollars between the mesh fence, Harry bought their cheap whisky. The raw liquor tasted better than the concoction his friends were fermenting from medicinal alcohol in clandestine stills. Harry had never shied away from risk, but if the military police patrolling the boundary saw him, they could arrest him, and if he were caught drinking, he could be charged with a federal violation for consuming alcohol on government land. Harry didn't give a damn. "I possessed more than the average bitterness against everybody and everything."

IN EARLY NOVEMBER, A CAMOUFLAGE NET FACTORY run by an outside contractor opened. Eligible only for citizens, the work sounded like an escape from camp, with the satisfaction of making a home-front contribution to the war effort. Harry liked the idea that 70 percent of the workers were slated to be women. On paper, the description was appealing. He applied for and landed a job.

On his first day, he boarded a factory-bound truck that bumped down dirt roads at the northwest end of camp and stopped at a guardhouse. When the guards opened the flaps, Harry hopped out. The factory lay in a fenced-in compound, beyond which the desert expanded. In the distance Harry saw something sinister and familiar: a towering barbed-wire perimeter fence glinting under a brass sun. He still stood firmly within Gila.

The factory buildings were little more than open scaffolds covered by modest roofs, providing scant shade. Beneath the watchful eyes of Southern California Glass Company foremen, Harry climbed a ladder and wove strips of colored burlap through fishing nets suspended from twenty-four-feet rafters. Coarse, loose threads stuck to his sweaty hands, and the handiwork made his fingers ache and swell; the piecework also paid poorly.

When he and the other workers completed a net, it was rolled, wrapped, and stacked. At regular intervals, hundreds of pounds of netting, precious as silk carpets, were whisked seventeen miles to the Casa Grande station, the first step in their passage thousands of miles overseas. Harry's hopes of temporarily leaving the 790-acre Butte Camp inside the 16,500-acre Gila concentration camp vanished.

In early November, interned laborers went on strike at Heart Mountain in Wyoming. Although wages and working conditions were at stake, smoldering anger over the internment propelled them to act. In mid-November, at Poston, also in Arizona, an internee suspected of being too close to the Caucasian administration was beaten with a pipe. Two suspects were arrested, a general strike erupted, and the term *inu*, or "dog"—a slur signifying an informer—gained currency across all ten concentration camps. More often than not, the detested *inu* were pro-American *nisei*, and the accusers and attackers were *issei* and *kibei*. The camp population was dividing, coalescing, turning on its own. No one, it seemed, could avoid taking sides.

Harry struggled to find common ground. Gila, too, was a tinderbox of trouble. One could smell it in the dry, resinous air. As the tamarisk leaves yellowed, another rumor infected camp. Both the *nisei* and the *issei* would be deported to Japan after the war. This climate of fear, a *Gila News-Courier* editorial countered, was "engendering a philosophy of defeatism." Harry sensed his own character hardening. The bitterness was "overwhelming," and he wasn't certain how long he could contain it.

• • •

AROUND MID-NOVEMBER, HARRY SPIED A mimeographed announcement on a bulletin board. Army recruiters were coming to interview Japanese speakers for a language school in Minnesota. They were looking for men fluent in high school Japanese. On a whim, Harry signed up.

At the appointed time, he entered a drab administration office, where one *hakujin* officer and two *nisei* privates rose to greet him. The officer chatted with Harry a few minutes, inquiring about his educational background and work, while the *nisei* listened. They needed linguists to translate Japanese documents, the officer said, and he wondered whether Harry knew any military terminology in Japanese. Sure, Harry replied. The officer slapped a book on the table and asked Harry to read aloud and translate.

This was the moment of reckoning. *Nisei*, who had only been exposed to written Japanese in after-school classes in the States, could not decipher the tiny characters, consisting of as many as twenty-six strokes, carrying multiple meanings depending upon their combination, and many forms of pronunciation. Harry looked down and paused.

He recognized the book at once, a field manual virtually identical to the one he carried in his back pocket throughout high school. He had spent so much time memorizing the contents that he had even packed it in his trunk when he sailed for Seattle, so accustomed to studying it that he hadn't realized that he wouldn't need it any longer. The text was part of his mandatory military training. Harry couldn't graduate from Sanyō without obtaining a high score on a test about the contents. If he didn't graduate, his mother would not have let him leave Japan. Harry had worked hard to pass the exam. In essence, he had committed to memory Japanese weaponry, armaments, and formations in order to return to the United States, the very country the officers at his school regarded as Japan's adversary.

Harry opened the book, several hundred onionskin pages long, as musty as a humid afternoon during the rainy season. There were photographs of rifles, cannons, tanks, even camouflage netting. But most of the pages were dense text about the conduct of war. So detailed were the contents that those who still held the books after the war would burn them before they fell into the hands of the Occupation forces. Harry began reading aloud, transported back to high school and the drone of drills led by retired military officers. He switched smoothly from guttural Japanese to translating in English. The terms were as comfortable on his tongue as abacus beads were to his fingers—smooth to the touch and easy to slide. He was warming to his task when the officer abruptly stopped him.

The recruiters glanced at each other. Harry couldn't read their expressions. The test had ended too quickly. To Harry's surprise, the officer rose, put out his hand, and said, "Congratulations!"

Harry had not only passed, he had excelled. His acceptance into language school was immediate and unconditional. "My eyes are bad," Harry cautioned. His nearsightedness, at 20/200 in each eye, was so pronounced that he couldn't make out the "Big E" on an eye chart from twenty feet away without glasses. This condition should have disqualified him, but the recruiters didn't balk. If he were recruited under the category of "limited service," he would not be posted where eyesight was critical. Harry didn't have to go abroad or serve with the infantry. How about it? they asked. If he agreed to enlist, he would leave after Thanksgiving. The men advised him to pack lightly and bid farewell quietly, lest tempers flare among the extremists opposed to recruitment. They wished him the best. Harry could hardly believe it. A few smiles and laughs later, he left the building blinking, the wire frames on his glasses glinting in the sun.

SHORTLY AFTER, HARRY TALKED WITH AN OLDER immigrant, a friend of his father who also hailed from Hiroshima and was a veteran of Japan's stunning 1905 victory in the Russo-Japanese War, the first major Asian defeat of a European power. "Fukuhara-san, why are you volunteering in the Army?" he asked. Japan would win this war, too, he declared.

Harry was puzzled by the man's thinking. "Your son is in the army," he said. The son, Harry's friend from Hiroshima, had already served in the United States Army before Pearl Harbor and entered the same language program.

"That's different, my son was drafted. But you are volunteering to go into the army and on top of that you went to Japan and you studied in Japan and you had military training in school," he said. "All the more reason you shouldn't be volunteering for the United States Army, especially since it was the army that locked us up in camps."

Harry understood. The man had a point: the army, through its Western Defense Command, had emptied the West Coast of virtually all ethnic Japanese and imprisoned them in the middle of nowhere. He would be entering the very service that had deprived him of his freedom.

Still, Harry had a retort in an ancient Japanese proverb. "*Umare no ie yori sodachi no ie.*" "To thy parents be truly respectful and to thy country be utterly loyal." Immigrant parents had raised their American children on this value, crossing a generational divide. John Aiso, the lead instructor at the language school, would expand on the meaning: "For the Samurai of Old

Japan, the path of loyalty would have been the only honorable one to take, even at the price of warring on one's own kin." Harry was certain that his father would have agreed.

The *issei* urged Harry to talk with Mary, who, as always, was forthright. She knew that Harry was miserable at Gila. She was grateful for his unwavering support when she had fled Seattle for Los Angeles and knew Harry could have avoided incarceration at Gila if she had not been with him. He had passed up an invitation to live with the Mounts' relatives in Ohio; he had forsaken his own comfort to find a place for three when no one wanted to rent an apartment to Japanese Americans. Mary understood her brother. "He didn't want to end up in a cage," she said.

She would be safe in camp, she assured him. She had food and shelter. She had neighbors and friends. She had Jeanie. Mary would miss Harry. People would talk more behind her back once he left, but she urged him to do what he wished.

ON EARLY FRIDAY MORNING, NOVEMBER 27, 1942, Harry stood shivering at Butte Camp's gate under a rose and marigold sky. He had dressed for the occasion in his summer sport coat, the finest clothing he owned, but it offered little resistance to the grip of a 35-degree dawn. A group of family and friends milled around, waiting to see off the twenty-seven men leaving Gila. The crowd would have been bigger, but those opposed to the men's enlistment stayed away. Mary and Jeanie stood in the thick of it, craning their heads. Harry jumped aboard one of the idling military trucks. From his vantage point, he couldn't see his sister and niece.

The truck started and moved slowly forward, the crunch of sand and stones grating underneath the wheels. The men were headed for Gila Bend station, where they would travel to Fort Snelling and then Camp Savage, both in Minnesota. At Savage, Harry, the once-casual student, would enter language school. From that point, he had no idea what he would be doing or how long he would be gone.

As the truck exited the camp, it picked up speed. His view was clear, but he didn't turn to see the dust choking in the truck's wake. As the road changed from packed earth to smooth asphalt, the Gila River Relocation Center, which had held him for eighty-eight days, receded, dwarfed by the stark hills, dotted with scaly tamarisk, thorny mesquite, and proud saguaro.

Beyond the distant western horizon, the war in the Pacific raged. Earlier that autumn, General MacArthur's command, the Southwest Pacific Area (SWPA), had formed the Allied Translator and Interpreter Section (ATIS) in Australia to handle captured documents. In October, its head, Colonel Sidney F. Mashbir, sat at his desk in Brisbane with a tray of documents before him. "They were covered with blood and body fat," he wrote, "and were typical of the documents that came into our hands in the early part of the campaign, while we were still being chased by the Japanese before the tide had turned." The stained, gruesome papers were all that the Allies had seized. Japanese soldiers did not surrender. American soldiers did not take Japanese alive. The cry for American linguists at the front sounded, as yet, faint.

Harry had no idea what was happening in the Pacific. But almost one year after Pearl Harbor, life was looking up at last. "I was so glad to leave," Harry reflected later. "But I did not know what I was getting into."

He could not know about an activity taking shape in another secluded, sand-swept desert in a nearby southwestern state. In late November, while Harry was packing his bag to leave Gila, Brigadier General Leslie Groves approved the selection of Los Alamos as a top-secret "demolition range" in New Mexico. The Manhattan Project, the race to build the first atomic bomb, had commenced in earnest.

14

A Balmy Winter in Minnesota

On Monday, December 7, 1942, one year after being fired in Santa Monica while the USS *Arizona* burned in Pearl Harbor, Private Harry Fukuhara in full uniform got off a train at Camp Savage, twenty miles south of Minneapolis. He hoisted a duffel bag on his shoulder and walked toward the entrance of yet another camp, his laced leather boots sliding over packed snow and black ice.

Harry could see his breath in the cold air. The smell of pine needles reminded him of Auburn and Miyajima but, at first glance, his surroundings were disappointing. Garbage cans stood at the entrance of dark barracks. Other buildings, their façades dripping with crackling icicles, appeared to be under construction. Beyond the shoveled paths, snowdrifts reached waist-high. Savage looked like a wintry version of Tulare and Gila—remote, unwelcoming, and harsh. Yet it was already vastly improved from its earlier incarnation.

Little more than six months before, Camp Savage had become the site of the Military Intelligence Service's (MIS) Japanese school by default. The fledgling program at the Presidio of San Francisco, with its Japanese American students and faculty, had been forced eastward in the wake of the evacuation. Minnesota, which in the 1940 census counted fifty-one people of Japanese descent in the entire state, did not share the West Coast's fear of the alleged Yellow Peril. Lieutenant Colonel Kai Rasmussen, the language school commandant, was drawn to the Twin Cities region "because the area selected not only had to have room physically, but room in the people's hearts."

Savage, consisting of 132 acres, had been constructed on farmland by the Civilian Conservation Corps as a log cabin facility and most recently had been used as a shelter for homeless men. The first class of *nisei* students, who were expected to bring their Japanese up to speed in six short months, pulled weeds, burned stained straw mattresses, and scoured the dilapidated compound before commencing their intensive study. They held a dance in a campus barn but only after the farmer using it had milked his cows and led them outside. By the time Harry arrived with the next class, Savage was spartan and spotless and the cows mooed in a different pasture.

ONCE HARRY SETTLED IN, HE BEGAN TO relax. The northern air was so different from that of Tulare and Gila. Thinner and more frigid, but tremulous with hope. Although most of the population was largely enlisted *nisei* supervised by *hakujin* officers, the community seemed cohesive. Everyone at Savage had elected to be there.

Camp Savage pulsed with purpose. The army's Military Intelligence Service had determined in early 1941 that combat intelligence would be vital when the United States and Japan went to war. At the time, only a few dozen officers were considered proficient in Japanese, an alarming figure. The army would need thousands who could translate and interpret. Three officers who spoke Japanese, including Commandant Rasmussen, envisioned a boot camp–style language school to teach the terminology of war to those who already had some ability in the language.

So challenging was written and spoken Japanese that it was perceived as inscrutable. Imperial Army soldiers battling in the Pacific counted on this advantage, an assumption that would prove costly. Admittedly, the Japanese had good reason to regard their language as indecipherable code. Literate Japanese used more than two thousand *kanji* characters originating from China, in addition to the native fifty-letter phonetic syllabary called *kana*, of which there were two forms. Certain *kanji* could be read more than two dozen ways. "The complexities of the Japanese language are almost beyond occidental comprehension," wrote Brigadier General John Weckerling, one of the leaders supervising the creation of the language school, in 1946. "A rough equivalent understandable to occidentals would be the incorporation of the entire French language into English plus a highly complicated and revolutionary system of picture writing."

In an effort to find qualified men, the army had interviewed all 1,300 *nisei* soldiers on the West Coast during the summer and fall of 1941. Thirty percent had immediate family in Japan, like Harry, and they were categorically disqualified on suspicion of divided loyalty. Only sixty met expectations. After Pearl Harbor, the organizers scrounged and recruited 150 more, including Harry's friend Walt Tanaka.

By May 1942, thirty graduates of that first class were dispersed to a vast battleground, ranging from Alaska in the north to Guadalcanal and Papua New Guinea in the Southwest Pacific. At first, Army and marine units didn't know how to utilize the few linguists and regarded them as suspect. They were kept far from the front, translating captured material—enemy numbers, disposition, plans—that arrived weeks after it might have had any tactical value. But by autumn, a paltry dozen or so *nisei* had proved their worth on short assignments to forward units in the Southwest Pacific, providing timely intelligence that influenced battles.

At a time when roughly one hundred thousand American soldiers battled in the Pacific, the Military Intelligence Service asked for three hundred *nisei* for its second class to commence in December 1942. To meet their target, recruiters ventured to the ten concentration camps, relaxed the IV-C "enemy alien" category for ethnic Japanese not already in the military, and applied flexibility regarding family in Japan. Captain Joseph K. Dickey, an officer key to establishing the language program, had recruited bilingual Ben Nakamoto with "I need you, I want you." "What could I do?" Ben reflected.

ARMY HOPES RESTED ON SAVAGE'S SECOND CLASS, composed of 444 *nisei*, including Harry. On December 15, he took his language placement exams and bared his upper arm for the last of three typhoid vaccinations. He didn't question why a man with terrible eyesight, who ought to stay stateside, might need protection from typhoid fever, endemic to and prevalent in the tropics.

Harry was assigned to the third section out of twenty-two. The first three sections were for those who were truly bilingual. The next few were for *kibei* whose Japanese was stronger than their English or who knew less Japanese. Harry's rank in the upper division was a marked improvement for the perennial second grader at the Auburn Buddhist Church. His years in Japan had made a difference.

At 6 a.m., the morning reveille blasted Harry awake. Breakfast in the mess hall began at 7 a.m., to be followed by classes at 8 a.m. The men devoted seven hours daily to class, two to homework, and Saturday mornings to exams. They worked on reading, Japanese-to-English translations, and interpreting skills.

The students were expected to memorize fifty to sixty *kanji* daily, a frenzied pace to learn one of the world's most difficult languages. Harry didn't study much at all. He even found *sōsho* (cursive) easy, although this shorthand confounded non-*kibei*. At the front, Japanese soldiers scrawled their orders on scraps of paper or in notepads and left them behind in the chaos of battle. Twenty percent of captured documents were written in *sōsho*, and the majority represented immense tactical value.

Savage's *nisei* instructors watched Harry tear through the coursework with ease.

Harry was regaining his bounce. Unburdened by the need to cram, he used his free time on weekends to walk into town. The absence of restrictions and suspicion was exhilarating. No rifle-toting guard blocked him from leaving the compound, no hypervigilant neighborhood warden questioned his movements, no skittish shop clerk refused to sell him goods. Returning to the barracks with a paper bag bulging with cheap groceries, Harry felt free for the first time in years.

He soon ruled Barrack F, where the Gila boys were housed, regaling them with jokes and his Charlie Chaplin waddle. His houseboy days of cooking served him well. "No one had any money," said Harry, who boiled hot dogs and rice on the pot-belly stove. Sho Nomura needed every minute to manage his studies, but he couldn't help laughing. "Everybody thought," said Sho, "that Harry was a kick in the pants."

Harry, in turn, drew energy from the companionship of his fellow student linguists. For both the West Coast and Hawaii *nisei*, Minnesota's coldest month wreaked havoc. When the mercury plunged to 40 degrees below zero, their priority became homework and survival. Noby Yoshimura placed a bottle of Coke between the window and the screen one night to chill it. By morning, it had exploded. He developed frostbite on his ears three times. "I didn't know better." Rusty Kimura felt his freshly shampooed hair ice as he walked from the shower to his barrack next door. The men studied the vagaries of winter as fastidiously as their *kanji*, the weather far more unyielding.

SO, TOO, WAS THE WEATHER EXTREME IN steaming Guadalcanal, a hemisphere away, where the fierce fighting that had erupted in August 1942 still raged. In January, the American offensive took hold. When combat ceased in February, American forces held more than three hundred prisoners and thousands of documents, all of which they were too shorthanded to capitalize on. The isolated Savage students were oblivious to the fluid events in the Pacific, but their instructors, privy to secret intelligence, perceived that needs in the field were rapidly evolving.

Guadalcanal revealed that only a few could effectively interrogate and instantly glean the value of documents. Yet fresh intelligence, arising from both these tasks, had infinitely strengthened the marines' tactical maneuvers. There was no question that the *nisei*, and particularly the *kibei*, with their fluent, if not native, Japanese and innate understanding of Japanese psychology, were needed near the front.

"Without front-line intelligence," wrote army historian James C. McNaughton, "units could only blunder into the enemy." Yet truly bilingual men were so scarce that forming pairs, each with a corresponding strength in Japanese and English, would become the norm. The Camp Savage faculty surveyed their rosters to respond to the rapid uptick in demand.

ON MARCH 15, 1943, PRECISELY THREE MONTHS after classes began, Harry answered as a buck private no more. The Savage instructors had determined what his classmates already knew. Harry, said fellow Gila pal Shizuo Kunihiro, was a "one-man team" who could read, write, and speak Japanese, as well as operate proficiently in English. Although he was not commissioned, the "ninety-day wonder" was promoted to sergeant and told that he was heading overseas.

Astonished, Harry questioned how he could possibly go overseas without basic training. Didn't he need at least six to eight weeks of physical conditioning on obstacle courses, experience doing marathon-length runs, and weapons' practice? "Well, we'll catch up with you," he was told. "Don't worry about it."

"I'm not worried," Harry said. "But I just don't feel very confident about anything."

ON APRIL 18, 1943, HARRY DEPARTED CAMP Savage with several dozen men from its top sections, including Ben Nakamoto. The last time Harry had boarded a train in California, he had been en route to Gila, guarded by soldiers, the window shades pulled down. This time he *was* a soldier. When the train stopped at stations, residents welcomed the men with coffee and doughnuts. Harry watched the landscape brighten from an anemic blur to washed pastels. Fog-free, San Francisco glistened.

The sun appeared to smile on the *nisei* linguists chugging west. On the same day as their departure, air force P-38 fighters flying over Bougainville in the South Pacific had downed the plane of Admiral Isoroku Yamamoto, commander of the Japanese Combined Fleet and architect of the Pearl Harbor attack. His corpse was found sitting upright among the jungle wreckage. In New Guinea, Harold Fudenna, a MIS linguist and *kibei* from California whose parents were imprisoned in a concentration camp, had translated the crucial radio message concerning the admiral's plans. But so secret was the MIS mission that Fudenna's crucial contribution would not be reported.

Other news gripped the nation. Yamamoto's death occurred

on the one-year anniversary of Lieutenant Colonel James Doo-little's raid on Tokyo, the first to hit Japan. Shortly after Harry reached California, the White House belatedly announced that three Doolittle-raid pilots captured by the Japanese had been condemned to death and shot the previous October. President Roosevelt called the executions "barbarous," "uncivilized," "in-human," and "depraved," evoking a burst of intense emotions similar to those that had galvanized Americans immediately af-ter Pearl Harbor.

Meanwhile, Lieutenant General John L. DeWitt continued to spew anti-Japanese rhetoric, directed particularly toward *nisei*, despite the success of those who had trained at the language school at his own headquarters on the Presidio and the total ab-sence of any reports of espionage or sabotage. Appearing before a congressional committee in mid-April, DeWitt stated unequiv-ocally, "A Jap's a Jap. They are a dangerous element, whether loyal or not. There is no way to determine their loyalty. . . . It makes no difference whether he is an American; theoretically he is still a Japanese and you can't change him. . . . You can't change him by giving him a piece of paper." By the time Harry caught wind of these comments, which rattled the students still at Sav-age, he had disembarked in San Francisco.

Harry and his fellow *nisei* weren't permitted to stay in the city. They were sent by ferry to Angel Island in San Francisco Bay for a few weeks before their departure. Angel Island, the Ellis Island of the West, had processed sixty thousand Japanese when they landed in the first two decades of a bright century. Here was hallowed ground where young *issei* men had queued for immigration processing, followed later by their kimono-clad picture brides. Now it was the temporary home for *nisei* bound for war and German POWs. The irony was not lost on Harry. "As if history was repeating itself, it was not too far-fetched to claim that we too, were confined to this island." Harry wrote the Mounts that he was heading overseas. Other linguists who were native to the Bay Area and wished to visit friends requested passes into San Francisco. Their applications were repeatedly rejected.

In mid-May, after more of the "hurry up and wait" mode of military life, Harry finally boarded a transport ship in San Francisco. When the ship, its wake roiling, passed beneath the Golden Gate Bridge, Harry didn't look up. The enormous swells made his stomach heave. He could do "nothing but lie down in the hold watching the ship rise and fall with the appearance and disappearance of the sky and the ocean through the port holes." No matter how sick he felt, he had to stay sharp. By now, he knew he was headed to Australia, though the linguists were explicitly forbidden from explaining their mission to others on board. Harry and the other linguists were assigned to the galley; the rest of the troops assumed they were Chinese cooks.

BACK ON FIRM GROUND IN GLENDALE, CLYDE and Flossie Mount ran the Stars and Stripes up the flagpole that Harry and Clyde had planted in the backyard. In her front window Flossie hung a white flag bordered in red with a blue star in the middle, signifying immediate family in the military. "They were proud of me and wanted the neighbors to know," Harry noted. For the rest of their lives, the Mounts would treasure the banner.

UNABLE TO FIND HIS SEA LEGS, HARRY grew conscious of danger for the first time. After about ten quiet days, the ship reached the combat zone of the South Pacific. The troops were ordered to climb to deck every night between 3 and 4 a.m. Stars blazing above, there they stayed for several hours, until the sky blushed in the east. In the wee hours, they conducted lifeboat drills in case the enemy attacked. They played poker and bridge. They waited. Smoking cigarettes was forbidden since the glow from a single match might attract the enemy. Japanese submarines, like sharks prowling at dawn, preyed beneath the seemingly placid Pacific. Harry reread the letter from the president to the troops that he had received before leaving. "Upon the outcome depends the freedom of your lives: the freedom of the lives of those you love—your fellow-citizens—your people." The president added, "Never were the enemies of freedom more tyrannical, more arrogant, more brutal." For Harry, the purpose of this war, his sense of freedom as an American, and the polarization of adversaries did not line up so neatly.

When the ship steered through the Coral Sea, the Southern Cross constellation graced the sable sky. The night drills turned more vigilant. At last, on the seventeenth day of the voyage, the port of Brisbane on the east coast of Australia appeared. "A truly welcome sight!" marveled Harry, worn-out from seasickness. "I didn't know where we were and didn't care in the least." Once he recovered, he cared very much where he was. For the second time in his life, he had crossed the Pacific. On June 4, 1943, he reported for duty.

15

Mary's North Star

As Harry's California-bound train chugged across the midwestern prairies in mid-April 1943, his sister Mary was eager to put her one-year internment behind her, too. Mary and Jeanie had swallowed enough sand and bitterness. There was a resettlement process for internees in place and many had secured clearance for leave. People had been departing Gila for several months, heading for Denver, Salt Lake City, and Chicago, where jobs abounded in the booming wartime economy and anti-Japanese sentiment was less pronounced than on the West Coast. But the WRA was worried that these destinations had reached a "critical stage of saturation." If internees attracted too much attention and took too many jobs, anti-Japanese sentiment might erupt. Mary watched in despair as these outposts closed to new arrivals. Then came the headlines of the Japanese executions of three air force pilots involved in the previous spring's Doolittle raid on Japan. Upon orders from Washington, all departures immediately ceased for the foreseeable future. The measure, the internees were told, was for their own safety.

"We hope this will blow over soon," Gila project director Leroy H. Bennett said, "but until the public cools down we cannot issue any more leaves."

THE DISAPPOINTING NEWS, HOWEVER, WAS MITIGATED BY a surprise visit from none other than the first lady herself. Eleanor Roosevelt arrived at Gila the same day that the leave cancellations were announced. In her floppy hat and sensible tie shoes, Mrs. Roosevelt engaged the residents in conversation, toured the facilities, and signed autographs in the burning heat. Utterly unflappable, she moved freely, without her FBI detail, never betraying a wink of fatigue or a blink of irritation. When she arrived in Los Angeles after her stop at Gila, she promptly gave a press conference. Responding to charges from fervently anti-Japanese senators and pundits who viewed the internees as coddled, Mrs. Roosevelt stated emphatically, "They are not being pampered—I would not choose their situation as a way to live."

Her statement was a righteous arrow shot in the bosom of the Western Defense Command. Mrs. Roosevelt was an outspoken American woman who conveyed the kind of *moga* modern dignity to which Mary aspired. The stop order on leaves was soon rescinded and Mary took heart. Her first step would be to divorce her estranged husband, Jerry, interned at Tule Lake in California.

THE MOOD AT GILA WAS TENSE. ANXIETY simmering over months of unjust incarceration had reached a boiling point by early February when the army announced that it was seeking volunteers for a segregated Japanese American combat unit to go overseas. If the *nisei* demonstrated their loyalty, army and WRA officials posited, public sentiment toward American citizens of Japanese ancestry would improve. To be sure, gifted *nisei* like Harry were already doing just that, but the secrecy of the MIS mission prevented publicity.

In conjunction with the registration drive, everyone in camp was required to fill out a leave application, regardless of whether residents actually left for the military or for jobs outside the Western Defense Command. Two questions concerned loyalty. Number twenty-seven asked whether an internee "would be willing to volunteer for the Army Nurse Corps or the WAAC," the Women's Army Auxiliary Corps. Number twenty-eight—the spoiler— read: "Will you swear unqualified allegiance to the United States of America and forswear any form of allegiance or obedience to the Japanese emperor, or any other foreign government, power, or organization?" These questions infuriated the internees particularly when the War Department clarified that the only correct answer was "yes" for both.

The questionnaire drove some outraged internees to extremes. Some of Harry's disillusioned *kibei* friends donned a *hachimaki* (headband)—white with a crimson sun—in protest and prostrated themselves, pledging allegiance to Imperial Japan. A few would eventually renounce their American citizenship and be disastrously repatriated.

Gila, the camp that had caused less consternation for authorities than hotbeds like Tule Lake and Manzanar, soon attracted the attention of FBI director J. Edgar Hoover. He was concerned that fifteen *issei* were discouraging a majority of *nisei* from answering "yes" to both loyalty questions. Moreover, Hoover wrote to Dillon Myer, the director of the WRA, the *issei* "have also persuaded the parents of those individuals to threaten to commit suicide if they enlist in the United States Army."

In this heightened atmosphere, Mary second-guessed her own answers. Even with two affirmative responses, would she still be doubted because of her close association with Japan? On a first draft she recorded Aunt Kiyo, a mere "CANDY STORE" owner, as her only relative in Hiroshima. She did not list her own years there, only her junior and senior high school education in Auburn. Although she had no one to help look after Jeanie, she asserted that she would be willing to volunteer for the Army Nurse Corps or the WAAC. As for employment, she would go anywhere for any work. Her first choice was Chicago, which she thought was in Ohio.

By March 3, when Mary filed her final applications for leave, she truthfully listed her three brothers as relatives in Japan, although she omitted her mother Kinu. Mary realized she could not volunteer for the Army Nurse Corps or the WAAC because of Jeanie. Instead she regarded her employment pragmatically. She was receptive to a job anywhere and, ideally, hoped to work in an office. Her second choice was as a domestic, the job Kinu dearly wanted her only daughter to avoid. If she were a man, Mary might have followed in Harry's footsteps. In the end, those long, lonely years of refined education in Hiroshima, which might have made Mary a valued *kibei* in the army, had not helped a bit.

AMID THE CAMP TURMOIL AND A STEADY trickle of resident departures, Mary lived for Jeanie, who, unlike Mary, would never be "hungry for a mother's love." In her spare time, she sewed Jeanie clothes with fabric from Sears, Roebuck and Montgomery Ward, played a game with a favorite red handkerchief, and balanced her in a woven bicycle basket while they teetered and tottered the length of the Canal Camp, careful lest they fall in the six-foot-deep ravines. Mary was aghast when people warned her, "Maybe, you better get married while you're young." As for Jeanie, they shrugged. "You could always put her up for adoption."

This jarring intrusion into Mary's affairs may have been motivated more by compassion than condescension. Mary could rebound more quickly with a husband. Even if she moved to a new city alone, she could find a room in an employer's home or in a women's hostel more easily than if she brought Jeanie and tried to secure a private apartment and regular employment. Regardless of the convenience to be gained, Mary was horrified. "No matter what happens, I'm never going to give Jean up, you know," she said years later.

MARY FELT FAR LESS WARMLY TOWARD MEN, although she was not immune to the attentions of the opposite sex. At twenty-seven, she was tall and slim, carried herself regally, spoke in refined Japanese and English, and mixed genuine humility with a dry, disarming wit. The severe physical conditions and emotional distress of Gila did nothing to diminish her charm.

Before Harry had left Gila, he had approached Fred Ito, an internee who was their block manager, and asked him to look out for his sister. Fred was a forty-six-year-old *nisei*, the former owner of a large grocery store with forty-two employees in San Gabriel, and lately an elected councilman at Tulare. He was also a *kibei*, fluent in Japanese, who had spent ten years in Japan. In a letter of recommendation, F. W. Heckelman, a Methodist minister and longtime missionary in Japan, wrote, "He has such a fine personality that it would seem he could fit into almost any position of trust," adding, "Fred is a modest man—a gentleman."

MARY THOUGHT SO, TOO. FRED WAS SOLICITOUS and kind. He gave her gifts—candy and lightbulbs, as valuable as sapphires and diamonds. He courted her, taking her to dances led by the Music Makers, Gila's big band, where they swayed to "Moonlight Serenade." Mary heard the rumors that Fred was married. He assured her that he was divorced; his ex-wife and three children lived in

Japan. As spring ripened and the saguaro cactus bloomed, Mary's heart filled. Although Fred was twenty years older, she wasn't bothered by the age difference. She adored him.

Fred was drawn to Mary, but he was also the eldest son in a large and noisy clan, responsible for his seven siblings and elderly parents. Unfortunately, almost all Fred's sisters lived at Gila. His father, a wizened *issei* who had labored in Maui's sugarcane fields, was polite. Fred's four sisters, however, belittled her, a single mother from Seattle who did not know anyone at Gila. Mary was not good enough for their brother. "You're a gypsy, a gypsy," they snickered. Mary didn't have much money and dressed poorly. Years later, she sobbed, "I hadn't brought a kimono or anything like it."

Despite her growing feelings for Fred, Mary yearned to leave Gila's hothouse atmosphere. Over the course of May, she watched more residents bid farewell to friends and depart camp forever. By the end of the month, 567 people had left, a pace in keeping with that of the other concentration camps. While this number was small relative to the more than thirteen thousand Gila residents, the flow would increase. Although Minneapolis– St. Paul, Cleveland, St. Louis, and New York were possibilities, Mary still set her sights on Chicago, where the WRA had opened its first field office earlier in the year to assist evacuees. Elmer L. Shirrell, the WRA relocation supervisor in Chicago, would describe the city as the "nation's warmest and most generous host to thousands of American citizens of Japanese ancestry."

Mary needed a job offer in order to secure her leave. So motivated was she to escape that she was willing to take a job for as little as ten dollars a week. She had made seventy-five dollars a month, plus housing, when she had worked for the Johnsons. Present openings for domestics in the Chicago area advertised a range from $50 to $75 to more a month. Mary downplayed her worth, explaining, "I don't mind because I am not expecting to get more wages for I have my daughter." Wherever Mary worked, three-year-old Jeanie would accompany her. In a letter, Elmer Shirrell reassured her. He was "certain that with your experience you will be able to earn $15 a week even though it is necessary for you to keep your daughter with you."

The gradual exodus from the concentration camps of more than one-third of the 120,000 ethnic Japanese driven from their West Coast homes was an authentic refugee migration. Such flights often bear a pattern. The able-bodied men venture first, scouting for and securing a safe haven while the women attend to aged relatives, children, and a displacing move. At the concentration camps, elderly immigrants asked their adult *nisei* children, American citizens fluent in English, to lead. Mary Hisae Fukuhara Oshimo, charting her own course, decided that she would wait for no one—neither Harry's friends the Nagatas and Matsumotos nor the Ito clan. Despite her avowed fear that her estranged husband would search for and physically threaten her, she was prepared to leave alone.

ON JUNE 9, 1943, MARY PACKED HER bags in Apartment B in Barrack Seven in Block Forty-Nine. It was her sweetheart Fred's forty-seventh birthday but her time had come. After nine months, six months longer than her brother, Mary's sentence at Gila was ending. The next morning, she clutched Jeanie's hand while they took a last look at the mesas of sand, mesquite, and saguaros. When the bus pulled up and its door clanged open, Mary gathered her daughter in her arms.

They would transfer from bus to train and travel northeast to Chicago over the course of four days. The landscape unfolded in bold contrast: from the bleached vistas of the Southwest desert to the grassy spread of the Midwest plains. In May, the farmlands near St. Louis had been submerged by heavy rainfall; the Missouri, Mississippi, Wabash, and Illinois Rivers had swollen to record levels and the surrounding districts had been classified disaster areas. When Mary and Jeanie neared the end of their journey, a flash flood drenched Peoria, 130 miles south of Chicago, washing out several hundred feet of tracks on the Rock Island railroad. One day later, on Monday, June 14, 1943, the locomotive, coughing a plume of coal smoke, blustered into the Windy City. Mary took to heart that it was a good sign that it was no longer raining.

A taxi deposited Mary and Jeanie at 537 North Wells Street. Crammed electric trains on elevated tracks screeched overhead. Mary searched for the Mutual Service Center, an agency facilitating resettlement that would shelter them temporarily. She fingered the memo with her brother Harry's army post office address. If she wrote him and he received her letter, she knew he would reply. She would not write the rest of the family in Hiroshima.

Mary would not be alone with Jeanie for long. A few weeks later, Fred headed to a brother in Mokena, Illinois, outside Chicago. Soon he would go to Mary. Most of his siblings would follow, including his four vocal sisters, and most would live in the same building and continue to rankle her.

Fred wrote lyrically of his impending Gila departure: "Being on the inside looking out, there appear many clouds of doubt and insecurity. . . ." Such was his ambivalence toward a fresh start as a middle-aged man in a strange city in an unfamiliar region of his mercurial country. Fred's heartfelt words might have just as easily applied to his ravishing Mary, an American from Auburn and Hiroshima, a woman who resolutely refused to dress in a kimono.

16

Rations and Spies in Hiroshima

n the summer of 1943, Kinu was still storing Mary's kimonos. From time to time, she opened the fragrant paulownia chest, unfolded the rice paper protecting the garments, and checked the silk for moth holes and mildew. Kinu intended to hold on to Mary's kimonos as long as possible. They were proof of her maternal bond to her estranged daughter, whom she missed more than she could express.

The kimonos were worthless in the present bloomer-bound society. People needed necessities, not luxuries. It could take an entire year to accumulate enough ration points to buy one blouse for one member of a family, let alone afford the cost of a tailor. "It was not the time to buy new items," said Masako, "and whatever you did, you needed thread." Women wished for a single spool, for repairing remnants over and again.

The nation was in the throes of another metal collection effort. In its insatiable hunger for scrap metal to manufacture armaments, the government no longer paid for contributions as it had in the massive drives of 1939 and 1941. The latest appeal, beginning in March, clamored for donations, particularly of iron.

As Hiroshima emerged from a moss-damp winter into a willow-green spring, priests unscrewed temple bells from their mountings, city workers dismantled streetlights, and mailmen detached mailboxes from their posts. The large cone-shaped bronze bell that Katsuji had generously donated to his favored Gion temple, Shōsōji, where his ashes were interred, tumbled into the arms of bureaucrats. To Kiyo's distress, Hondōri's filigreed *suzuran* lampposts were wrenched from the ground and carted off without ceremony. Summoning patriotic zeal, citizens continued to scrounge up metal objects at home. A jumble of pots, pans, kettles, buckets, and brass buttons, some piles higher than a four-foot-tall child, soon cluttered schoolyards and vacant lots commandeered by officials.

Kinu, too, surveyed her furnishings—Japanese and American, selected with flair by her late husband—to determine what she could do without. The hanging-bowl Art Deco lamp in her foyer? The Victorian ceiling light in her living room? She decided to keep her Seattle treasures. Kinu selected a few cast-iron pots and aluminum pans to donate but not all. She still had to cook. A few, with their American imprints on the copper bottoms, stayed.

Kinu looked at her hands, raw and wrinkled from cleaning with soap blended with mud and ashes, a grimy substitute for foamy detergent. Her hands were ruined but, after thirty-two years, her platinum-and-diamond wedding ring from Seattle still glittered. Platinum could be used for the mechanism of a gun. The war effort demanded sacrifice. She wiggled the ring from her finger. With so many families experiencing the grievous loss of husbands, sons, brothers, and uncles, how could she mourn a piece of jewelry? She had her children. Kinu buried her sadness and pushed on.

THAT THERE MIGHT BE ANY LINK BETWEEN the metal drive and reversed fortunes at the front did not occur to Kinu and Frank. So steady was the loss of normalcy from their lives that it was difficult to discern the course of the war. In early February, newspapers nationwide had reported that the battle of Guadalcanal had ended victoriously. The nation's troops were engaged, journalists wrote euphemistically, in a "sideward advance." From this point on, this perplexing phrase would be frequently employed. People folded their newspapers and wondered how a sideward advance, so odd to picture, differed from forward movement. The newspapers and radio broadcasts did not elaborate.

Twenty-four thousand Japanese soldiers had died during the brutal six-month battle of Guadalcanal, the first of many campaigns where desperate troops, educated from childhood to never surrender, made their final attack in suicidal banzai charges. Called *gyokusai*, literally meaning "shattered jewels" and signifying "glorious self-destruction," this act of violent futility proved gruesome. On the battlefield there was little dignity in dying in a fusillade of enemy bullets. Those who were not killed instantly often perished crying *"Okāsan,"* a last gasp for their mother.

Citizens, educated to accept and persevere, tolerated obfuscation from their military regime and waited for mail from their loved ones sent abroad. They adjusted to the diminution of their quality of life. *"Shikata ga nai."* "It cannot be helped." War, they knew from years of practice, was an extraordinary circumstance. When new regulations were announced, they held on.

Indeed, since the beginning of the year, listening to and playing jazz, that beloved American import, was prohibited. One thousand songs were banned. Other British and American tunes disappeared, too. Kinu felt compelled to discard the favorites that Harry once spun on his American Victrola, disposing of his records "Blue Moon" and "Home on the Range."

Stores no longer sold Japanese musical instruments like the *shamisen* or *koto*, with their materials diverted to the war effort and necessities for the home front. Fortunately, Kinu had her own instruments, sturdy survivors of two Pacific crossings. The government advocated military songs—poignant ballads or solemn marches. But Kinu couldn't get excited over "Hawaii Naval Battle," "At the Corner of Manila," and, the latest hit, "It's Getting Late in Batavia."

In a nod to the times, Kinu no longer played the piano. Chieko and Masako still visited, but making music was frowned upon since the whole neighborhood could hear. Kinu couldn't risk it. Besides, her piano might be misconstrued as excessive wealth. Restricted but not silenced, Kinu and Kiyo plucked the *koto* and strummed the *shamisen*, summoning their comforting twang. Chieko watched. And Masako danced, her soft-socked feet barely making a sound.

Kinu's family had shrunk significantly. Victor, back from the army, was working in a steel factory and living in a dormitory in the district of Misasa downtown. Pierce was still living near Tokyo, studying at Yokohama Technical School. Frank was the most present in her life. Kinu missed Katsuji, particularly his confident way with people. When she moved to Hiroshima, she had estimated her expenses in a world at peace, without a nefarious black market. Her costs were soaring. Katsuji would have bartered better than she did even on her most determined day.

Kinu and Frank needed rice. It had been rationed since 1941 and was regulated even more as farmers departed their fields for the front. When citizens lined up for their rationed portions, they were occasionally handed sweet potatoes instead. As prices dashed upward in the black market, Frank foresaw no respite. With neither Katsuji nor Harry to step in, he turned to a friend.

Jikki Fujii was Frank's best friend at *Icchū*. His father was responsible for rice distribution in western Hiroshima, a job with enormous clout. When Frank explained how arduous it was for his mother to obtain rice, Jikki and his father immediately understood. The Fukuharas had persevered without a male head of house for longer than most. Mr. Fujii took pity on them, figuring that his own bosses wouldn't notice the occasional loss of half a sack of rice in the warehouse. Whenever Jikki secreted away a partially open bag, still weighing between fifty and sixty pounds, his father cast a blind eye.

For the next year, after school Jikki would regularly place one of these bags on a special bike designed to hold heavy loads. In the murky broth of dusk, he pedaled to a bridge where Frank would be waiting. Jikki's magnanimity was fraught with risk. Had the boys been caught, they would have been accused of larceny.

Frank stepped up in other ways, too. One friend had access to *sake*, another to fish, a third to vegetables, all employing their fathers' connections. Frank paid them less than he would have on the black market. The bounty saved Kinu from the backbreaking work of planting and tending a garden.

Kinu had her persimmon, loquat, pomegranate, and fig trees but, unlike the other housewives who had repurposed their meditative gardens to plant hardy root vegetables—potatoes, sweet potatoes, and pumpkins, with some scallions thrown in—she would not dig up her yard for a vegetable patch. Did some neighbors resent her fragrant steamed rice when they could only afford *genmai* unmilled brown rice, mixed with two parts potatoes? Frank and Kinu ate that sometimes too; Frank spent hours stirring the *genmai* with a dowel to flake off the coating. Was someone critical of her Western living room, missing a portrait of the emperor? Cocooned in her bicultural home, Kinu did not bend to societal pressure.

She was not even intimidated by the *kempeitai* military

police. Officers patrolled Takasu and other neighborhoods on bicycles, hawkeyed for hints of disloyalty. Imperious in their belted uniforms and wide armbands, they jingled their bicycle bells, rattled residents' nerves, and, by their presence alone, raised the nightmarish prospect of an interrogation. The *kempeitai* had been concerned with counterintelligence even before Pearl Harbor. Only one neighbor needed to whisper a word to a *kempeitai* officer for the police to bang on Kinu's door. Kinu did not waver. She might cut corners to obtain food, but otherwise her behavior was upstanding. She participated in her neighborhood association by attending monthly meetings, showing up on parade routes to cheer departing soldiers, and taking part in air-raid drills. In her neighborhood bucket-brigade drills, she tied a bandanna around her head, sloshed relay buckets, and beat out imaginary fires with her broom.

It was Frank who feared the *kempeitai*. Neighbors were "nosy," he said, lurking behind windows, pausing at hedges, calling over others to whisper. Where did one draw the line between conversation and gossip? In Japan girls and boys weren't supposed to say more than "*Konnichiwa*" to one another. But what was the harm of talking with Masako? Some neighbors had admonished them for chatting. This was a minor transgression, but just one person who was envious of his family could create problems. The adage "*Tonari no kurō wa kamo no aji*" cut to the quick. "The neighbor's suffering is the taste of a duckling."

The memory of his own encounter with the *kempeitai* disturbed him. Once, before moving to Takasu, he had stopped along the bank of the Ōta River for a swim. Upstream, soldiers in loincloths were washing their horses, their dry uniforms piled onshore. While they were occupied, their clothing had been pickpocketed. Frank, who was questioned by a *kempeitai* detective, had provided information crucial to the criminal's arrest. When Frank was asked to stop by headquarters to receive a gift, he had acquiesced. But when he walked down the hall, he heard screams and moans. He tried not to look to the side but couldn't help but sneak a glance at the holding cells. "They were being yanked, slapped, and kicked." At the detective's office, Frank bowed deeply, accepted the tin of biscuits, and left quickly.

Anyone whose behavior was considered unpatriotic could be interrogated by the *kempeitai*. *Nisei* were particularly at risk. Societal acceptance of the unobtrusive minority had worsened following Midway and the "sideward advance" of Guadalcanal. "Japanese could afford to feel some generosity toward the Nisei in the early days of the war, while Japan was winning one victory after another. But once Japan began to lose the war, they began to treat 'American-borns' as if they were spies," wrote historian Rinjirō Sodei. Frank sensed the tension and devoted extra effort to appear wholly Japanese.

Late that summer, on August 24, he turned nineteen. Several months into his final year of *Icchū*, Frank was certain he would graduate but he still needed to find a way to stave off the draft. Barring a miraculous end to the war, his absolute deadline was his twentieth birthday, the age for compulsory service. Frank had to take care. His American roots could be easily traced to his family register at city hall, which listed the Seattle birthplace of the Fukuhara siblings as well as proof of Mary's 1938 marriage. Only Harry, for want of documentation, left no footprints.

PART FOUR

THE WAR IN THE PACIFIC THEATER

煮たった鍋から、こんどは火の中へ
Nitatta nabe kara, kondo wa hi no naka e
Out of the frying pan into the fire.

17

Suspicious from the Start

I n June 1943, it was winter in Brisbane, on the northeast coast of Australia. Sunny days and temperatures in the low seventies were a balm for Harry after his tumultuous weeks at sea. Trucked eight miles inland to Camp Chelmer at Indooroopilly, he was assigned to the Allied Translator and Interpreter Section (ATIS). He and four other *nisei* would be housed in a tent, one of a cluster, near the mosquito-infested Brisbane River.

Colonel Sidney F. Mashbir, a dashing cigar-smoking World War I veteran and former language attaché in Tokyo, was transforming ATIS from a makeshift organization into a highly regarded military unit. Despite ATIS's shabby campus, Mashbir envisioned far-reaching roles for the unit—supporting both American and Australian combat forces with intelligence; supplying language teams for regiments, divisions, and corps; and generating reports based on extensive translations.

Mashbir was an unabashed fan of the *nisei*. Likening the predicament of Japanese Americans to the Jews in Nazi Germany, Mashbir would declare, "almost without exception, you are volunteers, [and] that you are doing a brave, courageous, and patriotic thing in volunteering for this service." He believed this sentiment to his fastidious core.

Like many Americans but not his president, the colonel was as yet unaware of Nazi Germany's systematic efforts to murder the Jews of Europe. No matter how ill-fitting his comparison, Mashbir's clearheaded denunciation of prejudice toward *nisei* was the opposite of public opinion prevailing in the States. His vehement support motivated his charges, including one young sergeant from Auburn, Washington, whom he would come to know well over time.

Camp Chelmer hummed with purpose. Over the course of two months in an ATIS training program, Harry would learn to hone his interrogation skills, apply fresh intelligence to interrogations, convince American soldiers to capture prisoners alive, and encourage troops to hand over captured documents, rather than secret them as souvenirs. Mashbir proposed that his linguists serve "forward," near the front but no lower than the regimental level; otherwise, the scarce, increasingly indispensable *nisei* might be killed in combat. Mashbir envisioned that over time, "[t]his would give me a trained nucleus of about four hundred men, battle-tested, thoroughly indoctrinated, and thoroughly trained, which would be the cadre for the language units for the reinforcement, and the redeployed divisions as they arrived."

Harry, who was not privy to the colonel's thoughts, didn't think that he would be assigned to the field, in part due to his poor eyesight. But the boy who had once stared out the window during Japanese class at the Auburn Buddhist Church chafed under his present task, translating stacks of water-wrinkled, mud-encrusted papers, the volume rising as American and Australian troops pushed back the Japanese on New Guinea. The bloodstained diaries, letters, and reports reeked, even when dry-cleaned for easier handling, but Harry did not overthink the circumstances under which they had fallen into Allied hands.

Harry's work at ATIS might have been professionally draining, but the town was appealing. Indooroopilly—graced by camphor trees, porch-lined homes, and amiable townspeople—was a far cry from Savage, Gila, and Tulare. The residents welcomed the *nisei*. In Australia Harry wasn't a "Jap" or a lowly Chinese cook but another "Yank." The national penchant to "give a bloke a fair go," as one of Harry's Australian acquaintances would write, transcended racial and ethnic barriers.

For all its conviviality, Indooroopilly's outward calm belied Australia's vulnerable position. Central to the U.S. Army's Southwest Pacific Area (SWPA) command, Australia lay only one hundred miles south of New Guinea. By the time General MacArthur reached Australia from the embattled Philippines in March 1942, Japan had established a fleet base at Rabaul on the northern end of New Britain Island just north of New Guinea, bombed the Australian port of Darwin, shelled Sydney and Newcastle, and landed troops on New Guinea. One year later, entrenched Japanese troops were, increasingly, on the run. But if the United States and its allies did not regain control of New Guinea and Rabaul in New Britain, MacArthur would not be able to island-hop to the Philippines, from which he had withdrawn, famously vowing, "I came through and I shall return."

IN AUSTRALIA, HARRY KNEW THAT HE AND the other *nisei* linguists were still on probation. It didn't matter how much they had prepared at Savage and ATIS. The army higher-ups were dubious. One day, Harry overheard a white officer say that the *nisei* could not be trusted. Harry challenged him. "Well, why are we doing this work if we can't be trusted?" The officer backed off; he had spoken without thinking.

By the end of 1943, more than 300,000 American soldiers would be posted in Australia. Only 149 were Japanese American.

They would be dispersed with combat units throughout the Southwest Pacific, a vast region composed of Australia, most of the Solomons, New Guinea, the Bismarcks, the Philippines, and part of the Netherlands East Indies. Every *nisei* knew that he would have to work extra hard to avoid being misjudged as suspicious. When white American soldiers boarded transports for the distant Pacific, they did not leave their prejudices behind.

That summer the army ordered that all photographs of the MIS language school and its graduates be considered confidential. The *nisei* were a covert intelligence tool, and the army sought to protect them from Japanese retaliation should they be captured. The less the enemy knew about the *nisei*, the better their chances of survival. This tiny minority became virtually invisible.

Harry was soon placed on a ten-man *nisei* team, including one leader, three translators to work on documents, three interpreters to handle oral conversations, and three interrogators to interview new POWs. The team was supervised by a white officer. Terry Mizutari, a tech sergeant from Hawaii, served as the *nisei* leader. Shortly after, the team was whittled further when six members were sent elsewhere. Terry, Harry, Harry's Camp Savage friend Ben Nakamoto, and an experienced linguist named Howard Ogawa were assigned to serve the 112th Regimental Combat Team (RCT).

The men of the 112th, a Texas National Guard unit mobilized back in 1940, were cohesive. Many had grown up in the same hometowns. They regarded strangers warily, especially those who looked like "Nips" or "Japs." The Texans didn't mince words with the *nisei*. "What are you doing here?" "We don't want you." "We don't need you."

The 112th, which had neither combat nor amphibious experience, rushed to train. In mid-December, about five thousand men would land at Arawe, New Britain, to establish a PT boat base and divert the Japanese while the marines approached Cape Gloucester on New Britain's northwestern shore. Seizing Cape Gloucester was a vital step in the Allies' ultimate taking of Rabaul. In support of the overall operation, the First Marine Division would man the amphibious vehicles transporting the army troops to Arawe.

The marine division had just completed nine months rest in Melbourne after the battle of Guadalcanal, the first American land offensive against Japan. The troops were haunted by the horror. Men slaughtered in a bullet-and-bayonet ambush where the Japanese had pretended to surrender. Beheaded buddies. Genitals stuffed in the mouths of corpses. The rules of engagement were, the marines concluded, different with the Japs. Already roused by "Remember Pearl Harbor—keep 'em dying" and "A good Jap is a dead Jap," the leathernecks sharpened their motivation further. "Kill or be killed!" they warned.

This angry ethos—born of hatred, blood, and loss—meant that not many Japanese prisoners were brought in alive. The rare Japanese—invariably an enlisted man as opposed to a proud officer—who did surrender was often shot on the spot. "When we began our work the feeling was so bitter because of Japanese brutality that it was almost impossible to get either the Australians or the Americans to take prisoners," Colonel Mashbir would comment, "and it took a terrific amount of indoctrination to make them see the importance of it."

Amid the tense dynamic of the pressed 112th and the driven marines, the 112th's intelligence officer, who should have been the *nisei*'s natural ally, regarded the team warily, as if they were a burden. They needed protection from fellow American troops, as well as the enemy. Zealous Japanese troops were known to infiltrate American lines disguised in American uniforms pulled off the dead. The translators would be difficult to distinguish from the enemy, especially at night, the time the Japanese favored for attacks. Friendly fire was always a danger. The intelligence officer doubted that the *nisei* were worth the trouble. Mashbir acknowledged that his linguists were often perceived as doing "nothing but pry around among enemy dead and among abandoned enemy equipment, talking with prisoners, and reading scraps of paper that look like Chinese laundry tickets."

Harry and his teammates were assigned two Caucasian bodyguards and told to stick with them at all times, a practice put in place from the Aleutians to the Pacific. One was an armed, burly, six-foot Texan, whom the shorter linguists nicknamed "Bigfoot." He covered them wherever they went.

By early December, the small linguist team had sailed to Goodenough Island, off the coast of New Guinea, from which the troops would head to New Britain. While steady rain streamed off their tents, the men packed. Like any soldier, the linguists readied a knapsack, bedroll, knife, weapon, canteen, grenades, and rations. But they also carried a portable typewriter, a *Webster's New Collegiate* English dictionary, bulky Japanese Kenkyusha dictionaries, office supplies, and folding tables and chairs. The GIs laughed at the librarians. Harry shoved four pairs of spare glasses into his backpack. Those final days before his first campaign were his last chance to remedy a potentially fatal lapse. Harry approached an officer and asked. "Am I to receive basic military training—now?" Against the cacophony of roaring jeeps, drilling troops, and the screeching rain forest, his plea went unanswered.

THE WAR IN EUROPE SHIFTED THAT SPRING, autumn, and winter. Japan's Axis partner Italy had surrendered in September, but not before its troops had become prisoners of war in droves.

As many as 230,000 Italian and German troops had waved white flags in Tunisia in May alone. But across the Pacific, Allied victories continued to be dogged, tough, and incremental, the number of prisoners negligible. More often than not, Japanese forces pursued "sideward advances" that were, in reality, chaotic retreats. Still, at the end of 1943, the Japanese military remained well indoctrinated, highly motivated, and, to varying degrees, adequately supplied. Although the prospect of victory was eddying in corpse-ridden streams on volcanic isles, Japanese soldiers did not—unlike their German and Italian allies—raise their hands in capitulation.

Moreover, that autumn, troop mobilization had dramatically increased in Japan. In October, the right to defer the draft until age twenty-six for technical school and university students who majored in the humanities was abruptly canceled. Aspiring poets, artists, and businessmen formed queues for physical exams and withdrew from college, a formality since entire classes had been conscripted. Among them stood Pierce, two years younger than Harry and a third-year commerce major at Yokohama Technical School, near Tokyo.

That month a massive send-off ceremony took place at the Jingū Gaien Stadium adjacent to Meiji Shrine in central Tokyo for more than twenty-five thousand students from schools all over eastern Japan. Amid a drenching downpour, the young men marched into the national stadium to the blare of bugles and trumpets. Sixty-five thousand student spectators sat soaked in the stands. Dignitaries, including Prime Minister Hideki Tōjō, addressed the audience atop a draped podium. The recruits sang the military ode "Umi Yukaba," "Across the Sea," vowing to die for the Emperor. After hours standing at attention in the chilling rain, they marched to cheer "*Banzai*" before the Imperial Palace.

One of the soft-skinned soldiers that day was surely Pierce, whose entire class had been summarily conscripted. By December 1, the day that Pierce was officially inducted, there was so much that he did not know. His brother Harry was in the Pacific, preparing for his first landing in an active combat theater. The United States, Great Britain, and China would announce in the Cairo Communiqué their determination to obtain Japan's unconditional surrender. The Manhattan Project was making progress. The air force would soon refit its Boeing B-29 Superfortress to transport a new and stunning weapon.

Up until this point, Pierce's perspective had not extended to global politics. All he wanted was a solid college education that would culminate in a sensible career. Introverted like Victor, nostalgic for Auburn like Harry, and assimilated in Japan like Frank, Pierce would have been happy in either country. But now Pierce Katsuhiro Fukuhara, a dual citizen of nations at war, would answer the Japanese Imperial Army's commands as a second-class private. Pierce understood his mission. He knew his lines by heart. What the students-cum-soldiers had expressed before the Tokyo crowd that dismal October morn was true to everything that Pierce had learned in Japan. *"Ikite kaeru koto o nozomazu."* They roared. "We don't wish to return alive."

18

To the Front with a Typewriter

arry knew nothing about New Britain Island before landing there. Few did. On a map, it appeared as a 370-mile-long, forty- to fifty-mile-wide crescent above New Guinea south of the equator. Its topography was tropical: steaming emerald rain forests and smoking purple volcanoes, its terrain punishing. The official Marine history would call New Britain "one of the evil spots of this world." In vine-threaded jungles with tree canopies smothering light, soldiers would confront alligators, pythons, wild pigs, leeches, and malaria-carrying mosquitoes, not to mention the enemy. The monsoons blew from the northwest beginning in mid-December through March, impeccably timed with the convoy that left Goodenough Island on December 14, 1943, with General MacArthur and General Walter Krueger bidding the troops farewell.

Harry sat aboard the *Carter Hall,* an LSD (Landing Ship, Dock) warship holding forty-one amphibious vehicles for five waves of assault forces. In another area of the ship, senior staff spread maps and aerial photographs across a table, piecing together the puzzle of New Britain. The army's newest maps were old, dating from the 1914 German occupation. Although Australian intelligence officers had consulted those few familiar with New Britain—missionaries, natives, administrators, and planters—they had assembled an incomplete picture. Scouts had ventured ashore a few days earlier, but they had surveyed the land, not the water. Reefs proliferated: Where and how best to navigate them was anyone's guess.

During the trip toward the Vitiaz Strait, separating New Guinea from western New Britain, a squall turned into a typhoon, lashing the convoy with sheets of rain. When the *Carter Hall* reached its debarkation position, Harry scrambled to find a place aboard an armored Alligator tractor, an amphibious vehicle in the back of the ship's cavernous hold that had been designated for support staff and war correspondents. It was packed with a jeep, trailers, and more men than Harry had expected.

At 5 a.m., the assault forces in forty-one landing vehicles began emerging from the belly of the *Carter Hall*. Their engines roaring, one after another, they clanged down a steel-ribbed ramp and plowed into the sea. The Alligator rocked heavily in the typhoon-tossed waves. Harry's glasses fogged, his stomach churned, he tasted bile. He marked the moment. "That was the first time I regretted volunteering for the Army."

In the dark, Harry heard a mass grinding of gears. He couldn't see the boat in front of him. Nor could he control his nausea, throwing up over the man next to him. He kneeled by the side and watched the rain and waves wash away the vomit. Every time the sergeant aboard called out to be alert for trouble, Harry's chest tightened. "I was in trouble already." Soon after, he accidentally threw his helmet overboard while bailing water.

At some point, he dozed off amid the turbulence. When he awakened, the vessel swayed in a nebulous dawn. But it wasn't long before the buzz of thirty Japanese Zero fighter planes pierced the air. In a staccato of machine-gun fire, Harry lost his carbine and lunged under a jeep. The man by his side was hit and bled all over him. By the time the attack ended minutes later, Harry had been baptized by fire. He would never recall being that frightened again.

The troops had to wade ashore, but the tide came in higher than expected. Harry jumped into six feet of water and lost his grip on his typewriter. He watched it sink heavily to the bottom. "Whoever heard of a soldier going on a landing with a typewriter?" Still laden with gear, he struggled to swim. What if he lost his glasses? When he slogged ashore, his bodyguards were nowhere to be found. Harry spied Terry and plodded after him.

That night, warned not to move while his bodyguards slept, Harry memorized a code word and countersign in case he happened to confront a trigger-happy soldier. He passed the hours in a sandy coral cave, dozing on a poncho.

The next morning, he awakened thirsty and went for a drink of water at one of the buckets nearby. The beach resounded with activity: engineers directing bulldozers, jeeps barreling down the shore, GIs talking on their way to the mess tent. Overnight, Arawe's House Fireman Beach had been transformed into American turf. Harry felt safe. But while he was walking toward the water, a GI leveled a rifle at his head.

The soldier didn't say a word. "Don't get excited," said Harry. The man's hands began to shake. The more Harry talked, the more the soldier became agitated.

Nothing Harry said improved the situation. The passing seconds were making it worse. At last, a bodyguard ran up. "It's okay," he assured the GI, "we're all on the same side."

"He looks like the enemy," the GI blurted.

From that point on, no one on the team ever wandered off without Bigfoot beside him.

HARRY TURNED TO HIS FRIEND TERRY TO learn what he should have known to avert errors in the jungle. Yukitaka Terry Mizutari, twenty-three like Harry, hailed from Hilo, Hawaii. He played a mellow ukulele, dashed off clever cartoons, and danced a fluid waltz. But he was a hard-core soldier through and through. Terry had served with the 100th Infantry Battalion, a largely *nisei* unit that would later fight with unparalleled courage in Europe, and had mastered military Japanese. Harry saw Terry as stalwart from the start.

At night when Japanese planes bombed Arawe at will, they crouched in a foxhole that Terry had taught Harry how to dig and line with coconut logs. When the raids passed, the men talked. Although most ethnic Japanese in Hawaii were not interned, Terry's father had been imprisoned on the mainland because of his prominent position as a principal of a Japanese-language school. Had Katsuji lived, Harry was certain that his father would have been detained immediately and sent to a special Department of Justice camp, too. Both men were working their way through college. Both loved women. Both wondered what would happen if they were captured.

The worst fate, Terry believed, would be to become a prisoner. If he were wounded and captured, he might be tortured, sent to Japan as a POW, and imprisoned under horrific conditions. In the eyes of the Japanese, a *nisei* soldier, regardless of whether he possessed dual citizenship or not, would be perceived as a traitor. If his life came down to capture or combat, Terry told Harry, "I want to die fighting."

Harry didn't think that he would have a choice. He figured that he would be killed in battle, not wounded. After his harried landing and the nightly bombings, Harry bore no illusions about the safety of a linguist. He was closer to the front than he had ever imagined.

Still, despite his anxiety, Harry's initial shock subsided. Soldiers routinely came upon carnage. "It didn't take long to get used to seeing the dead, dying, or wounded." Although he encountered many wounded Americans at Arawe, the corpses he happened upon were Japanese; enemy losses would be four times as great as the Americans during the major course of fighting. Harry smelled the bodies before he saw them, rotting, bloating, leaking fluid, and swarming with flies, ants, and maggots. In no time, only bones remained.

Live prisoners proved as rare as unbitten skin. During the first month or so of heavy combat, only three Japanese were captured. Harry would recall interrogating one, wounded, shocked, and incoherent. Harry thought the man was dying. A rapid death suited the intelligence officer in charge, who had made clear from the start that he did not want to take any prisoners at all.

The linguists concentrated on documents. If they could determine details about the enemy's numbers, location, name, composition, orders, and objectives, the intelligence could trim the risk and abbreviate the campaign. To gather timely information, they poked around corpses, fished into mildewed pockets, and extracted stained memos scribbled with secrets. But as odd as their tasks may have appeared to the men of the 112th and the marines, they also began to make a difference. Their information proved useful in the heat of combat, providing tactical intelligence that helped turn the course of battles. Harry sensed grudging acceptance from the Texans. At least he was no longer the enemy.

By mid-January 1944, the night raids and fighting had diminished, and the combat and support staff had tripled to 4,750 men. The soldiers and marines had accomplished their mission.

ONE DAY IN EARLY 1944, AN UNEXPECTED visitor boarded a PT boat in Lae, New Guinea, and motored to Arawe, New Britain. John

Wayne—six foot four, Stetsoned, broad-shouldered—sauntered into the clearing. Wayne scribbled down contact information for families he vowed to contact upon his return.

An intelligence division captain took Ben Nakamoto to meet the actor, introducing the linguist as a "Tamed Jap." Wayne shook Ben's hand and thanked him for serving the country. Harry took his turn, too. But he was no longer the gullible boy who had been mesmerized by his father's connection to Charlie Chaplin. All Harry and the Duke shared was Glendale, where Harry had been a houseboy and Wayne a high school football star destined for Hollywood. The men trod different paths; their meeting was mere coincidence.

When the actor asked Harry for his telephone number at home, Harry hesitated. He couldn't ask Wayne to contact his mother or brothers. Mary wrote once in a while, but was inconsistent. Mrs. Mount was his most reliable correspondent. He gave the actor his employer's information.

Within weeks, an envelope from Mrs. Mount landed in Harry's hands. She had answered the phone to the Duke's inimitable drawl, she wrote, and couldn't be more overjoyed that Harry was safe and well. Harry's spirits, too, were uplifted. For the rest of his life, westerns would bring him back to the double features he had watched at Auburn's Mission Theater and to the encounter with John Wayne by Arawe's makeshift pier.

As the fighting ebbed, Harry learned to improvise. Like many, he had contracted jungle rot, a fungal infection from damp conditions nicknamed the New Guinea crud. His body itched, his groin reddened. When he scratched, his skin peeled in blood-streaked chunks. To relieve his discomfort, he threw away his olive-drab underwear. The army wanted its men healthy and well nourished. Harry—who had tired of dry, dehydrated rations—would toss grenades into the ocean. When they detonated and fish rose to the surface, he would grill a fresh-catch dinner for the team and repurpose the remaining rations as padding in his leather boots.

Harry also addressed his isolation. He needed pen pals to combat his pathetic lack of mail. Terry had a large, devoted family and a girlfriend, but he joined the effort. They posted a letter to the *Pacific Citizen*, the newspaper of the Japanese American Citizens League that was popular among *nisei* readers. It appeared in March 1944 under the headline "Lonely Sergeants."

> For your information I'd like to say that mail out here is few and far between. Letters from back home are what we look forward to the most out here, except for maybe going home again. As the fellows leave the camps for the outside world and the girls marry some 4F-ers because they think it's too long waiting for us to come back, gradually our correspondence dwindles and morale lowers.
>
> So, sometimes in the future, when you have some space in the paper you don't know what to do with, could you sort of mention in a casual way that there are a lot of lonely nisei soldiers out here living in foxholes day in and day out who would appreciate a "sugar report" or "morale booster," especially from some cute chick.

The editor promised to forward all "sugar reports" and in no time, the sugar began to flow. "Thirty to forty girls each," Harry boasted. Some sent photos. Harry and Terry, savoring the sweetness, wrote back. Problem solved.

Harry held one letter dear that he did not share, lest anyone doubt his sympathies. Found on the body of a Japanese soldier killed in action, its pages were worthless in terms of intelligence. A woman named Kashiko had given birth to a healthy boy eighteen days earlier. "The baby has grown bigger and is very cute," she wrote in a new mother's hurried hand. "When I think about how much we would be overjoyed together if you were here, I become teary-eyed, but the situation cannot be helped."

Harry's eyes traveled down the vertical lines running from right to left. Kashiko wrote of stroking her newborn's face, adding, "If this letter reaches you somewhere in the south, please be happy. I will raise our little boy tenderly, tenderly until you return." She begged, "If this letter reaches you, please write back immediately. Please take care."

Harry didn't doubt that the man would have killed him given the chance. Harry would have shot him, too, had they confronted each other in combat. Like any GI, Harry called the enemy "Japs," but unlike many of his *hakujin* colleagues, Harry knew his foe was not a fanatical, bloodthirsty man. A fearsome, dedicated, often savage fighter, yes, but human, too. The man for whom the letter was intended was a loving wife's husband and, surely, an elated first-time father.

Harry possessed empathy, born of his familial connections and life experience. Regardless of how final the soldierly send-offs in Japan were, the truth was that this soldier's family ached for their loved one to come home. At some point, Harry lost the original letter but kept a crisp copy. Touched by its poignance, he safeguarded the pages for the rest of his life.

19

No Season for Cherry Blossoms

By early 1944, Frank was a student in name only. *Icchū* had committed its student body to *kinrō hōshi* (compulsory labor). On weekdays, he was assigned to factories, military arsenals, provision depots, or the port of Ujina. Occasionally, he helped farmers plant and harvest their rice, a reprieve from his regular routine, a treat. "The farmers fed us well." School took place on weekends, an afterthought.

Ujina still thrummed with activity. Ships anchored, belching smoke, spitting out soldiers, swallowing more. But fewer vessels moored these days, and those that did stayed longer in port for repairs. The merchant shipping fleet, which transported troops and supplies to and from areas of combat, was reeling. By the beginning of 1944, so many vessels had been sunk by Allied aircraft and submarines in the Southwest Pacific that at least 40 percent of the nation's fleet was now rusting on the ocean floor.

Frank gazed at mammoth gray transports where he would deliver sugar, rice, and salt. He tied a *tenugui* (towel) around his head and padded his shoulders with a cloth. Hoisting a burlap sack on his back, he staggered over a narrow board placed between the ship and the wharf. At little over 140 pounds, Frank didn't weigh much more than his cargo. The officers barking orders didn't make allowances for inexperienced students. "*Hai*," Frank said, bowing his head in respect, and finished the task.

As weeks turned into months, Frank became skinnier and more famished but resolved to be a *ganbariya* (hard worker). He took pride that he pushed himself when those bigger than he faltered. Blistered, bruised, and callused, he persevered. Running across five bridges to and from *Icchū* and pedaling home on his bicycle with Jikki's purloined rice, Frank had conditioned himself well.

ON CHRISTMAS EVE DAY—WHILE, UNBEKNOWNST TO FRANK, Harry dug in his foxhole in New Britain—the official draft age in Japan was lowered from twenty to nineteen, Frank's age. Young teachers, who had been exempt because of their *Icchū* postings, went absent, and Frank heard that they had been conscripted. Men were fast disappearing from the home front. Frank's turn could come anytime, and he could be sent anywhere.

Despite the acclamations of victory in the *Chūgoku Shimbun* newspaper, Frank was fatalistic. "Once drafted, I wasn't going to live long." Determined to seek an extension, he noted that those majoring in medicine, science, or engineering were not subject to the lowered age limit. Frank liked economics, bookkeeping, and accounting, but the times left him no choice. He would take any of the sciences over a stint in the trenches.

For Kinu the spring of 1944 was disheartening. In the press, the government urged citizens to consider weeds, bees, and insects as viable ingredients. Sweet potatoes could be grown atop roofs both as camouflage and cuisine, "killing two birds with one stone." Kinu disregarded the suggestions, though in response to air-raid warnings, she screwed four indigo blackout bulbs in her American chandelier. Amid the gloom, Kinu rejoiced when Frank graduated from *Icchū*, a veritable achievement.

His next step looked promising. Frank had passed the rigorous exam for Takaoka Industrial Technical Public School, the equivalent of college, where he would major in metal engineering. His strategy had succeeded. Takaoka was in a rural area where food would be more plentiful and mobilization less frequent than in militarized Hiroshima. Frank wasn't interested in the metal and metal alloy department, singled out by the military for its application to armaments. But he breathed easier, knowing that he had temporarily circumvented the draft.

As of April 1, the Saturday before Frank had to report to college, travel was restricted nationwide. Only those with police permission could venture more than sixty-two miles. Limited express trains, sleeping cars, and dining coaches were abolished. Transporting soldiers, not troublesome civilians, was the green-lighted priority. Kinu did not envision making the three-hundred-mile, day-long trip to visit Frank in Takaoka often.

She would mourn his absence. Her baby from whom she rarely separated—taking him to Japan when she brought Mary and Victor back to Seattle, nursing him through pleurisy that first sorrowful Hiroshima winter, turning to him as her confidant when Harry departed. Frank—thwomping down the stairwell with his *kendō* sword, rushing home with a track-and-field trophy, devouring Kiyo's *castella* pound-cake slices—brightened her spirit.

Kinu would also lose her valued source of rice when Frank's best friend, Jikki, left for Waseda University in Tokyo. In the past year, the cost of rice on the black market had more than doubled; at some points, it had nearly quadrupled. Frank sometimes thought, "Jikki was the only reason I lived." Otherwise he might have become weak from malnutrition and become ill. One less mouth to feed did little to ease Kinu's burden.

She looked for possessions to barter on the black market, her gaze falling on her lustrous Monarch piano. Too bulky, too likely to attract police notice. Although Kinu no longer played it, she couldn't bear to give it up. Chieko would look back on those wretched days and sigh: "Rather than being one who tried hard, I did what I had to do." So it was for Kinu. When she was at her most anxious over her empty cupboards, she turned for help to her older sister Kiyo, still caramelizing sugar and steaming rice at Meijidō for the military's tins of provisions.

That fleeting spring, neither Frank nor Kinu celebrated the cherry blossoms, though the trees blossomed on schedule, carpeting the parks and the Ōta River. This year there were no vendors, picnickers, or revelers. By the time the wilted petals floated along the Ōta toward Hiroshima Castle, plans were under way to increase the fortress's massive military presence.

In battle-soaked New Guinea, Harry readied for his second landing.

20

Taking New Guinea

Harry fumed in the briefing tent at Finschhafen, New Guinea. His next landing would be with the 163rd RCT of the 41st Division. The 163rd members hailed from the Montana National Guard, and they had trained together for years. Harry had been pulled from the 112th just as he was becoming comfortable and trusted and he was now the team leader. Terry had returned to Australia for rest and relaxation, even though he and Harry had discussed waiting for a furlough together. Harry and three rookie linguists faced new bodyguards, officers, and troops who instinctively recoiled at Japanese faces.

Moreover, New Guinea, the world's second-largest island, which from the air looked like a winged dinosaur in flight, resisted being tamed. The topography was challenging, and the Japanese were heavily embedded. Although the Japanese were engaged in their "sideward advance," retreating west along the rocky coast, they were receiving reinforcements. Harry would be on their heels, invading Aitape, Dutch New Guinea.

The 163rd was experienced and edgy. In early 1943, they had fought a fierce battle in Sanananda, Papua New Guinea, and discovered evidence of cannibalism perpetrated against their men who had gone missing, their bodies recovered half-eaten. Then as now, the 163rd did not relish taking prisoners.

It was true: on occasion, Japanese troops devoured their own and others. Japanese provisions were running short, in part owing to the vast number of ships sunk. Malaria, dengue fever, and scrub typhus were ravaging the ranks of able-bodied men expected to forage for food and fight. Approximately two-thirds of Japan's total military deaths in the Pacific would arise from illness or starvation. Cannibalism stalked the troops, and some succumbed. "It's a matter of survival," recalled linguist Min Hara, who had taken confessions from wild-eyed POWs.

IN LATE APRIL 1944, THE 163RD LANDED on Aitape. This time, to his relief, Harry touched ground in shallow water. The team's typewriters, dictionaries, and folding chairs had been loaded separately on a jeep trailer. Armed with their carbines, the linguists waded to shore, free of enemy fire. The 163rd's mission: to seize a Japanese airdrome to aid Allied operations at Hollandia, 124 miles up the New Guinea coast. They accomplished their goal within hours. By the end of D-Day, only two men from the 163rd had been killed and thirteen wounded. At least one evaded friendly fire. "I saw a yellow man moving parallel at a crouch, so I slipped off the safety," recalled Hargis Westerfield, a soldier with the 163rd. The soldier behind him recognized the *nisei* as one of theirs. "Take it easy!" he grunted.

Harry focused on the prisoners: three had been taken in the first two hours. In the course of two weeks, more than half of the thousand-odd Japanese troops in the Aitape area would be killed; only twenty-five were captured. Sometimes, Harry would interrogate two or three prisoners a day, other times none, but he was heartened.

Harry talked to the POWs in hospital tents, where, often wounded, they lay bandaged, bleary-eyed, and bewildered. He offered them cigarettes to ease the tension and explained the

Geneva Conventions, the international treaties that protected human rights. Japan had pointedly not signed the 1929 Convention concerning prisoners of war. Unlike American soldiers who had been trained to provide only their names, ranks, and serial numbers, Japanese soldiers received no instructions in the case of capture. ATIS's Colonel Mashbir deplored the "ridiculous fact that the Japanese government, having officially boasted that no Japanese ever permitted himself to be taken prisoner, could not instruct its men in the proper procedure if they were captured."

Yet, despite their despair about their status, prisoners rallied when they realized that they would receive medical treatment, which they might have been refused in their own unit. They were treated humanely. The majority opened up and began to talk. Harry expanded his repertoire of tactical questions from the "What? Where? When?" to more strategic queries, as well as questions about food supplies, morale, and attrition. "The more meaningful questions had more meaningful answers."

Harry found that he could not interrogate well if he could not anticipate the enemy's reasoning. One day, he jetted in a PT boat to bring in three Japanese who had been floating offshore for hours. Two were clinging together while the other drifted about one hundred yards apart. Their life preservers kept them afloat, and they refused to surrender.

Leaning overboard, Harry told them that their safety was assured by the Geneva Conventions, but the men did not want to become prisoners of war. The sun blazed, the minutes ticked, and the officer in charge grew anxious that his troops were exposed out in the open. Another soldier in the boat lobbed a grenade in the water to frighten the Japanese into surrendering, but it didn't detonate. Harry stood stymied by the Japanese soldiers' intransigence. "Then why don't you drown yourself if you don't want to be saved?" he yelled, exasperated. Finally, another soldier aboard the patrol boat extended a pole and hooked a life preserver to pluck one man in. As soon as he was pulled aboard, the others threw up their arms and waited to be captured.

After the POWs had slept and eaten, Harry interviewed each man separately. He was perplexed by their behavior. "What happened to you guys?" he asked. The POW, who had been floating on his own, was a first-class private. "Well, I was senior and I couldn't surrender in front of these two who were subordinates," he said, dragging on a cigarette. The other POWs, second-class privates, could not surrender without permission from their superior, whom they hesitated to ask, lest they appear cowardly and disloyal. Harry understood the men's logic. They were cooperative, and the crisis passed.

Unlike the *nisei* linguist, his fellow American troops found it hard to understand this sort of intricate hierarchy. The social structure preserved order within the ranks at all costs—until retreats, hunger, illness, and despair began to fray the ropes of rigorous Japanese training.

FOR ALL THEIR DEFICIENCIES, JAPANESE TROOPS WERE still armed and favored night attacks. The 163rd conducted a classic perimeter defense, employed throughout New Guinea and the Solomon Islands. Officers commanded, "Dig in before dark and don't move until daylight." Even in daylight, the jungle could conceal a prone man ten yards away. Soldiers' sense of hearing heightened; the scratch of a scuttling hermit crab could be terrifying. A single grenade tossed in panic ignited a barrage of gunfire. Harry pulled his trigger, too. "Everyone was firing. It feels better to fire." The risk of being so tightly wound? "There was a lot of friendly fire."

By day, Harry didn't dwell on the events of the night before. He maneuvered. "Harry could sweet talk just about anybody," marveled his fellow linguist Gene Uratsu. When Harry wanted rice, he convinced the officers it was for softening up the prisoners so they would talk. The team thirsted for cocktails? Harry obtained pure alcohol from a field hospital and mixed it with grapefruit juice. Someone craved comfort food? He procured onions and eggs from navy sailors and bacon from the mess hall. Before long, Gene recalled, the "mouthwatering aroma of fried rice filtered through the coconut trees and attracted Commanding General's nose." Harry's pièce de résistance was far less fragrant. He assembled a portable outhouse from lumber gifted by the engineers. His commode endeared the linguists to the troops, who needed their privacy while reading "Dear John" letters from back home.

Each time, Harry provided something in return for the favors, often a *hinomaru* flag for men to send home to impress loved ones with their conquests. Cutting rectangles from hospital sheets, he drew and filled in a red circle against a white background. In his convincing Japanese cursive, he then autographed the flags with fictitious signatures.

This cottage industry combated a serious problem. Linguists missed opportunities to obtain valuable information when GIs sent home found documents that hadn't been analyzed first. The Japanese were prolific journal writers. Even the diary of a bottom-tier second-class private—the rank at which Victor and Pierce had entered the Japanese Imperial Army—could reveal morale issues, troop movements, and supply shortages. In early campaigns, most documents ended up in the troops' personal belongings. Later, even after they had been urged to turn in seized documents immediately, the outgoing mail of one unit turned up no less than five thousand documents with intelligence value over the course of eight months. One 41st Division memorandum warned, "These selfish individuals not only lower the high standard set by their fellow soldiers, but contribute to loss of life and imperil the success of an operation."

That spring *Life* magazine published a photograph of a young woman with a Japanese skull sent by her navy boyfriend in the Pacific. A few months later, after flying missions over New Guinea with the air force, the renowned aviator Charles A. Lindbergh touched down in Hawaii, where a customs official nonchalantly asked whether he had packed bones in his luggage. Lindbergh was not surprised: in New Guinea he had heard that soldiers routinely worked over corpses—removing shinbones to carve into letter openers and pen trays, extracting teeth to pocket the gold fillings, and placing heads in swarming anthills—all the better, Lindbergh was told, "'to clean them for souvenirs.'"

In the end, Harry's faithful reproductions of Japanese flags tapped what he knew at heart: Japanese soldiers cherished their autographed *hinomaru* flags as talismans for battle.

IN MAY 1944, ON THE EVE OF another campaign, Harry felt more confident than at any point since his ninety days at Camp Savage. He sensed a growing camaraderie with the men of the 163rd. G-2 intelligence-division staff in Aitape stepped in to act as bodyguards for the linguists, and there was less of a need for guards. His presence and work were increasingly valued. Gene was amazed by Harry's energy. "In the combat zone of steaming New Guinea jungles, everything was in short supply except K rations, insects, and enemy bullets. I just could not understand how in the world God could make a place so miserable, but Harry didn't seem to mind." Gene was correct. New

Guinea didn't distress Harry. "I was not particularly anxious to go home," he would remember.

In mid-May, Harry headed west for Sarmi, where the Japanese lay entrenched. A veteran of two landings, he didn't flinch. The outhouse came along with his translation paraphernalia.

21

Pierce's Stay of Execution

Harry understood that his brothers might be in the Japanese Imperial Army. Victor was serving when Harry had left for the States in 1938. He had a "hunch" that Frank and Pierce might be too, but he could not possibly know that Pierce was heading his way.

In early spring 1944, twenty-one-year-old Pierce was posted to Hamada, about forty miles from Hiroshima in Shimane prefecture, near the Japan Sea. Hamada was small, rural, and parochial, especially in comparison to cosmopolitan Hiroshima. Pierce's fellow soldiers, who had been born and raised locally, saw Pierce as an outsider.

The superior officer also singled out the second-class privates for torment. Pierce found the man unreasonable, especially in comparison to his genial college professors. Pierce could do nothing right but he was not alone. All draftees nationwide were chastised, forced to surrender their privacy and independence, and made to feel worthless. As one recruit put it, "Thus we had to live under circumstances which made us feel that we were always tied up with invisible hands." Everyone knew that second-class privates were considered less valuable than their horses.

Unfortunately, Pierce had fallen sick before his rigorous training. Perhaps the bitter autumn rain that soaked the military procession at the national stadium was to blame. His chest ached, his weight dropped, his appetite ebbed. Pierce's lungs had always been fragile—prone to infection, filling with fluid, warranting X-rays. Kinu, her memories raw from losing Katsuji to pleurisy and nursing Frank, wrote Pierce often, reminding him to take care. She worried. How could he recover in a military battalion?

That spring Kinu rushed to see him, winding her way through knots of soldiers and police to stand in line at Hiroshima Station. Huge placards remonstrated, "Stop Unnecessary, Nonurgent Trips!" For a concerned mother, her journey to Hamada was neither.

In Hamada, Pierce looked gaunt, pasty-skinned, his eyes receding in their sockets. Even worse than his troubling appearance were his prospects. Kinu and Pierce caught wind of a rumor. Townspeople murmured that the troops would soon board a transport ship for a southern isle, shorthand for a trouble spot in the Pacific.

If Pierce went overseas, he could end up in a place like New Guinea. In Japanese they called the mammoth island *Nyū Ginia*, the *G* hard and guttural, spoken with a groan. New Guinea, lamented bereaved families, devoured the young. New Guinea, declared survivors, was a disaster. New Guinea "will be your grave," warned Allied propaganda.

And then, out of the blue, the Imperial Army delivered a stay. Pierce, miserable in Hamada, had volunteered for guard duty in Hiroshima at electric power plants and ammunition depots. His request was granted and he received his orders to move in mid-May. By mid-June, Pierce would march the Hiroshima Castle grounds. Although he would be billeted on base, Kinu could visit him on his day off, smuggle him *omusubi* (rice balls), and monitor his health.

THAT JUNE, DOWNPOURS DRENCHED THE DELTAS, BUT the city was not yet saturated by *tsuyu* (plum rain), the euphemism for the rainy season. The days were damp but not intolerable. Kinu had three of her four sons close at hand. She could gauge their health from their faces, their mood from their voices. In 1944, she took solace that they were safe in Hiroshima.

PART FIVE

DOOMSDAY OVERTURE

豆を煮るにまめがらを焚く

Mame o niru ni mamegara o taku

There is strife among one's own flesh and blood.

22

A Stunning Encounter in Sarmi

New Guinea was, indeed, one of the world's most dangerous destinations, deserving of its fearsome reputation. It would tax even Harry, whose good cheer would prove of limited duration.

In Sarmi in northern New Guinea, he prepared to land with the 163rd on nearby Wakde Island, a coral gash of land desired for its rudimentary runway and airport. Intelligence reports indicated minimal opposition. At the last moment, Harry was told to stay behind and interrogate prisoners, and a white intelligence officer took his place.

The Japanese general in charge of the Wakde-Sarmi garrison was expecting the assault. He had warned his troops, "The enemy American military is coming before your eyes." He urged them to strike during the landing when the Americans were most vulnerable. "Be victorious unto death and exterminate the enemy."

His men complied, hitting each successive wave of amphibious craft with machine-gun and rifle fire from foxholes, slit trenches, and camouflaged bunkers. Still, the 163rd's men crawled onshore and up an incline. Lobbing grenades and firing their rifles, they cleared one pillbox at a time. Japanese soldiers emerged, shouting, flashing bayonets. By the end of the day, nineteen American army troops were dead, including the intelligence officer who had gone instead of Harry. As soon as he had charged off the landing craft, he had been shot in the head.

"It really kind of shook me up at the time," Harry said. The men had worked together to compile a massive list of Japanese officers that would help G-2 understand more about the units they confronted. They had eaten together, joked, bonded. Harry already knew that combat rotations were psychologically challenging. "You would become very close for several months and then some people would move on." But this was the first time that someone with whom he worked closely had perished.

A few days later, Harry went to Wakde for the first time. "We had bombed the island mercilessly." Yet, that morning, some three dozen Japanese, who had infiltrated the beachhead during the night, had made a *banzai* charge. The Americans quashed the assault and continued to mop up, exploding demolition charges in coral caves where the enemy hid, and shooting snipers perched in palm trees. Many Japanese committed suicide rather than surrender.

To do right by his duties, Harry needed Japanese soldiers who were alive. He was standing near a bunker where several Japanese were holed up and trying to talk them into surrendering when an American flamethrower stepped forward and set fire to the entrance. The soldiers ran out, screaming and burning. Harry was horrified. "They were a ball of fire." An odor of charred flesh permeated the air. The panicked men were shot one after another, falling face-first or bursting backward onto the sand. Harry was stunned by the violence. "That really scared me because I hadn't seen anything like that before."

He returned to Sarmi that day without a single prisoner. Within two days, the campaign's assault phase ended and the island hummed with hammers and drills as it was readied for

American fighter planes. The Japanese garrison had been eliminated: 759 had been killed and four Japanese captured.

At night, Harry and Gene talked quietly in their hammocks, resolutely avoiding the topic of war. Gene missed his family and Harry his friends, especially Terry. Neither man mentioned an unsettling development: one of the four Japanese taken prisoner at Wakde was a *nisei* from Hawaii who spoke English.

By this point, Harry was suffering from malaria that he had contracted in New Britain, despite taking atabrine. The *nisei* in the American military were nicknamed the "yellow bastards of New Guinea" because their skin turned particularly jaundiced from the antimalarial tablet that they downed daily at the chow line. Harry's bouts worsened in New Guinea with sweat-drenching fevers, teeth-rattling chills, stunning headaches, and nausea. He lost weight and stamina. The spells lasted for a few days, abated, and returned. Thin and tinged with atabrine's copper pallor, Harry rested but did not stop working. He was managing a huge load of documents, determined to stay in New Guinea, and defiantly, radiantly alive.

ONE DAY A JAPANESE SOLDIER CLOSE IN age to Harry, a man from Hiroshima, approached Sarmi weakened from malaria. In another lifetime, he had waved flags at farewell parades near Hakushima Elementary School, hosted soldiers in his family's home, and walked to school by Hiroshima Castle. In another lifetime, he had been a desultory student, baseball pitcher, and bully. His father thought the military would straighten him out. He had left Hiroshima as a teenager, serving in the field artillery in Manchuria and China. He had survived the blistering heat and guerrilla battles of the Philippines and Palau. By the time he reached New Guinea, he had been promoted to master sergeant, posted to the Akatsuki Butai, or Dawn Unit, a shipping force originating in Ujina that provided transport, equipment, and personnel throughout the Pacific. In his mid-twenties, he appeared a decade older than his years. "They all listened to me," said the hardened man in charge of two hundred.

He told his subordinates only what they needed to know. There was no reason to tell them what he had heard at the General Staff Office before coming to New Guinea: 99 percent of the troops would die. The preposterous prediction would destroy morale. There was no reason to tell them that Japan was losing the war. This they could see for themselves.

Once, he had watched with pride as dogfights played out in the sky. For every two Japanese planes battling three American fighters, the Rising Sun prevailed. Eventually there was only one Japanese plane to fight off three opponents. By the time he reached New Guinea, he watched in horror as Nippon's planes spiraled, nosediving, and exploding upon impact. "The sea and the sky went to America."

The Dawn Unit, too, faltered. Friends and subordinates were perishing in the jungle from combat, wounds, disease, starvation, and exhaustion. Japanese commanders would estimate that, among all their troops in the area, only 7 percent would survive to reach Sarmi. As May bled into June, the soldier's superior officer reached the end of his endurance, placed a pistol to his head, and pulled the trigger. The master sergeant had despised the man when he was alive. "He was not very humane," he scoffed. His suicide did not redeem him; this was not death before dishonor but a complete collapse of leadership and character. The master sergeant turned his back on the corpse and focused on concrete matters. The troops needed food. Two superiors and one subordinate joined him to forage.

They carried knives, pistols, and bayonets, but no compass or map. They scavenged enough food for themselves and did not go back to their unit. Did they lose their way in the jungle where faint trails hacked by natives ended in thickets of razor-sharp, six-foot-high kunai grass? Did they desert their battalion? The soldier would skirt the former and deny the latter. But at some point, he acknowledged, their hunt for food turned into "a separate action." They were no longer thinking about their unit. If they did not come back, they would be assumed dead. If they were caught and questioned by other Japanese troops, they would be deemed traitors and shot on the spot. "*Shikata ga nai.*" He was resigned. "The situation could not be helped." They wanted to survive.

They lunged down mountains, licking their cracked lips, craving salt, dreaming of an improbable rescue by a naval unit that would not doubt their circumstances. If they did not succeed, they would succumb to dehydration, starvation, or exhaustion. Within a week, two of the men went their own way, while his subordinate stayed by his side. They subsisted on coconuts, cracking the shells with rocks, devouring the chewy flesh, guzzling the chalky milk. They cornered crabs, dug up mountain potatoes, and shinnied up banana trees. Sometimes they found cans of American beef and slit open the tins with their bayonets. They shivered in the torrential rains and slept when they could in dank caves.

They fashioned a raft from fallen branches and crossed one surging brown river, then another; altogether, the soldier from Hiroshima counted four or five. His subordinate, who hailed from a mountainous area in Japan and was not a strong swimmer, lay on the raft, and his master sergeant pushed him. Finally they reached another shore, backed into the jungle, and wondered where they were. They had reached Sarmi, and the natives were watching.

One morning the soldier from Hiroshima was resting under a

palm tree when a native and an enemy scout emerged from the brush. The soldier's fever was so high that, dazed, he didn't understand what was going on. More enemy soldiers approached. No longer able to move his legs, which had cramped and stiffened from dehydration, he fumbled for two pistols. "This is it," he thought. After more than six years at war, this was the moment he would die. He vowed not to go without fighting.

That same morning, June 3, 1944, Harry strode into another clearing where a few prisoners at a time were being brought in. All told, he would interview six men. By this time, he was attached to the 158th Regimental Combat Team. Under tents or in the open, lashed by whipping rain, Harry conducted individual interrogations that lasted about thirty minutes, depending on the value of the intelligence.

"Very few good soldiers came in as prisoners," Harry said, certain that this day would be no different from all the others. Most enlisted men simply followed orders. "They didn't have any idea who was winning or losing the war." Many hadn't wanted to surrender but were too physically compromised to resist. Those who had become separated from their units had little information of tactical worth. When Harry heard that two more POWs were being brought in and one was "a little belligerent," even "cocky," he didn't blink. He would elicit what he could. Yet, he admitted that he was intrigued by the drama of their capture. The stragglers had been combative when they were caught floating down the river on logs, nothing like the hapless trio who had surrendered in Aitape.

TRANSPORTED ON A STRETCHER BY MILITARY POLICE to an area swarming with the enemy, the man from Hiroshima saw from afar a man in an American uniform with Japanese features. Even in his diminished state, he kept his wits about him. He never forgot a face. "*Masaka!* No way! Surely I have seen this person before." He pointed and asked his interrogator who the man was.

The linguist standing over the stretcher was startled. Generally, prisoners didn't ask questions. When they did, it was usually "Are you Japanese?" Captives wondered whether their interrogators were former Japanese prisoners who, unable to return home without bringing shame upon their families, had switched sides and allegiances.

Harry's counterpart was not about to reveal Harry's name to the prisoner, which was ATIS policy for the interrogators' protection. This prohibition extended to reports. A March 1944 41st Infantry Division G-2 report commanded, "Interrogation reports will *not* reveal the names of Nisei interrogators or interpreters."

The linguist yelled for Harry to come over. Harry approached the POW and saw a lanky, skeletal man with a scruffy beard that reached his chest. He reeked of perspiration, filth, and urine. The prisoner's eyes were hard, challenging, unblinking; most would have averted them in such a compromised situation. He was ill, Harry gathered, but his spirit was not broken. No sooner had Harry sized up the POW than the man spoke, his voice gravelly, his words brazen.

"I went to Kōryō, and you went to Sanyō," he said. "Do you have a cigarette?"

Taken aback, Harry said nothing. He looked at the prisoner's name on the white tag similar to the one he had worn when he was first interned at Tulare. Matsuura. Harry was stunned but betrayed no expression. Although the man was an emaciated specter of the glowering bully he remembered, the dark, sloping eyes and the grim, thin-lipped mouth were the same. "Are you that Matsuura?" he said.

"*Hai*." Yes.

Matsuura, Harry's nemesis from Hiroshima with whom he had once tussled at the night market. Matsuura, whom he had eyed warily from across the street every day on his way to school. Matsuura, whom Harry thought he had seen the last of six years earlier when the local tough boarded a military transport for China.

Yet here was his neighbor, a seasoned soldier but an adversary. Harry had little time to talk, especially since his colleague had already started the interrogation, and he had one to finish. He handed Matsuura a cigarette and left. But, later that day, he searched out the POW, gave him a can of American beef, and a helping of Japanese rice. Harry would not deny their roots, however tangled.

MATSUURA LASTED THE NIGHT. IN THE MORNING, Harry stopped by the pit and explained that he would be transported to Australia for medical treatment. Loaded on an amphibious vehicle, Matsuura was taken to Wakde and placed on a plane. When the plane took off from the coral-crushed runway and banked over the lush mountains, Matsuura, who had never flown before, was convinced that he would be pushed out of the plane and killed.

Matsuura had good reason to believe that his life was in danger. In one of Charles Lindbergh's diary entries in June 1945, the aviator recounted the horrors of both Asia and Europe during the war. Among them were "the accounts of our machine-gunning prisoners on a Hollandia airstrip" and "of the Australians pushing captured Japanese soldiers out of the transport planes which were taking them south over the New Guinea mountains (the Aussies reported them as committing hara-kiri or 'resisting')."

Matsuura arrived in Australia unscathed. While recuperating in an immaculate hospital under the care of able nurses, he began to view his encounter with Harry through a sepia tint. "It was auspicious luck," he said. "When you fight while young, you remember well." If he and Fukuhara had not grappled at the festival in Hiroshima, he might not have recognized him in New Guinea. "Fighting brings intimacy," he reflected. By giving him special treatment and dispatching him promptly to Australia, Harry had saved his life.

That night, Harry lay awake, listening for the enemy on the prowl—the crunch of dead leaves, the crack of split branches, a grunt in Japanese. Against all odds, he had come face-to-face with an enemy he knew. He knew now what he hadn't wanted to admit. "There was the chance that I might run across someone else." A friend or relative, or even a brother. But he kept the encounter with Matsuura to himself, lest the news spread of his ties to Japan and raise suspicions about his loyalty to the United States. Harry told Gene only that he had run into an "acquaintance from Hiroshima." He said nothing about his family still living there.

In the midst of moving from beachhead to beachhead, one day Harry discovered abandoned *hangō* aluminum mess tins, Japanese rice, and Japanese canned beef. Thrilled with his stash, he steamed the rice and stir-fried the beef for Terry, who had returned from leave; a Camp Savage classmate named Min Hara; and a few others. The guys feasted, laughed, and reminisced. Min was astonished by Harry's hospitality in the heart of the jungle. "And to this day," Min would write, "I feel bad for our bad manners, leaving all those mess kits for Harry to wash."

This was a sublime moment in Sarmi, after which Harry would lose control over his health. His malaria flared. Without rest and treatment with quinine or higher doses of atabrine, the disease could be fatal. In late June, Harry was dispatched to a hospital in Brisbane, his first break after three military operations.

His war—complicated by his own torturous circumstances—remained far from over.

AFTER HARRY LEFT FOR AUSTRALIA, THE BATTLE of Lone Tree Hill proceeded with Terry. Named for the one tree atop a hill on an army task force map, Lone Tree Hill was actually an area of elevated rain forest near Sarmi. If there had been only one tree, it would have been easier to uproot the Japanese who were waiting embedded. The Japanese crouched in caves and bunkers, lay in log dugouts camouflaged by vines, and pressed against the sides of holes hewn between tree roots. Their artillery was strategically placed.

On June 23, 1944, Terry and fellow linguist Kiyo Fujimura settled into their hammocks next to the intelligence tent at the makeshift 41st Infantry Division command post. Terry had selected the spot near a large tree with a trunk resembling a turret, which could buttress the men in case of an attack.

The first shots rang out after sundown when the jungle pitched into darkness. Terry and Kiyo grabbed their rifles and dropped to the ground, seeking cover behind the tree. "Everyone was firing like mad," recalled Kiyo; the shots seemed to be coming from every direction.

Terry rose to his knees to cock his rifle and collapsed on Kiyo. "Terry, Terry!" yelled Kiyo, sitting up to cradle his buddy. "Then," Kiyo wrote, "I felt something warm on my hands and in front of my body. I felt a hole about a half inch in diameter near his chest—it was much larger in his back. I kind of sensed that he was dead."

Yukitaka Terry Mizutari, the twenty-four-year-old linguist leader, was the first *nisei* to perish in combat in the Pacific. The devastating news soon reached Harry, who had just been hospitalized in Australia.

Although the Americans would vanquish Japanese resistance, the eleven-day-long battle proved bitter. The Japanese would employ mortars, grenades, and rifle fire, and propel themselves in bayonet charges. The Americans would counter, using flame throwers, bazookas, grenades, explosives, and gasoline. Between June 20 and 30, 1944, 150 Americans would die. Japanese losses would figure almost ten times higher, with 942 confirmed deaths and 400 estimated sealed in caves and buried alive. But, for Harry, the Battle of Lone Tree Hill would always be about Terry.

A few weeks later, two army officers in full dress uniform knocked on the Mizutari family's door in Hilo. Terry's mother, Sueme, answered; her husband, Yasuyuki, was still interned on the mainland. She was under the impression that her beloved "Taka-chan," her eldest son of nine children, was on furlough that month, and she was shocked by the news. While Mrs. Mizutari accepted the officers' condolences, Harry, who had temporarily recovered from his malaria, walked the streets of Brisbane alone. He was taking his first furlough, one that he had originally planned to spend with Terry.

In a span of three weeks, Harry had confronted his teenage adversary and lost his closest friend. The experiences upturned his assumptions. Once he had believed that he was unlikely to meet anyone he knew among the enemy, for the most sensible of reasons. "In the jungle, you could seldom see." Once he had taken comfort that while everyone was in danger during a landing, he would probably be safe at a command post. "We were not the infantry, so we didn't have to go in and fight, although one did have to defend oneself."

Had he been overly optimistic about not coming up against someone he knew? Not necessarily. Since the early 1940s, more than one hundred thousand troops from Hiroshima had been dispersed throughout Asia. On Sarmi, where Japanese strength was estimated at more than eight thousand, most of the soldiers did not hail from Hiroshima. American forces took only fifty-one prisoners during their mission that lasted between mid-May and the first of September. In its month of action, the 158th RCT captured a mere eleven prisoners. The encounter with Matsuura was extraordinary.

23

Glacial Change in the Jungle

By September 1944, Harry was back in Sarmi, where the airdrome and runway were in danger of being retaken by the Japanese. During his furlough, he had fallen in love with a beautiful *hapa* (mixed race) Australian woman whose father was Japanese. Harry was heartened that biracial children did not appear to raise eyebrows in Australia. In California, where he had lived the longest as an adult, miscegenation for whites and Japanese, among others, was against the law. Harry wrote to the Mounts about his budding romance, though it faded while he was at the front.

The front. Steaming Sarmi. Another division, this time the 33rd Infantry Division—the so-called Golden Cross on account of its insignia, made up of members of the Illinois National Guard. Another group of hometown buddies who would regard Harry as an outsider. Yet again he had to prove himself to others.

Sarmi challenged Harry's peace of mind. He had been promoted to tech sergeant in Terry's place and was haunted by his memory. "I felt sort of responsible," he said, as if he were profiting from Terry's misfortune. Compounding his misery, Harry was receiving Terry's stacks of pen pal letters. He didn't have the heart to break the news and substitute his name on the

V-Mail return address. He let the correspondence drift and began writing to some of Terry's sisters.

The one upside to this stay in Sarmi was meeting the 33rd
Division's commanding officer, Major General Percy W. Clarkson. The Texan was renowned for his brilliant mind and acces-
sibility. When Harry boiled rice and served the linguists *rakkyō*
(pickled shallots), *umeboshi* plums, and *miso* soup, Clarkson
was drawn to their tent by the aroma. Unlike the *nisei*, who ate
with chopsticks, Clarkson used a fork, but he relished their food
and forged a relationship with Harry.

Unbeknownst to the linguists, Clarkson had been in awe
of *nisei* sacrifice and courage well before setting foot in New
Guinea. In Kauai, Hawaii, a year earlier, Clarkson had spent
several Sundays presenting Purple Hearts to *issei* parents
whose sons, members of the largely *nisei* 442nd RCT and
100th Infantry Battalion, drawn from the Hawaii National
Guard, had been killed in combat in France and Italy. If
Clarkson had ever harbored doubts about *nisei* in the army,
they disappeared in the modest living rooms of sugar planta-
tion cottages. Diminutive, sun-wrinkled mothers guided the
general to fruit-laden Buddhist altars bearing black-and-white
beribboned photographs of their sons. The mothers knelt and
lit sticks of incense in devoted memory. Harry, who was the
team leader for nine other linguists and worked mostly at division headquarters, saw Clarkson frequently and sensed his
trust.

Over the next few months in late 1944, Harry realized the
war was changing for the better. Little by little, Japanese troops
were emerging in greater numbers from the jungle to surrender. GIs throughout the Pacific were recognizing the value of
taking prisoners alive and holding fire. Harry and his team
shelved their *hinomaru*-flag assembly line and began running

off propaganda and surrender leaflets on a rackety mimeograph. Weren't soldiers, they wrote, tired of dying of hunger? Wouldn't it be better to surrender and be sent alive to Australia? After the war, the soldiers could devote their energies to Japan. All POWs would be treated in accordance with the Geneva Conventions.

These papers, written in native Japanese with perfect *kanji* characters, were written from an American perspective. Japanese soldiers were sick at heart over the prospect of dying of hunger, but Japan had been at war in China and Asia for much of their youths, and the idea of returning to a munificent, pacific Japan bordered on the delusional.

Despite the culture gap, these papers proved increasingly effective, even if the evidence was inconclusive at first. When Harry questioned prisoners whether the papers had bolstered their will to surrender, some nodded, while others denied seeing the massive airdrops. Some confided that they had crumpled the sheets into wads, stuffing their pockets. Propaganda leaflets made good toilet paper, a rare commodity in a rain forest.

BY CHRISTMAS, HARRY HAD ISLAND-HOPPED TO MOROTAI, three hundred miles south of Mindanao, along with the 33rd Division. He brought his cooking and linguistic skills, his recurrent malaria, and his new affliction, dengue fever. Morotai, like Sarmi, was in danger of being retaken. Just months earlier, another division had landed on Morotai, meeting little resistance, but recent intelligence indicated that an entire infantry regiment had infiltrated the island.

Harry knew by now that all progress was hard-won and unreliable. On the one hand, he and his team had become so speedy and accurate with translations and interrogations that the division artillery commander bypassed subordinates and came directly to them to ask where he should place his next targets. On another level, Harry and the other linguists still felt they were not seen as trustworthy.

In keeping with procedure, they were under a white officer, a practice conceived with the best of intentions. Colonel Kai Rasmussen, Camp Savage's commandant, recalled, "The main purpose of this was to have an unmistakably Caucasian officer associated with Oriental faces in order not to have some trigger-happy G.I. pop a gun." In practice, their supervising officer was invariably an inferior linguist and a less experienced soldier. Second Lieutenant Horace Feldman, plucked from Harvard to train in Japanese at the University of Michigan and Camp Savage, was greener than most. He was younger than his subordinates, and his textbook Japanese may have sounded "brilliant" at Savage, but in the field it fell short. "I would make gentlemen of us," Horace said of his proficient use of Japanese honorific vocabulary. He knew nothing about combat. When the night sky lit up on Christmas with tracers, shells, and explosions, he was too embarrassed to ask his own men whether the spectacle was a fireworks show or shooting. "I telephoned another division." The extravaganza was an attack.

One of Horace's responsibilities was to review and, if necessary, censor outgoing mail. Harry and his teammates watched Horace peruse their letters. "We were upset that our mail was being monitored." Horace, oblivious to Harry's discontent, was busy looking for signs of "psychoneurotic disorders," or what would now be called post-traumatic stress disorder. "If someone was going wild, we would try to address it."

Harry may have had nothing to fear from Horace, but frustration over their precarious status increased as the war progressed. Only the officers' names appeared on reports no matter how invaluable the linguists' contributions. While the regulation that *nisei* interrogators' names could not be mentioned arose from safety concerns should the documents fall into enemy hands, the linguists felt as if they were not receiving due credit.

They also felt unrewarded. No matter how hard they worked and how much they achieved, they were rarely promoted. In the Southwest Pacific before 1945 most received no promotions and fewer than a dozen received commissions. Try as he might, Colonel Mashbir could not convince the War Department to increase its table of allowances for ATIS—an ad hoc unit arising from need more than advance planning—until the summer of 1945. In Morotai, Harry was permanently assigned to the 33rd Division since the number of linguists in the Pacific had increased, yet he remained outside the 33rd's structure. It was true, Horace said. "There was hardly any place to promote him."

Harry swallowed his exasperation over his stagnating status. In time, he and Horace reached an understanding and grew friendlier. One day Harry entrusted him with his secret, confiding that he had been incarcerated in Arizona and had family in Hiroshima. There were other soldiers, too, he said, with immediate family in Japan. The second lieutenant listened.

About this time, in December 1944, the U.S. Supreme Court ruled in *Ex parte Endo* that the government could not hold "concededly loyal" persons against their will. In January restrictions against resettling on the West Coast would be stricken and general release from the concentration camps, including Gila River, would commence. This decision was a vindication, but it was not unequivocal. In another case, *Korematsu v. United States*, the Supreme Court had upheld the constitutionality of the original exclusion order. A wave of vigilante incidents shook the West Coast to discourage ethnic Japanese from returning to their hometowns; in one incident, the American Legion removed the names of sixteen *nisei* soldiers from its county honor roll in Hood River, Oregon. One of the *nisei* was a linguist in the Pacific Theater named Frank Hachiya.

The home front was more rabid than the field, where racial barriers evaporated in the confines of coral foxholes and vine-tangled bunkers. When Harry and his teammates waited for documents, they talked with soldiers from the 33rd. Sometimes the conversation turned to where the *nisei* boys had come from; they paused, wondering how to respond, admitting that, most recently, they had been deported from their hometowns and relegated to internment.

The Illinoisans were astonished. "They had never heard about it, and they wouldn't believe it. They said it was impossible," said Harry. "But we did explain to them that it was possible and that it did happen." Harry pulled out his letters from his female pen pals in the camps and showed them to his 33rd buddies.

Shortly after the Supreme Court cases, a *nisei* linguist in the Philippines was returning to his headquarters under escort when he was shot in the abdomen by a sniper. He crawled to the front lines to give a critical report and collapsed; field surgeons operated but could not save him. The man was the same age as Harry, a bilingual *kibei* with a mother and brother in Japan and immediate family interned in the States. A "ninety-day wonder" from the same Camp Savage class, a tech sergeant, a division team leader. He shared the same first name as Harry's baby brother. His name was Frank Hachiya. A rumor ran the ranks of linguists throughout the Pacific. Frank, they said, was taken out by friendly fire. The account was never substantiated. Nevertheless, bodyguards returned to Harry's side. Back in Hood River, there was a public outcry. The late Frank Hachiya's name was hastily repainted on the county honor roll.

·   ·   ·

BY FEBRUARY 3, 1945, HARRY WAS ABOARD a troop transport churning across the Philippine Sea as the 33rd Division's convoy headed for the island of Luzon. In little more than a year, he had covered well over a thousand miles. Luzon wasn't that much farther from Japan. It was Victor's thirty-first birthday. Harry remembered his oldest brother's birthday; it was one day after their father's.

Victor was not yet married. Despite graduating from book-keeping school, he didn't have a career, either. He had been tossed to and fro since childhood by circumstances beyond his control. The threat of prejudice hindering his prospects in the States had led to his formative years in Japan; his father's death during the Great Depression had pushed the family across the Pacific. A global war had propelled him into the Japanese Imperial Army. At every step, Victor had soldiered on.

February 3 also marked the date of an ancient Japanese ritual called Setsubun. On the cusp of spring, people dispatched the evil of the previous year and welcomed luck by tossing roasted soybeans outside their entrances. *"Oni wa soto. Fuku wa uchi!"* "Demons out! Luck in," they called. Harry had once celebrated this custom in Hiroshima, where children wore devil masks and chewed one crispy bean for each year of their lives. This year there were no beans to throw and gather. In better days, Aunt Kiyo would have sold out dozens of powdery *daifuku mochi* (good-luck rice cakes) stuffed with *anko* (bean-paste jam). Now the tradition seemed naïve and ludicrous, her recipe relegated to a box.

Harry, heading for Lingayen Gulf, and Victor, biding his time in a steel factory in Hiroshima, needed every bit of good fortune they could muster. Failing to observe Setsubun with soybeans and laughter meant nothing. Protection from the agony that would engulf Victor's thirty-first and Harry's twenty-fifth years could not be gained from observing a quaint tradition.

24

The "Red Paper" Draft

J apan's fortunes at war were in dramatic decline well beyond the ports in New Britain, New Guinea, and Morotai where Harry had seen action. *Banzai* charges were occurring with greater frequency across battlegrounds throughout Asia. On July 9, 1944, this concept of *gyokusai* (shattered jewels)—or sacrifice for the sake of the Empire—metamorphosed to include civilians. Allied forces advancing in Saipan watched in horror as hundreds of Japanese residents killed themselves en masse— exploding hand grenades or jumping from rocky cliffs to the whitecap-tossed ocean far below, a phenomenon that would be repeated elsewhere. Three months later, on October 25, 1944, six Zero fighters loaded with 551-pound bombs, so-called *kamikaze*—named after the "divine wind" typhoons that had rescued Japan in 1274 and 1281 from Kublai Khan's convoys— crash-dived into carriers in the Leyte Gulf. The decimated Japanese navy had few other weapons at its disposal. Like the *banzai* charges, the element of terror exceeded military effectiveness.

When 111 B29s lifted off from Saipan and Tinian to bomb Tokyo on November 24, 1944, Japan's future darkened. Over the coming months mass raids would spread to sixty-three other cities, becoming so common that residents would call these formations *teikibin* (regular flights). On the seas, the U.S. Navy dominated, blockading Japan and preventing the arrival of food from other ports. The populace was gradually starving. Close advisors had tried and failed to convince the emperor to surrender in early 1945. Instead, the embattled nation persevered abroad and at home, for worse. "March on! 100,000,000 United in One Fireball!" beseeched a popular slogan. Citizens knew these words by heart, even if privately they struck some as hollow.

By the end of 1944, Hiroshima residents rushed preparations to repel an air raid. Mobilized citizens dismantled buildings in November to clear fire lanes and create open spaces to contain conflagrations at 133 locations designated the previous March. Central neighborhoods reverberated with the clatter of saws and axes, the heave-ho of workers pulling ropes attached to buildings, and the crescendo of crashing timber. By the end of the year, the first stage of the process was complete. More than one thousand buildings had been destroyed and 4,210 citizens evacuated. According to plan, the city   prior to any bombing was being systematically taken apart.

Kinu was fortunate. Her home in Takasu was not located in a demolition zone. Although the city hall repeatedly issued notices that residents in her area should evacuate to rural villages, almost no one in Takasu did. Rather, the neighborhood would serve as an escape route for people from more densely populated parts of the city.

In early 1945, an air of languor still bathed Takasu. Mr. Kaneishi proved a lenient leader of Kinu's neighborhood association. He was supposed to have organized and led *takeyari* (bamboo-spear) drills, beginning in the heat of the previous summer. Throughout the country, women were sharpening bamboo-laundry rods to a point, lining up in *monpe*-clad formation, and jabbing back and forth, housewives-cum-foot soldiers. Their sessions were deadly serious preparations for war when it reached the homeland. Mr. Kaneishi, rejecting the order, chose to concentrate on the less ominous bucket relays instead—fire drills, not death thrusts. Masako questioned the need for relays since the result was inevitably fatigue and muscle strains. "Everyone's back hurt."

Kinu was more lackadaisical than her neighbors. "Where should we dig a hole?" people asked while discussing air-raid shelters. Masako and her father shoveled a shallow pit in their yard for two to squat. Some built elaborate structures. Kinu, with her spacious garden, did not break ground. Farther away from central Hiroshima, on the oasis of Miyajima, Kinu's cousins applied black tape in a crisscross pattern to protect windows from breaking in the event of bombing. Kinu taped some windows in the front of her home, but that was it. And, with all her boys away, she took in a lodger. The idea of a widow and a younger man may have struck wagging tongues as scandalous. To Kinu, doing what she could to survive black-market inflation seemed a harmless and profitable solution.

Kinu had reason to slack off. She was fifty-two years old, a ripe age in Japan, where, Masako said, "fifty years was a lifetime." In 1945, the average life span for women in Japan was 37.5 years, a milestone Kinu had passed before the war had even started. Although she was not certain of the cause, Kinu's stomach often ached. Mr. Kaneishi, who worked for a company that manufactured calcium products, obtained packets of medicinal powder and handed it to her for relief.

Kinu, like most everyone, was famished. Food by-products that would have been discarded in times of peace were now part of daily meals. People used *aburakasu* (the oil-cake residue from cooking oil), instead of fish or vegetables in their daily soup. The greasy clots had flavor, an antidote to the bitter, tasteless, and rotten ingredients that all too often comprised rations. Masako explained, "We were malnourished but we could live."

Even Kiyo, Kinu's last resort, could not help her sister. Meijidō, though it remained one of twenty-six registered stores on Hondōri, was no longer operating. The previous summer, sugar rations nationwide had stopped. In a world without sugar, sweets had vanished for civilians. Nor was Meijidō receiving military contracts.

Yet, despite her indifference to some proclamations, Kinu continued to fulfill her community obligations. She donated her American cast-iron stove and refrigerator to the war effort, both losses diminishing her quality of life. But she refused to part with her American chandeliers, casting light on the dark corners of her dream home, and her beloved Monarch piano.

Mr. Kaneishi did not make demands on Kinu, to whom he was grateful. That February his wife had died, leaving him— old enough to be a grandfather—as a single parent. Kinu helped fill the void in Masako's life. In turn, Mr. Kaneishi viewed Kinu as kin. When Masako crossed the lane from Kinu's house to her own on her days off from school, she became the buoyant girl her father remembered.

Whatever fragile equilibrium residents of Hiroshima and its suburb of Takasu maintained would totter, however, after March 10, 1945, the day that Tokyo burned. From the night of the ninth, more than three hundred B-29s buzzed low over the city, releasing almost 2,000 tons of seventy-pound napalm bombs over the course of two hours. The jellied gasoline ignited houses made of pine, paper, and bamboo; fires rampaged and screamed through vast swaths of the city. When the raid was over, sixteen square miles of the nation's capital had been reduced to smoldering debris, more than one million homeless residents sought shelter, and as many as 100,000 had perished.

During the next week, American bombers flew missions against Nagoya, Osaka, and Kobe, less than two hundred miles away. In the wee hours of March 18, a minor raid occurred over Hiroshima itself, too insignificant to be noted outside the city limits. Earlier that day, schools nationwide, with the exception of elementary school students in the public school system, had been officially suspended for one year. Most students would work in factories devoted to the war effort. Instead of maintaining a pretense of study, they would labor.

When Kinu opened her *Chūgoku Shimbun* newspaper two days later, a photograph greeted her of the emperor reviewing the rubble of a bombed shrine in a densely populated district of Tokyo. No sign remained of the ancient shrine, once crammed with congregants holding celebrations for kimono-swathed newborns, purchasing festooned *kumade* bamboo rakes as symbols of prosperity for their shops, and praying for every kind of luck that calendar year. On the same front page, a bold headline announced "Launching a Violent Attack against Enemy Mobile Forces" about the air force effort to destroy enemy aircraft carriers and ships. Although the article's tone was encouraging, the location southeast of one of the archipelago's four main islands, Kyūshū, was terrifyingly close. In another article, Kinu read that Nagoya, about 250 miles away from Hiroshima, had suffered an air raid. "B29s in Nagoya: More Than a Hundred Jets in Evening Blitz." In fact, 290 bombers had descended over the city for close to three hours, subjecting the metropolis to its second major raid in a week.

Hiroshima's citizens redoubled their activities to create three fire prevention zones spanning across the city. A total of 8,401 buildings would be demolished by August. The growing

expanses—devoid of buildings, color, noise, and life—were just
the beginning. At the prefectural police headquarters, officials
were poring over blueprints to deflect the damage foreseen by a
future raid of three hundred bombers. Residents would have to
clear much more space.

That same March, the city lost not only lively neighborhoods
but its most cherished population. More than 23,000 young children were evacuated by train to rural temples and shrines, and
to country homes of friends and relatives. As steam rose from
the idling trains at Hiroshima Station, mothers wiped their eyes
with handkerchiefs.

In Takasu, where members of the neighborhood associations,
including Kinu, were gathering regularly to tramp toward Hiroshima's center and dismantle designated districts, the verdant
spring of 1945 passed without comment. Green buds swelled
on the branches of Kinu's fig trees; nearby, peach tree blossoms
fluttered in the breeze, and wayward petals landed on sweet-
potato tendrils carpeting the ground. The mild air wafted
sweet. Yet Masako would describe the spring as "lukewarm,"
nothing more than *"namajikka."*

And then, on the first of April, Frank came home for vacation
after completing his first year of college. The snow still reached
halfway up his shins in Takaoka and it had taken him all day by
various trains to reach Hiroshima. But he was elated to be back.

It was true, he told his mother over *genmaicha* (green tea
mixed with brown rice), that Takaoka was more pastoral than
Takasu. Unlike Hiroshima, Takaoka was not a military town.
His military drills were "nothing compared" with those at
Icchū. And yet the war had touched the small city. Frank hadn't
run marathons because the school's dirt track had been planted
with pumpkin and sweet potatoes. Nor had college progressed
according to the standard curriculum. Takaoka had lost so many

men to the draft that students had to step in to help elderly farmers, who had less produce to share than Frank had hoped. The dormitory food was not enough: at breakfast, he received only three boiled potatoes, one bowl of *miso* soup, and two slices of pickled radish. At lunch and dinner, two more potatoes rolled around his aluminum plate. But, thanks to his mother's occasional envelopes of money, Frank could line up at a department store where a cafeteria offered rice porridge that did not require ration tickets. Although he had never been excited about his major, he "didn't mind" his coursework. And while he was hungry, he was healthy. All in all, humble Takaoka offered a soothing respite from the strains of Hiroshima.

Frank held back one story from his mother, lest he upset her. In Takaoka, a second-lieutenant acquaintance, who had recently returned home after a three-year stint in the army, confided to Frank that he doubted Japan's prospects. Frank would be drafted, he said. "But it was no use trying your best." Japan would lose this war. Frank was stunned to hear such defeatist words from an officer. Despite his aversion to *Icchū*, he believed much of what he was told—by the government, by the press, by his *sensei*. He had never contemplated the possibility that Japan might lose, let alone be stalemated. He believed that Japan was still winning, but he could not banish the veteran's prediction from his thoughts.

A day or two into his visit, Frank received a bright pink postcard in the mail. His heart skipped a beat. He didn't need to read the contents to understand. The mere sight of the *akagami* (red paper) destroyed his world. The paper was the deep pink hue of the *sakura* (cherry blossom) long appropriated as a symbol for the fleeting lives of youthful soldiers. At age twenty, at the height of the once-joyous cherry blossom season, Frank had been drafted. Calculating his odds of survival, he figured on a year or two. His draft notice was nothing less than a "death sentence." During the course of Japan's excruciatingly lengthy conflict, from 1931 to 1945, every family would point to specific days to commemorate, often in sorrow. Frank would describe his own in a letter, and the delivery of his conscription notice became "THE DAY I CANNOT FORGET."

Ironically, the event that Frank had sought to avoid since entering *Icchū* in 1939 had occurred the same year that he, as a dual citizen, became eligible to select a single citizenship. In some deep recess of his mind, Frank was still drawn to America, but he never remotely contemplated filing the paperwork at city hall as it would be tantamount to giving himself up to the authorities. His sentence would be merciless: either execution by a single bullet or an extended prison term. Resisting the draft was treason.

Despite Frank's mighty effort, he could not have prevented his draft. The previous July, the draft age had been raised from forty to forty-five and in the autumn, it had been lowered from nineteen to eighteen. On the basis of age alone, Frank had held out for two years since late 1943. The April draft was a mass mobilization, so sweeping that Japan's vaunted bookkeepers lost track of many military records. Frank and Pierce were destined to be two of the more than six million soldiers staging the homeland's last stand.

Kinu strained to protect her youngest son the only way she knew how—by burnishing his luck. She stitched him a *senninbari* stomach warmer, as she had for Victor and Pierce. In theory, the sash would be embroidered in auspicious red thread by a thousand women, each knot symbolizing a wish for a soldier's well-being, the homely undergarment transformed into a symbol of caring. In practice, Kinu didn't have time to ask others and rushed to sew it herself, with bits of thread and the odd needle.

On April 10, 1945, Frank reported to the military grounds south of Hiroshima Castle, now the Second General Army Headquarters under Marshal Shunroku Hata. Frank's official assignment: the 417th Infantry Regiment of the 145th Division, Imperial Second Army; the First Army was based in Tokyo. Frank's status: a second-class private, an untrained recruit, the lowliest of the low, nicknamed *issen gorin* (one sen, five rin), the equivalent in change of less than a penny. Frank despaired. "I thought this was the end."

For a short time Frank had faith that his elite *Icchū* training would insulate him from the humiliations of basic training but he came up against a "mean one." The first-class private, who Frank reckoned was thirty, had a glass eye from a war wound and saw Frank, who was physically fit and well trained at drills, as a threat. He would taunt, hit, and slap Frank, who silently withstood the assaults. But when his commander called him in one day and said, "You're a *nisei*," Frank was terrified. The army knew Frank's secret. Yet nothing came of his suggestion that Frank transfer to another company where the commander also happened to be *nisei*.

Three days into Frank's draft, on the evening of April 13, Tokyo was bombed for the third time that year. A wing of the Imperial Palace was unintentionally hit and burned; the emperor and his family emerged unharmed. No one realized then that earlier that same day, an event of greater consequence had passed without incident in Hiroshima. An American reconnaissance plane had hovered over the city during daylight hours. Through a window, an army photographer angled, framed his scenes, and shot.

Frank had been drilling all day on the Hiroshima Castle grounds below. He did not see the plane's streaming contrail through the clouds nor hear the distant buzz of the engine over

Katsuji and Kinu Fukuhara on their wedding day in Seattle in September 1911. Kinu was a picture bride, her marriage arranged in Japan through an exchange of photographs with Katsuji's family. She met her husband for the first time in Seattle. *Courtesy of Harry Fukuhara*

Katsuji Fukuhara with the actor Charlie Chaplin. Katsuji became friendly with Chaplin through the actor's secretary, who hailed from the same area of Hiroshima. *Courtesy of Harry Fukuhara*

Victor at age four in Seattle, 1918. One year later, he was sent to Hiroshima for his education, before his three brothers were born. *Courtesy of Harry Fukuhara*

Harry, Frank, and Pierce with their parents. Victor and Mary were already living with Kinu's sister in Hiroshima. The three boys grew up largely unaware of their older siblings. *Courtesy of Harry Fukuhara*

Mary (bobbed hair) with Cousin Tazuko and Aunt Kiyo in Hiroshima. Mary never liked Japan and did not understand why her parents sent her there when she was seven. *Courtesy of Jean Furuya*

Victor after graduating from an accounting program in Japan. The nation was at war in China. In 1935 he was conscripted into the Japanese Imperial Army. *Courtesy of Harry Fukuhara*

Harry, Pierce, and Frank with their mother, Kinu, in Hiroshima in the mid-1930s. Harry and Pierce attended a private school that catered to *nisei* high school students. Frank was on a traditional track, bound for an elite middle school, a precursor to a military academy. *Courtesy of Harry Fukuhara*

Harry departing Japan for the United States in 1938. His cousins Toshinao and Kimiko accompanied him to Hiroshima Station with Aunt Kiyo, his mother, Kinu, and his brothers Pierce and Frank. It was the last time that the group would be together. Kimiko would die of injuries sustained from the atomic bomb. *Courtesy of Harry Fukuhara*

Shigeru Matsuura in the Japanese Imperial Army in Dairen, in the Japanese puppet state of Manchukuo, 1941. Shigeru and Harry fought as teenagers in Hiroshima and would confront each other again in New Guinea in 1944. *Courtesy of Shigeru Matsuura*

Mary's 1938 bridal portrait in Seattle. Mary married a man whose family came from the same area as her father, but her marriage ended in divorce several years later. *Courtesy of Jean Furuya*

Harry as a greengrocer in Los Angeles, 1938. After a series of short-term jobs, he hoped that this one would last. He was fired after Christmas. *Courtesy of Harry Fukuhara*

Interpreters Ben Nakamoto, Howard Ogawa, Terry Mizutari, and Harry Fukuhara at play with captured enemy equipment in Arawe, New Britain, January 1944. The Army classified photographs of *nisei* linguists during the war, lest the enemy realize that their communications were providing valuable intelligence. Five months later, Terry would become the first Japanese American to die in combat in the Pacific. *National Archives and Records Administration*

Harry interrogating Japanese prisoners of war in Aitape, New Guinea in April 1944. *National Archives and Records Administration*

Major General Percy W. Clarkson pinning an award on Harry in the Philippines, summer 1945. *Courtesy of Harry Fukuhara*

Frank, Harry, and Pierce in Kobe in autumn 1945. Frank was wearing American clothing issued by Major General Clarkson; only his cap was Japanese. Skinny from malaria, Harry was commissioned a Second Lieutenant on August 10, 1945, four days after the atomic bomb exploded over Hiroshima. *Courtesy of Harry Fukuhara*

Harry and Frank in the village of Shirakawa, 2005. Frank had attended college nearby until he was drafted in April 1945. Harry was posted close by in Toyama with the Occupation forces in 1948; Frank joined him there. *Courtesy of author*

his commander's barking orders. He could not possibly know that the American military would become more focused on this particular working castle than the imperial residence in Tokyo. Southwest of the castle, a short stroll away, lay the Aioi Bridge, a steel and reinforced-concrete structure that served both pedestrians and electric trains. To the north were the neighborhoods of Hakushima, where Chieko lived, and Misasa, where Victor toiled in a steel factory. Close to the bridge sat the Japan Red Cross, where Frank had once delivered letters to Harry, and immediately to the south, the landmark, copper-rotunda Industrial Promotion Hall; farther down lay Kiyo's cherished Meijidō. For U.S. Army strategists, the Aioi Bridge stood out. For a B-29 flying above the clouds, it was shaped like the letter T. Someday, strategists reckoned, the Aioi Bridge might be the perfect target.

25

Extremes in the Philippines

L uzon—the largest, most populous, and central of more than seven thousand tropical isles forming the ragged green lace of the Philippine archipelago— represented a turning point in the war. If the Allies succeeded, a final victory against Japan seemed likely. If not, the war could become—on Luzon's humid rice-latticed central plain and in its chilly, soaring northern mountains—a protracted quagmire. Harry, in charge of a language team and serving as General Clarkson's interpreter, was one of more than one hundred *nisei* linguists sprinkled among three corps head-quarters and ten divisions in the battle to retake Luzon from the Japanese.

General Tomoyuki Yamashita, who had conquered Malaysia and Singapore in February 1942, was prepared to defend the Philippines with some 275,000 troops. His seasoned soldiers knew every crag and crest of the volcanic island. In January Yamashita had moved from Manila to Baguio, the summer capital 155 miles to the north. Over the next two and a half months, the U.S. Army's 33rd Division would drive toward the city, perched almost five thousand feet above sea level, tucked among evergreen-and-moss mountain peaks, shrouded by rush-ing fog and mist. The precipitous ascent would tax even the strongest men.

Anticipating the Americans' arrival, the Japanese troops were prepared to hold out for as long as five years. "The mountainous terrain in the vicinity of Baguio is suitable for this purpose," wrote one of Yamashita's division commanders. Above cliffs that could only be navigated by ladder and rope, behind hairpin curves on roads that zigzagged for miles, in the slashing kunai grass along the jungle thickets lining the walkways and main thoroughfares, the Japanese had dug in. They waited, concealed in trenches, pillboxes, and caves, armed with whatever weapons they could muster.

Harry believed that since he was in the forward element but behind front lines, he was not necessarily safe nor was he in mortal danger. Still, the journey was treacherous. The Japanese had knocked out bridges to slow the American advance on roads strewn with bombed debris and avalanches of boulders. The men of the 33rd trudged, often under intermittent sniper fire from the enemy who were strapped to trunks or nestled in tree crotches. The division accumulated casualties, although, throughout the Philippines, Japanese losses were more than five times higher.

Coupled with the physical challenges of the rugged terrain, Harry reeled from more frequent bouts of malaria and dengue fever, flare-ups triggered by the drop in temperature in the mountains relative to the plains and the other tropical locales where he had been most recently. He rode the waves of fevers and was rocked by nightmares. Luzon tested his physical and emotional fortitude. But he didn't have the luxury to submit to illness and fall behind the advancing troops. Japanese prisoners were surrendering in high numbers. The Sixth Army would capture 7,297 prisoners in Luzon. Interrogating one after another in northern Luzon, Harry had never been so busy.

One reason for the influx was the increasing success in

psychological warfare. Allied planes commanding the skies above Luzon continued to spill some 25 million leaflets encouraging surrender. The papers struck many as finally worth believing. Japanese soldiers advanced, as instructed, to the recommended surrender spots during daylight, humbly holding over their heads printed passes in English.

Harry, who was not producing these fliers, gathered some for reference, including the *Rakkasan News*, or Parachute News, a newsletter for Japanese soldiers prepared by ATIS *nisei* with the input of Japanese POWs. Headlines blared. "The American Military Already Occupies One Fourth of Okinawa," "Sea Routes to the South Completely Closed," "The Battleship *Yamato* Sinks." All the news was true, including the fate of the *Yamato*, the pride of the Japanese fleet, built in the Kure shipyard.

The Japanese were also engaging in a propaganda war. In one cartoon, a hand squeezed red paint from a tube, fashioned as a soldier; the cap, which had been removed, appeared as a decapitated helmeted head. The paint dripped on the word Philippines. "CAPITALISTS DEMAND RED ENDLESSLY!" the cartoon exhorted. "IT'S YOUR BLOOD, DOUGHBOYS! BUT MORE AND STILL MORE IS TO BE SQUEEZED OUT!" "FAREWELL, AMERICAN SOLDIERS!" bellowed another paper with a drawing of the skeletal head of an Allied soldier. Nonetheless it was clear that the war was escalating in favor of the Allies.

It was the tender personal correspondence in Japanese—missives on tissue-thin paper that few others could read—that continued to touch a nerve in Harry in a way that neither side's propaganda did. One day, a soldier turned a document in to the language team that he had found on the body of an enemy killed in a skirmish. Harry knew, from first glance, that the paper possessed no military value. The dead soldier's sister had written "Our Family Newspaper," dated Sunday, September 5, 1943. It included colored pen-and-ink drawings with light-hearted captions: A plate of *makizushi* (rolled sushi), a fish on a rod, a ripe tomato, talking eggplants, a rotund cat. The page captured the rhythm of daily life—its sweet joy and inevitable sorrow. Through the delicate dipping of ink to paper coursed a sibling's luminous love for her distant brother. The soldier had held on to the folded paper for almost two years. By the time Harry received it, bloodstains the size of large thumbs had bled through the folded layers and blotted the border.

The furious flurry of words was matched by a spiking intensity in jarring prisoner encounters. When Harry received information from Philippine guerrillas and civilians about wounded and sick Japanese troops who had been abandoned by their units, he raced to the cave where they were allegedly waiting to die. On Wakde, he had been too late to intervene and had watched the flamethrowers spew cascades of jellied gasoline. This time he reached the site before bulldozers driven by army engineers were about to seal those within, dead or alive. Harry wanted survivors: They might throw caution to the wind and reveal who their commander was, where they were headed, what they planned and when, as well as how much longer their units could persevere.

Harry crouched at the caves' opening. The stench of urine, feces, blood, and putrid flesh was overpowering. He entered and kneeled over the men inside. Since he had no idea whether the enemy soldiers were dead or alive, he held a mirror close to their mouths. A couple of times, the glass fogged and Harry had the GIs carry out the few who were still breathing. The moment the ailing men were exposed to the brash sunlight, they succumbed.

One day in the midst of combat taking place nearby, Harry

rushed to a division operating room, where a critically wounded Japanese POW lay bleeding from a bullet to his stomach. He was conscious but, Harry recalled, "in great pain." The attending surgeon advised Harry that the prisoner's wound was critical, death a matter of time. Harry leaned over the patient on a table slick with blood; he needed him to answer some questions that could influence the outcome of a skirmish. "I repeated the questions over and over, and the man did not give much." Coughing up blood, the POW groaned out a question of his own. Would he live? His question stunned Harry, who debated telling the truth. "We have," he assured the dying man, "the best doctors in the world." When Harry looked up from his notes to continue his questions, the prisoner had died. This exchange, lasting only minutes, would resonate among Harry's wartime experiences forever. On a rational level, Harry knew that pursuing intelligence was justified by the exigencies of war. The source of his discomfort was something more subtle: the heartbreak of intruding on the sanctity of the man's final moments.

In the steep approach to Baguio—a blur of jade slopes, white tents, chalky cliffs, and crimson flames—Harry propelled himself to the next interview, the next stop on the campaign, the next breakthrough for the 33rd. Against a backdrop of hissing shells and thundering gunfire, General Clarkson took notice of his interpreter's tireless work and sent positive evaluations that reached the top echelon of ATIS.

With each passing week, Japan's situation turned more grave. Harry, accustomed to the surrender of low-ranking soldiers, began to see officers plodding forward, their heads lowered. One of the first he interviewed was voluble and wounded. Admitted to a Japanese camp hospital for his injuries before he fled and surrendered, he had overheard instructions that patients who were not mobile should be lethally injected when the troops withdrew. The officer had witnessed Japanese nurses going from bed to bed with syringes, carrying out what they had likely been told was *anrakushi* (euthanasia). In Japanese, the term meant "peaceful death." But this act—administering fatal doses of medication to the lightly wounded or those fit enough to recover in time—struck the officer as anything but humane. He was angry and bitter and resolved, he said, to tell the Americans everything.

On Sunday, April 29, the American and Philippine flags were raised on two flagpoles over ravaged Baguio. The city had fallen to the 33rd and 37th Divisions. One day later in Berlin, Adolf Hitler committed suicide, shooting himself in the mouth. On Monday, May 7, Nazi Germany unconditionally surrendered. The Axis was crumbling. American troops in Europe would soon be dispatched to Asia. The troops of the 33rd were elated.

After dark, when the official business of the day was over, Baguio pulsed with the electric air of a county fair. Each battalion had its own bar, and enterprising Filipinos opened more to sell *basi*, their fermented sugarcane wine. Dances, movies, and USO shows abounded. Most of all, the 33rd had fulfilled its battle cry, "Take Baguio!" To the jubilant riffs of big-band music, the men savored victory and celebrated.

The one bittersweet note was that General Yamashita had evaded capture by stealthily withdrawing from Baguio, and he would continue to direct his troops to battle. And although the American and Philippine flags had been proudly raised, they trembled in the mountain breeze at half-mast. President Franklin D. Roosevelt had passed away earlier that month from a cerebral hemorrhage and the 33rd Division would soon find that its final mission was far from over.

Harry had reason to feel exuberant. In March he had been

promoted to master sergeant, the highest rank for an enlisted man. At a time when few *nisei* were as yet commissioned, he felt like a "king" with his six white stripes placed below the 33rd Division's Yellow Cross. "My arm looked like a zebra." And in June General Clarkson, beloved by his troops for conferring awards in a warm manner, smiled and pinned a ribbon signifying another Bronze Star.

Harry was gratified that he was being recognized, but a sense of foreboding cast a shadow over his joy. A violent climax loomed in the Pacific. He was attuned to the frightful carnage—including the "shattered jewels" of civilian *gyokusai*—occurring in Okinawa, the Japanese territory closest to its mainland. Japanese commanders had ordered the Okinawans never to surrender. The populace was complying.

The fighting was terrible. As one *Rakkasan News* headline noted, it was a battle of "bloody mud." In the end, after three months of pitched battle, including *kamikaze* attacks, 95,000 civilians would commit suicide, be killed by their own friends and family, die at the hands of their own country's soldiers, or perish from enemy fire. Japanese military losses would exceed 100,000. For the Americans, casualties would reach 12,520, the highest figure for a campaign in the Pacific. Ten MIS *nisei* would perish on Okinawa before the end of the war.

All Harry knew at the moment was that Okinawa was a killing field reminiscent of Saipan and an unsettling harbinger of what Allied soldiers would confront when they set foot on Japanese soil. He assumed, like many, that the United States would invade.

An invasion was in the works. In Washington, the Joint Chiefs of Staff and President Harry S. Truman were discussing multiple landing options in the autumn. In Luzon, General Clarkson was pondering the future, too. Sometimes, he would ask

Harry in the course of conversation, "Do you think . . . ?" Harry understood what followed. Shaking his head, he said, "I don't think Japan will surrender."

What the respected general and his capable master sergeant could not know was that the American arsenal was growing. In late May, several Japanese cities considered possible targets for a remarkable weapon were deemed exempt from B-29 air raids. These locales would be kept pristine to observe the effects of a new bomb should it be detonated. One of the three cities selected was the western military nexus of Hiroshima.

BEGINNING IN LATE JUNE, THE 33RD DIVISION regrouped to retrain in the sweltering lowlands near Manila, taken by the Americans earlier that year. In the immediate present, the men were safer than they had been for a long time in the Southwest Pacific. Except for the *nisei* linguists.

Harry faced the menace of a recently liberated local population that had been savagely repressed during Japan's more than three-year occupation. The Filipinos were hankering for revenge. Anyone who appeared to have a Japanese face, regardless of his uniform, was vulnerable to violent retribution. "The local Filipinos," said Harry, "couldn't make the distinction."

Harry understood their rage. The Filipinos had suffered subjugation, murder, rape, torture, and pillage under Japanese occupation. The brutal Bataan Death March in 1942 had involved Filipino soldiers, as well as Americans. And, in February 1945, as the nation's capital fell, Japanese troops had massacred approximately 100,000 residents. Manila, "the Pearl of the Orient," was cracked and damaged, a shell of its lustrous nature. Its residents lacked basic necessities and livelihoods.

Harry sensed the threat, caught the sneers. "*Nisei* had to be careful about not getting into fights." Division troops were sensitive to the simmering resentment toward the *nisei* and sought to protect them. Harry once again needed to be shadowed by bodyguards.

The Philippines were a prelude to combat in Japan. Hundreds of replacements were flooding the 33rd Division. Harry's responsibilities involved training those new to the Pacific Theater about what to expect in an invasion. He had to actively picture battles in Japan. Colonel Mashbir would describe the ideal intelligence agent: "A vivid but logical imagination is a highly important tribute. You must be able mentally to put yourself in the enemy's brain." Harry possessed this talent, as Mashbir already knew, and it would cause him considerable pain.

At first Harry, now twenty-five, found that the young recruits were not so much prejudiced as ignorant. How, some asked, did one make the distinction between Japanese, Chinese, and Koreans? Was it the gap between the toes, from wearing sandals or those split-toed boots in battle? Harry and the other linguists explained that one could not tell at all. "The enemy looks like us." Up until now, Harry told the troops, one hadn't necessarily seen the enemy during combat in pockets of dense jungle and mountain terrain. That would change in Japan. The entire country would be enemy territory and much of the population lived in villages, towns, and cities along the coast where invasion forces would come ashore after a massive aerial and naval bombardment. "If and when we land in Japan, anybody and everybody is your enemy," he warned.

One day, a photograph of a Japanese women's volunteer home defense unit emerged from a pile on the linguists' desk; it had most likely arrived with some captured documents and offered a visual for the troops on how women would defend their country. In the photo, several dozen women, dressed in *zōri* (sandals), *monpe,* and caps, stood at attention in a dusty schoolyard.

Those in the front shouldered old bayonets. Those in the back held bamboo spears.

Harry held on to the photograph. One of the girls bearing a bayonet, her full cheeks in the bloom of youth, could easily have been Chieko. The fine-boned older woman with a white kerchief on her head looking down in the row behind, she could have been his mother.

26

Brothers at War

Around the same time in June that Harry was preparing to teach recruits about Japanese troops, Frank marched with his unit along the narrow streets toward Hiroshima Station. The air was sticky in the rainy season; the clouds hovered low and leaden. Frank was under the impression that his unit was bound overseas, and the railroad depot marked the first leg of an arduous journey.

He couldn't help but feel anxious: his unit was not close to combat-ready. His fellow soldiers were nothing like his alert, disciplined, and muscular *Icchū* classmates. Frank's *nisei* friend Henry Ogura, drafted one year earlier, was training up north as a *kamikaze* pilot in Sendai. Another classmate had graduated from an air force academy and was serving as an officer in China. The *Icchū* elite who had not delayed their draft were surrounded by men of a similar caliber on a more revered path than that of a mere second-class private.

An abbreviated training schedule had barely addressed the deficits in Frank's unit. Still, the training was toil, something that everyone was glad to finish at the end of the day. The recruits also had housekeeping obligations. Required to prepare breakfast for the others, they cleaned up, drilled all day, then made and served dinner. "My superiors did nothing," Frank recalled, feeling less like a soldier and more like a servant.

The training had only highlighted the men's vulnerabilities. Frank's backpack had to weigh twenty-nine pounds; otherwise, he had to top it with rocks and sand. The troops marched the equivalent distance—twenty-nine miles a day—on the extensive castle grounds and around Hiroshima. When a weak former neighbor fell out of line, Frank grabbed the man's rifle or sandbag, placing it on his free shoulder. Some men were so old and feeble that they could barely place one foot in front of another.

At Hiroshima Station, Frank was handed "new" clothing, "winter clothes in the summer," he recalled, perplexed. When he looked closely, he realized that the uniforms were second-hand and the sizes too large or too small for someone of his standard build. His *jikatabi* (rubber-soled, split-toed shoes) did not come as a pair; the right and left were different sizes, troubling for a *hohei* (foot soldier). After accepting extra socks to stuff into the shoe that was too big, Frank put on the one new item he received—his hat with one star proclaiming his humble second-class-private status.

Frank was among the privileged. Only one third of the nation's recently drafted soldiers carried weapons, and primitive ones at best—often, bamboo spears. In its rush to mass for all-out war, the Imperial Army came up short.

"That's it," Frank thought. He did not want to leave Hiroshima and lose contact with his mother. Part of his unit had remained on the castle grounds, where Frank wished that he had stayed, too. Pierce had been transferred from Hiroshima with his division for points unknown in late April.

Later Frank would discover how fortunate they both were.

The troops waited aboard a train in Hiroshima Station for

almost a week with no word of their destination. Frank no longer cared where he went. He had been unable to notify his mother of his whereabouts, or she would have passed him, at least, a rice ball through the window. There was nothing redeeming, Frank found, about living in a stationary train-cum-barrack.

One night about a week later, the train abruptly lurched out of the station. Frank fell asleep to the motion of wheels rhythmically clicking on the tracks. When the train came to a stop the next morning, he awakened to find himself at a station in northern Kyūshū; his train had crossed the islands—so close that the tips almost touched—via a tunnel overnight. A rumor ran through the coach that the ship the troops had been waiting for in Hiroshima had been lost.

FRANK AND HIS TRAIN MATES WERE IGNORANT of the vast toll Allied attacks had already taken on Japanese shipping. Not many vessels remained. Those moored in ostensibly safe homeland harbors were not seaworthy until repaired, but the materials were scarce. By this time, Allied air and sea domination over sea routes from Japan to resource-rich areas in the south greatly restricted the Empire's access to fuel.

Those who lived near major ports had already gleaned the truth without knowing the particulars. Paul Yempuku, a *nisei* teenager in Kure, had noticed in late 1944. "We used to wonder why we were now spending all of our time digging tunnels, instead of building submarines. We used to wonder, too, why all the ships were in the harbor, instead of out in the ocean fighting."

By the time Frank's train rolled into Kyūshū, the port of Kure was crippled. In the black, early hours of July 2, 152 B-29s had swarmed over the city, dropping 1,081 tons of bombs, killing

1,817 residents. The downtown of Kure, home base to the now-sunken battleship *Yamato*, had disappeared.

Frank, isolated in distant Takaoka, had not seen the changes in these once-booming harbors. In his transit to Kyūshū, he had missed the crisis in Kure. Privates were not allowed to read newspapers or listen to radios. "I was so tired, I didn't even ask," he said.

Kinu, however, had her newspaper, although its size had steadily shrunk to one page folded. She sat by her radio, although the news was government-censored. She chatted with relatives and friends, although they knew that they must whisper. Her *Chūgoku Shimbun* newspaper suggested that the military was looking furtively to the south.

That spring, the newspaper openly referred to locations of conflicts—Luzon, Iwo Jima, and Okinawa. Lately there was mention of Kyūshū, firmly Japanese soil. More and more, references to *tokkōtai* (the special attack forces) popped up. Early in the war, the term had applied to planes and submarines that were expected to return to their Japanese launch sites. Since late 1944, however, those involved were expected to damage the enemy and forfeit their lives, all to thwart the invasion of Japan. The *kamikaze*, the elite *tokkōtai*, were glorified, but when the term *tokkōtai* was applied to the general populace, it no longer summoned awe and respect but rather, cold fear.

Kinu's newspaper coverage was a cloudy mirror of current events. Behind closed doors in Tokyo, the Japanese command had correctly surmised American strategy for an autumn invasion of its homeland, first of Kyūshū, followed by Honshū. In early April, just before Frank reported for duty, Operation Ketsu-Go had been formulated in response, a massive plan for the homeland's last stand. "*Ketsu*," meaning "decisive," expressed the nation's grim determination to repel the enemy or—with the nobility of failure—to die trying.

THE SECOND GENERAL ARMY, HEADQUARTERED IN HIROSHIMA, had been assigned to defend Kyūshū against an invasion, and Frank's division had been formed for this very confrontation. By mid-July 1945, the number of Japanese forces massing on Kyūshū would reach 375,000, or six divisions, accelerating at a faster pace than the Americans had estimated possible at that point. Later that month, nine combat divisions would be in place. By early August, Kyūshū would be crowded with more than 545,000 soldiers, let alone civilian defense units. Day by day, the number would climb.

Frank, in his warm clothes and ill-fitting shoes, disembarked in the nondescript town of Orio. No thought had been given to barracks. The troops lodged in a sweltering elementary school, where they slept, pressed as tightly as silkworms, on wooden floors, the aged planks damp with their perspiration. They drilled in a dusty schoolyard, reminiscent for Frank of *Icchū*. And they waited, an all-too-familiar routine since hurriedly assembling in Hiroshima.

A few days later, the foot soldiers walked for about an hour to an area near the city of Wakamatsu, also located in northern Kyūshū. The area was heavily forested, lightly farmed, and sparsely populated. Told that they could not rest, the unit was assigned to carve a regimental headquarters on a mountain near the northern coast. They dynamited rock to form caves, used pickaxes to clear debris and burrow tunnels. Kyūshū would soon be hollowed out and threaded by bases, tunnels, and caves, which would be topped with emplacements and camouflaged with foliage, much as the Japanese had done throughout the Pacific. Nevertheless, the efforts were haphazard and incomplete. The 145th Division would, overall, reach less than half of its planned goals for base, arsenal, and fortification construction.

One day, Frank was marching in the hills with about two dozen other soldiers, divided into pairs. Nothing seemed out of the ordinary until Frank heard the roar of a plane above. The commander barked, *"Tategata sankai,"* an order to split down the middle and fan out vertically. Frank knew the procedure by heart. He had learned it at *Icchū*, practiced it in Takaoka, and reviewed it during basic training. Frank looked up and saw a small American naval fighter with its telltale insignia, a white star in a navy-blue circle, bordered by white bars. The plane was flying low, and Frank caught a flash of machine guns. His survival instinct kicked in. He darted to the side as rounds of bullets whizzed and ricocheted right down the path. The fusillade bisected and scattered the troops, raising puffs of dirt, just missing everyone's feet. Fortunately, the plane did not return. Miraculously, no one was hurt.

Later, Frank would assert that it must have been a P-51 Mustang, a small plane used to take reconnaissance photographs and escort B-29 bombers on daily raids that were occurring in Honshū. At this point, Japan had few planes to deter raids; those it had were being safeguarded for its decisive battle. For Japan, the loss of bases on the Mariana Islands—including Guam, Tinian, and Saipan—and closer to home on the Ogasawara chain south of Tokyo hindered air defense patrols. The American military was free to toy with troops like Frank's unit or take valuable surveillance pictures.

After work, Frank and other troops filed into a school auditorium. An officer stood in the center of the room and made the announcement. Consider yourselves *tokkōtai*, he commanded. Holding a bomb, he demonstrated how to place it on one's back or wrap it around the waist. He brought forward a cardboard cutout, backed by plywood, of an American M-2 tank. Pointing where the men should jump, he showed them how to detonate the bomb as they dove under the oncoming tank. The delivery was low-key but the collective anxiety was palpable. Frank's heart pounded. "I was really scared then."

His fear was understandable. School-age boys had drilled with papier-mâché tanks in the 1930s when the war with China was still young and the battlefield lay across the Yellow Sea. But the drills were no longer child's play, and the front stretched directly before them. All over Japan, troops and civilians were preparing to hurl themselves as human weapons. Although the population had long been less than *ichioku* (100 million) and was dropping—from the ravages of protracted war, growing starvation, and related illness—citizens were told that they must unite as "*ichioku tokkōtai*" ("the 100 million Special Attack Forces"). American military strategists took this number seriously, but it hardly expressed the reality of Japan's paltry preparations.

For starters, M-2 tank facsimiles had already become obsolete. Most American M-2s had only been used for training, and the one version that had been employed in the Pacific had not been used since 1943. Newer tanks were faster, better armed, and more thickly armored. To make matters worse, Frank's division was running short of explosives to equip its *tokkōtai* and had to request them from a major supply depot in nearby Kokura, where Frank would increasingly spend time.

Kokura, like Hiroshima, was an old castle town with a grand, white-tiered jewel of a citadel, surrounded by mossy moats. And like Hiroshima, Kokura was militarily significant. Hiroshima was a major army headquarters, housing officers and soldiers; Kokura was valued for its arsenal. Frank had no idea that months earlier, Kokura, at the tip of northern Kyūshū, had attracted the intense scrutiny of American military planners. By the time Frank walked its pine-studded hills, the city had been selected as a possible target for a top-secret American weapon.

All Frank knew was that, with each passing day, he became hungrier. He wrapped his belt around his trim waist, pulling it in too many notches; for a twenty-year-old man, he was much too skinny. Either he had already adjusted to the slight increase in food at the mess hall or the allocation had begun to contract, but hunger pangs drove him and others to farmers' fields in the black of night. There Frank tugged firm, ripe tomatoes from thick stems. Hours later, in the silken light of morn, the farmers found that their plants had been picked clean, not by pests, they rightly suspected, but by uniformed men.

By this point, Frank conjectured that his prospects of survival were, at best, "fifty-fifty." Suicide units were becoming "common" even though his superiors kept declaring that Japan was winning. How Frank swallowed assurances of victory while running suicide drills might seem like a lesson in forbearance or denial but Frank wasn't thinking very hard about very much. He didn't have access to news, any distractions to lighten his mood, or even sufficient nutrition. By the time he returned to his barracks after a day of dispatching and diving under flimsy fake tanks, Frank was too exhausted to think. "Dying doesn't mean too much to you," he reflected. "Little by little, you get convinced that losing your life for a country is not too hard."

And then, at the end of a numbing July, Frank received a message at the dispatch center in the countryside. His mother was waiting for him in Wakamatsu. Frank was overjoyed that she had figured out where he was. He requisitioned a two-wheeled cart to drag into town. The cart was empty, but Frank wanted to give the appearance of being occupied on military business.

They were ecstatic to see each other. Kinu had just visited Pierce, too, who was stationed nearby, training as a heavy machine-gun specialist in the 418th Infantry Regiment of the same division. Frank had had no idea. He wanted to stretch their time together, but after just twenty minutes, he worried that his absence on base might be noticed. He thanked his mother for coming so far, placed the cart's posts on his shoulder, and pulled it like a mule, the wheels creaking in his wake. Kinu watched her youngest child recede into the distance.

In this taxing summer of 1945, Kinu had weathered the grinding bureaucracy for permission, the expense of tickets, and an uncomfortable trip, elbowed by throngs of Kyūshū-bound soldiers. She had given up time haggling at the black market. Yet any tribulations paled in light of her jubilation. She had succeeded in seeing two of her sons. Once a retiring wife mincing three steps behind her husband and deferring to his authority outside the home, the widow of more than a decade had turned bolder than she had been raised to imagine.

PIERCE, TWENTY-THREE AND HIGHER IN RANK THAN Frank, was in a slightly less perilous position than his younger brother. He, too, was charged with helping to protect the northern coastline, but he was a proper soldier, manning heavy machine guns, not an insignificant *tokkōtai*. Still, Pierce didn't have enough access to food because of his irregular schedule. Tall and too lean, he subsisted on cigarettes. Whorls of smoke curling above his head, he sat on his coastal perch and mulled over his situation: Whatever happened on Kyūshū, Pierce decided, would be *"unmei"* (fate).

By August Frank had grown glum. A photograph taken at

that time shows him looking young and clean-shaven, more like a boy of twelve than a man of twenty. But the downturned line of his mouth and the lack of animation in his eyes give his age away. Frank was a man of resolve, ingrained by now from education, training, and resignation. *Bushidō*, the martial philosophy he had learned at *Icchū* and practiced in *kendō*, motivated his behavior. Its approach to war and suffering pervaded Japanese life. "Rectitude is the power of deciding upon a certain course of conduct in accordance with reason, without wavering;—to die when it is right to die, to strike when to strike is right."

At the Kokura weapons arsenal, Frank, like Pierce, accepted his fate. "In my mind I didn't want to die," he would later write. Regardless, he was determined to prove his worth as a soldier. "We decided to die to the last man. We all felt that way at the time."

IN LUZON IN LATE JULY, HARRY FOUND himself geographically closer to Japan than he had been since 1938, when he had left Hiroshima in high spirits for the United States. He continued to prepare American troops for the invasion of the islands, which would be defended by seasoned soldiers and determined civilians. In explaining how to understand the Japanese psyche, Harry expressed much of what his brother Frank believed, although Harry perceived the world through American eyes. "The enemy didn't fight to live, they fought to die," he said. "The Japanese would fight to the end, every man, woman, and child."

A master sergeant in an immense military apparatus, Harry knew little about the discussions occurring in Washington over estimated forces on both sides and the projected casualties. The initial landing would require more than three-quarters of a million American troops. Estimates for American losses started as low as 31,000 and escalated, depending on rapidly evolving estimates for Japanese troops. If the battle lengthened and involved another major operation, casualties could soar to six digits or more.

Harry was only aware that the 33rd was among the first divisions slated to invade Japan that autumn. Although he would not be in the very first wave of 33rd combat troops, alighting from amphibious vehicles and crawling upon shore in the face of withering fire, he would not be far behind. Once on land, every beach, grove, and village would descend into a savagely contended front line.

The "Okinawa story" dismayed him. The island had finally been relatively, but not completely, subdued in late June after three months of unmitigated horror. One-third of the American forces had been killed, declared missing, or treated as wounded, a figure that did not bode well for an invasion of Japan. For the first time since his first landing, Harry became fatalistic about his own chances of survival. He had talked quietly with a colonel who had privately reckoned that the forces might lose half their men. Harry put his own chances as "fifty-fifty" for lasting a few days beyond reaching the initial beachhead.

Where his brothers were he did not know. His mother was surely in Hiroshima. "I didn't like the idea of going on an invasion of Japan." Faltering from another bout of malaria, he had finally had enough and decided to request a long-overdue leave to the United States.

Harry asked two other linguists, team leaders with immediate family in Japan, to join him in his petition. One was Pat Neishi, born in California, who had been raised by his grandmother in Hiroshima. The three men, who were initially rebuffed by the counterintelligence division as too subordinate to speak with a general, approached ATIS's high command. They believed that they had a strong case. They had been in combat far longer than white soldiers with fewer points who had already headed home. Even a transfer would be welcome, as long as it didn't involve Japan.

Colonel Mashbir, now in Manila, received the men, whom he knew as "three of my best Nisei officers." He gathered that they were hesitant to ask for special attention and offered them cigarettes as they sat before him. Harry pleaded their case, explaining that there were now sufficient linguists available. His language team had expanded from ten to twelve men, and he no longer seemed as necessary.

Mashbir, buttoned up and as exacting as ever, stated emphatically that the men were "indispensable."

Harry explained that they were all *kibei* with relatives in Japan. "I didn't want to be responsible for any inimical act leading to their demise," he said of his family.

Harry found the colonel "pleasant" and "sympathetic but not encouraging." Mashbir promised only to take their concerns into consideration.

In private, he grasped the significance of the men's request. "They had been turning this thing over in their minds for weeks," he wrote in his subsequent memoir.

"They had had long and solemn discussions among themselves, and had arrived at the perfectly logical conclusion that, as the combat divisions fought their way inland, there would, in addition to the regular prisoner of war camps, unquestionably be separate internment camps for civilians, and that many of their relatives would be in those camps. It was a foregone conclusion that someone would recognize them as all three had gone to universities in Japan. It was also unquestionable that in the frenzy and hysteria incident to battle, their relatives—and, in fact, two of them had mothers there, and one had other very close relatives—would probably be brutally mistreated as a result of their presence in our Army."

Mashbir noted that he instructed all forward-echelon commanders to transfer any linguist bound to invade his home prefecture to a different area of attack in Japan.

American forces were not slated to invade Honshū until the following spring. Mashbir assumed that Japanese citizens would stay put in their hometowns. That was hardly the case, especially as soldiers from other prefectures—like Pierce and Frank—streamed into Kyūshū. And only those who survived the battlefield would end up in camps. Mashbir's directive may have helped Pat avoid coming into conflict with his relative, an elderly grandmother in Hiroshima, but it wouldn't help Harry at all.

Later, Harry received a telephone call from an officer on the colonel's staff stating that he should stay with his unit. "I didn't think it would work anyway," he shrugged. He had to accept the decision, but he was unable to dispel a gnawing sense of foreboding.

Come Thursday, November 1, 1945, Harry would—barring an unforeseen circumstance—climb down an amphibious craft and wade fully armed onto the sandy shore in southern Kyūshū, one soldier in Operation Olympic, a massive landing on three separate beaches encompassing more men, aircraft, and vessels than Normandy. How far north he would proceed would depend on how long he could evade friendly fire, how well he could survive relentless combat, and how long the fierce battle lasted.

That frenzied summer, all over the island of Kyūshū, the Rising Sun flag billowed as Japanese troops readied for their defense, Operation Ketsu-Go. They gouged foxholes and trenches facing the coast, practiced age-old drills, manned camouflaged machine guns, and trained placing bombs against their *senninbari* thousand-stitch-belted bellies. In the northern hills, ready to push south upon command to halt all incursions, Harry's brothers, *hohei* foot soldiers Pierce and Frank, braced for the Empire's last stand.

27

The Atomic Bomb

n early August, soon after Kinu had returned from Kyūshū, her sister Kiyo arrived at her door. She was holding the hand of her adopted grandson, the little brother of Toshinao and Kimiko, cousins who adored the Fukuharas. She had come for a stay, not a visit.

Kiyo had left her home after finding a leaflet, dropped by one of the glinting enemy B-29s, warning women and children to leave the city. She concluded that Takasu, a few miles from downtown, would be safe. Rumor had it that one should discard such inflammatory papers, so after showing it to Kinu, they burned it.

Several family members would attest to this account, but history would show that no such leaflets were ever scattered over the city. Sixty thousand sheets rained over Kure, twenty-five miles east of Hiroshima, and its prefecture environs on July 28, predicting more air raids to come and urging surrender. From a distance, some residents saw a B-29 hurtling toward the city after being shot down in the vicinity of Kure and Hiroshima. Could wayward messages, whether jettisoned or carried off course, have accidentally floated into Hiroshima city limits?

The air in Hiroshima quivered with tension. Everyone expected a major bombing in Japan's seventh-largest city. Few major urban areas had avoided what people called "the rain of fire." By the end of July, sixty-four cities had been attacked nationwide, 188,310 people had perished, 250,000 had been left wounded, and nine million wandered homeless among the rubble. Newspapers mentioned the raids, but not the casualty count. The people, however, were well aware of the losses.

Yet Hiroshima had been largely spared. At the end of April, one B-29 had lobbed a small bomb in the center of the city, resulting in eleven casualties. Kyōto—the ancient capital beaded with astonishing temples, shrines, gardens, and imperial palaces—glittered as the other notable exception on the main island.

Hiroshima residents were frightened and awed by the B-29s, and thankful when the droning formations, comprising hundreds of planes, glided past. Takiko Sadanobu, a high school student from Takasu, recalled, "We looked forward to seeing the white contrails of the B-29s." Children listened and pointed with excitement, "That's the roar of B." Masako, too, watched the planes en route to dropping bombs elsewhere in Honshū. "Why aren't they falling in Hiroshima?" she wondered.

Hiroshima's mystified citizens came up with theories. President Truman's mother lives here. Actually, his cousin does. Did you know that General MacArthur's mother was Japanese and born in Hiroshima? A son of an important American official happens to be a POW here. The American military will leave us alone because Hiroshima has sent so many immigrants to America. No one mentioned that several thousand Japanese Americans lived in Hiroshima; the *nisei* had long since been assimilated.

So it was that people braced for the inevitable. Sleeping fully clothed under a mosquito net, wearing exercise shoes and a quilted air-raid hood, Masako resolved, "Tomorrow I don't know whether I will die."

• • •

ON SATURDAY, AUGUST 4, KINU AND KIYO danced classical *buyō* while Masako performed as their musician. Playing popular, even classical, music was forbidden, but they could not dance to martial anthems. So the women took the risk even if it meant a prying neighbor informing a policeman that she had overheard the thumping of socked feet on *tatami* and the spontaneous tinkle of laughter. Kinu, Kiyo, and Masako didn't care.

Resisting the urge to strum Kinu's banjolike *shamisen*, Masako practiced *kuchi-jamisen*, humming in imitation. Listening intently and taking slow steps, Kinu and Kiyo raised invisible fans close to their chins, moved the fans in a graceful arc, and folded them to insert into their imaginary *obi* sashes. In their minds, they were wearing not baggy *monpe* but shimmering kimono.

Outside, the merciless summer sun steamed and stifled the dark house. The draining humidity didn't matter; Kinu and Kiyo were transported by the nearly silent music they had learned long ago. The women were engaged, united, and content. The cicadas whined, muffling and protecting Masako's earnest *kuchi-jamisen* and Kinu and Kiyo's beloved *buyō*. They had defied the overbearing war. Masako laughed: "No one could hear."

The next day, Kinu and Masako walked into town and joined more than two dozen others on a mobilization shift to tear down a grand home for a firebreak to contain the kind of napalm raids that many cities were suffering. They labored from early morning, trudging back in late afternoon *hetoheto* (exhausted).

When Kinu returned stoop-backed to her house, Kiyo asked for a bath. Kinu did not have enough firewood to heat bathwater. She would have to walk back to town to gather the debris from the demolition site with a cart, a task that she could not accomplish alone. Kinu, who could not ask her elder sister to assist, had no choice but to ask Masako.

In better days, a bath would not have become a topic of neighborly discussion. But hot baths had become expendable. Kinu and Masako had each reduced their soaks to a few each month, depleting their wood-scrap piles. Firewood, which was not rationed, was only available from the carcasses of houses destroyed for firebreaks. "People would burn books," said Masako, "to heat their baths."

Kiyo, however, believed that luxury was never frivolous. It was a waste to leave the wood from a hard day's work on an empty lot. "If you can get it for free, why don't you?" Masako could hear her saying. "Theoretically," Masako remarked drily, "she was correct."

When Masako and her father heard Kinu's request, they blanched. Since spring, Mr. Kaneishi had worried about Masako; she tired easily. The problem may have been their diet: mealy rice bran buns with mushy figs and tough shepherd's purse weeds in place of rice. As everyone's nutrition suffered, the incidence of disease had spiked. Masako was fragile. A few months earlier, Mr. Kaneishi had obtained permission for her to miss mobilization duty on occasion. As it was, most days she worked in a torpedo factory, bent over an assembly line producing *tokkōtai* weapons. Collecting firewood required pulling a cart more than a mile and bending in the heat for hours. As fond as he was of Kinu, he turned her down.

But Kinu insisted, virtually begging. Knowing that she could not refuse her elder sister, Mr. Kaneishi finally gave in. Kinu promised that they would leave before the mercury and humidity soared. Mr. Kaneishi grumbled, "Go early then." They agreed to meet at 5:30 a.m.

That night Kinu and Masako did not sleep well. Hardly

anyone in Hiroshima did. A warning siren sounded at 9:20 p.m. and an air-raid siren seven minutes later. Another air-raid siren whined at 12:25 a.m. The all-clear signal for the air-raid alert came at 2:10 a.m., almost two hours later. In fits and starts, the day that would change Hiroshima forever had begun.

WHEN MR. KANEISHI AWAKENED MASAKO BEFORE DAWN on Monday morning, August 6, she was groggy. Her father had grown even more anxious since the night before. Giving her a small breakfast, he fretted, "Don't get sick."

In the street Kinu waited, looking sleepy, at an hour most suited to the night-soil collectors. But it was too late to change their plans: Kinu had gone to the trouble of borrowing an old pushcart, weighted by two wooden tires. Masako grabbed the cart's long handles and Kinu pushed from behind. They headed for the site of the firebreak project of the day before.

As the sky blushed violet, the women labored in silence, heaving to the tune of the battered cart's rattle. The bush warblers and swallows chirped as the sun rose. The heat thickened. But the streets were still pleasantly empty, and the women were well on their way.

By the time they reached their destination, the humidity had climbed. Grateful for a slightly overcast sky, Kinu and Masako began looking for "junk," small sticks that would burn quickly, but the lot had already been picked over. The remaining remnants of pillars and walls were heavy and too long for the cart and the women had not brought tools. "We just did what was necessary, we weren't really looking for good wood," recalled Masako. As soon as they could, they tossed some pieces in the cart and turned to go.

"Auntie pushed hard," said Masako of their slog. Masako

leaned against the cart, feeling the strain of the day before, a massive "tug of war" to pull apart the building. Kinu must have ached, too, but said nothing. Masako should have been the one bearing the cart's weight, assisting her elder, but she rested while Kinu "half-carried" her home.

An enemy weather observation plane circled the city above, triggering an air-raid alert. Since raids usually occurred at night, most people assumed that there was probably nothing to worry about. Sure enough, at 7:31 a.m., the siren blasted the all-clear. Kinu and Masako soon reached Koi, where Hiroshima turned more rural, and met several friends in a neighborhood association en route to a demolition site inside the city.

"*Ohayō Gozaimasu.*" "Good morning!" they called to one another. How early Kinu and Masako had ventured into the city! How the sun baked! The women waved and continued on their way, the neighbors heading east and Masako and Kinu plodding west, their cart creaking over the unpaved roads. All over Hiroshima, students, including Kiyo's granddaughter Kimiko, were laboring at their assigned areas. All over the city, workers, including Victor, were pouring into factories. All over the city, residents, like Chieko, were tinkering in kitchens.

Masako's doting father had prepared a second breakfast. As soon as she entered the house, she washed her hands and joined him at the table. Through the kitchen window, she could see Kinu bent over her pump scrubbing the dirt caked between her toes; a mild breeze tousled her hair.

AT 8:15 A.M. A BRILLIANT ORANGE GLOW illuminated the sky. "*Pika!*" "A bright flash!" people called the sight. The unthinkable had happened: an atomic bomb had been detonated over Hiroshima.

In an instant, glass windows and doors exploded throughout Takasu. Masako dashed to a futon closet and jumped inside. Kinu bolted for the safety of her kitchen. Kiyo was elsewhere in the house.

Although the experience varied widely depending on where one was in Hiroshima, many in Takasu would not remember a single sound—neither that of a massive explosion nor the sudden rupture of glass. The world, for Masako, turned absolutely silent. "All in an instant." When it seemed as if the worst had passed, Masako emerged to find the house in disarray. Everything had scattered; glass littered the floor, the *fusuma* partition doors were warped off their tracks, and the ceiling had buckled, opening to the sky. The house itself seemed askew. Yet the refrigerator and stove sat in place, and the spoons rested neatly in their appointed drawer. Masako rushed outside.

Kinu came running, too. In place of a helmet, she was wearing an American cooking pot. "Auntie was upset and all alone." Masako said. Kinu's home, too, was topsy-turvy. All the closed windows and doors on the side of the house facing the city had shattered, but open windows, which had allowed the wind to pass through, were untouched. The hallway was carpeted with splinters of shining glass. Crystal bullets studded the stairwell. The air-raid tape crisscrossing windows lay in sticky tatters. When Kinu stepped into her garden, she found it pitted with shrapnel glass. Her house stood slightly tilted from its foundation. Her trees and hedges were singed. The most puzzling sight of all was a shadow of the hedges etched on the house; this phenomenon of radioactive imprinting would later be called ghosting.

"What happened?" cried Kinu. Masako had no idea. Had an explosion occurred at the station, practically next door?

Whatever it was, the neighborhood seemed strangely still. Overhead, an enormous black cloud tumbled and swelled. In time, this would be called the *kinokogumo*, or mushroom cloud, the chilling iconic image that ushered in the Atomic Era.

THAT MORNING TOSHINAO, KINU'S FIFTEEN-YEAR-OLD NEPHEW, WAS bicycling to the hospital to seek treatment for a chronic stomachache. But when he accidentally punctured his tire, he changed course to go to a friend's to borrow a bike. Mount Hiji shielded him from the blast. Toshinao immediately tried to walk home but everywhere he moved was a "sea of flames." Dark smoke roiled as fires erupted and spread, sparks flying. It would take Toshinao an entire day to return home.

His younger sister Kimiko, a twelve-year-old middle school student, had reached downtown earlier than Toshinao and by 8:15 a.m. was pulling down a building near the city hall. Looking up, she saw an unexpected sight—a parachute. It was secured to instruments that would record the air pressure and other effects of the blast. In a fraction of a second, a flash lit the sky. Kimiko, a little over half a mile from the epicenter of the T-shaped Aioi Bridge, instantly lost her sight.

She did not see her clothing burn, leaving her naked and branding her skin with the cloth's indigo pattern; she did not see her skin swell, color, and crack. She did not see that her classmates—those who were still alive—had the same injuries. Kimiko stumbled east toward the port of Ujina, away from her home, the only route possible, tripping over the fallen, swallowing the billowing smoke, somehow outstepping the raging fires through an acutely heightened sense of hearing and smell.

Chieko was in her kitchen at the time of the earth-shaking jolt. "I felt as if a bomb had dropped in our garden," she recollected.

In a creak of falling timber, the house collapsed over her and her bedridden, 103-year-old grandmother. As air defense drills had intensified, Chieko had practiced covering her grandmother with a blanket to smother flames. Her grandmother had resisted, crying, "Are you trying to kill me?" With kin in the United States, "she couldn't comprehend war." Now Chieko and her grandmother were trapped. Chieko clawed herself out of the rubble. But the flames were spreading fast, hissing and weaving toward them. She could do nothing to save her grandmother.

Stunned, Chieko fled to a refuge center. Many of those heading in the same direction were nude and held their hands before them, their skin dangling like limp strands of *wakame* (seaweed). Their eyes bulged in crimson faces. Their bodies were smeared with blood, a ferric odor mingling with the stench of charred flesh. "It was hell," Chieko said. People were dropping before her, imploring, *"Tasukete kudasai."* "Please help me."

One-third of a mile away, Shigeru Matsuura's house crashed, planks landing helter-skelter. His father, who was at the castle military headquarters, somehow survived the complex's conflagration. Glass slivers piercing his neck, he lunged toward the Ōta River for relief. Fires snaked through the river choked with wide-eyed, blackened corpses. He struggled around searing embers and roaring fires the short distance to his home and collapsed before it. Miraculously, his wife, elsewhere and unharmed, would find and nurse him.

In this corner of Hakushima, only a few of 285 buildings, a mere one percent, would stand. The upscale neighborhood would smolder for days before turning ashen.

Slightly northwest of the Aioi Bridge, Hiroshima Castle, and Hakushima lay Misasa, where Victor worked. The factory imploded from the shockwave rippling from ground zero less than a mile away. Caught underground, he struggled to find a way out. He crawled through the debris and standing in the fiery, acrid, smoking street, he saw that many had perished. The elementary school designated as a shelter had collapsed and was burning. Victor followed the crowd heading for the northern hills. He knew the drill: those in Misasa were supposed to seek refuge in the northern village of Asa. Whether driven by necessity or inclination, Victor walked toward Gion, his father's ancestral home, the site of Shōsōji Temple, where his father was laid to rest and had donated a bronze bell, only for it to be smelted in wartime for guns, explosives, and heavy weapons.

Victor's cousin Aiko, the daughter of his father's older brother, lived in Gion, about three miles north of Hiroshima. Aiko, a newlywed, had been sleeping late that morning when her windows shattered. Thirty minutes after the mighty blast, the water of the Ōta River inked black. Aiko thought that the scourge was ash.

It was that and more. A curious black rain had begun to fall, as showers in the city center and thunderstorms beyond Gion and, particularly, over Takasu. The weather darkened, becoming cloudy and *torihada* (chicken-skin) chilly. The sky opened, spitting raindrops as large as thumbs, muddy, oily, and black. They stung to the touch, stuck to surfaces, and puddled in thick clumps. The precipitation was a ghastly mix of dust, vapor, and radioactive soot. In Takasu, Masako's futons were soaked by the rain that poured through the roof. No matter how many times she later washed the cushions, the stains remained.

"Zombies," Aiko called the figures, limping and dragging along the road, single file or holding each other up. They were genderless, hairless, virtually skinless, badly burned and blistered. Aiko took the lost souls in. Those who could speak moaned for *"mizu"* ("water"). With the bomb, the waterworks had ceased operating. Aiko raced back and forth to her emergency well, dipping in desperation.

Aiko was surprised when Victor, whom she knew as Katsumi, turned up at her door. He had braved a firestorm, whirlwind, and black rain to reach her. His shoulders and back appeared pale, swollen, and on the verge of blistering, but his face looked fine. "He walked easily," said Aiko. "He talked." His injuries were relatively light. She couldn't accommodate him in her house, overflowing with victims. Katsumi didn't want to trouble Aiko; he told her that he might walk home. Aiko wasn't sure whether he continued his trek or spent the night in a nearby school-turned-refuge.

As day descended into night, the colossal cloud still hovered over the city. People were filing into villages and neighborhoods outside Hiroshima. In Gion, Aiko felt as if "everyone came here." But the road through the mountains leading to Takasu also reverberated with cries—"like the howling of wild animals," a Takasu resident said.

In her home, Kinu digested the day with Kiyo, trying to recover. None of their extended family who lived downtown had reached Takasu. The local hospital, elementary school, city office, lecture hall, and shrines were jammed with the injured. It was the same in the neighborhood next door. More than a thousand people were seeking help, pleading for water. Kinu feared another momentous explosion and worried desperately for the safety of her family.

THE DAY AFTER HIROSHIMA WAS DEVASTATED BY a bomb still not understood, the sun broiled and the fires burned. Undeterred, Kinu walked downtown to look for family and friends while Kiyo stayed at the house. The mountain road was clogged with two-way pedestrian traffic—an exodus from the city of the terribly injured seeking refuge and an influx of frantic friends and family searching for survivors. "It was a natural instinct to go find those close to you," Masako said.

Toshinao reached his home that morning. Although his sister Kimiko had been on mobilization duty a manageable walk away, she had not yet returned. Toshinao and his distraught mother set out to find her.

It was night by the time they reached Ujina, the last stop before the sea. Toshinao and his mother scanned the posted scribbled lists of hundreds of people being cared for in the area. "Strangely, we saw her name immediately," he said. Kimiko Nishimura. They ran to a large warehouse and called out, *"Kimiko-chan, Kimiko-chan!"* To Toshinao's astonishment, his sister answered.

Toshinao and his mother did not recognize Kimiko, lying on a thin mattress in a crowded row. Her face was swollen, her body bloated and blistered; her skin *"zuruzuru"* ("peeling"). They thought about taking her home and decided to let her rest overnight. Toshinao's mother handed a doctor some money for medicine.

She did not realize how limited were the options. Medical staff and first-aid volunteers were using cotton, torn newspaper, and bits of curtains as bandages. They were applying rustproofing oil and cooking oil to mitigate the burns' incessant itching. Doctors dabbed a waning supply of mercurochrome antiseptic on wounds. None of this treatment was appropriate, and all of it was too little and too late.

"We quieted Kimiko down," Toshinao said, as he and his mother cared for her into the night. The hot air stagnated; it was infused with the sickly sweet and sour odor of blood, feces, and urine. The room echoed with sobs, and cries. *"Okāsan."*

"Mother," people whimpered. Exhausted, Toshinao fell asleep beside his sister on the slatted floor. At some point that agitated night, his mother nudged him awake. Kimiko was dead.

Years later, he would be grateful. It was a blessing that Kimiko had not died alone, that the family had not anguished, wondering what had happened. More than four hundred of Kimiko's schoolmates on duty were killed, a figure dwarfed only by the losses at Sanyō, Harry and Pierce's alma mater, and one other school. In all, citywide, more than seven thousand mobilized students died. Toshinao, aware of the toll, later reflected. "I was happy," he said, "I found my little sister."

That day and night, Toshinao and Kinu did not cross paths, although she was looking for him and his family. Kinu would learn later that Kimiko—once a cherry-cheeked girl in a smock who had seen off her cousin Harry at the station when he left for the United States—was swiftly cremated, her body piled with countless others, covered with straw, and ignited.

Kinu would someday briefly mention the horrific sights that met her eyes—the staring, nude, bloodied, and burned apparitions, but little more. The devastation was stunning. The domed Industrial Promotion Hall and the Red Cross still stood, but its gleaming copper dome was gone. The Red Cross, where Frank had posted letters to Harry, was a windowless concrete shell, its surrounding landscape flattened.

Hiroshima Castle was extinct. The white behemoth had disintegrated into a mound of fallen, scorched boards. The adjacent military barracks had collapsed and burned. Some tree trunks still stood, split through the middle or sprouting leafless, spindly, black branches. The concrete pillars, marking the entrance to the grounds where Frank and his unit had drilled, remained, but the imperious wrought-iron gates that joined the pillars had melted and disappeared. To say nothing of the men in the environs.

Kinu tried to reach Meijidō, but she could not get close to Hondōri Street, instantly incinerated. Fires still crackled and burned. The once magical Meijidō, situated only 328 yards southeast of the bomb's epicenter, had vanished. One hundred percent of the buildings on the street had been completely destroyed.

At a shelter, Chieko was rapidly weakening. Curling up, she had become nauseated. She was vomiting, running a fever, and doubled over with diarrhea; no one knew why. In the coming days, when Chieko had to leave the shelter, one of her distant relatives would hammer together a rough, two-*tatami*-mat shack, equaling six by twelve feet, in the rubble of the once-rollicking family compound she called home. Her face inflamed, her organs ailing, Chieko prayed for the return of her elder brother, a soldier abroad. If he were still alive, he was her sole surviving immediate family.

Two days later, on Thursday morning, August 9, while Kinu still combed Hiroshima and Victor still gathered strength at a school in Gion, two B-29s circled over Kokura, the primary target for the second atomic bomb. Smoke and haze clouded the view of the Arsenal, the bomb's objective. After trying twice to pinpoint its location, the B-29 pilot aborted the drop and headed southwest. At 11:02 a.m., the second atomic bomb to hit Japan would detonate over Nagasaki.

When the B-29s approached Kokura, Frank was milling between the town and its military armory, looking for two conscripted Korean soldiers who had escaped. Although the newspapers were already referring to a "new-type bomb," Frank, as usual, did not have access to the press. Nor had any hushed talk reached him of the *pikadon*—the "flash-boom" bomb, as it was called in Hiroshima. Frank didn't have an inkling of what had happened. Newly appointed a squad leader, despite his humble rank, he wondered whether the captain thought that a *nisei* could control the Koreans since both were foreigners, namely misfits and outsiders. Frustrated, he searched for them to no avail.

Oblivious to the B-29 course plotted for Kokura, Frank was a lucky man. He had avoided catastrophe twice—once when part of his unit had been stationed in the heart of Hiroshima, and then at the key weapons depot in the castle town of Kokura.

Five days or so after setting out for the city center, Kinu returned to her damaged home. She was thoroughly depleted. Victor had not yet surfaced. Sad news filtered in and friends gathered in grief and despair. The women whom Kinu and Masako had met in Koi that fateful morning, one cluster among fifty-one neighbors from the area on mobilization duty, were almost all gravely injured. One by one, they were dying.

In Takasu, blowflies swarmed over corpses into deep summer and the doleful cremation ceremonies would stretch from August into November.

AMID THE OVERWHELMING SIGHTS OF STRICKEN HIROSHIMA, the deaths of neighbors, and the loss of her young niece Kimiko, Kinu brightened a day or two later when Victor opened the front door, calling, "I'm home!" "*Tadaima!*"

His journey had lasted a week. For a fit person in normal times, the solid hike from Gion to Takasu took a morning or afternoon; sturdy country people habitually walked it as a matter of course. Now a robust trek had stretched into a death-defying odyssey for the injured stragglers. "They walked for dear life," said Masako; "they wanted to come home."

Kinu's eldest son retreated to his futon on the second floor. He was worn-out, ill, and flinching from oozing burns on his back. Kinu cared for him the best she could. She, like everyone in Takasu, had pitifully few rations. The neighborhood distributed a few pumpkins and sweet potatoes to tide residents over. There was no medicine. The electricity resumed before the water and gas, but everything clanged, cranked, and sputtered, the service spotty. The fancy flush toilet couldn't operate without electricity. Masako spied Victor digging holes and defecating in the garden where glass fragments glinted between blades of grass. Each day loomed agonizing, pinched by shortages, pulsing with pain, charged with uncertainty. The war dragged on. Victor's condition worsened. Kinu, too, was ailing.

PART SIX

THE AFTERMATH

死期腹中に勝着あり
Shiki fukuchū ni shōchaku ari
The darkest hour is that before the dawn.

28

Bittersweet Reunion

Harry was in Manila when he first heard about the atomic bomb in Hiroshima. His first thought was that finally, the war would be over and he wouldn't have to take part in the invasion. "We were all happy about it," he said. But as the enormity of the news hit, he was shocked. The city had apparently been decimated.

Specific numbers were still foggy and would be subject to change, but casualties were staggering. Tens of thousands had died immediately. President Truman took to the airwaves sixteen hours after the explosion, pronouncing, "If they do not now accept our terms they may expect a rain of ruin from the air the like of which has never been seen on this earth."

Japan did not surrender. Allied military preparations to invade Kyūshū proceeded on schedule. On August 10, one day after an atomic bomb exploded over Nagasaki, Harry was shown aerial photographs of the terrain and instructed on the order of battle for enemy forces. He was also promoted to second lieutenant, a commissioned officer at last.

The prospect of an invasion had heightened the need for linguists and the War Department had produced a new table of allowances for ATIS. Authorizations for lieutenants soared almost tenfold, from 38 to 300. After more than two years in the Pacific, Harry added a gleaming gold bar to his shoulder.

Colonel Mashbir was swearing in men in Manila and, as always, was impressed by his charges. "Any group on earth would have taken Manila apart, because seven hundred promotions in two days is not a thing that a bunch of soldiers will pass over lightly," he wrote of several levels of promotions. "But the Nisei received this news with the same dignity and reserve with which they had received bad news in the past."

As vague news about the swath of devastation in Hiroshima trickled in, Harry's mood darkened. He didn't know whether his family was affected. "Each day it became worse for me." His spirits dipped further when his duties were expanded to include explaining the bomb to hundreds of Japanese prisoners in POW camps. Since no Japanese term yet existed for the weapon, Harry and the other linguists strung together "atomic" and "bomb," coming up with a literal translation, *genshi bakudan*. As it was, the same terminology was being used in Japan.

This powerful weapon, Harry told the POWs seated in rows before him, was "equivalent to thousands of tons of TNT," in which "one single explosion had completely wiped out the entire city of Hiroshima." That, anyway, was what he had been told to convey. He couldn't expand on the nature of nuclear fission since "I didn't know what an atomic bomb was." Nor could he describe the damage, since he had difficulty picturing the devastation. News on the effects of radiation, a mystery in itself, varied daily. What information dribbled in was alarming, including the dire prediction that nothing would grow in Hiroshima for at least a century.

Some of the prisoners were most likely from Hiroshima or had relatives there. In the clinging heat of a heavy day, the POWs sat dumbfounded while mosquitoes buzzed around them. Speechless, they didn't ask a single question. Harry understood well how stillness could conceal surging emotions.

Several days later, at noon on August 15, the POWs' compatriots in Japan would hear the voice of the so-called "Sacred Crane" for the first time. As the emperor took to the airwaves, neighbors gathered. Heavy static obscured his high-pitched nasal tone and his formal court language. The distance between the ruler, regarded as a living god, and his humble subjects loomed as vast as ever. In a brief address, the emperor asked his people to "endure the unendurable and bear the unbearable." The war was over: their nation had surrendered. Heads down, people cried—some with relief, others with anguish—and with a host of complex emotions retreated to the privacy of their homes in a funereal silence.

At the same time, giddy jubilation swept every far-flung locale in the Pacific Theater, where more than 1.5 million American soldiers were posted, with 750,000 in the Philippines. Manila was instantly transformed from a rubble-strewn city into a raucous American and Filipino fiesta. That night on the traffic-snarled streets, drivers honked incessantly, soldiers clanged their jeeps with iron pipes and fired their guns upward, while tangerine-hued tracers looped across the sky. The next day, 33rd Division soldiers nursed bruising hangovers while grinning over the headline on the *Guinea Pig*, their division newspaper: "WAR OVER: 24 HOURS OLD BUT HEADLINES STILL LOOK 'PRETTY.'"

HARRY STRUGGLED TO COME TO TERMS WITH his thoughts. The war had lasted three years and eight months; he had spent more than two years of it island-hopping in the Pacific. He had been bracing himself for an invasion. "Then, the war ended just like that." Harry wanted to go home. But, unlike most American soldiers, he hesitated. For him, his strong family ties and the physical place where he belonged were not necessarily one and the same.

Harry doubted that his mother and brothers, if they were in Hiroshima, had survived. "The more I thought about it, the more depressed I became. My thinking degraded to the point that I blamed myself that they had died because I had volunteered to fight against them." After denying for so long that enlisting in the U.S. Army had anything to do with his family, Harry could not avoid a crushing sense of complicity.

And, initially, he could not bear the thought of going to Japan. "I thought it would be no use going." But, then, he decided to try. Many *nisei* were released from their extended service in the Philippines, but Harry decided to proceed with the 33rd Division to Japan. From wherever he might be based, he would determine whether it would be possible to venture to Hiroshima.

LITTLE MORE THAN TWO WEEKS LATER, SEPTEMBER 2, 1945, dawned cool and overcast in Tokyo Bay, where hundreds of American and British ships surrounded the battleship *Missouri* for the official surrender. Shortly before 9 a.m., the eleven-man Japanese delegation, led by General Yoshijirō Umezu and diplomat Mamoru Shigemitsu, walked the gangway of the last American battleship built before the end of the war. The *Missouri* resonated with significance. Named after President Truman's home state and christened by his daughter Margaret at the New York Naval Shipyard, it had recently seen action at Iwo Jima, Okinawa, and points along Japan. That particular morning, the *Missouri*'s nine 16-inch guns faced Tokyo primed to blast, if necessary, 2,700-pound shells more than twenty miles in less than sixty seconds.

Sailors craned over the towering superstructure, foreign correspondents and photographers watched from the massive gun mounts, and rows of admirals and generals stood near a green-felt-covered table. Guided by Colonel Mashbir, the Japanese delegation climbed to the teak deck, where they were met by stares of loathing and utter silence. Amid the officers were three *nisei* lieutenants: Tom Sakamoto and Noby Yoshimura, both from California, and Jiro Yukimura, from Hawaii. Tom and Noby, like Harry, had been partly raised in Japan. Noby, like Harry, had military-age brothers there. No one understood the Japanese representatives' intense discomfort better than they did.

Tom and Noby were taken aback by how dwarfed the Japanese were by the Allied presence. The linguists felt the silence stretch for fifteen excruciating minutes while the Japanese delegates were left waiting. "This was the scene of a nation disgraced in total defeat," Tom would write, "a scene that brought home to me how sad a defeated nation can be."

The proceedings commenced with an invocation by the ship chaplain and a recording of "The Star-Spangled Banner." General Douglas MacArthur, representatives from nine Allied nations, and the two leading Japanese officials signed two copies of the formal instruments of surrender. Everything was over within minutes.

While the ink dried, thousands of navy carrier planes and B-29 Superfortresses roared low over the bay, the sea, and sky, a shining display of Allied military and industrial might at the dawn of an uncertain occupation.

Wrote Tom, "As for myself, after 25 months of combat in the hot jungles of the southwest Pacific islands, this moment aboard battleship *Missouri* was by far the most emotional event that I had the privilege of witnessing."

Within one week, Tom would be overwhelmed by Japan's circumstances. Accompanying foreign correspondents as their interpreter on a brief stop to Hiroshima, Tom felt as if the bomb "had sucked the air out of the city." Patients—largely old men, women, and children—lay in the hospital, horribly burned, their faces covered with pus. Flies swarmed. When the correspondents quickly boarded their plane for Tokyo, "nobody spoke," Tom said, his voice trembling decades later.

The reactions of Tom and Noby—among the first Americans to reach Japan—did not bode well for Harry, who had not yet stepped foot in the vanquished Empire.

ON SEPTEMBER 25, THE 33RD DIVISION LANDED on beaches in Wakayama Prefecture, located about 150 miles east of Hiroshima. Under a clear sky, amphibious vessels disgorged troops, including Harry, who waded in knee-high water to the shore. A few Japanese sat on the dunes, watching grimly. Marching down the empty streets, Harry noticed groups of children crowded along the edges, their bony shoulders partially covered by buttoned shirts that billowed over their concave stomachs. They all seemed to be scratching their scalps. Their heads, he realized, were covered with lice.

Harry's colleague Mas Ishikawa, who also had family in Hiroshima, saw shoreline trenches and stacks of sharpened bamboo spears when he had landed near the harbor. "That's what you might have faced," he thought. "What," he asked himself, "would you have done?"

Harry and Mas, with their complicated pedigrees, were not the only ones wrestling with their emotions. In the crowd stood a teenager named Hideyoshi Miyako, who did not know any Americans. He hated the enemy, and yet he watched transfixed. He hadn't wanted to come but his mother had made him; she had heard that the Americans were distributing candy and she wanted a treat for his sister. Everyone had heard the rumor that women would be raped, so Miyako had to go in the family's place. He took one look at his younger sister, who had never tasted the intense sweetness of sugar, and left the house.

He was amazed. Although it was daytime, jeeps and trucks drove off the transport ships with their headlights on, so different from the charcoal-spewing buses that had to be pushed uphill in Japan. Although the soldiers were well armed, they were young, cheerful, and smiling. Some waved. "They looked like friends back from a trip, not the enemy with whom we had been fighting," marveled Hideyoshi, who until recently had been a *tokkōtai* suicide bomber in training. When the soldiers tossed chocolate, he grabbed the bars. He had not tasted the sweet for five years; it thoroughly disarmed him. He heard himself joining the crowd, yelling, "Give me chocolate!" In that moment, his animosity, simmering all these long, hard years, "vanished like a bubble popping."

Harry did not recognize anyone in the crowd, but he was struck by the scene as well. There was no opposition. "I couldn't believe it," he said. A glimmer of hope, so subtle he did not articulate it as yet, began to lighten his burden of complicity. If there were a way he could come back someday, he remembered later, "I felt some responsibility to help postwar Japan recover."

Posted to division headquarters in Kobe, Harry served as the 33rd's chief interpreter. Assigned to liberate American POWs, demilitarize Japanese forces, and maintain security, he filled his days with work. In his free time, he tried to learn about Hiroshima, which, as the crane soars, lay 156 miles away. No one seemed to know what was going on there. Shortly before Harry had landed, the Occupation authorities had imposed a ban on the military and Japanese press regarding news about the atomic bombs. When Harry privately asked American officials and Japanese police in Kobe, they didn't have any off-the-record information, either.

In early October, military censorship was lifted, although the Japanese media ban remained in place. Discovering whether his family was alive, however, would prove a challenge. The *Pacific Stars and Stripes*, the newspaper for American forces in Asia, carried articles about *nisei* hunting for family in Hiroshima. One soldier had found his three sisters but his mother had perished. Another story reported that three others were searching for their loved ones in Hiroshima and Nagasaki. "All efforts to find these relatives have failed so far."

"What little news there was was worse than expected," Harry said. "Even in areas not bombed, people were on the verge of starvation." He wasn't certain that he should risk his own emotional stability for a heart-wrenching search. "I feared the futility of looking for my family and I feared that whatever I found could make me very bitter."

Yet Harry also sensed the faintest hint of possibility, which he traced to his remarkable encounter in New Guinea with Shigeru Matsuura. Their meeting had haunted him for more than a year. "The odds were slim regarding Matsuura," Harry reflected, turning the troubling encounter on its head. But both he and Matsuura had survived this war, and their futures awaited. Perhaps an equally unlikely scenario could unfold in Hiroshima. "Maybe," Harry thought, "the miracle of finding my family could happen."

Harry talked with General Clarkson, who gave him permission to travel to Hiroshima, still largely off-limits, save occasional reporters and a growing cadre of scientists. Plants were blooming in strange profusion. At military headquarters at the castle, now no more than ruins, a lush canna plant had sprouted from the debris with a stalk of giant blossoms. Illness was also proliferating. Physicians arrived in Hiroshima, trying to determine why so many patients were dying every two to three days. They were calling this baffling new illness *genbakushō*, or radiation sickness.

Harry tried to reach the city twice and failed. After loading a small convoy with clothing, blankets, and foodstuffs, he was forced to turn back because the narrow roads were in disrepair. Yet, despite the frustration and uncertainty, waiting to start over would prove wise. Hiroshima, lying partly below sea level, had been flooded by a September typhoon of historic proportions. Rain had poured for days, swelling the city's seven rivers, taking out more than half its bridges, tearing up its gravel roads, and halting its railroads, which had swiftly resumed service after the bomb. The trains would be unable to operate fully again until November. So torrential were the downpours that eleven Kyōto Imperial University scientists researching the effects of the bomb had died when the hospital they were in was swept away by a booming landslide. A second storm pounded the area on October 8. The city's tribulations seemed unending. In the district of Takasu, the rain created deep ponds from rice paddies and waterlogged bomb-damaged houses. The city lacked the staff and services needed to provide rescue and relief.

Residents coped. In beautiful Miyajima, Harry's cousins placed rocks on the shore as a dike to prevent the waves from tunneling down its serpentine lanes, toppling crowded houses and shops. From Takasu, Masako bypassed the fallen bridges and boarded river ferries to cross into the city. The bridges often collapsed in floods, she recalled. No one could deny that autumn that the skies over Hiroshima wept.

• • •

ON OCTOBER 16, HARRY BEGAN HIS THIRD attempt to get to Hiroshima. He secured a driver and packed what he could in a single
jeep to facilitate speed and mobility. At the wheel sat Harry's
driver Chester, a six-foot-three, blue-eyed, blond farm boy from
Michigan. The duo—Chester, by Harry's account, "scared," and
Harry, hopelessly bereft of a sense of direction—left at 10 a.m.
Harry's hopes rose, eager as he was to return to his family's
home.

The pair traveled west, passing villages where the residents
had never seen an American soldier or jeep. They churned
clouds of dirt on rutted roads and entered the city of Okayama,
not yet recovered from having been badly bombed. Some of the
bridges were washed out, forcing them to cross railroad tracks
and a river, which ran wide but not deep. When they stopped at
a railroad station to ask about the train schedule in order to avoid
oncoming trains, the stone-faced stationmaster claimed not to
know. The men forged ahead, bouncing over trestles, moving
too slowly for comfort, testing their luck. Chester steered and
Harry directed. "I didn't think about turning back."

At one junction, they were almost across a track when the
jeep's wheels became stuck in the trestles. They heard a train
rumbling their way; Harry ran to the back and jostled the jeep
up and down; it groaned, but the tires did not budge. Several
rice farmers, who were watching, fled, but a few other passersby
stepped forward and lifted the end. The jeep jerked "in the nick
of time," Harry said. "My adrenalin was pumping."

By the time they reached heavily bombed Fukuyama, only
thirty-five miles or so from Hiroshima, the streets were cloaked
in darkness, the city's lights and signage long consigned to the
war effort. They had been traveling all day. They stopped at
a police station to inquire about the road conditions in the
approach to Hiroshima. The chief, who had been sleeping,

descended from the second floor, astonished by the Americans who greeted him. Harry had Chester step in, acting like an officer and Harry his humble interpreter. "Just stand there," Harry said, hoping that the nineteen-year-old's towering physical presence and rifle would lend an air of authority. It was a tough act. The boy seemed mute, "shaking all the time." Gaining some sense of the lay of the land, they continued without pausing to rest.

Once in a while, they passed gangs of demobilized Japanese soldiers. They were drunk on rubbing alcohol, singing, yelling, and arguing. Harry and Chester skirted around them, following police advice about avoiding confrontations.

At last in Kure, familiar ground for Harry though B-29-devastated, they stopped for gas at an American base. When the guard asked where they were headed, Harry replied, "Hiroshima."

"You can't get in," the soldier said. Harry and Chester left quickly. "After all," said Harry, "there was nobody to stop us." From Kure, the road was paved, a welcome sight for the adventurers. At around 1 a.m., they crossed the city limits.

AT HIROSHIMA STATION, HARRY STEPPED DOWN FROM the jeep. The imposing reinforced-concrete landmark was a flame-singed, cracked shell, missing windows, ceilings, and floors. From its vantage point, Harry could see several unrestricted miles across the city; only a few ruins broke the flattened vista. "All was eerie and lifeless," he later wrote. "There was no movement or noise. The only things that appeared undamaged were streetcar tracks and gravestones near where Buddhist temples once stood." His chest heavy with emotion, Harry believed it was unlikely that the house in Takasu stood untouched.

He spied two men sitting around a bonfire in a streetcar that had been flung from its tracks, landing upright, surrounded by debris. Where, Harry asked, could they cross the river en route to Takasu? The men, who appeared drunk and reeked of alcohol, did not bother to look up. Light from the flames flickered across their faces. "Zombies," Harry thought.

Ultimately, Chester and Harry would need several hours—for what should have taken at most one hour—to get to Takasu. As they approached, the sun was rising; their journey from Kobe had consumed nearly one day.

The gracious town of Takasu appeared caught in an unearthly slumber. At least, Harry expected to hear a dog barking in response to the jeep's roar, but there was not a living thing in sight. Later, Harry would hear that during the war domesticated animals had either starved or been eaten. In a daze, he motioned Chester to stop in front of his mother's house, where he had lived for a few months back in 1938. The hedges at the entrance were charred. The house sat at a slight tilt and its roof appeared ripped. Harry paused before going to the door. The window on the front door was missing every pane of glass.

Inside, Kinu and Kiyo, who happened to be visiting, had been sleeping in a *tatami* room on the first floor when they were startled awake by the sound of the jeep and watched in horror as it cranked to a stop. Thinking that the house was about to be plundered by enemy forces, they had fled upstairs to hide on the second floor. They had heard rumors of rape, even of old women.

With Chester standing beside him, Harry knocked and waited. At last, the door opened and there stood the two sisters. If Harry had not known the women, he would not have recognized them—so emaciated, ill, and aged did they appear. What was worse, his mother and aunt met Harry with blank stares.

Kinu looked up at Chester and then down at Harry, back and forth, over and again. Harry knew his skin was jaundiced from the side effects of the antimalarial atabrine, but he had anticipated a flash of recognition. There was none.

"All they saw was an American soldier," he thought. The women seemed frightened. Finally, Kinu's eyes met Harry's, and he took a deep breath. "*Okāsan, Katsuharu desu. Tadaima kaette mairimashita,*" he said, using polite, humble language and his Japanese middle name. "Mother, I am Katsuharu. I have come home."

Kinu blinked. No one said a word. At last, Kiyo recognized her nephew and cried out, "Harry!" Kinu's eyes filled with tears and, silently, she opened her arms. The years and distance disappeared as Kinu and Harry held on to one another.

When they separated, Kinu struggled to gather her wits. Harry's uniform and pistol had thrown her off. He was supposed to be in the United States; she had no idea that he had enlisted. "What are you doing here?" Had he run away from somewhere? He must hide the jeep.

"Why would she say something like that?" Harry wondered, concealing the jeep near the Oitoshi Shrine, which had recently harbored atomic bomb victims. Maybe his mother feared neighbors' reactions to a vehicle belonging to the Occupation forces. She could have been trying to shield them from retaliation or avoid causing the neighbors' undue alarm. There was so much about his family's life that he did not understand.

FOR THE FIRST TIME IN MORE THAN seven years, Harry went inside his mother's house. There in the foyer was the Art Deco ceiling lamp and the mirrored hat stand that used to hold his dad's fedora. Kinu told him that Victor was on the second floor.

Climbing the stairs, Harry noticed shards of glass embedded in the stucco walls. He opened the sliding door to his brother's room and was overwhelmed by the odor of sweat, dried blood, and pus. Victor lay prone on a futon. There was hardly any skin on his back.

Victor did not recognize him at first but when Harry spoke, his brother looked him in the eyes. "He couldn't talk much," Harry remembered, but he smiled and listened.

Harry kept his eyes on Victor's face. He did not fully register that Victor was suffering from severe burns. Victor responded kindly, trying—after all these years and tribulations—to make conversation. They talked for a few minutes. Victor never said a word about his wounds.

Downstairs Kinu rushed about mortified. She had little to offer Harry and Chester besides slivers of sweet potatoes and teacups of water. As much as Harry appreciated his mother's attempt at hospitality, he didn't want to eat. He was anxious to find Pierce and Frank, both of whom Kinu said had recently returned and were working. It was still early morning when Harry walked into Frank's office.

Since his recent return, Frank had understood acutely that the family needed food and medicine. With inflation raging, he had been forced to exploit the black market, for which he needed as much cash as he could quickly earn. He had started a lucrative job a few days earlier. Dusting off his rusty English, he was assisting an American atomic bomb research team to pinpoint the epicenter of the blast. Knocking on the doors of buildings in the vicinity of the target, Frank had spent the past few days asking in Japanese, "Where were you when the bomb was dropped?"

Answers were not forthcoming. "People didn't like that we would say *'Dōzo yoroshiku'*" ("Please treat us kindly") and continue with questions. The physicians on the team would examine the residents' faces and backs but offer no treatment. Some people weren't strong enough to communicate, but they could not refuse the victors. The encounters made Frank squeamish. When Harry showed up, Frank was preparing for another day of distressing rounds with these researchers.

Frank was overjoyed to see Harry, if bewildered by his American uniform. He wondered how Harry possibly could have enlisted after the letters Frank had posted on their mother's behalf. Besides, Harry still wore soda-bottle-thick eyeglasses; he could not have been drafted. Was he a repatriated *nisei*? Was the *hakujin* soldier Harry's guard or was Harry the American's driver? Frank couldn't understand a word the white man said to Harry, who seemed to sense Frank's confusion.

"Would you like to go with me to Kobe?" Harry asked Frank in Japanese. Frank—once a toddler perched on his brother's bike seat, a boy listening to tales of hijinks, a teenager winding their Victrola—did not hesitate. "*Hai*," he said. Even after all these years apart. Even though he needed to earn daily pay to take care of his infirm mother and brother. He made an excuse to his superior, and the brothers were off.

Together they took a boat to find Pierce on an island in the bay where he was working as an interpreter at a hospital with American scientists. Pierce, too, was thrilled to see his older brother. But when Harry asked him if he would like to go to Kobe, Pierce demurred. Ever comfortable on the sidelines, he would stay for the time being in Hiroshima.

Within hours, Harry, with Chester at the wheel, and Frank in the back, drove into devastated Hakushima. There they found Chieko alone in her hut. She, like Victor, did not dwell on her pain, although she was suffering from profound radiation sickness. Harry offered to take her to Kobe for medical care. Chieko declined and thanked Harry for his kindness. "I must wait for my older brother," she said, holding out hope that he would return from the front.

Harry, Frank, and Chester headed next to the lean-to a short distance away that the Matsuuras now called home. Neither Harry nor Frank had ever met the elderly couple. Like Kinu and Kiyo, the Matsuuras were caught off guard by their visitors. When Harry greeted them in Japanese and explained that he, too, used to live in Hakushima, they looked vacant. When Harry said that their only child was alive and well in Australia and would return, Mrs. Matsuura stiffened. She had received a notice that her son had perished one year earlier. His unit, she said, had been "annihilated." "He's dead," she said. No matter how much Harry tried to change her mind, it was obvious, Frank said, "they didn't want to listen to Harry, who was in an American uniform." Plus, if they chose to accept Harry's news, they would have to confront the shame that their son had been taken prisoner and not died a noble death. Harry's good intentions had fallen flat. Frank tried to comfort him. "It cannot be helped," he said.

THAT EVENING, KINU HAD ALL THREE OF her boys under her roof for the first time since 1938. Of course, Chester and Kiyo were there, too. Kinu appeared fatigued, with little appetite. In time, Frank would confide to Harry about their mother's condition. Nor was Kiyo as vigorous as usual, though her penchant for making her opinions known had not wavered. "She wanted that Caucasian boy out of the house," said Frank. Harry would not hear of her demand; that night in his mother's house he shared a room with Chester.

Before leaving Hiroshima for Kobe, Harry made the rounds of neighbors, thanking them for looking after his mother, a politesse customary for an eldest son. When Masako opened her door to Harry, she made no mention of the uniform that had unnerved the Matsuuras. Masako rejoiced, crying in her singsong voice, "*Buji de yokatta.*" "I am glad that you are safe!"

With promises to return soon with food and supplies, the men boarded the jeep—missing its toolbox and spare tires, which had been stolen that night near the shrine—and stopped at the base near Kure to fill up with supplies. When the guard saluted Harry, not the driver, Frank was baffled. He still didn't understand his brother's situation. When Harry began packing cases of military rations, candy bars, and tangerines, as well as tools and tires, Frank was stunned by the abundance and Harry's apparent authority. He clutched the food so that it wouldn't roll around during the ride, just as he had when their mother collected more produce than money that final summer in Auburn.

In the wee hours of the morning they reached Kobe. A guard again saluted Harry, Chester took leave for the enlisted men's barracks, and Frank followed Harry into the plush Oriental Hotel, the officers' quarters. This was the moment that Frank realized Harry's status. Unsettled, confused, and sick to his stomach from gorging bars of chocolate, Frank wouldn't sleep at all that night.

The next day, though, Frank rallied for a wondrous breakfast of fresh eggs, long rationed. General Clarkson permitted him to eat in any mess hall he wished, including the officers' area as long as Harry was present. He also granted Frank two brand-new winter and summer American enlisted-man uniforms, cotton underwear, leather shoes, everything except an official cap. Frank's *kokuminfuku* standard khaki, issued when he was in college in Takaoka, was threadbare; its humble wooden buttons, in place of brass, had been painted black and were heavily scratched. Frank was ecstatic with his fresh, pressed wardrobe. And still ravenous. He spent the next few days dining five times a day. Slices of beef, scoops of mashed potato, dollops of mayonnaise, everything he had ever craved, all served in cafeteria-style heaping portions.

The brothers did not sit down for a heart-to-heart conversation. Not knowing what either had suffered, Frank opted for unconditional trust. As long as he could remember, he had loved and respected his older brother. "Harry was like a father and a brother," Frank said. Despite the abyss of war, as far as Frank was concerned, nothing had come between them.

Harry's journey to Kobe had surpassed his expectations. In the emotional upheaval of finding his mother, he brimmed with joy. "I didn't think it possible that I'd ever see her again," Harry told a Japanese reporter.

His elation seemed merited. As the crimson in the brilliant Miyajima maples deepened, he stifled a throb of guilt over his own decisions and let his nagging worry about their well-being slip away. Including Mary in Chicago, the Fukuhara family had survived.

29

A Troubling Letter

At the end of October, the 33rd Division began to redeploy troops to the States as part of a naval operation code-named "Magic Carpet." Two million soldiers in the Pacific would be shipped home over the course of a year. Every two weeks, ecstatic Golden Cross troops slung bulging duffels over their shoulders and boarded trains in Kobe for the port of Nagoya. General Clarkson joined the crowd to see off the men amid the hoopla of friends yelling, "See you in Chicago!" As the trains huffed down the tracks, an army band played "Auld Lang Syne," the song Harry knew by heart in two languages.

He would have liked to have been among those leaving. But he couldn't leave, not yet. His mother and Victor were ill. Frank had told Harry that when he returned from Kyūshū their mother had been wearing a turban because she had lost her hair. Her gums were bleeding and she was doubled over from diarrhea, typical symptoms of radiation sickness. The acute phase had passed, but she was fatigued and susceptible to infections. Victor, especially, struggled; his painful burns were healing slowly and his bone-deep malaise had deepened.

Any relief that the war was over had dissipated in the dogged ordeal to survive. An array of illnesses erupted, everything from the minor to the grave: chilblains, an irritating inflammation of small blood vessels, often in the extremities; beriberi from a thiamine deficiency; contagious typhus, smallpox, and tuberculosis. When a serious disease infected a patient with a suppressed immune system arising from radiation exposure, the combination could be lethal.

Everyone in Hiroshima—including patients, their caretaking families, and investigating physicians—knew that better nutrition would facilitate recovery, but improving the populace's diet was daunting. The economy was decimated and inflation skyrocketed, hindering the ability to purchase healthy ingredients, both in the legal and black markets. Masako, like most, would call this period her "*takenoko seikatsu*" (bamboo-shoot existence), peeling one layer after another of her former lifestyle, shedding items to sell or barter in exchange for food or yen. Others described their lives as an "onion existence," expressing not only the agonized sorting but also the tears shed when parting with cherished possessions.

"Everyday clothes were expensive," said Masako, "more than jewels, even diamonds." In the first year of the occupation, wholesale prices in the legal market, ostensibly subject to price controls, would rise by 539 percent. The black market, offering a greater supply and variety, was even higher. Luxury items became expendable. Masako sold the silk kimono that she would have ordinarily passed down to her own daughter. Desperate for a treat, she splurged on a bar of chocolate.

No one suffered more than Kiyo, once so prosperous. There was less demand for her *konpeitō* (star-shaped rock candy) and her other sweets, not enough rationed sugar to produce the little she needed, and no place of business. The postwar race to purchase land had not yet started; even if she had sold Meijidō's land, inflation would have consumed the profits. Her other properties were damaged, eliminating rental income. For the first time, Kiyo, the magnetic saleswoman, did not, according to her grandson Toshinao, "have expectations about the future." American servicemen were hungry for souvenirs. To make ends meet, Kiyo began selling her resplendent kimonos.

Kinu, too, could not keep up with black-market prices. She no longer mentioned holding on to Mary's kimonos. One day she met a middleman representing a school in the countryside that was willing to pay cash for a piano. Although Kinu considered hers a treasure of tender memories—from the early years when she bounced Victor and Mary on her lap in Seattle, to the blurry days raising three active boys in Auburn, to the sweet afternoons running her fingers over the keys with Chieko and Masako in Hiroshima—she needed money for rice. During the war, selling a cumbersome item would have attracted police attention. Now she could get away with it. For one sack of rice weighing a standard 132 pounds, which she and the boys would consume within a few months, she watched the stately Monarch, swathed in quilts, carried out of her house. At least she could console herself that the young students who would gather around the piano would now be permitted to sing, loudly and in unison if they liked. Most of all, her sons would not starve.

AFTER THE 33RD DIVISION WAS INACTIVATED, HARRY moved his family to Kobe, renting the upstairs of a house with several rooms, a lucky find in a city that had been heavily bombed. In Hiroshima the hospitals had been too full of grievously wounded patients to treat the relatively well such as Victor and Kinu. In Kobe they could be seen, though the doctors were at a loss as to how to treat atomic bomb patients.

That winter, the brothers posed for a formal portrait. Harry, as skinny as ever partly from malaria, sat in the middle in uniform with his younger brothers perched on either side. Frank was dressed in American khakis and his Japanese cap. His face, thanks to extra helpings of American food, had filled out. Pierce wore a tie and suit, looking every bit the gentleman scholar. The American second lieutenant flanked by his two brothers, the former Japanese privates. As was customary in Japanese portrait photography, no one smiled. Victor, who was missing from their Auburn photo albums, was too ill to attend the session.

Harry hoped his family was making gradual headway. Frank, a natural entrepreneur, started a gift shop, capitalizing on his dusted-off English to sell curios to the Occupation forces. Pierce was back on track, determined to complete college. The boys were not aware of the severe anemia that plagued both their mother and brother. "Sometimes, Victor could talk," Frank said, but as Harry acknowledged, "he was in bad shape." Harry averted his eyes—hoping the scars on Victor's back would fade and the pain diminish—desperate for an optimistic future.

No one pressured Harry to stay in Japan. He processed his paperwork to leave, holding out as late as March 1. The family believed that Harry would come back after he completed his military obligation, though no one was certain precisely when that would be. Shortly after their reunion, Harry and Frank had sat for a *Kobe Shimbun* newspaper interview, and Harry had told the reporter that, after a sojourn in the States, he would like to move to Kobe to run a trading business, making use of his college major. Caught up in the spirit of the moment, Harry was elated over having just reunited with his family. It was a spontaneous idea, though, not a concrete plan.

In truth, Harry had no desire to live in Japan. It was, after all, a ruined country to which he had never truly warmed. He had already helped his family weather the tough postwar months, and while he would leave them with as much financial security as he could, America beckoned. Harry and his family would part with affection. It was not the first time that Kinu, Pierce, and Frank had seen him off.

ON MARCH 14, 1946, HARRY ARRIVED AT Fort Lewis, Washington, setting foot on familiar ground. He was no longer an irrepressible eighteen-year-old eager to renew old acquaintances; he hadn't forgotten his frosty Auburn receptions. After staying one night in Seattle, Harry turned his back on his hometown and headed south by train for sunlit California, where he would visit the Mounts. More than half a century would elapse before he would return to Auburn's fragrant strawberry farms and drive down its pleasant brick-fronted main street again. "I never made any effort."

Harry went next to Mary's place in Chicago. She had married Fred Ito and had another daughter. Mary was happy to see her brother, as was Jeanie, almost six. It was clear to Harry, though, that his sister had a full life and he must find his own way.

In Chicago he reconvened with fellow *nisei* veterans and 33rd Division buddies, picking up odd jobs here and there. He bought and sold rice and meat, both rationed, operating in the "gray market," a murky world at best. With the help of some friends from the 33rd, he converted an empty building into a boardinghouse. But Harry was uncomfortable in the extreme cold. It triggered the malaria that had stalked him since the tropics.

By the holiday season, as the frigid wind hissed off Lake Michigan, Harry had escaped to Los Angeles—awash in brambles of bougainvillea—to stay with Amy and Kaz, his old friend from Auburn and his best friend from Hiroshima. Amy and Kaz were picking up their lives after Tulare and Gila River, but Harry had nothing to do in Los Angeles. Whenever he applied for work, the problem of his ethnicity would surface. He felt the sneers cast his way as he walked down the street. "It was real bad in California," he remembered. "When I had on my uniform it was okay." Even so, he couldn't get a job. Harry suspected that if he were Chinese, his job search would not be so dire.

Indeed, it would take more than a 1944 Supreme Court decision outlawing the internment of loyal citizens and an Allied victory for negative Japanese stereotypes to abate. Although internees had been permitted to return to the West Coast from January 1945 on, profound social change would take time. As Harry struggled to reintegrate into American culture, he wondered if his commitment and loyalty to the United States had been appreciated. "It really bothered me," he said. His friend Ben Nakamoto also experienced overt racism after his return. "One afternoon a Hakujin drove into the yard, dragging cans behind the car creating all kinds of noise and telling me to get 'the hell out of here,'" he wrote. "This is the welcome I got for putting my life on the line," he fumed decades later.

Amy was concerned at how altered Harry seemed. He had always been her wisecracking pal, quick with a plan and ready to have fun. "Harry was totally lost," she said.

SOMETHING ELSE WAS EATING AT HARRY BESIDES the pall of discrimination. Burning a hole in his pocket was a postcard from Victor asking him to return to Japan because their mother was weakening with tuberculosis and hoped to see him: "As soon as this letter arrives, please let me know whether you can come back or not." Kinu also wanted to move from Kobe to Takasu. As is often the case in Japanese, the absence of crucial information was more revealing than what was explicitly expressed. On the surface, the card was brief, straightforward, and very polite. But what lay beneath the fluid penmanship consumed him.

The postcard had been signed by Katsumi—that is, Victor—but it was not in his hand. The cursive writing looked like a woman's, surely his mother's. Most alarming was that the author had not mentioned Victor's precarious condition. All he could think of were the horrifying images of his brother's burned back—the missing and oozing flesh, the exposed tissue. Harry feared that Victor, too weak to even write a few sentences, was failing. It was the only letter that he had ever received in the name of his brother.

Japan had no diplomatic relations; the occupied nation operated under the aegis of the United States, Harry had no job, and without employment and a special visa, there was no chance he could return. But the more he thought about it, a solution presented itself. The army, Harry believed, could deliver him to his mother and brother.

BY FEBRUARY 1947, HARRY, TWENTY-SEVEN, HAD REENLISTED, less than one year after being released. The man who only a year earlier was anxious to leave Japan now felt differently. "I mostly wanted to get back." Forty-nine percent of American college students that year were veterans, exchanging pistols for pencils and books, charting a solid future in a growing middle class, tantalized by the prospect of a career and home ownership. Harry, still clinging to society's margins despite his accomplishments, realized that his dream of a parchment diploma would have to wait.

He reentered the army without a physical exam. He would not have passed. No one dwelled on his chronic malaria, which would finally peter out in 1952, the same year that the Occupation ended. No one mentioned his poor vision and thick glasses. No one registered him for basic training. The army, particularly the branch of military intelligence, needed experienced linguists in Japan as much as Harry needed a way back to the defeated nation. The enlisting officer nodded after one look at Harry's military record with its superlative comments on his character and the neatly typed listing of ribbons, medals, and honorary citations.

Just as he had been convinced that he had to enlist in 1942 to save his soul, Harry was certain of his decision in 1947 to devote his energies to his mother and brothers. "I felt I had an obligation to the family," he said, figuring on "two to three years out of my life to go back and help them out." Then, he would resume college in California.

Harry could not know then that he would not graduate from college until a decade later. He could not envision that he would not reside permanently in California, the Golden State, which had both harbored and hurt him, for four more decades. He could not predict how close he would become to Frank nor what would happen to Victor. Lingering in Los Angeles, Harry could not know how proud his mother would be of his loyalty to the land of his birth nor imagine how high he would rise in a service that he had first joined to escape internment.

IN EARLY 1947, KINU, VICTOR, PIERCE, AND Frank Fukuhara waited in Kobe for the son and brother they had lost for almost four years during the war and found in its shattered aftermath. Peace was dawning and, unlike their previous wartime correspondence, they believed their one letter, a model of Japanese restraint, would be enough for Harry to comprehend the urgency of their situation. He might lose his way but he would reach them. Not tomorrow, next week, or even next month, but, as soon as he could, Harry would come.

30

Peace and Redemption

Despite Harry's best intentions, the army had its own timetable. Before leaving for Japan, he had to take a refresher course in Japanese for military intelligence; presumably, he could have taught it. Then he attended a basic course in intelligence; this subject matter, too, was hardly new. By the time he stepped foot in Japan, it was September 1947. Victor, at age thirty-three, had passed away from the effects of his radiation burns four months earlier. Harry had missed the passing of both his father and brother.

Frank was absent for Victor's death, as well. Straining to support his family—including Aunt Kiyo—Frank was involved in a pearl farm venture and had been away on a one-week business trip. Before he left, he had stopped by Victor's room. Victor wasn't feeling well. Frank recalled that he said, "Try to come back as soon as you can."

Victor had been ailing since the atomic bomb, but his quiet end came as a shock. At least Pierce and Kinu were beside him when he died. By the time Frank raced upstairs to their rented rooms in Kobe after his trip, the funeral was past and Victor had been cremated. Frank lit incense before a Buddhist altar in the apartment. He grieved. "I couldn't believe that he was gone."

Victor, a tender soul of early promise whose life was

repeatedly interrupted by sweeping circumstances, had never found his footing in either the United States or Japan. Dispatched to Hiroshima as a young boy to preempt American discrimination, shuttled back to Washington state as a youth, drafted as an adult into the Imperial Army, where, as a *nisei*, he was vulnerable, and consumed by the Japanese war apparatus, Victor did not achieve a career commensurate with his intellectual ability and professional training. He never had his own family. His life cut short, Victor took his last breath without having spoken of the bomb.

Kiyo, enervated by mild radiation sickness, was not bouncing back emotionally. Suffering from a low white blood cell count, she fretted even when minor bug bites would not heal. She worried when she saw Kinu, in and out of the hospital, hacking with tuberculosis. Adding to Kiyo's anxiety was her depleted financial status. The grand dame of the clan had gone, Masako would comment, "from privileged to penniless." By 1948, Kiyo, after more than a decade of war and its aftermath, was vaguely sick and bone tired.

Most of all, she was disheartened. Kiyo had not found anyone to help her resuscitate Meijidō, her nearly half-century-long glorious achievement. Toshinao's family, still recovering from the death of Kimiko, showed no affinity for business. Frank, who had no desire to stay in Hiroshima, had declined Kiyo's request to take over. Mary, Kiyo's once-intended successor, lived in America, where she would stay. Victor was dead. For the first time, Kiyo did not roll up her own sleeves and forge on.

In the early hours of July 28, 1948, Kiyo went for a walk in Takasu, where she was visiting Kinu. The cicadas whirred and the sky was as black as the bottom of the Ōta River, but the air was mild and the neighborhood in repose. Kiyo headed to Takasu Station, the first stop for the train from Koi to the ferry bound for her hometown, Miyajima, where relatives would have welcomed her at any hour. She listened for the train's slow roar and watched its glow brighten from afar. Kiyo was drawn to the light. As Harry had once timed riding the rails toward Seattle, she made her next move with precision. Ever efficient, she stepped forward. The rumble grew louder and the pool of light spread. It beckoned. Kiyo waited. Seconds before the train slowed in its approach to the station, she jumped. At 3:30 a.m., the sixty-two-year-old matriarch was pronounced dead.

KIYO COULD NOT KNOW THAT THE JAPANESE economy would pick up in 1950 and register double-digit growth in the 1960s. The Hondōri district, obliterated by the bomb, would be resuscitated; modern *suzuran* lily-of-the-valley lights would rise over the block where Meijidō had stood, and shoppers would flock to the shops again. Kiyo's living standard and quality of life would have improved if she could have held on. Yet suicide, more accepted in Japan than in the West, was not uncommon during the state of postwar national malaise called *kyodatsu*, a generalized despondency arising after the relief of surrender waned. Still, in Hiroshima, where residents suffered from *kyodatsu*, radiation illness, and survivor-related anxiety and depression, suicide would account for only one-half of one percent of the deaths between 1946 and 1954. But Kiyo, a career woman since the turn of the century, had never followed society's norms. Even in death she decided her singular path, walking alone, leaving her husband a widower.

Some in the Fukuhara circle would seize a second chance. Shigeru Matsuura, the POW in New Guinea who had been Harry's nemesis in Hiroshima, had read about the atomic bomb and seen a photograph of the mushroom cloud while interned in a POW camp in Australia. Assuming that his parents could not have survived, he had no desire to return to Japan but was given no choice.

When he boarded a repatriation ship in Sydney in the spring of 1946, Matsuura had no idea that he was one of five million Japanese soldiers repatriated that year and one of more than eight thousand shipped from Australia. He was convinced that, upon reaching Japan, he would be executed for the cowardice of having been captured alive. After all, everyone knew that becoming a POW was the "most shameful thing."

Upon his arrival at a Japanese port, Matsuura was hosed down in a cloud of pungent DDT to prevent typhus; his beard was shaved, and his hair was roughly cropped to prevent lice. He felt uneasy, but nothing sinister occurred. Slinking into the crowd, he headed for chaotic Tokyo to look up some women he knew, only to discover they had married during the war. After a week he was out of options, so he reluctantly grabbed a train to Hiroshima, where, to his astonishment, he found his parents.

He expected to be met with stony looks and frigid shoulders. He was, after all, an *ikite iru eirei*, or "living war dead," persona non grata, a man who should have perished in glorious battle. Many returning soldiers were treated as pariahs, ostracized by their towns and villages. Matsuura hung his head in shame, but, to his relief, his parents did not betray anger, shock, or disappointment.

An American had prepared them, his mother blurted, a *nisei* who had once lived in their neighborhood. They had needed time to embrace the idea that their only child was alive "to some extent." If they accepted this possibility, they had to forget what they had heard about the noble demise of his unit, his tragic death, and his heroic status. They did just that, savoring the prospect of reuniting with their only child, overjoyed to have him back.

For Matsuura, who would have difficulty readjusting to civilian life after close to a decade in the military, this warm reception was life-affirming. To Harry, with whom he would reunite in 1989 for the first time in forty-five years, Matsuura was forever grateful.

Another who recovered from her trials was Chieko Matsumoto. Chieko had led a life meager with joy, heavy with obedience and obligation. So ill after the bomb that she had contemplated suicide, Chieko had rallied in spirit when her older brother returned from abroad in 1946. And, to her bafflement, she had a suitor, a kind man one year her junior, who was her brother's friend and had known her before the war. Chieko could not imagine what the ramrod-straight veteran saw in her. "He must have felt badly for me," she said. Despite the societal stigma of being an atomic bomb survivor, spurned by outsiders as if her symptoms were contagious, Chieko received an offer of marriage. Her symptoms gradually receded, her marriage proved loving, and she would give birth to two daughters, who revered her. In her immaculate sunlit home, fashioning delicate Japanese dolls with rice paper, Chieko flushed with contentment. "I worked so hard to live," she said, "I became happy."

Others, too, would defy tragedy and throw themselves into life and Japan's heady progress. Rushing toward the future, the brothers charged in various directions. Pierce had finished college in Kobe by day and interpreted for the U.S. Army at night. He would use his English and work for one of Japan's largest trading companies, so crucial to the nation's rebirth as an export-oriented economy. Harry took his brother Frank under his wing, hiring him as a civilian interpreter. Within four years, Frank would settle in the Nagoya area, work as a civilian at an American base, and open several small, successful businesses catering, at first, to Americans.

But Frank and Pierce also paid for their past. As Frank had feared, upon his draft he had lost his American citizenship; so had Pierce. No matter how many times Frank inquired at the local consulate, the answer was inconclusive. In 1954 the outcome turned bleak when Frank, who still had fervent hopes of returning to America, was issued a "Certificate of Loss of Nationality." He wondered if his fate had anything to do with his wartime assignment to an Imperial Army suicide unit.

Harry and Mary, at this point, were the only American citizens in their immediate family. Harry, who had reenlisted in the army as a first lieutenant, would rise, by 1960, to become a major and the chief of the liaison office for the army's Tokyo-based counterintelligence detachment.

Before that, he would be posted to six Japanese cities, where the local administrators, though initially skeptical, would warm to the bilingual, proactive, and unabashedly American officer. "This man is different," recalled Hideo Miwa, a Tokyo bureaucrat, of his first impression of Harry in 1947. For one thing, Harry didn't regard the Japanese as enemies. "The government couldn't deny anything that the United States' military wanted," said Kiyoshi Hashizaki, a prefectural official in Toyama, where Harry was posted in 1948, but Harry "didn't ask for anything impossible."

Harry did not tell his Japanese counterparts in the government and police forces about his own background. Yet he felt driven by a sense of mission to aid Japan in the service of the United States. His drive was underpinned by guilt. Harry worked very hard on his specific tasks. But he also engaged in the community. In those early years, among other activities, he held parties—an unheard-of luxury—for every stratum of Japanese society, from officials to war orphans; dispatched fire trucks to neighborhoods where fires broke out at a time when Japanese resources fell dangerously short; and handed packets of scarce penicillin—the medicine that, had it been available, might have saved his father—to acquaintances whose loved ones would die without it. To his Japanese peers, time and again, Harry's behavior revealed an unexpected, deeply appreciated empathy.

In midlife, Frank noted, "Harry started to like Japan." And the longer he stayed, other than occasional stateside stints for training, the more Harry realized how advancing American military and political objectives involved finding common ground. It was an "ambitious" undertaking, he said. "I felt that I was accomplishing some of what I wanted to do."

The man who had once envisioned a career in international trade had ended up specializing in intelligence, trading secrets. He would not talk in detail about his projects, but he was involved in operations that spanned the Cold War, touching upon the growth of Japanese unions, the surge of leftist protests, the developing Japanese Communist Party, and the eruption of the Korean War, among others. The 1950 conflict in Korea became an impetus to rearm Japan, leading to the formation of the Self-Defense Force. Although a conventional military was outlawed by Japan's postwar constitution, its Self-Defense Force and police agencies were large, powerful organizations with which Harry closely consulted.

IN 1960, FRANK AND PIERCE, AT LAST, received positive news. If they chose, their American citizenship could be reinstated, almost fifteen years after the war had ended. Frank, in his mid-thirties, ran the idea of settling in Washington State by Tamiko, his wife and business partner, who did not speak a word of English. She could take American citizenship, too. Tamiko, aghast, didn't hesitate to refuse in English: "No go!" Nor would her family concur; they hadn't even wanted to acknowledge that Frank was *nisei*, which, in their conservative upbringing and wartime experience, was sufficiently distressing. Resigned, Frank acknowledged how uphill his prospects would be in the States, but even though he was too old to start over, he did make an audacious choice. In the coming months, Frank formally renounced his Japanese citizenship, obtaining permanent residency in Japan through his wife. Never again, Frank vowed, would he find himself torn by two countries. Frank, like Mary and Harry, was—wherever he resided—an American.

So, too, was Pierce, who took a subtler stance, becoming a dual citizen of both nations, holding two passports. He would live, work, and raise a family in Japan, but he would never forsake his ties or downplay his affection for his country of birth.

Among the siblings, it was Mary, who had been interned but not witnessed the scourge of war, who struggled. She lived in Los Angeles with her husband, Fred, and three children, Jean, Lillian, and Clyde, who had been named after Harry's beloved employer. Mary was a devoted mother, cleaning houses to cover costs. Her children admired her energy, humor, and grit. She was opinionated, too. "If you live in America, you should speak English," Mary reminded Jean. Of course, English was Jean's dominant language since Mary only used Japanese to argue with Fred. But, as much as she tried to bury her concerns in hard work and wit, Mary's daughters could see that their mother was unhappy.

Mary had never been able to forgive her mother. For her part, Kinu did not give up on her only daughter, sending her letters in flowing script. Mary did not read her mother's correspondence. The mere appearance of these letters enraged her. Mary would tear the stationery into bits, place them in the envelope, and write "Return to Sender." "When she dies, won't you feel bad?" her daughter asked.

"Never, never!" Mary replied. She could not reconcile her sense of hurt, neglect, and abandonment. Like Victor, she had never fully regained her step after being sent to Hiroshima even though she knew that her mother had sent her to Japan thinking, as many *issei* first-generation immigrant parents did, that a traditional education would give Mary a comfortable future as the wife of an affluent man. Between seven and fourteen were the ages that children needed to be with their mother, Mary asserted. "If not, they won't come back to you," she sobbed.

In Japan, Kinu focused on alternating stays with her three boys, taking pride in their careers, and cherishing their thriving families. The stylish matron in pleated-skirt dresses and cat-eye glasses shared Japanese folk tales with Harry's children, played the piano with Frank's daughter, and even spent time in the States with Harry's family when he was temporarily transferred. She kept writing to Mary, to no avail.

By 1967, Frank was profiting from his shops, and Pierce and Harry were working around the clock in Tokyo. A few years earlier, Kinu, longing to return to Hiroshima, had moved back. In time, she sold her house in Takasu, complete with its American ceiling lamps and furniture; the new owners would care for the house as if it were a vintage museum. Kinu briefly entered a nursing home. Like calendar pages flipping in a cinema newsreel, life was passing.

In August 1967, the same month that Kinu turned seventy-five, she was diagnosed with stomach cancer, prevalent in Japan and not necessarily linked to her *hibakusha* (atomic bomb survivor) status. Harry, a lieutenant colonel, traveled from Tokyo to the Atomic Bomb Hospital to see her. "I didn't feel like going to Hiroshima," he said. Like Auburn and Gila River, Hiroshima was a place he best avoided.

Kinu—the picture bride with porcelain skin, the gaunt

Depression-era widow, the furrowed-brow mother of boys at war, and the fashionable grandmother—was dying. She had legally emigrated from Japan in the early 1900s, when immigration was an economic-release valve for the impoverished in an over-populated land. She had returned in 1933 to Hiroshima when her nation was already embroiled in China. She had survived the atomic bomb and witnessed the Japanese economy, like a phoenix, be reborn and soar. Although her only daughter remained alienated, Kinu had, for better or for worse, been guided by *"kodomo no tame ni"* (for the sake of the children).

Her boys conferred. They wanted every measure taken to prolong their mother's life. Masako, living far away on one of her husband's corporate transfers, did not know how ill Kinu was, but Chieko came running, one of the last confidantes to bow at her sickbed and hold her hand.

After a last-ditch surgery in January 1968, Kinu contracted pneumonia. Three days later, shortly after midnight, her life ebbed. She died in the city that she cherished on February 3. It was Victor's birthday.

MARY TRIED TO MAKE AMENDS BY HONORING her late mother. In 1975, she traveled to Japan for the first time since leaving in 1937. "Be sure you go to Mama's grave," Harry told her. "Of course!" she answered. Mary intended to place a bouquet of red carnations on her mother's headstone at Shōsōji Temple in Gion, where her father and Victor rested as well. She wanted to bring thirty-eight stems, one for each year that the women had been separated. When Pierce and Frank came up nine or ten short, the trio dashed frantically from florist to florist. Finally, at the last shop, they found precisely thirty-eight perfect blossoms.

By 1970, Harry had been promoted to colonel, as high as he could rise in his field. In the Military Intelligence Service arm of the army, approximately six thousand *nisei* served in World War II and approximately three dozen of them would subsequently reach full colonel. A number of these had volunteered from the concentration camps. Harry would be among the most renowned and energetic, nicknamed "Mr. MIS" by his peers. When he retired from the army in 1971, his MIS army position was especially reconfigured as a civilian one, which he would hold for twenty more years. He would, by his own account, work in Tokyo with "the major Japanese civilian and military intelligence and security agencies at the national and regional level on intelligence matters of mutual interest." Emperor Hirohito would pass away in 1989, marking the end of Japan's postwar period. It was also the sunset of Harry's career, for he would fully retire in 1990 at age seventy. During the previous four-plus decades, his Japanese colleagues had risen from the debris of war to the nation's highest offices. They walked the glistening corridors of the National Diet, held forth in Tokyo's downtown brick bureaucracies, and conferred in the spartan quarters of the Self-Defense Forces. The politicians, elite bureaucrats, and generals had never forgotten the humiliating days of the Occupation. Nor could they fail to remember the dignity that Harry had consistently accorded them. "Everything went back to the period when these guys were nothing, had nothing," said Major General Stanley Hyman, Harry's boss in the early 1980s, who became his admiring friend.

In September 1990, before he left Japan to permanently move to the States at long last, Harry was awarded the Order of the Rising Sun, third class, one of Japan's most coveted decorations, signed by the prime minister. He was one of the few chosen Americans and only three *nisei* to have been recognized at that point. It was a personal and political coup of sorts that the Japanese government was, for the first time, publicly honoring an American intelligence officer. The following day, Harry was presented with "the President's Award for Distinguished Federal Civilian Service," one of the highest awards from the American government. Side by side, the elegantly framed certificates adorned his apartment. Through decades of service, he had become a bridge between the United States and Japan.

Harry had married Terry, a fellow bilingual *nisei* who had spent the war years in Japan, in 1949. Together they had four children who would experience none of the discrimination their parents and grandparents had endured. Harry and Terry's children would, variously, graduate from college, attend an Ivy League graduate program, select the professions of their choice, and climb the ladder to executive corporate suites on the mainland and in Hawaii. Raised primarily on American army bases in Japan, they are wholly American; yet they are also at ease with Japanese ways, embodying their late immigrant grandfather's vision.

PIERCE AND FRANK WOULD LEAD PRIVATE LIVES. Few knew of Pierce's *nisei* background. To all appearances, his life embodied platinum success; he had ridden the corporate escalator of one of Japan's most prestigious companies, arranging joint ventures with fluent ease, hard work, and quiet relish. But when anyone asked where he had learned his native-accented English, he never hesitated to mention the White River Valley town of Auburn.

Frank invested wisely in real estate. At its height, during Japan's dizzying economic bubble, the value of his holdings increased a thousandfold from the original purchase price. Never able to fully adapt to strict Japanese organizations, Frank stayed self-employed and independent. He was a prosperous man. His only child, his daughter, Hitomi, became a conservatory-trained pianist. Frank may not have graduated college and his mother's treasured Monarch piano may have been bartered for a single sack of rice, but his daughter would be inspired by her grandmother's pastime and blessed with her talent.

The brothers, in particular, would look back upon their lives with serenity and satisfaction, expressed with humility. Bilingual, bicultural, and thoroughly assured, they were proud of their careers and surrounded by loving families and, for Harry, convivial, mahjong-playing friends. Their days were placid, sweet, and full, and, for Harry and Frank, often spent in Honolulu, where Frank owned a spacious apartment overlooking Waikiki. There Tamiko tinkered in her kitchen with her shining American pots and pans, preparing her brother-in-law Harry's favorite, delicately seasoned Japanese dishes.

BUT A SHADOW HAS DARKENED HARRY'S DREAMS since the mid-1990s, several years after he retired and the frenzy of his overworked days was behind him. The dreams, he takes pains to point out, are not always nightmares, though they are deeply troubling and he awakens screaming. Sometimes Harry dreams of his stultifying military drills in 1930s Hiroshima, sometimes of the possibility of being drafted into the Japanese army, and sometimes of his frightening first landing. More often than not, though, it is Victor—with his burned back that Harry could not bear to look at—who comes to Harry in his dreams. Victor, Frank's and Harry's lost, kind, and gentle brother.

Epilogue: At Ease in Honolulu

人生朝露の如し

Jinsei chōro no gotoshi

Life is as passing as the morning dew.

n August 2006, Mary Fukuhara Ito died at age eighty-nine at home in Los Angeles. Her daughter Jean, whom Mary had refused to give up for adoption in Gila River, said that Mary regarded her three children as her greatest legacy. "Thanks to her strength and constant love," Jean wrote, "we have had an easy and wonderful life."

Like her aunt Kiyo, Mary was a bold and unpredictable woman, striving to live fully within the constraints of her era. Jean described her mother as an "enigma" and "a rebellious teenager all her life." Mary adored Mickey Mouse, could touch her toes until age eighty-eight, and never lost contact with her cousin in Hiroshima who had been her best friend. Mary may have been more like her own mother, Kinu, than she was aware. No matter what befell her, her priority was always *"kodomo no tame ni"* (for the sake of the children).

Mary had registered decades earlier with the Neptune Society to be cremated, telling Jean that "since she was going to heaven, she didn't need to be buried in the ground." In every choice she made—whether adapting to Hiroshima or Auburn, interned in Arizona or escaping to Chicago, or resettling in Los Angeles—she was resolute, from turbulent beginning to quiet end.

Pierce would pass away from colon cancer in September 2008 at age eighty-six. Patient and reserved like Victor, he did not complain about his pain. A few days before Pierce died, Frank had a premonition that he should rush to see him. He dashed on a sleek bullet train from Nagoya to Yokohama, a couple of hours away. Pierce, already failing, did not recognize his brother at first, but came around by the end of the visit. Pierce died a few days later, leaving one surviving son.

Harry and Frank, still the closest of siblings, had outlived their sister and two brothers. They saw each other as frequently as possible in Honolulu, where Harry lives and Frank spends a few months a year.

Several years ago, the Military Intelligence Service veterans in Hawaii held their new-year luncheon at the Japanese Cultural Center in Honolulu. Nearby stands a crimson, steel *torii* gate, a replica of the one in Miyajima and a gift from Hiroshima to its sister city. Harry and Frank passed by the monument when they drove to the hall.

"Good morning, Colonel." "How are you, Colonel?" Harry strode to the center table in the front of a banquet hall full of largely *nisei* veterans, greeting friends along the way. The room buzzed with Japanese and English conversations taking place at once. Terry, his wife of almost sixty years; their eldest son, Mark; his wife, Mona, and daughter Sara; and Frank and Tamiko sat together. That Frank had once been the enemy and was now joining a celebration of the Military Intelligence Service, no one found strange. Among the veterans were others who had family in Japan during the war, from the killing fields of Okinawa to the carpet-bombed waste of Tokyo to the ashen shell of Hiroshima. Frank had often been by Harry's side during festivities in both the United States and Japan over the years. He, too, nodded and smiled at a number of guests.

Speeches and a multicourse meal followed. A harmonica band played Hawaiian classics. Toward the end of the four-hour event, the guests stood to sing "God Bless America." The emcee asked the group to follow with "Auld Lang Syne." Everyone burst forth in Japanese, the words slipping effortlessly from their lips. This was the version that they had learned first in their mother tongue.

The decades faded. The elderly men could have been elementary school students climbing the steps of Buddhist churches—in California, Washington State, or Hawaii—for Japanese-language classes. They could have been teenagers, with shaved heads and military-collar uniforms, standing at attention in classrooms in prefectures like Hiroshima, Yamaguchi, and Kumamoto, sent back to their parents' homeland for an education. The men's voices never wavered. Their memories—the lyrics learned by heart—never flagged. They sang for their war-riven past, their secure present, and a new and joyous year.

Tamiko, Frank's wife of fifty-five years, and whose family had not approved of her marrying a *nisei*, watched as her husband and brother-in-law sang in unison. Struck by their intricately woven bond, Tamiko whispered in Japanese, *"Kyō hajimete wakatta."* "Today is the first time I understand."

As soon as the song ended, a hearty rendition in English began. Harry and Frank—brothers who had overcome the enmity of war and the anguish of personal loss, and who now lived in glorious peace—switched languages, barely blinking, their voices blending, vigorous and clear.

POSTSCRIPT: FRANK KATSUTOSHI FUKUHARA PASSED AWAY IN Nagoya in January 2015. Harry Katsuharu Fukuhara died in Honolulu three months later, on April 18, the anniversary of their father's death in Seattle.

ACKNOWLEDGMENTS

I am indebted to many.

Harry Fukuhara championed this project from its infancy. His brother Frank matched his enthusiasm. In many ways, this book is a paean to their sterling characters and unbreakable bond. Pierce Fukuhara and Mary Ito lent their precious recollections. I wish that Mary could have known how much her vital presence graces the book. Harry and Frank's family tolerated their attention to this project with hospitality and endless good humor. If only Harry's wife, Terry—every bit his equal in intelligence, bicultural heritage, and courage—could have known that the book would be published. I thank Frank's wife, Tamiko, for many a meal and her enduring warmth. Harry and Terry's children—Mark, Brian, and Shary Fukuhara—and Frank and Tamiko's daughter, Hitomi Okaniwa, have smiled on this project. I also appreciate Pierce's son Toshihiro and Mary's daughter Lillian Lam. For guiding us around Los Angeles, staying in touch, and sharing her memories, I am grateful to Jean Furuya, who is one of the world's finest people, Mary's daughter, and Harry's niece with whom he entered Gila River.

For their help with research in Auburn, I thank Stan Flewelling and Yosh Shimoi. Stan has stayed in helpful contact through the years. For taking luminous pictures of Harry and Terry

ACKNOWLEDGMENTS

Fukuhara, I thank the photographer Gay Block. Helene Yorozu and her brother Ben Tsutsumoto hosted Harry, Frank, and me in Seattle.

I spoke or corresponded with many in the United States. Some, unfortunately, have passed away. I am grateful to Ray Aka, Harry Akune, Ken Akune, Ed Arbogast, George Ariyoshi, Judy and Nobuyuki Azebu, Jim Delaney, Bill Endicott, Horace Feldman, Bob Fukuhara, Jack Herzig, Tom Hikida, Stanley Hyman, Grant Ichikawa, Mas Ishikawa, George Kanegai, Rusty Kimura, George Koshi, Spady Koyama, Irene Fujii Mano, Bob Menke, Norio Mitsuoka, Roy M. Mitsuoka, Atsuko Moriuchi, May Mori, Amy Nagata, Ben Nakamoto, Sho Nomura, Ray Obazawa, Esther Oda, Peter Okada, Doris Sagara, David Sakai, Calvin Sasai, Yoshi Shitamae, John Stephan, Walter Tanaka, David and Jean Toyama, Gene Uratsu, Roy Uyehata, Mae Yamada, and Noby Yoshimura.

In Japan, I talked with and benefited from the insights of the following people. Atsuko Hayashi at the *Chūnichi Shimbun*, Masamichi Bando, Jeffrey J. Chur, Tetsuya Enomoto, Takashi Hirano, Toshiko and Yasushi Fukuda, Joan Fujii, Masaharu Gotoda, Kiyoshi Hashizaki, Kenji Igarashi, Hirotsugu Iikubo, Misao Inoue, Chieko Ishida, Aiko Ishihara, Asako Kakumaru, Takeyoshi Kawamura, Hiromori Kawashima, Tohru Kobayashi, Masahiro Kunimi, John Masuda, Shigeru Matsuura, Hideyoshi Miyako, Hideo Miwa, Wataru Moriya, Hisatake Narita, Goro Nishimoto, Toshinao Nishimura, Henry Ogura, Tazuko Omori, Takao Sakamaki, Chiemi Sasaki, Takehiko Sasaki, Kiyotaka Shishido, Kiyoshi Suwa, Hiroshi Tanaka, and Saburō Takano. Michiko Shimamune, the curator with whom I first worked on a loan for the United States Holocaust Memorial Museum, became my friend and ally in the search for research nuggets at the Yokohama Maritime Museum. Masaaki Shiraishi has long guided me at the Diplomatic Archives. Masako Sasaki could not be more crucial to this book. Her openness revealed exciting layers of the story. Eiko and Kenji Maekawa opened their home in Hiroshima on multiple occasions.

There are four people integral to this book's journey. This book would never have been written without my friend and mentor, Ron Powers. When there was every reason to give up and move on, Ron, a writer among writers, urged me to persevere. His brilliant works, generous friendship, and radical amazement inspire me daily. Ron's wife, Honoree Fleming, a biochemist and dean, has lent her incisive wisdom and support. Pam Allyn, the great global literacy advocate and my friend since our freshman year at Amherst College, listened to my publishing saga and, without hesitation, put me in touch with her literary agent, Lisa DiMona. Lisa—indomitable, dedicated, and wise—embraced this project with passion and vastly improved it. Not a day goes by without my recognizing how lucky I am to have Lisa's sunshine illuminating my corner. At Writers House, Lisa's assistants Jean Garnett and Nora Long scrutinized the manuscript and provided advice.

My tremendous good fortune extends to HarperCollins, where the incomparable Gail Winston is the image of a consummate editor. Gail's efficient approach, sharp eyes, and editing finesse astonish. She finds the heart of the book and works magic. I thank Emily Cunningham and her successor Sofia Ergas Groopman for their terrific assistance, Tom Pitoniak for his meticulous copyedit, Michael Correy for the elegant design, Fritz Metsch for carrying through the process, Jarrod Taylor for the stunning cover, and Christine Choe for diligent marketing. The eminent translator and interpreter Beth Cary kindly reviewed the glossary. On short notice, Kiyoko Newsham checked the Japanese endnotes and bibliographical entries. Dr. James C.

McNaughton, chief of the Histories Division at the U.S. Army Center of Military History and the author of the definitive *Nisei Linguists*, took time from his busy schedule to read the manuscript. Any errors are my own, and I apologize in advance.

Dr. Karen L. Thornber at Harvard graciously permitted the use of an excerpt of the poem "Flames" from her translation of *Poems of the Atomic Bomb* by Sankichi Tōge. Dr. Thornber's translation may be found at: https://ceas.uchicago.edu/sites/ceas.uchicago.edu/files/uploads/Sibley/Genbaku%20shishu.pdf.

Ray Moore, my advisor from Amherst, treated me as a scholar when I was a naïve student. John Curtis Perry, my advisor at the Fletcher School of Law and Diplomacy, encouraged me to write a trade book. Sol Gittleman, the legendary Tufts University professor, has followed this book with enthusiasm. Sandra Kaiser, at the United States Holocaust Memorial Museum, has patiently accommodated my schedule.

In Honolulu, my close friends saw me through many stages. Debbie Funakawa cried when the first publisher showed interest and screamed with joy when HarperCollins committed. Outside of my parents, Debbie is hands down my biggest booster. Jan Oppie is the essence of kindness. Pam Tsuzaki is smart, indefatigable, and funny. We became friends over time; she is Harry's youngest daughter. We rarely discussed the story, and she never asked to read the manuscript or tried to influence the narrative. Debbie, Jan, and Pam rescued me from my enforced solitude of daily writing and showed me through example how to live with delight, integrity, and deep engagement.

I am buoyed by the friendship of Amy Forman, Atsushi Funakawa, Colette Higgins, Peter Hoffenberg, Winnie Inui, Julia Kim, Monica LaBriola, Christine Donnelly Lynch, Laura Ozak, Kirk Patterson, Cammie Russell, Megumi Sugasawa, Kat and Kent Uyemura, and Josh and Ann Woodfork. I tip my hat to the ebullient Honolulu Pen Women, particularly Shan Correa, Carol Egan, Sabra Feldstein, Victoria Gail-White, Ria Keltz-Remenar, Lavonne Leong, Susan Killeen, Jan McGrath, Nancy Moss, Nancy Mower, Vera Stone, and Sandra Wagner-Wright. I am forever grateful for the abiding love of Jeanine and Joseph Maglione, Ellen and Louis Marino, and Pat and Tom Sullivan. For their unwavering belief that I would complete this book and for their friendship since Amherst, I bow to Rick Hollander, Donna De Bernardo Marino, and Barbara Soojian.

My aunt, Judy Leeder, deserves enormous thanks. Putting aside painful health issues, she provided extraordinary support, empathy, and laughter during the most agonizing period of my life, which coincided with writing this book. Her daughter and my cousin Gayle Leeder Dublin has been right beside her. My cousins Eliot Young, and Sue and Herb Triedman have been attentive and caring. My siblings, Beth and Chip Davis, and Philip and Kim Rotner, are the best in the world, without exaggeration. I don't know how I would have survived this time without them. Even from afar, they have always been within a moment's reach.

I am profoundly grateful to my children, Masa and Anna, who have brightened my days, put up with this book for years, and cheered me on. On countless mornings, they have found me immersed in papers in front of my computer. Anna sweetly endured a summer when I was distracted, and never complained while waiting for me to finish my quota of pages. I called Masa at school when the contract was decided. The joy in his voice was one of life's sublime moments.

GLOSSARY

Note: In Japanese the singular and plural forms of nouns are the same.

aburakasu	oil-cake residue or clots from cooking oil
aizome	indigo-dyed
akagami	"red paper," denoting a draft notice
Amerika-gaeri	returnees to Japan from America, including the U.S.-born children of Japanese immigrants to the States
anrakushi	euthanasia
aozora	"blue skies," euphemism for black market
azuki	red beans
bakayarō	fool
banzai	"ten thousand years," often appearing as a patriotic cheer or battle cry
batakusai	stinking of butter
bentō	boxed lunch
Buji de yokatta	I am glad that you are safe

bushidō	the way of the warrior, a philosophy espousing martial values
buyō	classical dance
castella	sponge cake introduced to Japan by Portuguese merchants
chōchin	paper lanterns
daifuku mochi	good-luck rice cakes, often filled with bean paste jam
dōjō	studio, training center
Dōzo yoroshiku	Please treat us kindly, request
fukumimi	ears of happiness
fundoshi	loincloths
furisode	long-sleeved kimono
furoshiki	wrapping cloth
fusuma	partition door
gaman	self-restraint and perseverance
ganbariya	hard worker
genbakushō	radiation sickness
genkan	entry
genmaicha	green tea mixed with brown rice
genshibakudan	atomic bomb
geta	Japanese wooden clogs
gētoru	puttees
Gochisōsama deshita	Thank you for the feast, expression at the end of a meal
goshin'ei	portraits of the emperor and empress
gyōgi minarai	bridal training

gyokusai	"shattered jewels," euphemism glorifying suicidal charges
hachimaki	headband
hakama	traditional, pleated culotte-like trousers
hakujin	white person or people
hangō	rice pot for soldiers
hatachi baba	old maid at twenty, colloquial expression
hetoheto	exhausted
hibakusha	atomic bomb survivor
hinomaru bentō	a boxed lunch of white rice with one red pickled plum in the center
hinomaru	Rising Sun flag
hōanden	small shrine housing the imperial portraits and the Imperial Rescript on Education
hohei	foot soldier
ichioku tokkōtai	100 million Special Attack Forces, nationwide suicide units
ichioku	100 million
Icchū	abbreviation for Hiroshima First Middle School
ikite iru eirei	living-war dead
ikebana	flower arrangement
inu	"dog," pejorative for informer in the concentration camps
Irasshaimase	Welcome, greeting

issei	first-generation immigrants
issen gorin	"one sen, five rin," coins worth less than a penny, the cost of mailing a draft notice, slang for how expendable foot soldiers were
Itadakimasu	I humbly accept, said before eating, a form of nonsecular grace
jikatabi	rubber-soled, split-toed shoes
kagami mochi	traditional New Year decoration consisting of two rice cakes topped with a tangerine
kaki yōkan	persimmon-flavored bean jelly
kamikaze	"divine wind" suicide bombers
kanai	wife
kanji	Chinese characters, one of the major Japanese alphabets
kempeitai	military police
kendō	Japanese martial art of swordsmanship
kenjinkai	prefectural association
ketsu	kanji character meaning "decisive"
kibei	*nisei* educated in Japan who had returned to the United States
Kichiku Bei-Ei	devilish Americans and British
kimono(s)	traditional dress
kinokogumo	mushroom cloud
kinrō hōshi	compulsory labor
kiritsu, rei, chakuseki	stand, bow, sit down: instructions at school

kōden	condolence money
kodomo no tame ni	for the sake of the children
kokuminfuku	national uniform
konpeitō	star-shaped rock candy
kotatsu	low table, with heating source covered with a quilt; the tabletop is placed over the quilt for warmth
koto	long zither
kuchi-jamisen	humming the notes of the *shamisen*
kumade	decorative bamboo rakes considered good-luck charms
kyodatsu	despair
makizushi	rolled sushi
manjū	cakes filled with bean-paste jam
Masaka	No Way! Oh No! An exclamation of surprise
miso	soybean paste
mizu	water
mochi	rice cakes
mochigome	sticky sweet rice
modan	modern
moga	modern girl
monpe	bloomer-like pants
montsuki	formal-crested kimono
mushin	"no mind," state of grace in martial arts enabling acute mindfulness
namaikiya	spoiled brat

namajikka	lukewarm
natsukashii	nostalgic
nisei	second-generation Japanese Americans, children of *issei* immigrants
noren	shop curtain
obon	annual Buddhist festival honoring ancestors
Ohayō gozaimasu	Good morning.
Ojama shimasu	Sorry to interrupt you.
okāsan	mother
omusubi	rice balls
onīsan	older brother, honorific
otōsan	father
Oyasuminasai	Good night
pika	bright flash
rakkyō	pickled shallots
ramune	carbonated lemonade
sake	rice wine
sakura	cherry blossoms
seiza	position in which one sits and folds legs underneath
sekkyō	sermons, implemented as hazing
senbei	rice crackers
Senjinkun	Field Service Code
senninbari	thousand-stitch stomach-warmer, battle amulet

senpai	a superior
sensei	teacher
Setsubun	custom for the day before the beginning of spring
shamisen	Japanese lute
Shikata ga nai	It cannot be helped
Shintō	Japan's indigenous religion
shirokuro	"white and black," meaning black-and-white
shōchikubai	New Year pine-bamboo-plum-blossom flower arrangement that embodies discipline and endurance
shōji	latticed paper window screens
soba	buckwheat noodles
sōsho	cursive
sumi	ink
suzuran	lily-of-the-valley
Tadaima	I'm home, announcement upon returning home
taiko	drum
takenoko seikatsu	bamboo-shoot existence
takeyari	bamboo spear
tatami	straw mat
tategata sankai	military maneuver to split down the middle and fan out
tatemae seikatsu	a life of appearances
teikibin	regular flights

tenugui	towel
tokkōtai	Special Attack Forces
tonarigumi	neighbor association
torii	gate at the entrance to a Shintō shrine
torihada	"chicken skin" or goose bumps
toshikoshi	"crossing the year"
tsuyu	plum rain, expression for the rainy season
uchikake	wedding kimono
umeboshi	pickled plum
undōkai	track meet
unmei	fate
wakame	seaweed
yami	black market
yoki tsuma, tsuyoi haha	good wife and wise mother
zōri	sandals
zuruzuru	peeling

NOTES

PROLOGUE: SHOCKWAVE

1 "Japan has attacked Pearl Harbor": Conversation is in Harry Katsuharu Fukuhara, interview by Eric Saul and assistance by Lonnie Ding, January 7, 1986, transcript, National Japanese American Historical Society Oral History Project, San Francisco, 23; Harry Fukuhara, interview, transcript, MIS Association, Norcal, Civil Liberties Public Education Fund Program (CLPEFP), San Francisco, 14.

2 "wounded": Fukuhara, interview, CLPEFP.

3 "our victorious assault on Hawaii": Frank Fukuhara, interview, Tokyo, April 17, 2001.

4 "Defend and attack for our country": Radio broadcast information is from Tomi Kaizawa Knaefler, *Our House Divided: Seven Japanese American Families in World War II* (Honolulu: University of Hawaii Press, 1991).

4 "a declaration of war": https://archive.org/details/PearlHarborAttack Announcement.

4 "This is going to bring up": Harry Fukuhara, interview, Tokyo, January 10, 1999; Harry Katsuharu Fukuhara, interview by Eric Saul, 23.

5 Kinu opened her local *Chūgoku Shimbun*: *Chūgoku Shimbun*, December 9, 1941.

1: AT HOME IN AUBURN

11 By 1920 steam whistles: Josephine Emmons Vine, *Auburn: A Look Down Main Street* (Auburn, WA: City of Auburn, 1990), 57.

13 two stories down: Harry Fukuhara, interview, Tokyo, October 20, 2005.

14 in a glass case: Harry, Pierce, and Frank Fukuhara, interview, Tokyo, October 13, 1998; Harry Fukuhara, interview, Tokyo, January 9, 1999.

14 By the early 1920s, more than twenty-five thousand legal immigrants from Hiroshima: Zaibei Hiroshima Kenjin Shi (Los Angeles: Zaibei Hiroshima Kenjinshi Hakkōjo, 1929), 70-71.

17 "Many firms have general regulations": Eliot Grinnell Mears, *Resident*

Orientals on the Pacific Coast (Chicago: University of Chicago Press, 1928), 199–200.

17 "It seems a tragedy": Ibid.

17 He had attained white-collar status and attended some college: *Zaibei Nihonjin Jinmei Jiten* (San Francisco: Nichibei Shimbunsha, 1922), 147.

17 In 1929, almost four thousand: Rinjirō Sodei and John Junkerman, *Were We the Enemy? American Survivors of Hiroshima* (Boulder, CO: Westview Press, 1998), 16.

19 "The goal to be attained": Japanese Immigration Hearings Before the House Committee on Immigration and Naturalization, July 12–August 3, 1920, H.R. 66th Congress, 2nd Session, Points 1–4, quoted in Yamato Ichihashi, *Japanese in the United States* (Palo Alto: Stanford University Press, 1932), 329.

19 "We must talk and walk": Monica Sone, *Nisei Daughter* (Seattle: University of Washington Press, 1979), 24.

19 "With no amount of persuasion": Harry Fukuhara, interview, Tokyo, January 10, 1999. Other comments are from the same interview.

21 "When will your father become the mayor of Auburn?": Conversation between hometown friends and Harry Fukuhara, Auburn, WA, August 2, 2002.

21 "I wanted to get a different name": Harry Fukuhara, interview by Eric Saul, 13, 53.

22 "There will be many surprises": "2000 Lanterns Will Glow In Night Parade," *Auburn Globe-Republican*, July 25, 1929.

22 The festivities began with fireworks: Stan Flewelling, *Shirakawa: Stories from a Pacific Northwest Japanese American Community* (Auburn, WA: White River Valley Museum, 2002), 105-106.

2: HIROSHIMA SOJOURN

24 Frank was taking his first: Frank Fukuhara, telephone interview, September 2003.

24 After two weeks: *Port of Yokohama* (Yokohama: Yokohama Maritime Museum, 2004), in Japanese, chart 6.

26 They were his brother and sister: Frank Fukuhara, 1999, notebook prepared for author, 3.

26 "My parents fooled me": Mary Ito, interview, Torrance, March 21, 2003.

27 Kiyo possessed a single obsession: *Hiroshima Hondōri Shōtengai no Ayumi* (Hiroshima: Hiroshima Hondōri Shōtengai Shinkō Kumiai, 2000), 24; Toshinao Nishimura, interview, Tokyo, March 24, 2001.

27 Kiyo hung those panels: *Hiroshima Hondōri Shōtengai no Ayumi*, 50; Frank Fukuhara and Takehiko Sasaki, interviews, Hiroshima, April 10, 1999.

27 Every morning, Kiyo pulled her hair into a tidy chignon: Masako Sasaki, interview, Hiroshima, March 27, 2007. Masako supplied much of

this information, along with her relative whose family owned a rival shop.

28 largest and brightest venue in western Japan: *Hiroshima Hondōri Shōtengai no Ayumi*, 33.

29 her marriage ended: *Koseki Tohon* (Family Register), Sukesaburō Sasaki, Miyajima-chō, Hiroshima Prefecture. Kiyo married her first husband in 1903, when she was seventeen.

29 Victor was "very kind": Takehiko Sasaki, interview, April 10, 1999.

29 "People would pick on him": Mary Ito, interview, March 21, 2003; Takehiko Sasaki, interview.

30 a brash "Yankee" and a bully: Takehiko Sasaki, interview, April 10, 1999.

30 Etiquette was no longer as formal and rigid: Ben-Ami Shillony, *Politics and Culture in Wartime Japan* (New York: Oxford University Press, 1981), 148.

31 Tokichi had lost an eye: Frank Fukuhara, telephone interview, May 22, 2006.

31 "Let's wake up": Takehiko Sasaki, interview; Masako Sasaki, interview.

31 When Tokichi did leave the premises: Toshinao Nishimura, interview.

31 As the mistress of Meijidō: Masako Sasaki, interview, March 27, 2007.

32 "No, I didn't give you my girl": Mary Ito, interview, March 21, 2003.

33 "I bought my graduation diploma by money": Ibid.

33 Legend had it: Harry Fukuhara, interview, Tokyo, April 22, 2006.

3: GROWING PAINS

36 The boys had not removed their shoes: Mary Ito, interviews, Torrance, March 21, 2003, and March 24, 2003.

36 "It seemed like a long time": Harry Fukuhara, interview, Tokyo, October 20, 2005.

37 "I was a spoiled brat": Mary Ito, interviews, Torrance, March 21, 2003, and March 24, 2003.

37 "I was hungry": Ibid.

37 "born mouth first": Ibid.

37 six custom light fixtures: Information on ornamental lights is from Stan Flewelling, *Shirakawa: Stories from a Pacific Northwest Japanese American Community* (Auburn, WA: White River Valley Museum), 107-108.

37 "a tribute to the friendship": "Dedication Is Formal Affair," *Auburn Globe-Republican*, November 28, 1929, 1, 5.

38 "gratitude for what Auburn schools": Ibid.

38 "to be ready to serve": Ibid.

38 Kinu served him first: Mary Ito, interview, Torrance, March 24, 2003.

39 "Everything I say, I get": Frank Fukuhara, interview, Honolulu, February 7, 2008.

39 to carry him downstairs: Mary Ito interviews.

39 Victor, Mary, and Pierce were all second-grade students: Pierce Fuku-hara, interview, Tokyo, March 9, 2001.

40 "The f in food": Kazuo Ito, *Issei: A History of Japanese Immigrants in North America,* trans. Shinichiro Nakamura and Jean S. Gerard (Se-attle: Executive Committee for Publication, c/o Japanese Community Service, 1973), 627.

40 "rebellious tomboy": This and the quotations from Mary that follow are from Mary Ito interviews.

43 All across the West Coast and Hawaii: Mei Nakano, *Japanese American Women: Three Generations 1890–1990* (Sebastopol, CA: Mina Press, 1990), 122.

43 On New Year's Eve: Buckwheat noodles eaten on New Year's Eve are called "*toshikoshi soba,*" meaning "crossing the year" noodles, which are believed to carry luck into the new year.

4: THE GREAT DEPRESSION

45 They cultivated a cornucopia: David A. Takami, *Divided Destiny: A History of Japanese Americans in Seattle* (Seattle: University of Wash-ington Press and Wing Luke Asian Museum, 1998), 20.

46 he would drive Japanese from the county: David A. Neiwert, *Straw-berry Days: How Internment Destroyed a Japanese American Community* (New York: Palgrave Macmillan, 2005), 64–65; Stan Flewelling, *Shirakawa: Stories from a Pacific Northwest Japanese American Community* (Auburn, WA: White River Valley Museum, 2002), 76.

46 When *issei* first appeared in the White River Valley: Flewelling, *Shi-rakawa,* 24–25.

46 By 1925: John Adrian Rademaker, "The Ecological Position of the Jap-anese Farmers in the State of Washington" (Ph.D. diss., University of Washington, 1939), 35–36, quoted in Neiwert, *Strawberry Days.*

46 "swallowing their tears": Ito, *Issei:* 65–66.

46 *A History of Japanese Immigrants in North America,* trans. Shinichiro Nakamura and Jean S. Gerard (Seattle: Executive Committee for Pub-lication, c/o Japanese Community Service, 1973), 165.

46 "I used to make all my pastoral calls": Kitagawa quotation in Flewel-ling, *Shirakawa,* 215.

47 Unable to afford electricity: Tom Hikida, telephone interview, Decem-ber 1, 2003.

47 truck their produce: Takami, *Divided Destiny,* 20.

47 more than 4.5 million Americans: Timothy Egan, *The Worst Hard Time: The Untold Story of Those Who Survived the Great American Dust Bowl* (New York: Houghton Mifflin, 2006), 95.

47 Katsuji became the first Japanese trustee: Chamber of Commerce officers, Auburn 1930, in University of Washington Libraries Digital Collections.

48 "She went out of her way": Harry Fukuhara, interview, Tokyo, January 10, 1999.

48 "Their wallet folds had money": Ray Obazawa, telephone interview, January 27, 2004.

49 No more than 10 percent: Eliot Grinnell Mears, *Resident Orientals on the Pacific Coast* (Chicago: University of Chicago Press, 1928), 258–59, quoted in Yamato Ichihashi, *Japanese in the United States* (Palo Alto, CA: Stanford University Press, 1932), 168.

50 "potato blanket": Harry Fukuhara, interviews, January 10, 1999, and April 17, 2001. "Potato blanket" lunches were mashed potatoes with gravy.

50 "the 'ching' of the cash registers": Ito, *Issei*, 712–14, 851, 854.

50 "one by one": Ibid.

51 burlap sacks of produce: Harry Fukuhara, interview, Seattle, August 4, 2002.

51 He would leave the house: Information on riding the blinds from MIS Norcal Association, *Prejudice & Patriotism: Americans of Japanese Ancestry in the Military Intelligence Service of WWII*, video (San Francisco: National Japanese American Historical Society, ca. 2000); Flewelling, *Shirakawa*, 113; Harry Fukuhara, interviews, Tokyo, January 10, 1999; April 26, 2001; October 17, 2005.

51 Sometimes he sought out the men: Harry Fukuhara, interview, transcript, MIS Association, Norcal, Civil Liberties Public Education Fund Program (CLPEFP), San Francisco, 5; Harry Fukuhara, interview, January 10, 1999.

52 On his application for his first passport: list of passports issued, File 3.8.5.8 Tabi 21, Diplomatic Archives, Ministry of Foreign Affairs, Tokyo.

52 Yet in Auburn he had been selected: Flewelling, *Shirakawa*, 107.

53 massive anti-American riots: *Tokyo Asahi Shimbun*, July 1, 1924, 2.

53 On November 8: Frank Fukuhara, notes, April 6, 2002, interview, Seattle, August 2, 2002; letter to author, October 3, 2003.

5: IVORY BONES AND LEADEN ASHES

54 "He was never in robust health": Harry Fukuhara, interview, January 10, 1999.

54 Three days before the family's anticipated New Year's Eve celebration: information on Katsuji's treatment in Auburn and Seattle from probate court records of Superior Court of the State of Washington, Kings County.

56 "Stay in the hospital": Harry Fukuhara, interview, October 16, 2005.

56 "I just took off": Ibid.

57 "If my mother had scolded me": Ibid.

57 Priest Aoki: The funeral information is from Flewelling, *Shirakawa*, 107.

57 "A wide circle alike": "Death Calls H. K. Fukuhara," *Auburn Globe-Republican*, April 14, 1933, 4.

58 His savings account held: Probate court records.

59 "a family of moderate means": Ibid.

60 "That's not right": Harry Fukuhara, interview, Honolulu, February 7, 2008.

60 Harry was delighted: Harry Fukuhara, interview, Tokyo, July 3, 2006.

61 Kinu spread a blanket: Harry Fukuhara, interview, January 10, 1999.

61 "I didn't miss my father much": Frank Fukuhara, interview, Honolulu, January 21, 2009.

62 On the few occasions: Harry Fukuhara, interview, January 10, 1999.

62 "When you're thirteen years old": Harry Fukuhara, interview, Honolulu, February 7, 2008.

62 Japanese women may have been wearing bolder kimonos: *The Fabric of Life: Five Exhibitions From the Textile Collection*, July–October 2008, brochure and exhibition. In particular, Gallery 20, "Bright and Daring: Japanese Kimono in the Taisho Mode," July 23–October 5, 2008, at the Honolulu Museum of Art.

63 "The only problem": Harry Fukuhara, interview, January 10, 1999.

63 McLean devalued the initial estate estimate: Probate court records.

63 "She couldn't leave without me": Harry Fukuhara, interview, Tokyo, April 17, 2001.

63 "If I didn't like it, I could go back": Ibid.

63 On the afternoon: "N.Y.K. Seattle-Vancouver-Orient Service: Sailing Schedule for Nov. 1932–December 1933," NYK Maritime Museum, Yokohama, Japan.

63 Kinu had purchased: "Nippon Yūsen Taiheiyō Kōro Unchinhyō," NYK Maritime Museum, Yokohama, Japan.

6: LAND OF THE RISING SUN

67 First-class passengers: "Yōjō No Interia." NYK Maritime Museum, Yokohama, Japan, March 3–September 2, 2007.

68 Charlie Chaplin: Sanae Sato, *Nihon no Kyakusen to Sono Jidai* (Tokyo: Jiji Tsūshinsha, 1993), 46.

68 The cost of the trip: *Yokohama-shi Shitei Bunkazai,* "Hikawa Maru Chōsa Hōkokusho" (Yokohama: Kyōiku Iinkai, 2003), 85.

68 At the time: Ibid.

68 The more Harry explored: Ito, *Issei,* 13.

68 "Just kids": Harry Fukuhara, interview, Tokyo, December 7, 2004.

68 Gale-force winds: *Yokohama Bōeki Shimpo,* November 29, 1933, 5, 7.

69 The sun's spreading rays: Frank Fukuhara, telephone interview, May 28, 2007.

70 One of Kinu's brothers: Harry Fukuhara, interview, transcript, MIS Association, Norcal, Civil Liberties Public Education Fund Program (CLPEFP), San Francisco.

70 *"Kutsu o nuginasai"*: Harry Fukuhara, interview, Tokyo, July 3, 2006.

70 This house did not have a telephone: Masako Sasaki, interview, Hiroshima, March 27, 2007.

71 He hadn't liked Japan: Harry Fukuhara, interview, Tokyo, April 24, 2001.

71 Little more than two weeks: Nobufusa Bitow, Auburn, to Harry Fukuhara, Hiroshima, December 16, 1933.

71 "The Emperor and prince system": Frank Fukuhara, interview, April 17, 2001.

72 "Don't you long for": Hiroshi Sonobe, Tokyo, to Harry Fukuhara, late 1937 or early 1938.

72 "She was scared": Frank Fukuhara, interview, April 17, 2001; notes, April 2005.

73 "I couldn't speak": Harry Fukuhara, interview, Honolulu, September 29, 2008.

73 "What did you learn today?": Harry Fukuhara interview with Frank and Pierce, Tokyo, October 13, 1998; Harry Fukuhara, interview, December 6, 1998.

73 "I was all mixed up": Mary Ito, interview, Torrance, March 21, 2003.

74 "When you went into that house:" Chieko Ishida, interview, Fukuoka, April 9, 1999.

75 Despite his tutoring: Harry Fukuhara, interview, September 29, 2008.

75 Scarlet goldfish swam: Shigeru Matsuura, interview, Hiroshima, April 10, 1999.

76 The boys eyed one another: Shigeru Matsuura, interview, Hiroshima, November 16, 2002. Harry Fukuhara, interview, Honolulu, January 27, 2008. Note that Harry and Frank would forever call Shigeru Matsuura by his last name, as is the custom in Japan, whether enemies or friends.

76 There were a few more furious exchanges: Ibid.

76 Or did Matsuura simply resent: Harry Fukuhara, interview, Tokyo, April 10, 1999.

76 "For the first year in Japan": Harry Fukuhara, interview, Tokyo, October 20, 2005.

76 Until eight or nine at night: Harry Fukuhara, diary, July 15, 1936; Roy Mitsuoka, "Answers to Questions for the Fukuhara Project," December 20, 2001; Roy Mitsuoka to author, December 24, 2003.

77 In her breezy update: Ruth Woods to Harry Fukuhara, September 21, 1935.

77 Meanwhile, Victor: Frank Fukuhara, interview, Honolulu, January 21, 2009.

77 Just when Victor was finally regaining his stride: Katsumi Fukuhara, military record, Hiroshima Prefecture.

77 "A native American citizen": Consul Kenneth C. Krentz, Kobe, to Harry Fukuhara, November 29, 1935.

78 "Unique" among nations: Ulrich Straus, *The Anguish of Surrender: Japanese POWs of World War II* (Seattle: University of Washington Press, 2003), 35.

78 Among other skills: Harry Fukuhara, interview, Tokyo, April 17, 2001; April 26, 2001; Johnny Masuda, interview, Tokyo, April 3, 2001. Also see Straus, *The Anguish of Surrender*, 35, and MIS Norcal Associa-

tion, *Prejudice & Patriotism: Americans of Japanese Ancestry in the Military Intelligence Service of WWII* (San Francisco: National Japanese American Historical Society), video.

78 scooping up the errant shells with a handy net: Harry Fukuhara, interview, Honolulu, March 16, 2009.

78 "number one enemy": Harry Fukuhara, interview, Tokyo, April 19, 2006.

78 "kind of awkward": Harry Fukuhara, interview, March 16, 2009.

79 "Got pretty tired": Harry Fukuhara, Diary, June 2, 1936.

79 "and then marched around": Ibid.

79 "part of the curriculum": Harry Fukuhara, interview, Honolulu, February 7, 2008.

79 When Frank wound the phonograph: Harry Fukuhara, interview, Tokyo, April 20, 2001.

80 "*Bakayarō*": Ibid. Harry Katsuharu Fukuhara, interview by Eric Saul and assistance by Lonnie Ding, January 7, 1986, transcript, National Japanese American Historical Society Oral History Project, San Francisco, 11.

80 "To the Japanese": Harry Fukuhara, interview, transcript, MIS Association, Norcal, Civil Liberties Public Education Fund Program (CLPEFP), San Francisco, 9.

80 "Mary and my mother argued": Harry Fukuhara, interview, April 24, 2001; Frank Fukuhara, interview, Fukuoka, April 9, 1999.

80 But Mary was so tightly wrought: Mary Ito, interview, Torrance, March 24, 2003.

81 Instead of changing into a demure kimono: Masako Sasaki, interview, March 27, 2007.

81 Kinu promptly purchased: Harry Fukuhara, diary, March 28, 1936.

82 "I didn't want to stand for it": Mary Ito, interview, March 24, 2003.

82 "You ran away?": Ibid.

82 "I just couldn't take it anymore": Ibid.

83 "Oh, this is Hisae": Ibid.; Tazuko Omori, telephone interview, April 13, 2001.

83 But when she looked at her mother: Mary Ito, interview, March 24, 2003.

83 "Auntie still had a dream": Masako Sasaki, interview.

84 "Yes, I realize how difficult": Ellen Rutherford, Auburn, to Harry Fukuhara, March 21, 1937.

84 "You are torn between the wishes": Ellen Rutherford, Auburn, to Harry Fukuhara, May 2, 1937.

85 Kinu did worry: Harry Fukuhara, interview, April 20, 2001.

85 Harry and Matsuura: Shigeru Matsuura, interview, November 16, 2002.

86 "It was just a short while": Ruth Yamada, Hiroshima, to Harry Fukuhara, October 8, 1937.

86 "Oh yes, I have heard": Mary Okino, Gresham, Oregon, to Harry Fukuhara, October 27, 1937.

86 "Everybody over here": Kaz Kojo, Auburn, to Harry Fukuhara, February 19, 1938.

87 one-third of the cost of the house: Harry Fukuhara, interview, Tokyo, November 2, 1998; Frank Fukuhara, interview, Honolulu, January 29, 2008.

87 He wrote friends: W. A. McLean, Tacoma, WA, to Harry Fukuhara, Hiroshima, February 9, 1938.

87 And, on March 3, 1938: Sanyō Commercial School Graduation Certificate.

88 *Tatemae seikatsu* (a life of appearances): Masako Sasaki, interview.

88 "They hit him": Harry Fukuhara, interview, January 10, 1999.

89 both a father and brother: Frank Fukuhara, telephone interview, February 9, 2009.

7: A SORROWFUL HOMECOMING

90 This story reminded Harry: list of passports issued, File 3.8.5.8 Tabi 69, Diplomatic Records Office, Tokyo.

91 rickshaw rides and sumo tournaments: Frank Fukuhara, Komaki City, to author, Tokyo, December 1, 2001; Frank Fukuhara, interview, Honolulu, February 7, 2008.

91 When the tofu vendor: Frank Fukuhara, interview, November 20, 2001.

92 "never done that kind of work": Mary Ito, interview, Torrance, March 21, 2003.

92 Her *ikebana* skills: Ibid.

92 "He was my watchdog": Ibid.

93 A domestic was one of the few occupations: "Pride and Practicality, Japanese Immigrant Clothing in Hawaii," exhibition, Japanese Cultural Center of Hawaii, September 2008.

93 "Your old pal": Helen Hall, Auburn, to Harry Fukuhara, Hiroshima, December 8, 1934, and June 5, 1935.

93 "OH Harry": Mrs. Biddle, Auburn, to Harry Fukuhara, Hiroshima, undated.

94 He had missed: *The Invader 1937*, yearbook (Auburn, WA: Auburn High School, 1937).

94 "They were really nice girls": Amy Nagata, interview, Los Angeles, March 21, 2003.

95 "Step aside": Walt Tanaka, interview, San Jose, May 11, 1999.

95 "Do you think I'm dirty?": Ibid.

97 "drift": Harry Fukuhara, "Autobiography Highlights" (photocopied notes, undated, circa December 5, 1992).

99 Walt Disney, Hollywood, to Harry Fukuhara, Christmas card, 1938.

99 "I would just go from job to job": Harry Fukuhara, interview, Los Angeles, March 22, 2003.

100 "Don't end up like me": Harry Fukuhara, interview, Tokyo, January 17, 1999.

100 "tough guy": Bob Fukuhara, interview, Los Angeles, March 22, 2003.

100 The Mitchums: Harry Fukuhara, interview, January 19, 1999.

100 He enrolled part-time: Harry Katsuharu Fukuhara, military records, National Personnel Records Center, St. Louis, MO.

100 Hitchhiking to school: Harry Fukuhara, interview, Tokyo, October 20, 2005.

8: HAZING IN HIROSHIMA

102 Hiroshima First Middle School: Middle school was six years, comprising junior high school and high school.

102 "Everyone who went there": Masako Sasaki, interview, Hiroshima, November 16, 2002.

103 school motto: "Greetings from Principal," Hiroshima Prefectural Hiroshima Kokutaiji Senior High School, http://www.kokutaiji-h.hiroshima-c.ed.jp/koutyou/principa3_e23.html.

104 "You didn't salute me": Frank Fukuhara, interview, Toyama, March 24, 1999.

104 "*Namaikiya*": Ibid.

105 An *Icchū* student: List from Frank Fukuhara, various interviews; Henry Ogura, interview, Tokyo, June 27, 2001; Hiroshi Tanaka, interview, Hiroshima, November 17, 2002.

106 she and her son were "*batakusai*": Henry Ogura, interview.

106 "You don't wear that blue thing in Japan": Frank Fukuhara, interview, Tokyo, June 20, 1999.

107 "The older brothers seemed different": Toshiko Fukuda, interview, Hiroshima, November 16, 2002.

108 "Buy suffering when young": Frank Fukuhara, interviews, Tokyo, June 20, 1999, and April 17, 2001.

108 official bullying: Hiroshi Tanaka, interview.

109 "Spell *tulip*": Hiroshi Tanaka and Henry Ogura, interviews.

110 Now that Frank was enrolled: Frank Fukuhara, interview, Honolulu, January 21, 2009.

110 *Icchū* boasted: Hiroshi Tanaka, interview; Frank Fukuhara, April 17, 2001.

111 "If you were a soldier": Masako Sasaki, interview.

111 "*Sekkyō* had changed my life entirely": Frank Fukuhara, interviews, March 22, 1999; April 9, 1999; November 17, 2002; June 9, 2006.

112 "But nobody asked me": Frank Fukuhara interview, June 20, 1999.

116 "I was excited": Frank Fukuhara, 1999, notebook prepared for author, 9.

116 "Defend and attack": Radio broadcast information is from Tomi Kaizawa Knaefler, *Our House Divided: Seven Japanese American Families in World War II* (Honolulu: University of Hawaii Press, 1991).

117 "Japan shouldn't fight": Masako Sasaki, interview, Hiroshima, March 27, 2007.

117 "a tough, tough struggle": Knaefler, *Our House Divided*.

118 "I decided to behave": Frank Fukuhara, Komaki-shi, notes to author, April 6, 2002.

9: PANIC IN LOS ANGELES

119 "JAPS OPEN WAR": *Los Angeles Times*, December 8, 1941.
119 "classified for internment": "Japanese Aliens' Roundup Starts" and "City Springs to Attention," *Los Angeles Times*, December 8, 1941.
120 Glendale Junior College: Harry K. Fukuhara, graduation certificate, June 19, 1941.
121 "They were like my own family": Harry Fukuhara, interview with Frank, Tokyo, April 16, 2005.
122 "Bottoms up": "War Mutes New Year's Eve Hilarity," *Los Angeles Times*, January 1, 1942.
123 "some empathy": Harry Fukuhara, interview, transcript, MIS Association, Norcal, Civil Liberties Public Education Fund Program (CLPEFP), San Francisco, 15.
123 forced labor: John Dower estimates that between 1939 and 1945, almost 670,000 Koreans were taken to Japan to work, primarily in mines and heavy industry. More than 10,000 probably perished in Hiroshima and Nagasaki as a result of the atomic bombs. John W. Dower, *War Without Mercy: Race & Power in the Pacific War* (New York: Pantheon Books, 1986), 248.
123 "This Restaurant Poisons": Ibid., 92.
124 "climate of harassment": Harry Fukuhara, interview, Tokyo, December 7, 2004.
124 "I am a Chinese": Michi Nishiura Weglyn, *Years of Infamy: The Untold Story of America's Concentration Camps* (Seattle: University of Washington Press, 1996), 36; Robert A. Wilson and Bill Hosokawa. *East to America: A History of the Japanese in the United States* (New York: William Morrow, 1980), 249.
124 American college rings: Wilson, *East to America*, 189.
124 flashing messages to shore: "Jap Boat Flashes Messages Ashore," *Los Angeles Times*, December 8, 1941.
124 signs with arrows: Harry Fukuhara, interview, Seattle, August 2, 2002.
125 "Some perhaps many": "Death Sentence," *Los Angeles Times*, December 8, 1941.
125 "A viper is nonetheless a viper": "The Question of Japanese-Americans," *Los Angeles Times*, February 2, 1942.
126 "What's wrong with Japan?": MIS Association, Norcal, Civil Liberties Public Education Fund Program (CLPEFP), San Francisco, 14–15.
126 "The Japanese race": Quoted in Wilson, *East to America*, 234.
126 "I do not think": Doris Kearns Goodwin, *No Ordinary Time: Franklin & Eleanor Roosevelt: The Home Front in World War II* (New York: Simon & Schuster, 1994), 322.
127 "false alarm": "This Is No Time for Squabbling," *Los Angeles Times*, February 27, 1942.

128 the writ of habeas corpus: Harry Fukuhara, interview by Sheryl Narahara, undated transcript, National Japanese American Historical Society Oral History Project, San Francisco, 21.

128 "100% American": Harry Fukuhara, interview by Eric Saul and assistance by Lonnie Ding, January 7, 1986, transcript, National Japanese
American Historical Society Oral History Project, San Francisco, 28.

129 "Have you ever considered": Harry Fukuhara, interview, Tokyo, October 24, 2000.

129 Mary wanted a divorce: Tulare Assembly Center, Records of
Japanese-American Assembly Centers, ca. 1942–ca. 1946, RG 499,
Records of U.S. Army Defense Commands (WWII) 1942–46, micro-
film, National Archives and Records Administration; Evacuee Case
File for Mary Oshimo, RG 210, Records of the War Relocation Au-
thority, National Archives and Records Administration.

130 "we were going to be interned": Harry Fukuhara, interview, April 20,
2001.

130 some twelve thousand volunteer air-raid wardens: *Los Angeles Times*,
February 27, 1942.

131 Motioning Harry over: interview by Eric Saul, 25.

131 Charged with violating a blackout edict: Sho Nomura, interview, Los
Angeles, March 23, 2003.

131 "Count to ten": Harry Fukuhara, interview, Tokyo, April 20, 2001.
Harry Fukuhara, interview by Sheryl Narahara, 21.

132 "It was just the indignity": interview by Eric Saul, 26.

132 "To take a gun away": Harry Fukuhara, Interview, Tokyo, January 9,
1999.

132 Walt Tanaka had been inducted: Walt Tanaka, interview, San Jose,
May 11, 1999.

132 "cruel blow": Roy Uyehata, interview, San Jose, May 11, 1999.

133 In Little Tokyo: Farm Security Administration/Office of War Information Black-and-White Negatives, Library of Congress Prints & Photographs Division.

134 "It wasn't that much": Harry Fukuhara, interview by Sheryl Narahara,
19; interview by Eric Saul, 23.

135 On Wednesday, May 6, 1942: Tulare Assembly Center Records.

135 Harry handed him the keys: Harry Fukuhara, interview by Eric
Saul, 32.

135 Harry deposited: Tulare Assembly Center Records; – Records of U.S.
Army Defense Commands (WWII) 1942–46.

136 Harry and Mary attached: Ibid.

136 At 8:15 a.m.: Ibid.

10: SILENCE FROM GLENDALE TO HIROSHIMA

137 Frank had demonstrated: Frank Fukuhara, telephone interview, September 30, 2004.

137 Shortly after war broke out: Frank Fukuhara, during interview with Harry, Pierce, and Frank Fukuhara, Tokyo, October 13, 1998; Henry Ogura, interview, Tokyo, June 27, 2001.

138 The idea: Frank Fukuhara, interview, Tokyo, November 20, 2001.

138 "100 million hearts beating as one": Ben-Ami Shillony, *Politics and Culture in Wartime Japan* (New York: Oxford University Press, 1981), 5.

138 Frank had heard a joke: Reference to *Senjinkun* (Field Service Code) and "death before dishonor" from Ulrich Straus, *The Anguish of Surrender: Japanese POWs of World War II* (Seattle: University of Washington Press, 2003), 38.

139 "*Nisei* were sissies": Frank Fukuhara, interview, Tokyo, April 17, 2001; interview, Honolulu, February 7, 2008.

139 Two decades earlier: *Sensō to Kurashi* I, 50–51; John W. Dower, *War Without Mercy: Race & Power in the Pacific War* (New York: Pantheon Books, 1986), 248.

140 "The Great East Asia War": *Dōin Gakuto*, exhibition brochure, Hiroshima Peace Memorial Museum.

141 Kiyo negotiated: Masako Sasaki, interview, Hiroshima, November 16, 2001.

141 Her pantry brimmed: Frank Fukuhara, interview, February 7, 2008.

142 Frank packed tins: Ibid.

142 "No one knew": Ibid.

143 *nihon buyō*: Masako Sasaki, interview, Hiroshima, March 27, 2007.

144 She rejected their offer: Frank Fukuhara, interview, November 20, 2001; interview, Honolulu, January 29, 2008.

144 "70,000 American-born Japanese": "Tokyo Assails Evacuation," *Los Angeles Times*, March 6, 1942.

145 Forty-four Japanese citizens: *Chūgoku Shimbun*, March 17, 1942.

145 ten concentration camps: The use of "concentration camps" is the widespread, accepted terminology today. At the time, they were called "relocation camps" or "internment camps."

146 "I might join the Army": Harry and Frank Fukuhara, during interview with Harry, Pierce, and Frank Fukuhara, Tokyo, October 13, 1998. Kinu's response, as well, is from Frank during the same interview.

146 From December 19, 1941, on: Louis Fiset, "Return to Sender: U.S. Censorship of Enemy Alien Mail in World War II," *Prologue* 33, no. 1 (2001), http://www.archives.gov/publications/prologue/2001/spring/mail-censorship-in-world-war-two-1.html.

11: INCARCERATED IN CALIFORNIA

151. approximately five thousand: *Final Report, Japanese Evacuation from the West Coast, 1942* (Washington, DC: U.S. Government Printing Office, 1943), 158.

151 Already 2,400 had arrived: *Tulare News*, undated and May 9, 1942.

151 "volunteers": Claire Gorfinkel, ed., *The Evacuation Diary of Hatsuye Egami* (Pasadena, CA: Intentional Productions, 1995), 50–51.

151 Assigned to J-6-10: "Individual Record," Evacuee Case File for Mary Oshimo, Record Group 210, National Archives and Records Administration.

151 Although contractors had raced to fill: *Tulare News*, first issue.

152 Without street names: *Tulare News*, June 12, 1942.

152 "apartment": Michi Nishiura Weglyn, *Years of Infamy: The Untold Story of America's Concentration Camps* (New York: William Morrow, 1976), 80.

152 "It was a chicken coop": Harry Fukuhara, interview, Los Angeles, March 22, 2003.

152 to fill the mattress sacks with straw: *Final Report, Japanese Evacuation from the West Coast, 1942*, 186; Sho Nomura, interview, Los Angeles, March 23, 2003.

152 "New": Mary Ito, interview, Torrance, March 21, 2003.

152 The lights-out curfew: *Tulare News*, June 12, 1942.

152 he finally drifted off: Harry Fukuhara, interview by Sheryl Narahara, undated, transcript, National Japanese American Historical Society Oral History Project, San Francisco, 22.

153 "our financial situation was so bad": Harry Fukuhara, quoted in Shizue Seigel, *In Good Conscience: Supporting Japanese Americans During the Internment* (San Mateo, CA: Kansha Project, 2006), 78–79.

153 sodium chloride tablets: *Tulare News*, May 17, 1942.

153 "Their boughs are so interlocked": Gorfinkel, ed., *The Evacuation Diary of Hatsuye Egami*, 35.

153 to stay five feet from the perimeter fence: *Tulare News*, May 6, 1942.

153 a large tree, the only one in the area: *Tulare News*, May 27, 1942; Harry Fukuhara, interview, Honolulu, January 29, 2008.

153 11 mess halls: Also other details. *Tulare News*, May 9, 1942.

153 "Like the early American pioneers": This and following quote from *Tulare News*, first issue.

154 "a heck of a way to live": Harry Katsuharu Fukuhara, interview by Eric Saul and assistance by Lonnie Ding, January 7, 1986, transcript, National Japanese American Historical Society Oral History Project, San Francisco, 34.

154 six dollars a month: *Tulare News*, May 23, 1942.

154 a clerk in the accounting office: Tulare Assembly Center, Records of Japanese-American Assembly Centers, ca. 1942–ca. 1946, RG 499, Records of U.S. Army Defense Commands (WWII) 1942–46, microfilm, National Archives and Records Administration.

154 "skilled" worker: Ibid.; Harry Katsuharu Fukuhara, military records, National Personnel Records Center, St. Louis, MO.

154 he bought briefs and pajamas: Ibid.

154 "flickers": *Tulare News*, July 25, 1942, and August 1, 1942.

154 3,440 persons out of a total 4,893: *Tulare News*, June 3, 1942.

154 "A newspaper for better Americans": *Tulare News*, May 9, 1942.

155 Thirty percent of Tulare's citizen population: *Tulare News*, August 19, 1942.

155 "cheated out of living a normal life": Sho Nomura, interview, Los Angeles, March 23, 2003.

155 evacuee wages: *Final Report, Japanese Evacuation from the West Coast, 1942*, 222.

155 thirty-nine cents per day: Ibid., 186, 187.

156 "restless and upset": *Tulare News*, June 10, 1942.

156 second leading cause: *Tulare News*, August 19, 1942.

156 a check for seventy-five dollars: Harry Fukuhara, interview, Los Angeles, March 21, 2003; interview by Eric Saul, 32.

157 Tehachapi Mountains: Harry Fukuhara, quoted in Shizue Seigel, *In Good Conscience: Supporting Japanese Americans During the Internment* (San Mateo, CA: Kansha Project, 2006), 79.

157 "visiting house": *Final Report, Japanese Evacuation from the West Coast, 1942*, 226; *Tulare News*, May 16, 1942.

157 They "were defying public sentiment": Harry K. Fukuhara, "My Story, 50 Years Later," *Nikkei Heritage* 15, no. 1 (Winter 2003): 12.

157 "Mr. and Mrs. Mount": *Color of Honor*, video, directed by Loni Ding (San Francisco, CA: Vox Productions, 1989).

157 only emergency calls: *Tulare News*, June 20, 1942, 4.

157 roll call: *Tulare News*, June 17, 1942; June 24, 1942.

157 election of three *issei*: *Tulare News*, June 10, 1942; July 1, 1942.

158 "We had no idea": Harry Fukuhara, interview, Honolulu, January 29, 2008.

158 "My sadness": Gorfinkel, ed., *The Evacuation Diary of Hatsuye Egami*, 60.

158 full schedule: *Tulare News*, July 4, 1942.

158 "Swing and sway with Sammy Kaye": *Tulare News*, July 18, 1942.

158 "happy family": *Tulare News*, July 8, 1942.

159 "being kicked out for no particular reason": Harry Fukuhara, interview, Tokyo, January 9, 1999.

159 "Where was the justice": Harry Fukuhara, interview, transcript, MIS Association, Norcal, Civil Liberties Public Education Fund Program (CLPEFP), San Francisco, 18.

160 "very healthy climate": *Tulare News*, July 29, 1942.

160 "rich nut-brown color": *Tulare News*, August 1, 1942.

160 "hardened": Harry Fukuhara, interview, transcript, MIS Association, Norcal, Civil Liberties Public Education Fund Program (CLPEFP), San Francisco, 18.

161 516 people: *Final Report, Japanese Evacuation from the West Coast, 1942*, 283, 288.

12: THE EMPIRE'S HOME FRONT

162 more bulbs: *Jūgo o Sasaeru Chikara to natte: Josei to Sensō*, exhibition brochure, Hiroshima Peace Memorial Museum, 1998.

162 shield the citizenry from the navy's decisive defeat: Shunsuke Tsurumi, *An Intellectual History of Wartime Japan, 1931–1945* (London: KPI, 1986), 96.

162 The staggering truth: Ben-Ami Shillony, *Politics and Culture in Wartime Japan* (New York: Oxford University Press, 1981), 95, 96.

163 the training increased: Frank Fukuhara, interview, Tokyo, April 17, 2001.

163 students had to undress: Frank Fukuhara, interview, Honolulu, February 7, 2008.

164 The army and navy were counting on: Frank Fukuhara with Hiroshi Tanaka, interview, Hiroshima, November 17, 2002.

164 "In future combat": Akira Fujiwara, *Gunji Shi Nihon Gendai Shi Taikei* (Tōyō Keizai, 1961), quoted in Tsurumi, 87.

164 *Kichiku Bei-Ei*: John W. Dower, *War Without Mercy: Race & Power in the Pacific War* (New York: Pantheon Books, 1986), 248.

164 "If you said anything": Frank Fukuhara, interview, Honolulu, March 4, 2008.

165 ten-year-olds bayoneted: Shillony, *Politics and Culture in Wartime Japan*, 145.

166 a mural of Churchill: Masako Sasaki, interview, Hiroshima, March 27, 2007.

166 "*Hakujin* eat meat": Ibid.

166 The Furue neighborhood: *Shinshū Hiroshima-shi Shi* (Hiroshima: Hiroshima City Hall, 1961), 1.

167 "During the war": Masako Sasaki, interview, March 27, 2007.

168 More than ever: Frank Fukuhara, interview, Honolulu, January 21, 2009.

13: ARIZONA SANDSTORMS

169 Gila River Relocation Center: The War Relocation Authority (WRA) termed the camps "relocation centers." I am using the proper name here to keep the narrative in historical context.

169 Block 49: Evacuee Case File for Harry Katsuharu Fukuhara, Record Group 210, National Archives and Records Administration. Other details as well.

169 Camp construction: Jeffrey F. Burton, Mary M. Farrell, Florence B. Lord, and Richard W. Lord, *Confinement and Ethnicity: An Overview of World War II Japanese American Relocation Sites* (Seattle: University of Washington Press, 1999), 61.

170 "family apartment": Michi Nishiura Weglyn, *Years of Infamy: The Untold Story of America's Concentration Camps* (New York: William Morrow, 1976), 84.

170 beaverboard: Burton, *Confinement and Ethnicity*, 61.

170 "so very cheap": Weglyn, *Years of Infamy*, 84.

170 "sand and cactus": Roger Daniels, *Concentration Camps USA: Japanese Americans and World War* (New York: Holt, Rinehart, & Winston, 1980), 92.

172 "Haruko was cuckoo": Mary Ito, interview, Torrance, March 21, 2003.

172 "That made it kind of awkward there": Harry Fukuhara, interview, Tokyo, November 7, 1999.

172 "That was the reason": Harry Fukuhara, interview, Honolulu, January 29, 2008.

172 "Issei Father": *Gila News-Courier*, September 12, 1942, 6.

173 One tantalizing rumor: Harry Fukuhara, interview, transcript, MIS Association, Norcal, Civil Liberties Public Education Fund Program (CLPEFP), San Francisco, 18.

173 an attack by a lone submarine: Audrie Girdner and Anne Loftus, *The Great Betrayal: The Evacuation of the Japanese-Americans During World War II* (New York: Macmillan, 1969), 109.

174 The WRA reassured internees: *Gila News-Courier*, October 10, 1942, 1.

174 "constantly questioned": Harry Fukuhara, "Autobiography Highlights" (photocopied notes, undated, ca. December 5, 1992).

175 Harry bought their cheap whisky: Harry Fukuhara, interview, Tokyo, April 19, 2006.

175 clandestine stills: Harry Fukuhara, interview, Seattle, August 3, 2002.

175 a federal violation: *Gila News-Courier*, September 12, 1942, 4.

175 "I possessed more than the average bitterness": Harry Fukuhara, San Jose, to Andy Bode, September 25, 1998.

175 The factory lay in a fenced-in compound: Burton, *Confinement and Ethnicity*, 66–67.

175 strips of colored burlap: *Gila News-Courier*, October 7, 1942, and October 21, 1942.

176 *inu*, or "dog": Brian Niiya, ed., *Japanese American History: An A-to-Z Reference from 1869 to the Present* (Los Angeles: Japanese American National Museum, 1993), 177, 178, 286.

176 "engendering a philosophy of defeatism": *Gila News-Courier*, November 14, 1942, 2.

176 "overwhelming": Fukuhara letter to Bode.

177 Harry spied a mimeographed announcement: Sheryl Narahara, undated, transcript, National Japanese American Historical Society Oral History Project, San Francisco, 25; Stanley L. Falk and Warren M. Tsuneishi, *American Patriots: MIS in the War Against Japan* (Washington, DC: Japanese American Veterans Association, 1995), 19.

178 "My eyes are bad": Harry Fukuhara, interview, Tokyo, April 10, 2004.

179 "Fukuhara-san, why are you volunteering in the Army": Harry Katsuharu Fukuhara, interview by Eric Saul and assistance by Lonnie Ding, January 7, 1986, transcript, National Japanese American Historical Society Oral History Project, San Francisco, 35.

179 "Your son is in the army": Narahara, transcript, 26.

179 "All the more reason": Ibid.

179 "To thy parents be truly respectful": Tad Ichinokuchi, *John Aiso and the M.I.S.: Japanese-American Soldiers in the Military Intelligence Service, World War II* (Los Angeles: Military Intelligence Service Club of Southern California, 1988), 82.

180 "He didn't want to end up in a cage": Mary Ito, interview, March 21, 2003.

181 "They were covered with blood and body fat": Sidney Forrester Mashbir, *I Was an American Spy* (New York: Vantage Press, 1953), 220.

181 "I was so glad to leave": Harry Fukuhara, interview, Tokyo, December 7, 2004.

14: A BALMY WINTER IN MINNESOTA

183 On Monday, December 7, 1942: Harry Katsuharu Fukuhara, military records, National Personnel Records Center, St. Louis, MO.

183 Minnesota: James C. McNaughton, *Nisei Linguists: Japanese Americans in the Military Intelligence Service during World War II* (Washington, DC: Department of the Army, 2006), 94. Dr. McNaughton also references Theodore C. Blegen, *Minnesota: A History of the State* (Minneapolis: University of Minnesota Press, 1963), 521–49.

184 "in the people's hearts": Ichinokuchi, *John Aiso and the M.I.S.*, 47.

184 shelter for homeless men: McNaughton, *Nisei Linguists*, 96.

184 scoured the dilapidated compound: Ibid. Also Walt Tanaka, interview, San Jose, May 11, 1999; George Kanegai, interview, Los Angeles, March 24, 2001.

184 a dance in a campus barn: *The MISLS Album* (Nashville, TN: Battery Press, 1990), 38.

184 only a few dozen officers: McNaughton, *Nisei Linguists*, 15, 17. McNaughton elaborates that the army would need "hundreds and possibly thousands of interrogators and translators," 20.

185 "The complexities of the Japanese language": John Weckerling, "Nisei Language Experts: Japanese Americans Play Vital Role in U.S. Intelligence Service in WWII," in Ichinokuchi, *John Aiso and the M.I.S.*, 187.

185 In an effort to find qualified men: McNaughton, *Nisei Linguists*, 27, 33, 54.

185 By May 1942: Ibid., 61.

185 But by autumn: Ibid., 81.

186 "I need you, I want you": Ben Nakamoto, telephone interview, January 30, 2004.

186 composed of 444 *nisei*: McNaughton, *Nisei Linguists*, 107.

186 typhoid vaccinations: Harry Katsuharu Fukuhara, military records, National Personnel Records Center, St. Louis, MO.

186 third section: *The MISLS Album*, 125.

186 At 6 a.m.: Ibid., 48.

187 Twenty percent of captured documents: Sidney Forrester Mashbir, *I Was an American Spy* (New York: Vantage Press, 1953), 259, 260.

187 "No one had any money": Both this comment and Sho Nomura's that follow are from Sho Nomura, interview, Los Angeles, March 23, 2003.

188 "I didn't know better": Noby Yoshimura, interview, Tokyo, April 24, 2001.

188 Rusty Kimura felt: Rusty Kimura, interview, Los Angeles, March 22, 2003.

188 more than three hundred prisoners: McNaughton, *Nisei Linguists*, 74.

188 "Without front-line intelligence": Ibid., 76.

188 "one-man team": Shizuo Kunihiro, telephone interview, March 5, 2004.

189 "Well, we'll catch up with you": Harry Fukuhara, interview, Tokyo, April 11, 2004.

189 coffee and doughnuts: Harry Fukuhara, interview, Tokyo, December 11, 2004.

189 Harold Fudenna: McNaughton, *Nisei Linguists*, 185–86.

190 President Roosevelt called the executions: John W. Dower, *War Without Mercy: Race & Power in the Pacific War* (New York: Pantheon Books, 1986), 49.

190 "A Jap's a Jap": Quoted in many sources. See McNaughton, *Nisei Linguists*, 137, and *Gila News-Courier*, April 15, 1943.

190 "As if history was repeating itself": Harry Fukuhara, interview, transcript, MIS Association, Norcal, Civil Liberties Public Education Fund Program (CLPEFP), San Francisco, 21.

191 "nothing but lie down": Ibid., 22; Harry Fukuhara, interview, Tokyo, November 5, 1999.

191 "They were proud": Harry Fukuhara, "Autobiography Highlights" (photocopied notes, undated, circa December 5, 1992). Even after the Mounts died and their house was sold, the flag was displayed on the wall by the next owner.

192 lifeboat drills: CLPEFP, 22; Harry Fukuhara, interview, November 5, 1999.

192 "Upon the outcome": President Franklin Delano Roosevelt, White House, to Members of the United States Army Expeditionary Forces, undated copy.

192 "A truly welcome sight": CLPEFP, 23.

15: MARY'S NORTH STAR

193 "critical stage of saturation": *Gila News-Courier*, April 27, 1943.

193 "We hope this will blow over soon": *Gila News-Courier*, April 23, 1943.

194 "They are not being pampered": *Gila News-Courier*, April 29, 1943.

195 "would be willing to volunteer": War Relocation Authority Application for Leave Clearance, 4, in Evacuee Case File for Mary Oshimo, Record Group 210, National Archives and Records Administration.

195 "to commit suicide": Michi Nishiura Weglyn, *Years of Infamy: The Untold Story of America's Concentration Camps* (New York: William Morrow, 1976), 144, 145.

196 "hungry for a mother's love": Mary Ito, interview, Torrance, March 24, 2003.

196 "Maybe, you better get married": Ibid.

197 "a fine personality": F. W. Heckelman, El Monte, CA, to Dillon S.

Myer, Washington, June 8, 1943, in Evacuee Case File for Fred Hiroshi Ito, Record Group 210, National Archives and Records Administration.

198 "You're a gypsy": Mary Ito interview, March 24, 2003.

198 567 people had left: *Gila News-Courier,* June 8, 1943; June 10, 1943.

198 "nation's warmest and most generous host": Mei Nakano, *Japanese American Women: Three Generations 1890–1990* (Sebastopol, CA: Mina Press, 1990), 172.

199 "I don't mind": Mary Oshimo, Rivers, AZ, to E. L. Shirrell, May 21, 1943, in Evacuee Case File for Mary Oshimo.

199 "$15 a week": E. L. Shirrell, Chicago, to Mary Oshimo, May 25, 1943, in Evacuee Case File for Mary Oshimo.

200 the Missouri, Mississippi, Wabash, and Illinois Rivers: "Waive Credit Curb in Flood Stricken Area," *Chicago Tribune,* June 14, 1943.

200 a flash flood: "Flash Flood Near Peoria Routs a Dozen Families," *Chicago Tribune,* June 14, 1943.

200 "clouds of doubt and insecurity": Fred Ito, Rivers, AZ, to Dillon S. Myer, June 16, 1943, in Evacuee Case File for Fred Hiroshi Ito.

16: RATIONS AND SPIES IN HIROSHIMA

201 "It was not the time": Masako Sasaki, interview, Hiroshima, March 27, 2007.

202 Hondōri's filigreed *suzuran* lampposts: *Hiroshima Hondōri Shōtengai no Ayumi* (Hiroshima: Hiroshima Hondōri Shōtengai Shinkō Kumiai, 2000), 33.

202 platinum-and-diamond wedding ring: Frank Fukuhara, interview, Tokyo, November 20, 2001.

203 "sideward advance": Ben-Ami Shillony, *Politics and Culture in Wartime Japan* (New York: Oxford University Press, 1981), 96.

203 One thousand songs: *Kinokogumo no Shita ni Kodomotachi ga Ita,* exhibition brochure, Hiroshima Peace Memorial Museum, 1997.

204 sweet potatoes instead: *Onnatachi no Taiheiyō Sensō* (Tokyo: Asahi Shimbunsha, 1996), 385.

206 "nosy": Frank Fukuhara, interview, Honolulu, February 7, 2008.

207 "They were being yanked": Frank Fukuhara, telephone interview, February 19, 2010.

207 "as if they were spies": In Laura Hein and Mark Selden, *Living with the Bomb: American and Japanese Cultural Conflicts in the Nuclear Age* (Armonk, NY: M. E. Sharpe, 1997), 236.

17: SUSPICIOUS FROM THE START

211 "you are volunteers": Sidney Forrester Mashbir, *I Was an American Spy* (New York: Vantage Press, 1953), 243. Also quoted in James C.

McNaughton, *Nisei Linguists: Japanese Americans in the Military Intelligence Service During World War II* (Washington, DC: Department of the Army, 2006), 179.

212 "a trained nucleus": Mashbir, *I Was an American Spy*, 237.

213 another "Yank": McNaughton, *Nisei Linguists*, 181.

213 "give a bloke a fair go": Andy Bode, Arundel, Australia, to Harry Fukuhara, October 5, 1998.

213 "why are we doing this work": Harry Fukuhara, interview, April 24, 2001.

213 more than 300,000 American soldiers: McNaughton, *Nisei Linguists*, 188.

213 Only 149 were Japanese American: Ibid., 179.

214 all photographs: Ibid., 162.

214 Terry, Harry: Harry Fukuhara, interview, transcript, MIS Association, Norcal, Civil Liberties Public Education Fund Program (CLPEFP), San Francisco, 24; Ben Nakamoto, Sanger, CA, to author, February 11, 2004.

214 "What are you doing here?": *Japanese Americans Who Fought Against Japan*, video (Tokyo: NHK, 2006).

215 "Kill or be killed!": The most notorious incident was the Goettge Patrol ambush of August 12, 1942, when over twenty marines were killed after being deceived into believing that the Japanese were surrendering. John W. Dower, *War Without Mercy: Race & Power in the Pacific War* (New York: Pantheon Books, 1986), 64; Harry Fukuhara, interview, Tokyo, January 17, 1999.

215 "the feeling was so bitter": Sidney Forrester Mashbir, *I Was an American Spy* (New York: Vantage Press, 1953), 226.

216 "nothing but pry around": Ibid., 47.

216 a *Webster's New Collegiate* English dictionary, bulky Japanese Kenkyusha dictionaries: List in Joseph D. Harrington, *Yankee Samurai: The Secret Role of Nisei in America's Pacific Victory* (Detroit: Pettigrew, 1979), 136. Also CLPEFP, 24.

216 "basic military training": CLPEFP, 24; Sheryl Narahara, undated, transcript, National Japanese American Historical Society Oral History Project, San Francisco, 36.

217 massive send-off ceremony: Accounts in *Asahi Shimbun*, October 21, 1943.

217 "Umi Yukaba," "Across the Sea": The radio broadcast of Japan's declaration of war in 1941 ended with this martial song. Its graphic lyrics of death at war were rooted in the *Manyōshū*, one of Japan's oldest literary works. Funeral ceremonies aboard Japanese Imperial Navy ships also played this song.

217 to cheer "*Banzai*": YouTube has a number of clips of the induction ceremony and visit to the palace.

218 second-class private: Katsuhiro Fukuhara, military record, Hiroshima Prefecture.

219 "one of the evil spots of this world": Frank O. Hough and John A. Crown, *The Campaign on New Britain* (Nashville, TN: Battery Press, 1992), 2.

219 December 14, 1943: James S. Powell, *Learning under Fire: The 112th Cavalry Regiment in World War II* (College Station: Texas A&M University Press, 2010), 36; Harry Katsuharu Fukuhara, military records, National Personnel Records Center, St. Louis, MO.

220 Where and how best to navigate: Hough, *The Campaign on New Britain*, 23, 141.

220 Alligator tractor: Powell, *Learning under Fire*, 37–39.

220 It was packed: Sheryl Narahara, undated, transcript, National Japanese American Historical Society Oral History Project, San Francisco; interviews, Harry Fukuhara, Tokyo, November 5, 1999, and October 25, 2000; interview, Harry Fukuhara, Honolulu, October 20, 2009. Other details, too.

220 "That was the first time": Narahara, 37.

220 "I was in trouble already": Ibid.

221 "landing with a typewriter": Harry Fukuhara, interview, November 5, 1999.

221 "Don't get excited": *Color of Honor*, video, directed by Loni Ding (San Francisco: Vox Productions, 1989).

221 "It's okay": Harry Fukuhara, interview, Tokyo, November 5, 1999.

222 "I want to die fighting": Harry Fukuhara, interview, Tokyo, November 10, 1999.

222 "It didn't take long": Harry Fukuhara, interview, Tokyo, November 13, 1999.

223 4,750 men: Powell, *Learning under Fire*, 48.

224 "Tamed Jap": Ben Nakamoto, Sanger, CA, to author, February 11, 2004.

224 When the actor asked Harry: Harry Fukuhara, telephone interview, June 9, 2004; interview, Tokyo, December 11, 2004.

225 "Lonely Sergeants": *Pacific Citizen*, March 25, 1944, 6.

225 "Thirty to forty girls each": Harry Fukuhara, interview, Tokyo, November 10, 1999, 8.

226 "The baby has grown bigger": "Somewhere Another Woman Griefs [*sic*]: 'Letter Captured at Arawe, New Britain,'" copy of letter in Japanese with English heading, in possession of Harry Fukuhara, translated by author.

226 "Japs": Harry Fukuhara, interview, Tokyo, April 12, 2005.

19: NO SEASON FOR CHERRY BLOSSOMS

227 "The farmers fed us well": Frank Fukuhara, Komaki City, to author, December 2001.

228 "Once drafted": Frank Fukuhara, interview, Hiroshima, April 11, 1999.

228 "killing two birds": *Onnatachi no Taiheiyō Sensō* (Tokyo: Asahi Shimbunsha, 1996), 384.

229 "Jikki was the only reason I lived": Frank Fukuhara, telephone interview, June 9, 2006.

230 "I did what I had to do": Chieko Ishida, interview, Fukuoka, April 9, 1999.

20: TAKING NEW GUINEA

231 evidence of cannibalism: Martin J. Kidston, *From Poplar to Papua: Montana's 163rd Infantry Regiment in World War II* (Helena, MT: Farcountry Press, 2004), 56–57.

232 Approximately two-thirds: Allison B. Gilmore, *You Can't Fight Tanks with Bayonets* (Lincoln: University of Nebraska Press, 1998), 150.

232 "It's a matter of survival": Min Hara, "A True M.I.S. Action from a Sergeant's Diary Revealed for the First Time," in Tad Ichinokuchi, *John Aiso and the M.I.S.: Japanese-American Soldiers in the Military Intelligence Service, World War II* (Los Angeles: Military Intelligence Service Club of Southern California, 1988), 69.

232 "I saw a yellow man": Kidston, *From Poplar to Papua*, 90.

233 "ridiculous fact": Sidney Forrester Mashbir, *I Was an American Spy* (New York: Vantage Press, 1953), 226–27.

233 "What? Where? When?": Military Intelligence Report, 41st Infantry Division, March 31, 1944, G-2 Journals for 41st Infantry Division, Record Group 94, National Archives and Records Administration.

233 "The more meaningful questions": Harry Fukuhara, interview, Tokyo, November 10, 1999.

233 "Then why don't you drown yourself": Harry K. Fukuhara, "Japanese Prisoners of War," *Nikkei Heritage* 3, no. 4 (Fall 1991): 6.

234 "Well, I was senior": Harry Katsuharu Fukuhara, interview by Eric Saul and assistance by Lonnie Ding, January 7, 1986, transcript, National Japanese American Historical Society Oral History Project, San Francisco, 51–52.

234 "Dig in before dark": Frank J. Sackton, "Night Attacks in the Philippines," *Army Magazine* 54, no. 6 (June 1, 2004): 18.

234 "Everyone was firing": Harry Fukuhara, interview, Tokyo, April 11, 2004.

235 "Harry could sweet talk": Gene Uratsu, San Francisco, interview, May 8, 1999.

235 "mouthwatering aroma": Gene Uratsu, San Rafael, CA, to author, 5 December, 2003.

235 portable outhouse: Ibid. Gene termed the outhouse "another Fukuhara legacy."

236 "These selfish individuals": Military Intelligence Memorandum, 41st Infantry Division, May 16, 1944, G-2 Journals for 41st Infantry Division, Record Group 94, National Archives and Records Administration.

236 "'to clean them for souvenirs'": Charles Lindbergh, *The Wartime*

Journals of Charles A. Lindbergh (New York: Harcourt Brace Jova-novich, 1970), 993.

236 "everything was in short supply": Gene Uratsu, December 5, 2003.

237 "I was not particularly anxious": Harry Fukuhara, interview, Tokyo, October 27, 2000.

21: PIERCE'S STAY OF EXECUTION

238 "hunch": Harry Fukuhara, interview, Tokyo, November 10, 1999.

238 "tied up with invisible hands": Shunsuke Tsurumi, *An Intellectual History of Wartime Japan, 1931–1945* (London: KPI, 1986), 115.

239 reminding him to take care: Masako Sasaki, interview, Hiroshima, April 11, 1999.

239 "Stop Unnecessary, Non-urgent Trips!": *Onnatachi no Taiheiyō Sensō* (Tokyo: Asahi Shimbunsha, 1996), 396. These banners and placards were ubiquitous nationwide.

239 "will be your grave": Allison B. Gilmore, *You Can't Fight Tanks with Bayonets* (Lincoln: University of Nebraska Press, 1998), 157.

239 he received his orders: Katsuhiro Fukuhara, military record, Hiro-shima Prefecture.

240 *tsuyu* (plum rain): The rainy season coincides with the ripening of plums.

22: A STUNNING ENCOUNTER IN SARMI

243 Intelligence reports: Harry Fukuhara, interview, Tokyo, November 10, 1999. Martin J. Kidston writes, "Reports suggested that Wakde was unoccupied." *From Poplar to Papua: Montana's 163rd Infantry Regiment in World War II* (Helena, MT: Farcountry Press, 2004), 105.

243 "The enemy American military": "Kunji," 36th Division Commander Hachirō Tagami original military order, to troops, May 18, 1938, Harry Fukuhara collection.

244 "shook me up": Harry Fukuhara, interview, Tokyo, November 10, 1999.

244 "You would become very close": Ibid.

244 "We had bombed the island mercilessly": Ibid.

244 "ball of fire": Ibid.

245 759 had been killed and four Japanese captured: Robert Ross Smith, *The Approach to the Philippines: The War in the Pacific* (Washington, DC: Center of Military History, 1984), 231. See John W. Dower, *War Without Mercy: Race & Power in the Pacific War* (New York: Pantheon Books, 1986), 69 for the following anecdote. After the war, a 41st Division army captain would write in the *Saturday Evening Post*, "In a small but costly battle at Wakde Island off Dutch New Guinea the same year, 'the general wanted a pris-oner, so we got him a prisoner.'" Harry earned his first Bronze Star

for meritorious service in the campaign, but he and his team still struggled to contribute as fully as they were capable.

245 a *nisei* from Hawaii: Kidston, *From Poplar to Papua*, 118.

245 "yellow bastards of New Guinea": Gene Uratsu, San Rafael, CA, to author, December 5, 2003.

246 "They all listened to me": Shigeru Matsuura, interview, Hiroshima, November 16, 2002.

246 "The sea and the sky went to America": Shigeru Matsuura, interview, Hiroshima, April 10, 1999.

246 only 7 percent: *Approach to the Philippines*, 101.

246 "He was not very humane": Shigeru Matsuura, November 16, 2000.

247 "a separate action": Ibid.

247 "*Shikata ga nai*": Ibid.

248 "This is it": Shigeru Matsuura, April 10, 1999.

248 That same morning, June 3, 1944: June 3, 1944, Prisoner of War/Internee: Matsuura, Shigeru, Record Group MP1103/1, National Archives of Australia.

248 "Very few good soldiers": Harry Fukuhara, interview, Tokyo, November 10, 1999.

248 "They didn't have any idea": Ibid.

248 "a little belligerent": Harry Fukuhara, interview, Tokyo, July 5, 2006; Harry Fukuhara, interview, Honolulu, June 24, 2008.

248 The stragglers had been combative: Note that Matsuura's and Harry's accounts differ in the one respect of how Matsuura was captured. Matsuura said that he was captured resting under a tree while feverish with malaria. Why the discrepancy? Perhaps Matsuura did not want to be perceived as having surrendered—better that he be delirious with malaria than fail to fight to the death. Or what Harry heard from others may have been mistaken, though Harry was generally fastidious in verifying accounts.

249 "*Masaka!* No way!": Matsuura interviews.

249 "Interrogation reports": March 31, 1944, G-2 Journals for 41st Infantry Division, Record Group 94, National Archives and Records Administration.

249 "I went to Kōryō": Matsuura interviews.

249 "Are you that Matsuura?": "45nenburi Kangeki no Saikai," *Asahi Shimbun*, December 7, 1989.

250 a can of American beef: Shigeru Matsuura, April 10, 1999; Harry Fukuhara, interview, Tokyo, July 5, 2006.

250 placed on a plane: Shigeru Matsuura, November 16, 2002.

250 "our machine-gunning prisoners": Lindbergh, *The Wartime Journals of Charles A. Lindbergh*, 997.

251 "auspicious luck": Shigeru Matsuura, April 10, 1999.

251 "Fighting brings intimacy": Shigeru Matsuura, April 10, 1999, and November 16, 2002.

251 "There was the chance": Harry Fukuhara, July 5, 2006.

251 "acquaintance from Hiroshima": Gene Uratsu, December 5, 2003.

251 He said nothing: Gene Uratsu, May 8, 1999.

251 "our bad manners": Min Hara, "A True M.I.S. Action from a Sergeant's Diary Revealed for the First Time," in Tad Ichinokuchi, *John Aiso and the M.I.S.: Japanese-American Soldiers in the Military Intelligence Service, World War II* (Los Angeles: Military Intelligence Service Club of Southern California, 1988), 63.

251 In late June: Harry Fukuhara, military records, National Personnel Records Center, St. Louis, MO.

252 Named for the one tree: Smith, *The Approach to the Philippines*, 244.

252 "Everyone was firing like mad": Kiyo Fujimura, "He Died in My Arms," in *John Aiso and the M.I.S.*, 96.

252 "sensed that he was dead": Ibid.

253 Between June 20 and 30, 1944: Smith, *The Approach to the Philippines*, 275–76.

253 eldest son of nine children: Masako M. Yoshioka, "Terry Mizutari," *Puka-Puka Parade* 34, no. 3 (1980): 28. Terry's sister Masako Yoshioka also wrote in another article that Terry was supposed to be on furlough. "T/Sgt Yukitaka Mizutari: May 5, 1920–June 23, 1944," Internet source referenced as excerpt from University of Hawaii, Hawaii War Records Depository. *In Freedom's Cause: A Record of the Men of Hawaii Who Died in the Second World War* (Honolulu: University of Hawaii Press, 1949).

253 his first furlough: Harry Fukuhara, military records.

253 "In the jungle": Harry Fukuhara, interview, Tokyo, April 10, 2004.

253 "We were not the infantry": Ibid.

253 more than one hundred thousand troops from Hiroshima: *Shinshū Hiroshima-shi Shi* (Hiroshima: Hiroshima City Hall, 1961), 1, 558.

254 more than eight thousand: Smith, *The Approach to the Philippines*, 233, 256.

254 fifty-one prisoners: Ibid., 278.

254 eleven prisoners: Ibid., 262.

23: GLACIAL CHANGE IN THE JUNGLE

255 his budding romance: Harry Fukuhara, interview, Honolulu, September 29, 2008.

255 "I felt sort of responsible": Harry Fukuhara, interview, Los Angeles, March 22, 2003.

256 V-Mail: During the war, many Americans used this special stationery and envelope combination to communicate with soldiers posted overseas. The letters were microfilmed for lighter transport and converted into photographs at their destination V-Mail station. Members of the Armed Forces could send V-Mail for free.

256 Major General Percy W. Clarkson: Major General was Clarkson's official rank, but he was addressed as "General" in conversation. That custom is observed in this book as well.

256 Clarkson used a fork: Harry Fukuhara, interview, Tokyo, November 5, 1999.

256 Clarkson had spent several Sundays: "33rd Dominant as Luzon Campaign Winds Down," *The 33rd Infantry Division: A Newsletter for WWI and WWII Veterans* 16, no. 2 (June 2001): 6.

257 All POWs: Various documents from Harry Fukuhara.

257 Propaganda leaflets made good toilet paper: Harry Fukuhara, interview, Tokyo, October 25, 2000.

257 dengue fever: Harry Fukuhara, military records, National Personnel Records Center, St. Louis, MO.

257 artillery commander bypassed subordinates: Harry Fukuhara, interview, Tokyo, February 4, 2004.

258 "an unmistakably Caucasian officer associated with Oriental faces": Kai E. Rasmussen, speech, Defense Language Institute Foreign Language Center (DLIFLC), Monterey, CA, 25 June 1977, printed in *DLIFLC Forum* (November 1977), quoted in James C. McNaughton, *Nisei Linguists: Japanese Americans in the Military Intelligence Service During World War II* (Washington, DC: Department of the Army, 2006), 147.

258 "brilliant": Horace Feldman, telephone interview, February 4, 2004. All other quotations in this paragraph are from the same interview.

258 "We were upset": Harry Fukuhara, interview, Tokyo, April 10, 2004.

258 "If someone was going wild": Horace Feldman, February 4, 2004.

259 "There was hardly any place": Ibid.

260 "They said it was impossible": Harry Fukuhara, Eric Saul, and assistance by Lonnie Ding, January 7, 1986, transcript, National Japanese American Historical Society Oral History Project, San Francisco, 48.

260 taken out by friendly fire: Ben Nakamoto, interview, San Francisco, May 8, 1999; James C. McNaughton, *Nisei Linguists*, 297.

24: THE "RED PAPER" DRAFT

263 at 133 locations: *Shinshū Hiroshima-shi Shi* (Hiroshima: Hiroshima City Hall, 1961) 1, 558.

263 More than one thousand buildings: Ibid., 701.

263 the neighborhood would serve as an escape route: Ibid., 880.

264 "Everyone's back hurt": Masako Sasaki, interview, Hiroshima, March 27, 2007.

264 "Where should we dig a hole?": Ibid.

264 black tape in a crisscross pattern: Sasaki relatives, interview, Miyajima, April 11, 1999.

264 "fifty years was a lifetime": Masako Sasaki, March 27, 2007.

265 "We were malnourished": Ibid.

265 one of twenty-six registered stores on Hondōri: *Hiroshima Hondōri Shōtengai no Ayumi* (Hiroshima: Hiroshima Hondōri Shōtengai Shinkō Kumiai, 2000), 50.

265 sixteen square miles: John W. Dower, *Japan in War and Peace* (New York: New Press, 1995).

266 a minor raid occurred over Hiroshima itself: *Shinshū Hiroshima-shi Shi*, 560. *Hiroshima Hondōri Shōtengai no Ayumi*, 51.

266 "B29s in Nagoya": *Chūgoku Shimbun*, March 20, 1945.

266 8,401 buildings: *Shinshū Hiroshima-shi Shi*, 701.

267 More than 23,000 young children: Ibid. Other sources at Hiroshima Peace Memorial Museum cite the same figure.

267 "lukewarm": Masako Sasaki, interview, March 27, 2007.

267 His military drills were "nothing compared": Frank Fukuhara, interview, Toyama, March 22, 1999.

268 he "didn't mind": Frank Fukuhara, telephone conversation, May 22, 2006.

268 "But it was no use trying your best": Frank Fukuhara, telephone conversation, January 19, 2007.

268 symbol for the fleeting lives: Emiko Ohnuki-Tierney, *Kamikaze, Cherry Blossoms, and Nationalisms: The Militarization of Aesthetics in Japanese History* (Chicago: University of Chicago Press, 2002), 112, 135; John W. Dower, *War Without Mercy: Race & Power in the Pacific War* (New York: Pantheon Books, 1986), 212.

269 "death sentence": Frank Fukuhara, interview, Tokyo, November 20, 2001.

269 "THE DAY I CANNOT FORGET": Frank Fukuhara, Komaki-shi, to author, July 27, 2002.

269 more than six million soldiers: Pacific War Research Society, *The Day Man Lost: Hiroshima, 6 August 1945* (New York: Kodansha America, 1981), 80–81.

270 On April 10, 1945: Katsutoshi Fukuhara, military record, Hiroshima prefecture.

270 *issen gorin* (one sen, five rin): Saburō Ienaga, *The Pacific War, 1931–1945* (New York: Pantheon Books, 1978), 52.

270 "I thought this was the end": Frank Fukuhara, interview, Honolulu, March 4, 2008.

270 "mean one": Ibid.

270 "You're a *nisei*": Frank Fukuhara, telephone conversation, May 22, 2006; August 2008.

270 an army photographer angled: Aerial photograph, taken April 13, 1945, by the U.S. Army, Hiroshima Peace Memorial Museum Memorial Hall.

25: EXTREMES IN THE PHILIPPINES

272 more than one hundred *nisei* linguists: James C. McNaughton, *Nisei Linguists: Japanese Americans in the Military Intelligence Service during World War II* (Washington, DC: Department of the Army, 2006), 332.

273 "The mountainous terrain": Quoted in the 33rd Infantry Division Historical Committee, *The Golden Cross: A History of the 33rd Infantry Division in World War II* (Nashville, TN: Battery Press, 1948), 93.

273 in the forward element: Harry Fukuhara, interview, Tokyo, April 16, 2005.

273 Japanese losses: Allison B. Gilmore, *You Can't Fight Tanks with Bayonets* (Lincoln: University of Nebraska Press, 1998), 155.

273 The Sixth Army would capture 7,297 prisoners: Ibid., 154.

274 some 25 million leaflets: Ibid.

274 "The American Military": Headlines from leaflets in Harry Fukuhara collection.

274 "FAREWELL, AMERICAN SOLDIERS!": Ibid.

275 "Our Family Newspaper": Ibid.

275 they succumbed: November 10, 1999.

276 "in great pain": The entire encounter is from Harry Fukuhara, interview, Tokyo, November 10, 1999; April 17, 2004; July 5, 2006.

277 angry and bitter and resolved: Harry Fukuhara, interview, November 10, 1999.

277 "Take Baguio!": 33rd Infantry Division, *The Golden Cross*, 299.

278 a "king" with his six white stripes: Harry Fukuhara, interview, Tokyo, October 27, 2000.

278 "My arm looked like a zebra": Harry Fukuhara, interview, Honolulu, January 29, 2008.

278 And in June General Clarkson: Harry Katsuharu Fukuhara, military records, National Personnel Records Center, St. Louis, MO. Harry would also be awarded an oak leaf cluster, representing another Bronze Star, in August 1945.

278 "bloody mud": *Rakkasan News*, Harry Fukuhara collection.

278 95,000 civilians: John W. Dower, *War Without Mercy: Race & Power in the Pacific War* (New York: Pantheon Books, 1986), 212.

278 For the Americans: John Toland, *The Rising Sun: The Decline and Fall of the Japanese Empire, 1936–1945* (New York: Modern Library, 2003), 726.

278 Ten MIS *nisei* would perish: Tad Ichinokuchi, *John Aiso and the M.I.S.: Japanese-American Soldiers in the Military Intelligence Service, World War II* (Los Angeles: Military Intelligence Service Club of Southern California, 1988), 201.

279 "Do you think . . . ?": Harry Fukuhara, interview, Honolulu, February 22, 2010.

279 "The local Filipinos": Harry Fukuhara, interview, Tokyo, October 27, 2000.

279 "*Nisei* had to be careful": Ibid.

280 "You must be able mentally": Sidney Forrester Mashbir, *I Was an American Spy* (New York: Vantage Press, 1953), 33.

280 "The enemy looks like us": Harry Fukuhara, interview, Tokyo, November 11, 1999.

280 "If and when we land in Japan": Harry Fukuhara, interview, Tokyo, April 19, 2006.

280 One day, a photograph: Harry Fukuhara collection.

26: BROTHERS AT WAR

283 "My superiors did nothing": Frank Fukuhara, interview, Honolulu, March 4, 2008.

283 "winter clothes in the summer": Frank Fukuhara, interview, Honolulu, January 21, 2009.

283 Only one third: Discussion with archivist, Military Archives, National Institute for Defense Studies, Tokyo, October 19, 2001.

283 "That's it": Frank Fukuhara, March 4, 2008.

284 "We used to wonder": Tomi Kaizawa Knaefler, *Our House Divided: Seven Japanese American Families in World War II* (Honolulu: University of Hawaii Press, 1991), 82.

285 "I was so tired": Frank Fukuhara, interview, Honolulu, February 7, 2008.

286 with the nobility of failure: This concept is treated by Ivan Morris in his classic book, *The Nobility of Failure: Tragic Heroes in the History of Japan* (Fukuoka, Japan: Kurodahan Press, 2013).

286 The Second General Army: Donald M. Goldstein, and Katherine V. Dillon, and J. Michael Wenger, *Rain of Ruin: A Photographic History of Hiroshima and Nagasaki* (Brassey's: Washington, DC: 1995), 41.

286 By mid-July 1945: Douglas J. MacEachin, *The Final Months of the War with Japan* (Washington, DC: Center for the Study of Intelligence, Central Intelligence Agency, 1998) 12, 17, 29. Available online.

287 less than half: *Hondo Kessen Jumbi: Kyūshū no Bōei* (Tokyo: Bōeichō Bōei Kenshūsho Senshishitsu, 1972), 557.

287 The commander barked, *"Tategata sankai"*: Frank Fukuhara, March 4, 2008; February 17, 2010.

288 "I was really scared then": Frank Fukuhara, February 17, 2010.

288 a major supply depot in nearby Kokura: *Hondo Kessen Jumbi: Kyūshū no Bōei*, 558.

289 "fifty-fifty": Frank Fukuhara, interviews, Tokyo, December 6, 1999; June 20, 1999; telephone conversation, August 2008.

289 "Dying doesn't mean too much to you": Frank Fukuhara, December 6, 1998.

290 *"unmei"* (fate): Pierce Fukuhara during interview with Harry, Pierce and Frank Fukuhara, Tokyo, October 13, 1998.

291 "Rectitude is the power": Inazo Nitobe, *Bushido: The Soul of Japan* (Rutland, VT, and Tokyo: Charles E. Tuttle, 1969), 23.

291 "In my mind": Frank Fukuhara, Komaki-shi, notes to author, April 6, 2002.

291 "We decided to die": Frank Fukuhara, interview with Harry, Tokyo, April 16, 2005.

291 "The enemy didn't fight to live": Harry Fukuhara, interview with Frank, Tokyo, April 16, 2005.

291 "The Japanese would fight to the end": Harry during interview with Harry, Pierce and Frank Fukuhara, Tokyo, October 13, 1998.

292 The "Okinawa story": Ibid.

292 "fifty-fifty": Harry Fukuhara, interview, Tokyo, October 27, 2000.

292 "I didn't like the idea": Harry Fukuhara, interview, Tokyo, November 11, 1999.

293 "three of my best Nisei officers": Sidney Forrester Mashbir, *I Was an American Spy* (New York: Vantage Press, 1953), 252–53. Mashbir never states the officers' names, but Harry, who was interviewed separately with no knowledge of Mashbir's memoir, provided a compatible account.

293 "indispensable": Harry Fukuhara, interview, transcript, MIS Association, Norcal, Civil Liberties Public Education Fund Program (CLPEFP), San Francisco, 34.

293 "I didn't want to be responsible": Ibid.

293 "pleasant" and "sympathetic but not encouraging": Harry Fukuhara, interview, Tokyo, April 10, 2004; CLPEFP, 34.

293 "They had been turning this thing over": Mashbir, *I Was an American Spy*, 253.

293 "It was also unquestionable": Ibid.

294 "I didn't think it would work anyway": Harry Fukuhara, April 10, 2004.

27: THE ATOMIC BOMB

296 Sixty thousand sheets: *Hiroshima Genbaku Sensai Shi* I (Hiroshima: Hiroshima City Hall, 1971), 54.

296 hurtling toward the city: Ibid.

296–97 "the rain of fire": *Sensō to Kurashi* IV (Tokyo: Nihon Tosho Center, 2001), 4.

297 Newspapers mentioned the raids: Ben-Ami Shillony, *Politics and Culture in Wartime Japan* (New York: Oxford University Press, 1981), 81.

297 At the end of April: Rinjirō Sodei and John Junkerman, *Were We the Enemy? American Survivors of Hiroshima* (Boulder, CO: Westview Press, 1998), 28; *Hiroshima Hondōri Shōtengai no Ayumi* (Hiroshima: Hiroshima Hondōri Shōtengai Shinkō Kumiai, 2000), 51.

297 Kyōto—the ancient capital: See Otis Cary, "Mr. Stimson's 'Pet City'– The Sparing of Kyoto, 1945" (Kyoto: Amherst House, Doshisha University, 1987).

297 "We looked forward": Miyoko Watanabe, ed., "Still Surviving," in *Peace Ribbon Hiroshima: Witness of A-Bomb Survivors* (Hiroshima: Peace Ribbon, 1997), 30–34, in *Victims' Experiential Testimonies*, Memorial Hall, Hiroshima Peace Park.

297 "That's the roar of B": *Hiroshima Genbaku Sensai Shi* I (Hiroshima: Hiroshima City Hall, 1971), 56.

297 "Why aren't they falling in Hiroshima?": Masako Sasaki, interview, Hiroshima, March 27, 2007.

297 theories: Sodei, *Were We the Enemy?*, 28. *Hiroshima Hondōri Shōtengai no Ayumi*, 51.

297 "Tomorrow I don't know whether I will die": Masako Sasaki, March 27, 2007.

298 "No one could hear": Masako Sasaki, Ibid.

298 trudging back in late afternoon *hetoheto* (exhausted): Ibid.

299 "People would burn books": Ibid.

299 "Theoretically": Ibid.

299 "Go early then": Ibid.

300 "Don't get sick": Ibid.

300 "We just did what was necessary": Ibid.

300 "Auntie pushed hard": Ibid.

301 several friends in a neighborhood association: Masako Sasaki, interview, Hiroshima, April 11, 1999.

301 "*Ohayō Gozaimasu*": Ibid.

301 mild breeze tousled her hair: Eisei Ishikawa and David L. Swain, trans., *Hiroshima and Nagasaki: The Physical, Medical, and Social Effects of the Atomic Bombings* (New York: Basic Books, 1981), 77.

302 "All in an instant": Masako Sasako, interview, Hiroshima, November 16, 2002; March 27, 2007.

302 "Auntie was upset and all alone": Masako Sasaki, November 16, 2002.

302 ghosting: Masako Sasaki, March 27, 2007.

302 "What happened?": Ibid.

303 "sea of flames": Toshinao Nishimura, March 24, 2001. The account about Toshinao's sister Kimiko is from this interview as well.

303 "I felt as if a bomb": Chieko Ishida, interview, Fukuoka, April 9, 1999.

304 "Please help me": Ibid.

304 His father: Shigeru Matsuura, interview, Hiroshima, November 16, 2002.

304 only a few of 285 buildings: *Hiroshima Genbaku Sensai Shi* II (Hiroshima: Hiroshima City Hall, 1971), 197, 211.

304 The factory imploded: The account of Victor's experience is culled from multiple interviews with multiple family members over time.

305 The elementary school: *Senchū Sengo ni okeru Hiroshima-shi no Kokumin Gakkō Kyōiku* (Hiroshima: Hiroshima-shi Taishoku Kōchōkai, 1999), 307.

305 those in Misasa: *Hiroshima Genbaku Sensai Shi* I (Hiroshima: Hiroshima City Hall, 1971), 35.

305 Aiko thought: Aiko, Ishihara, interview, Hiroshima, April 11, 1999.

305 chilly: Eisei Ishikawa and David L. Swain, trans., *Hiroshima and Nagasaki*, 92.

305 They stung to the touch: Hitoshi Takayama, ed., *Hiroshima in Memorium* (Hiroshima: Yamabe Books, 1969); Miyoko Watanabe, ed., "Still Surviving," in *Peace Ribbon Hiroshima*, 31, in Memorial Hall, Hiroshima Peace Park.

305 mix of dust, vapor, and radioactive soot: Hiroshima Peace Memorial Museum, Permanent Exhibition.

305 Masako's futons: Masako Sasaki, March 27, 2007.

305 "Zombies": Aiko Ishihara, April 11, 1999.

306 firestorm, whirlwind, and black rain: Eisei Ishikawa and David L. Swain, trans., *Hiroshima and Nagasaki*, 55–56.

306 "He walked easily": Aiko Ishihara, April 11, 1999.

306 "everyone came here": Ibid.

306 "like the howling of wild animals": Miyoko Watanabe, ed., "Still Surviving," *Peace Ribbon Hiroshima*, 31.

306 The local hospital: *Hiroshima Genbaku Sensai Shi* II, 888.

306 More than a thousand people: Ibid., 886.

306 The mountain road was clogged: Ibid., 884.

307 "It was a natural instinct": Masako Sasaki, March 27, 2007.

307 "Strangely": Toshinao Nishimura, March 24, 2001.

307 "*zuruzuru*" ("peeling"): Ibid.

307 cotton: *For Those Who Pray for Peace* (Hiroshima: Hiroshima Jogakuin Alumni Association, 2005), 20. Other materials used as ointment and medicine from this source and Miyoko Watanabe, ed., "Still Surviving," in *Peace Ribbon Hiroshima*, 32–34.

307 "We quieted Kimiko down": Toshinao Nishimura, March 24, 2001.

308 more than seven thousand mobilized students: *Dōin* Gakuto, exhibition brochure, Hiroshima Peace Memorial Museum, 2. Chart breakdown of deaths per school.

308 "I was happy": Toshinao Nishimura, March 24, 2001.

308 the imperious wrought-iron gates: *Hiroshima Genbaku Sensai Shi* II, 157, 159, 160, 172, 175. The Hiroshima Castle complex is discussed at length.

309 One hundred percent: *Hiroshima Hondōri Shōtengai no Ayumi* (Hiroshima: Hiroshima Hondōri Shōtengai Shinkō Kumiai, 2000), 55.

309 At a shelter: Chieko Ishida, April 9, 1999.

309 When the B-29s approached Kokura: Frank Fukuhara, interview, Tokyo, June 20, 1999.

309 "new-type bomb": Ben-Ami Shillony, *Politics and Culture in Wartime Japan* (New York: Oxford University Press, 1981), 107.

310 both were foreigners: Frank Fukuhara, telephone conversation, August 2008.

310 one cluster among fifty-one neighbors: *Shashinshū Genbaku o Mitsumeru: 1945 Hiroshima, Nagasaki* (Hiroshima: Iwanami Shoten, 1981), 149. *Hiroshima Genbaku Sensai Shi* II, 887.

310 August into November: *Hiroshima Genbaku Sensai Shi* II, 889.

310 His journey had lasted a week: Harry Fukuhara, interview, Tokyo, December 11, 2004.

310 "They walked for dear life": Masako Sasaki, March 27, 2007.

311 a few pumpkins and sweet potatoes: *Hiroshima Genbaku Sensai Shi* II, 891.

315 "We were all happy about it": Harry Fukuhara, interview, Honolulu, February 22, 2010.

315 Tens of thousands: Specific figures for immediate and subsequent deaths vary widely to this day. Hiroshima City estimated that approximately 140,000 had died by the end of 1945. *The Spirit of Hiroshima* (Hiroshima: Hiroshima Peace Memorial Museum, 1999), 41. For further detail, see Eisei Ishikawa and David L. Swain, trans., *Hiroshima and Nagasaki: The Physical, Medical, and Social Effects of the Atomic Bombings* (New York: Basic Books, 1981), 113.

315 "If they do not now accept our terms": Donald M. Goldstein, Katherine V. Dillon, and J. Michael Wenger, *Rain of Ruin: A Photographic History of Hiroshima and Nagasaki* (Brassey's: Washington, DC: 1995), 62. (This quotation is available from many other sources as well.)

316 from 38 to 300: James C. McNaughton, *Nisei Linguists: Japanese Americans in the Military Intelligence Service during World War II* (Washington, DC: Department of the Army, 2006), 384.

316 "Any group on earth": Sidney Forrester Mashbir, *I Was an American Spy* (New York: Vantage Press, 1953), 250.

316 "Each day": *Japanese Americans Who Fought Against Japan*, video (Tokyo: NHK, 2006).

316 *genshi bakudan*: McNaughton, *Nisei Linguists*, 379.

316 the same terminology: Ben-Ami Shillony, *Politics and Culture in Wartime Japan* (New York: Oxford University Press, 1981), 108.

316 "equivalent to thousands of tons": "My Story, 50 Years Later," *Nikkei Heritage* 15, no. 1 (Winter 2003): 12.

316 "I didn't know": Harry Fukuhara, interview, Honolulu, January 29, 2008.

316 nothing would grow in Hiroshima: Harry K. Fukuhara, "My Story, 50 Years Later," *Nikkei Heritage* 15, no. 1 (Winter 2003): 12. Residents of Hiroshima believed that the city would be uninhabitable for seventy-five years. Michihiko, Hachiya, *Hiroshima Diary: The Journal of a Japanese Physician, August 6–September 30, 1945* (Chapel Hill: University of North Carolina Press, 1995), 65.

317 Speechless: Harry Fukuhara, interview, Tokyo, July 5, 2006.

317 "endure the unendurable": Quoted in John W. Dower, *Embracing Defeat: Japan in the Wake of World War II* (New York: Norton, 1999), 36.

317 the Pacific Theater: more than 1.5 million from "Army Reports Half Its Men Returned Home," *Pacific Stars and Stripes*, October 22, 1945. Figure of 750,000: James C. McNaughton, *Nisei Linguists*, 411.

317 "WAR OVER": "The *Guinea Pig* told it all," *The 33rd Infantry Division Newsletter for WWI and WWII Veterans* 17, no. 1 (March 2002): 1.

317 "Then, the war ended": Harry Fukuhara, interview, Tokyo, April 16, 2005.

318 "The more I thought about it": "My Story, 50 Years Later," *Nikkei Heritage*, 13.

318 "I thought it would be no use going": Harry Fukuhara, January 29, 2008.

318 Sailors craned: "Japan Signs the Surrender," *Life*, September 17, 1945, 27–35.

319 three *nisei* lieutenants: They were present to accompany Japanese journalists covering the surrender ceremony. Note from Dr. James C. McNaughton, April 13, 2015.

319 "a nation disgraced": Thomas T. Sakamoto, "Witness to Surrender," *Nikkei Heritage* 15, no. 1 (Winter 2003): 8.

319 "As for myself": Ibid., 9.

320 "had sucked the air": *Japanese Americans Who Fought Against Japan*, video (Tokyo: NHK, 2006).

320 "That's what you might have faced": Mas Ishikawa, telephone interview, February 18, 2004.

321 "They looked like friends": Hideyoshi Miyako, August 6, 2004, to author.

321 "vanished like a bubble popping": Ibid.

321 "I couldn't believe it": Harry Fukuhara, interview, Tokyo, November 13 1999.

321 "I felt some responsibility": Ibid.

321 Posted to division headquarters: Headquarters Sixth Army, Special Orders, Number 143, Extract, 31 May 1945, Harry Fukuhara collection; "WITH THE SIXTH ARMY IN JAPAN," undated fragment, Harry Fukuhara collection.

322 military censorship was lifted: "Censorship Is Cut for Press but Not Japs," *Pacific Stars and Stripes*, October 7, 1945, 8.

322 One soldier had found: "Nisei Soldier Visits Hiroshima to Find Mother Atom Victim," *Pacific Stars and Stripes*, October 5, 1945, 4.

322 "All efforts to find": "After Service During War, Nisei Still Have Large Job," *Pacific Stars and Stripes*, October 7, 1945, 2.

322 "What little news": Harry Fukuhara, interview, Tokyo, April 19, 2006.

322 "the verge of starvation": Ibid.

322 "I feared the futility": "My Story, 50 Years Later," *Nikkei Heritage*, 12.

322 "The odds were slim": Harry Fukuhara, interview, Tokyo, July 5, 2006.

322 "Maybe": Ibid.

322 a lush canna plant: Hiroshima Peace Memorial Museum, *The Spirit of Hiroshima* (Hiroshima: Hiroshima Peace Memorial Museum, 1999), 83.

323 patients were dying: "Oppose Hiroshima as Anti-War Shrine," *Pacific Stars and Stripes*, October 4, 1945, 4.

323 a September typhoon: Eisei Ishikawa and David L. Swain, trans., *Hiroshima and Nagasaki: The Physical, Medical, and Social Effects of the Atomic Bombings*, pages 6, 80, 94, 505 for misfortunes, including the landslide.

323 In the district of Takasu: *Hiroshima Genbaku Sensai Shi* II (Hiroshima: Hiroshima City Hall, 1971), 892.

323 Harry's cousins placed rocks: Sasaki relatives, interview, Miyajima, April 11, 1999.

323 The bridges often collapsed: Masako Sasaki, interview, Hiroshima, March 27, 2007.

324 Harry's driver Chester: "WITH THE SIXTH ARMY IN JAPAN," fragment. This document is similar to a newspaper article. "Hachinenburi ni Boshi Saikai," *Kobe Shimbun*, October 22, 1945.

324 "scared": "My Story, 50 Years Later," *Nikkei Heritage*, 13.

324 "I didn't think": Harry Fukuhara, January 29, 2008.

324 "in the nick of time": Ibid.

325 "Just stand there": Ibid.

325 "You can't get in": Ibid.

325 At around 1 a.m.: "Hachinen buri ni Boshi Saikai," *Kobe Shimbun*, October 22, 1945.

325 "All was eerie and lifeless": "My Story, 50 Years Later," *Nikkei Heritage*, 13.

326 "Zombies": Ibid.

326 nearly one day: Harry Fukuhara, April 19, 2006; January 29, 2008.

326 The window on the front door: Harry Fukuhara, during interview with Pierce and Frank Fukuhara, Tokyo, October 13, 1998; Pierce Fukuhara, interview, Tokyo, June 9, 1999.

327 "All they saw was an American soldier": *Japanese Americans Who Fought Against Japan*, video (Tokyo: NHK, 2006).

327 "*Okāsan*": "Hachinenburi ni Boshi Saikai," *Kobe Shimbun*, October 22, 1945.

327 Kiyo recognized her nephew: Harry Fukuhara, interview, Tokyo, April 19, 2005.

327 Kinu and Harry: "Hachinen buri ni Boshi Saikai," *Kobe Shimbun*, October 22, 1945.

327 "What are you doing here?": Harry Fukuhara, January 29, 2008.

327 "Why would she say something like that?": Harry Fukuhara, interview, Tokyo, April 19, 2006.

328 "He couldn't talk much": *Uncommon Courage: Patriotism and Civil Liberties* (Davis, CA: Bridge Media, 2001).

328 "Where were you": Frank Fukuhara, telephone conversation, December 15, 2006.

328 "People didn't like": Ibid.

329 "Would you like to go": Frank Fukuhara, telephone conversation, June 9, 2006.

330 "I must wait for my older brother": Chieko Ishida, interview, Fukuoka, April 9, 1999.

330 "annihilated": Harry Fukuhara, interview, Tokyo, April 26, 2001.

330 "He's dead": Frank Fukuhara, telephone conversation, June 5, 2005.

330 "they didn't want to listen to Harry": Frank Fukuhara, interview, Tokyo, November 2, 1998.

330 "It cannot be helped": Frank Fukuhara, interview, Hiroshima, April 10, 1999.

330 "that Caucasian boy": Frank Fukuhara, interview, Tokyo, December 6, 1998.

331 *"Buji de yokatta"*: Masako Sasaki, March 27, 2007.

332 "Harry was like a father": Frank Fukuhara, telephone conversation, May 22, 2006.

332 "I didn't think it possible": "WITH THE SIXTH ARMY IN JAPAN" fragment.

29: A TROUBLING LETTER

333 "Magic Carpet": "'Magic Carpet' to Take Vets Home: 2,000,000 Pacific Troops Due Boat Ride," *Pacific Stars and Stripes*, October 3, 1945, 1.

333 "See you in Chicago!": *Golden Cross: A History of the 33rd Infantry Division in World War II* (Nashville, TN: Battery Press, 1948), 369–70.

333 An array of illnesses erupted: "Typhus Cases Highest In 32 Years Among Japanese," *Pacific Stars and Stripes*, March 13 1946, 1.

334 bamboo-shoot existence: Masako Sasaki, interview, Hiroshima, March 27, 2007.

334 "onion existence": John W. Dower, *Embracing Defeat: Japan in the Wake of World War II* (New York: Norton, 1999), 95.

334 "Everyday clothes were expensive": Masako Sasaki, interview, Hiroshima, November 16, 2002.

334 wholesale prices: Dower, *Embracing Defeat*, 115.

335 "have expectations about the future": Toshinao Nishimura, interview, Tokyo, March 21, 2001.

335 Mary's kimonos: Kinu sent Mary a wedding kimono when Mary first married; Mary lost it between her separation from her husband and internment. No one ever said anything about Mary's other kimonos.

335 For one sack of rice: Masako Sasaki, interviews, November 16, 2002, March 27, 2007.

336 "Sometimes, Victor could talk": Frank Fukuhara, interview, Honolulu, February 18, 2008.

337 On March 14, 1946: Harry Katsuharu Fukuhara, military records, National Personnel Records Center, St. Louis, MO.

337 "I never made any effort": Harry Fukuhara, interview, Tokyo, April 16, 2005.

338 "It was real bad in California": Harry Fukuhara, interview, Tokyo, April 19, 2005.

338 "It really bothered me": Harry Fukuhara, interview, Tokyo, April 26, 2001.

338 "a Hakujin drove into the yard": Ben Nakamoto, Sanger, CA, to author, February 11, 2004.

338 "Harry was totally lost": Amy Nagata, interview, Los Angeles, March 21, 2003.

338 "As soon as this letter arrives": Victor Fukuhara to Harry Fukuhara in care of Mrs. Fred Ito, undated postcard.

339 Harry feared that Victor: Harry Fukuhara, interview, Tokyo, January 9, 1999.

339 "I mostly wanted to get back": Harry Fukuhara, interview, Tokyo, May 16, 2000.

340 "I felt I had an obligation": Ibid.

30: PEACE AND REDEMPTION

341 "Try to come back": Frank Fukuhara, telephone conversation, January 19, 2007.

341 "I couldn't believe": Frank Fukuhara, interview, Honolulu, March 4, 2008.

342 Suffering from a low white blood cell count: Information about Kiyo's maladies is from Toshinao Nishimura, interview, Tokyo, March 24, 2001.

342 "from privileged to penniless": Masako Sasaki, interview, Hiroshima, March 27, 2007.

343 At 3:30 a.m.: *Koseki Tohon* (Family Register), Tokichi Nishimura, Hiroshima-shi. Accounts of Kiyo's suicide are from interviews with Aiko Ishihara and Frank Fukuhara.

343 only one-half of one percent of the deaths: Nihon Gensuibaku Higaisha Dantai Kyōgikai, "Genbaku Shibotsusha ni kansuru Chūkan Hōkoku no Gaiyō," November 9, 1987, 64–65.

344 "most shameful thing": Shigeru Matsuura, interview, Hiroshima, April 10, 1999.

344 treated as pariahs: John W. Dower, *Embracing Defeat: Japan in the Wake of World War II* (New York: Norton, 1999), 59–60.

344 "to some extent": Shigeru Matsuura, interview, April 10, 1999.

345 "He must have felt badly for me": Chieko Ishida, interview, Fukuoka, April 9, 1999.

345 "I worked so hard to live": Ibid.

346 "Certificate of Loss of Nationality": Referenced in letter from Harvey J. Feldman, American Vice Consul, Nagoya, to Frank Katsutoshi Fukuhara, March 23, 1960. The certificate was dated December 29, 1954.

346 "This man is different": Hideo Miwa, interview, Tokyo, February 9, 1999.

346 "The government couldn't deny": Kiyoshi Hashizaki, interview, Toyama, March 22, 1999.

346 underpinned by guilt: Harry Fukuhara, interview, Tokyo, April 19, 2006. "I had a mission to do that was in a way a guilt complex for what happened during World War II."

347 "Harry started to like Japan": Frank Fukuhara, telephone conversation, April 11, 2007.

347 "ambitious": Harry Fukuhara, interview, Tokyo, April 22, 2006.

347 "No go!": Frank and Tamiko Fukuhara, interview, Honolulu, January 29, 2008.

348 "If you live in America": Jean Furuya, conversation, Honolulu, January 27, 2008.

348 "When she dies": Lillian Lam, conversation during interview with Mary Ito, Torrance, March 24, 2001.

349 "If not, they won't come back": Mary Ito, interview, Torrance, March 21, 2003.

349 her *hibakusha* (atomic bomb survivor) status: Kinu fell under two categories for her *hibakusha* designation; Takasu was located within the bomb exposure range, and Kinu had ventured close to the hypocenter within two weeks of the explosion.

349 "I didn't feel like": "Haha to Ani Hibaku . . . Tomo o Horyo ni," *Chūnichi Shimbun*, September 26, 1994.

350 "Be sure": Mary Ito, interview, March 24, 2001. Entire anecdote.

351 "Mr. MIS": From a plaque awarded by the Military Intelligence Service of Northern California.

351 "the major Japanese civilian and military intelligence": Harry Fukuhara "Biography," prepared by Harry Fukuhara.

351 "Everything went back to the period": Stanley Hyman, interview, Washington, DC, July 22, 1999.

353 since the mid-1990s: Harry Fukuhara, interview, Tokyo, July 5, 2006.

353 The dreams: Harry Fukuhara, interview, Honolulu, June 24, 2008; conversation, Honolulu, October 20, 2009.

EPILOGUE: AT EASE IN HONOLULU

355 "Thanks to her strength": Jean Furuya, Torrance, CA, to author, November 2006.

355 "enigma": Ibid. Typed insert in handwritten note above.

355 "since she was going to heaven": Jean Furuya, email, to author, October 14, 2006.

357 "Today is the first time I understand": Tamiko Fukuhara to author, MIS New Year and Installation Luncheon, Honolulu, February 1, 2009.

SELECTED BIBLIOGRAPHY

PRIMARY SOURCES

Chūgoku Shimbun, December 1935–October 1945. Microfilm, Japan Newspaper Museum, Yokohama.

Diplomatic Archives. List of Passports Issued. File 3.8.5.8 Tabi 21, 38, 69 Microfilm, Ministry of Foreign Affairs, Tokyo.

Evacuee Case Files for Harry Katsuhara [*sic*] Fukuhara, Fred Hiroshi Ito, Harue Jean Oshimo, Jerry Takao Oshimo, and Mary Oshimo, RG 210, Records of the War Relocation Authority, National Archives and Records Administration, College Park, Maryland.

Final Report: Japanese Evacuation from the West Coast, 1942. Washington, DC: U.S. Government Printing Office, 1943.

Gila News-Courier. September 1942–September 1945. Online, Densho Digital Archive.

G-2 Journals and Periodic Reports. RG 94, Adjutant General's Office, World War II Operation Reports: 1940–1948: 41st Infantry Division, National Archives and Records Administration, College Park, Maryland.

"Hachinen buri ni Boshi Saikai." *Kobe Shimbun*, October 22, 1945.

"Haha to Ani Hibaku . . . Tomo o Horyo ni." *Chūnichi Shimbun*, September 26, 1994.

Harry Katsuharu Fukuhara. Collection of letters from 1933 to 1938, 1936 diary, books, and wartime Japanese and American letters and propaganda.

Harry Katsuharu Fukuhara. Military Records. Paper, National Personnel Records Center, St. Louis, Missouri.

Harry Katsuharu Fukuhara. Interview by Eric Saul and assistance by Lonnie Ding, January 7, 1986, transcript, National Japanese American Historical Society Oral History Project, San Francisco.

Harry Katsuharu Fukuhara. Interview, transcript, MIS Association, Norcal, Civil Liberties Public Education Fund Program (CLPEFP), San Francisco.

Harry Katsuharu Fukuhara. Interview by Sheryl Narahara, Undated, Transcript, National Japanese American Historical Society Oral History Project, San Francisco.

Harry Katsuji Fukuhara. Probate Court Records. Superior Court, State of Washington, King County, 1933.

The Invader. Auburn, WA: Auburn High School, 1937.

"Japan Signs the Surrender." *Life*, September 17, 1945.

Katsuhiro Fukuhara. Military Record. Hiroshima Prefecture.

Katsumi Fukuhara. Military Record. Hiroshima Prefecture.

Katsutoshi Fukuhara. Military Record. Hiroshima Prefecture.

Koseki Tohon. Family Registers for the Sasaki, Fukuhara, and Nishimura families. Hiroshima Prefecture.

Los Angeles Times, December 1941–May 1942. Online.

Military Archives. *Akatsuki Butai* and *Yuki Butai* Records, including field diaries for New Guinea. National Institute for Defense Studies, Tokyo.

The MISLS Album. Nashville, TN: Battery Press, 1990.

"Nihon Shinchū no Nisei Shōi: Hachinenburi ni Boshi Taimen." *Chicago Tsūshin*, October 1945.

Pacific Stars and Stripes, September 1945–April 1961, Tokyo.

Records of Japanese-American Assembly Centers, ca. 1942–ca. 1946, RG 499, Records of U.S. Army Defense Commands (WWII) 1942–46, National Archives and Records Administration, College Park, Maryland.

Registers containing "Service and Casualty" forms (Form A112) of enemy prisoners of war and internees held in camps in Australia MP1103/1, National Archives of Australia.

Tokyo Asahi Shimbun. July 1–3, 1924. Microfilm, National Diet Library, Tokyo.

Tulare News. May–August 1942. Paper, National Archives and Records Administration, College Park, Maryland.

Yank magazine. August–September 1945. National Archives and Records Administration, College Park, Maryland.

Yokohama Bōeki Shimpo, November 29, 1933.

Zaibei Nihonjin Jinmei Jiten. San Francisco: Nichibei Shimbunsha, 1922.

SECONDARY SOURCES

Abe, Mark Normes, and Yukio Fukushima, eds. *The Japan/America Film Wars: WWII Propaganda and Its Cultural Contexts.* Switzerland: Harwood Academic Publishers, 1994.

Allen, Frederick Lewis. *Only Yesterday: An Informal History of the 1920s.* New York: Harper & Row, 1931.

Alperovitz, Gar. *The Decision to Use the Atomic Bomb.* New York: Vintage Books, 1996.

Ambrose, Stephen E. *Citizen Soldiers: The U.S. Army from the Normandy Beaches to the Bulge to the Surrender of Germany.* New York: Touchstone, 1998.

Asahina, Robert. *Just Americans: How Japanese Americans Won a War at Home and Abroad: The Story of the 100th Battalion/442nd Regimental Combat Team in World War II.* New York: Gotham Books, 2006.

Benedict, Ruth. *The Chrysanthemum and the Sword: Patterns of Japanese Culture.* New York: New American Library, 1946.

Berg, A. Scott. *Lindbergh.* New York: Berkley, 1999.

Bix, Herbert P. *Hirohito and the Making of Modern Japan.* New York: HarperCollins, 2001.

Bock, Dennis. *The Ash Garden.* New York: Knopf, 2001.

Borg, Dorothy. *Pearl Harbor as History: Japanese-American Relations, 1931–1941.* New York: Columbia University Press, 1973.

Bradley, James, with Ron Powers. *Flags of Our Fathers.* New York: Bantam Books, 2006.

Brendon, Piers. *The Dark Valley: A Panorama of the 1930s.* New York: Knopf, 2000.

Burton, Jeffery F., Mary M. Farrell, Florence B. Lord, and Richard W. Lord. *Confinement and Ethnicity: An Overview of World War II Japanese American Relocation Sites.* Seattle: University of Washington Press, 2002.

Cary, Otis. "Mr. Stimson's 'Pet City'—The Sparing of Kyoto, 1945: Atomic Bomb Targeting—Myths and Realities." Kyoto: Amherst House, Doshisha University, 1987.

———, ed. *From a Ruined Empire: Letters—Japan, China, Korea 1945–46.* Tokyo and New York: Kodansha International, 1984.

Cook, Haruko Taya, and Theodore F. Cook. *Japan at War: An Oral History.* New York: New Press, 1992.

Crost, Lyn. *Honor by Fire: Japanese Americans at War in Europe and the Pacific.* Novato, CA: Presidio Press, 1994.

Daniels, Roger. *Concentration Camps USA: Japanese Americans and World War II.* New York: Holt, Rinehart & Winston, 1972.

———. *The Decision to Relocate the Japanese Americans.* New York: J. B. Lippincott, 1975.

———. *Prisoners Without Trial: Japanese Americans in World War II.* New York: Hill & Wang, 1993.

De Bary, William Theodore, ed. *Sources of Japanese Tradition.* Vol. 2. New York: Columbia University Press, 1958.

Doi, Sakuji. *Zusetsu Hiroshima-shi no Rekishi.* Nagoya: Kyōdō Shuppan, 2001.

"Dōin Gakuto." Hiroshima: Hiroshima Peace Memorial Museum.

Dower, John W. *Cultures of War: Pearl Harbor, Hiroshima, 9-11, Iraq.* New York: Norton, 2010.

————. *The Elements of Japanese Design*. New York: Weatherhill, 1971.

————. *Embracing Defeat: Japan in the Wake of World War II*. New York: Norton, 1999.

————. *Japan in War and Peace: Selected Essays*. New York: Free Press, 1993.

————. *War Without Mercy: Race & Power in the Pacific War*. New York: Pantheon Books, 1986.

Egan, Timothy. *The Good Rain: Across Time and Terrain in the Pacific Northwest*. New York: Vintage Departures Edition, 1991.

————. *The Worst Hard Time: the Untold Story of Those Who Survived the Great American Dust Bowl*. New York: Houghton Mifflin, 2006.

Falk, Stanley L., and Warren M. Tsuneishi, eds. *MIS in the War Against Japan: Personal Experiences Related at the 1993 MIS Capital Reunion, "The Nisei Veteran: An American Patriot."* Washington, DC: Japanese American Veterans Association, 1995.

Flewelling, Stan. *Shirakawa: Stories from a Pacific Northwest Japanese American Community*. Auburn, WA: White River Valley Museum, 2002.

For Those Who Pray for Peace. Hiroshima: Hiroshima Jogakuin Alumni Association, 2005.

Gibney, Frank, ed. *Sensō: The Japanese Remember the Pacific War*. Armonk, NY: M. E. Sharpe, 2007.

Gilmore, Allison B. *You Can't Fight Tanks with Bayonets*. Lincoln: University of Nebraska Press, 1998.

Girdner, Audrie, and Anne Loftus. *The Great Betrayal: The Evacuation of the Japanese-Americans During World War II*. New York: Macmillan, 1970.

Goldstein, Donald M., Katherine V. Dillon, and J. Michael Wenger. *Rain of Ruin: A Photographic History of Hiroshima and Nagasaki*. Washington, DC: Brassey's, 1995.

Goodwin, Doris Kearns. *No Ordinary Time: Franklin & Eleanor Roosevelt: The Home Front in World War II*. New York: Simon & Schuster, 1994.

Gorfinkel, Claire, ed. *The Evacuation Diary of Hatsuye Egami*. Pasadena, CA: Intentional Productions, 1996.

Harrington, Joseph D. *Yankee Samurai: The Secret Role of Nisei in America's Pacific Victory*. Detroit: Pettigrew, 1979.

Henry, Mark R. *The US Army in World War II (1): The Pacific*. Oxford: Osprey, 2000.

Hachiya, Michihiko. *Hiroshima Diary: The Journal of a Japanese Physician, August 6–September 30, 1945*. Trans. and ed. Warner Wells. Chapel Hill: University of North Carolina Press, 1995.

Hein, Laura, and Mark Selden. *Living with the Bomb: American and Japanese Cultural Conflicts in the Nuclear Age*. Armonk, NY: M. E. Sharpe, 1997.

Hersey, John. *Hiroshima*. New York: Vintage Books, 1989.

Hillen, Ernest. *The Way of a Boy*. Toronto: Viking, 1993.

Hiroshima and Nagasaki: The Atomic Bombings as Seen Through Photos and Artwork: The True Face of the Bombings. Tokyo: Nihon Tosho Center, 1993.

Hiroshima City Museum of History and Traditional Crafts. *Taishō Jidai no Hiroshima.* Hiroshima: Hiroshima City Museum of History and Traditional Crafts, 2007.

Hiroshima Genbaku Sensai Shi I and II. Hiroshima: Hiroshima City Hall, 1971.

Hiroshima Hondōri Shōtengai no Ayumi. Hiroshima: Hiroshima Hondōri Shōtengai Shinkō Kumiai, 2000.

Hiroshima Peace Memorial Museum. *The Spirit of Hiroshima.* Hiroshima: Hiroshima Peace Memorial Museum, 1999.

Hiroshima-ken Shi: Kindai Gendai Shiryō. Hiroshima: Hiroshima-ken, 1973.

Hondo Kessen Jumbi: Kyūshū no Bōei. Tokyo: Bōeichō Bōei Kenshūsho Senshishitsu, 1972.

Hornfischer, James D. *The Last Stand of the Tin Can Sailors: The Extraordinary World War II Story of the U.S. Navy's Finest Hour.* New York: Bantam Dell, 2004.

Hough, Frank O., and John A. Crown. *The Campaign on New Britain.* Nashville, TN: Battery Press, 1992.

Houston, Jean Wakatsuki, and James D. Houston. *Farewell to Manzanar.* New York: Laurel-Leaf, 2006.

Ibuse, Masaji. *Black Rain.* Trans. John Bester. New York: Kodansha USA, 2012.

Ichihashi, Yamato. *Japanese in the United States.* Palo Alto: Stanford University Press, 1932.

Ichinokuchi, Tad. *John Aiso and the M.I.S.: Japanese-American Soldiers in the Military Intelligence Service, World War II.* Los Angeles: Military Intelligence Service Club of Southern California, 1988.

Ichioka, Yuji. *The Issei: The World of the First Generation Japanese Immigrants, 1885-1924.* New York: Free Press, 1988.

Ienaga, Saburō. *The Pacific War, 1931–1945.* New York: Pantheon Books, 1978.

Inada, Lawson Fusao. *Only What We Could Carry: The Japanese American Internment Experience.* Berkeley, CA: Heyday, 2000.

In Freedom's Cause: A Record of the Men of Hawaii Who Died in the Second World War. Honolulu: University of Hawaii Press, 1949.

Ishikawa, Eisei, and David L. Swain, trans. *Hiroshima and Nagasaki: The Physical, Medical, and Social Effects of the Atomic Bombings.* New York: Basic Books, 1981.

Ito, Kazuo. *Issei: A History of Japanese Immigrants in North America.* Trans. Shinichiro Nakamura and Jean S. Gerard. Seattle: Executive Committee for Publication c/o Japanese Community Service, 1973.

"Jūgo o Sasaeru Chikara to Natte: Josei to Sensō." Hiroshima: Hiroshima Peace Memorial Museum, 1998.

Kessler, Lauren. *Stubborn Twig: Three Generations in the Life of a Japanese American Family.* New York: Random House, 1993.

Kidston, Martin J. *From Poplar to Papua: Montana's 163rd Infantry Regiment in World War II.* Helena, MT: Farcountry Press, 2004.

"Kinokogumo no Shita ni Kodomotachi ga Ita." Hiroshima: Hiroshima Peace Memorial Museum, 1997.

Knaefler, Tomi Kaizawa. *Our House Divided: Seven Japanese American Families in World War II.* Honolulu: University of Hawaii Press, 1991.

Kono, Juliet S. *Anshū: Dark Sorrow.* Honolulu: Bamboo Ridge Press, 2010.

Lindbergh, Charles A. *The Wartime Journals of Charles A. Lindbergh.* New York: Harcourt Brace Jovanovich, 1970.

Little Tokyo Historical Society. *Los Angeles's Little Tokyo.* Charleston, SC: Arcadia, 2010.

MacEachin, Douglas J. *The Final Months of the War with Japan.* Washington, DC: Center for the Study of Intelligence, Central Intelligence Agency, 1998.

Mashbir, Sidney Forrester. *I Was an American Spy.* New York: Vantage Press, 1953.

Matsumae, Shigeyoshi. *The Second World War—A Tragedy for Japan: Plunge from High Government Official to Private Soldier on the Waterfront.* Tokyo: Tokai University Press, 1981.

McCullough, David. *Truman.* New York: Touchstone, 1992.

McNaughton, James C. "Nisei Linguists and New Perspectives on the Pacific War: Intelligence, Race, and Continuity." 1994 Conference of Army Historians.

———. *Nisei Linguists: Japanese Americans in the Military Intelligence Service during World War II.* Washington, DC: Department of the Army, 2006.

———. "Training Linguists for the Pacific War, 1941–42." Defense Language Institute, Foreign Language Center. Presidio of Monterey, CA, 1991.

Mears, Helen. *Year of the Wild Boar: An American Woman in Japan.* Westport, CT: Greenwood Press, 1973.

Military Intelligence Service Association of Northern California and the National Japanese American Historical Society. "The Pacific War and Peace: Americans of Japanese Ancestry in Military Intelligence Service, 1941–1952." San Francisco, 1991.

Military Intelligence Service Veterans Club of Hawaii. "Secret Valor: M.I.S. Personnel: World War II Pacific Theater." Honolulu: Military Intelligence Service Veterans of Hawaii, 2001.

Minear, Richard H., ed. and trans. *Hiroshima: Three Witnesses.* Princeton, NJ: Princeton University Press, 1990.

Moore, Ray, and Donald L. Robinson. *Partners for Democracy: Crafting the New Japanese State under MacArthur.* Oxford: Oxford University Press, 2002.

Morimatsu, Toshio. *Teikoku Rikugun Hensei Sōkan.* Tokyo: Fuyō Shobō, 1987.

Morison, Samuel Eliot. *The Two-Ocean War: A Short History of the United States Navy in the Second World War.* Boston: Little, Brown, 1963.

Morris, Ivan. *The Nobility of Failure: Tragic Heroes in the History of Japan.* Fukuoka, Japan: Kurodahan Press, 2013.

Murata, Alice. *Japanese Americans in Chicago.* Charleston, SC: Arcadia, 2002.

Myer, Dillon S. *Uprooted Americans: The Japanese Americans and the War Relocation Authority During World War II.* Tucson: University of Arizona Press, 1971.

Nakano, Mei. *Japanese American Women: Three Generations 1890–1990.* Sebastopol, CA: Mina Press, 1990.

Neiwert, David A. *Strawberry Days: How Internment Destroyed a Japanese American Community.* New York: Palgrave Macmillan, 2005.

New York Times. Hiroshima Plus 20. New York: Delacorte Press, 1965.

Nihon Gensuibaku Higaisha Dantai Kyōgikai. "Genbaku Shibotsusha ni kansuru Chūkan Hōkoku no Gaiyō." November 9, 1987.

Niiya, Brian, ed. *Japanese American History: An A-to-Z Reference from 1869 to the Present.* Los Angeles: Japanese American National Museum, 1993.

Nikkei Heritage. San Francisco: National Japanese American Historical Society, Fall 1991–Winter 2003.

Nishina Kinen Zaidan, ed. *Genshi Bakudan: Hiroshima • Nagasaki no Shashin to Kiroku.* Tokyo: Kōfūsha Shoten, 1973.

Nitobe, Inazo. *Bushido: The Soul of Japan.* Rutland, VT, and Tokyo: Charles E. Tuttle, 1969.

Norman, Michael, and Elizabeth M. Norman. *Tears in the Darkness: The Story of the Bataan Death March and Its Aftermath.* New York: Picador, 2009.

O'Donnell, Patrick K. *Into the Rising Sun: In Their Own Words, World War II's Pacific Veterans Reveal the Heart of Combat.* New York: Free Press, 2002.

Ohnuki-Tierney, Emiko. *Kamikaze, Cherry Blossoms, and Nationalisms: The Militarization of Aesthetics in Japanese History.* Chicago: University of Chicago Press, 2002.

Okihiro, Gary Y. *Common Ground:Reimagining American History.* Princeton: Princeton University Press, 2001.

———. *Whispered Silences: Japanese Americans and World War II.* Seattle: University of Washington Press, 1996.

Okuzumi, Yoshishige. *B-29 64 Toshi o Yaku.* Tokyo: Yōransha, 2006.

Onnatachi no Taiheiyō Sensō. Tokyo: Asahi Shimbunsha, 1996.

Otsuka, Julie. *The Buddha in the Attic*. New York: Knopf, 2011.

———. *When The Emperor Was Divine*. New York: Anchor Books, 2002.

Pacific War Research Society. *The Day Man Lost: Hiroshima, 6 August 1945*. New York: Kodansha America, 1981.

Perry, John Curtis. *Beneath the Eagle's Wings: Americans in Occupied Japan*. New York: Dodd, Mead, 1980.

Pitt, Leonard, and Dale Pitt. *Los Angeles A to Z: An Encyclopedia of the City and County*. Berkeley: University of California Press, 1997.

Port of Yokohama. Yokohama: Yokohama Maritime Museum, 2004.

Powell, James S. *Learning under Fire: The 112th Cavalry Regiment in World War II*. College Station: Texas A&M University Press, 2010.

Sasaki, R. A. *The Loom and Other Stories*. Saint Paul, MN: Graywolf Press, 1991.

Sato, Sanae. *Nihon no Kyakusen to Sono Jidai*. Tokyo: Jiji Tsūshinsha, 1993.

Seigel, Shizue. *In Good Conscience: Supporting Japanese Americans During the Internment*. San Mateo, CA: Kansha Project, 2006.

Senchū Sengo ni okeru Hiroshima-shi no Kokumin Gakkō Kyōiku. Hiroshima: Hiroshima-shi Taishoku Kōchōkai, 1999.

Sensō to Kurashi. Tokyo: Nihon Tosho Center, 2001.

Shashin de Miru Hiroshima Ano Koro. Hiroshima: Chūgoku Shimbun, 1977.

Shashinshū Genbaku o Mitsumeru: 1945 Hiroshima, Nagasaki. Hiroshima: Iwanami Shoten, 1981.

Shillony, Ben-Ami. *Politics and Culture in Wartime Japan*. New York: Oxford University Press, 1981.

Shinshū Hiroshima-shi Shi I and II. Hiroshima: Hiroshima City Hall, 1961.

Shishido, Kiyotaka. *Jap To Yobarete*. Tokyo: Ronsosha, 2005.

Shōwa Niman-nichi no Zenkiroku 7. Tokyo: Kodansha, 1989.

Sides, Hampton. *Ghost Soldiers: The Epic Account of World War II's Greatest Rescue Mission*. New York: Anchor Books, 2001.

Slesnick, Irwin L, and Carole E. Slesnick. *Kanji & Codes: Learning Japanese for World War II*. Bellingham, WA: Authors, 2006.

Smith, Robert Ross. *The Approach to the Philippines: The War in the Pacific*. Washington, DC: Center of Military History, 1984.

Smurthwaite, David. *The Pacific War Atlas: 1941–1945*. New York: Facts On File, 1995.

Sodei, Rinjirō. *Dear General MacArthur: Letters from the Japanese During the American Occupation*. Lanham, MD: Rowman & Littlefield, 2001.

Sodei, Rinjirō and John Junkerman. *Were We the Enemy? American Survivors of Hiroshima*. Boulder, CO: Westview Press, 1998.

Soga, Yasutaro. *Life Behind Barbed Wire: The World War II Internment Memoirs of a Hawai'i Issei.* Honolulu: University of Hawaii Press, 2008.

Sogi, Francis Y. *Riding the Kona Wind: Memoirs of a Japanese American.* New York: Cheshire Press, 2004.

Sone, Monica. *Nisei Daughter.* Seattle: University of Washington Press, 1979.

Straus, Ulrich. *The Anguish of Surrender: Japanese POWs of World War II.* Seattle: University of Washington Press, 2003.

Swift, David W. *First Class: Nisei Linguists in World War II: Origins of the Military Intelligence Service Language Program.* San Francisco: National Japanese American Historical Society, 2006.

Takaki, Ronald. *Strangers from a Different Shore: A History of Asian Americans.* Boston: Little, Brown, 1989.

Takami, David. *Divided Destiny: A History of Japanese Americans in Seattle.* Seattle: Wing Luke Asian Museum, 1998.

Takayama, Hitoshi, ed. *Hiroshima in Memorium.* Hiroshima: Yamabe Books, 1969.

Terkel, Studs. *"The Good War": An Oral History of World War II.* New York: New Press, 1984.

33rd Infantry Division: A Newsletter for WWI and WWII Veterans.

33rd Infantry Division Historical Committee. *The Golden Cross: A History of the 33rd Infantry Division in World War II.* Nashville, TN: Battery Press, 1948.

Thomson, James C., Jr., Peter Stanley, and John Curtis Perry. *Sentimental Imperialists: The American Experience in East Asia.* New York: Harper Torchbooks, 1985.

Tobin, James. *Ernie Pyle's War: America's Eyewitness to World War II.* New York: Free Press, 2006.

Toland, John. *The Rising Sun: The Decline and Fall of the Japanese Empire, 1936–1945.* New York: Modern Library, 2003.

Truman, Harry S. *Memoirs by Harry S. Truman.* New York: Doubleday, 1955.

Tsurumi, Kazuko. *Social Change and the Individual: Japan Before and After Defeat in World War II.* Princeton, NJ: Princeton University Press, 1970.

Tsurumi, Shunsuke. *An Intellectual History of Wartime Japan, 1931–1945.* London: KPI, 1986.

Uchida, Yoshiko. *Picture Bride.* Seattle: University of Washington Press, 1987.

University of Hawaii, Hawaii War Records Depository. *In Freedom's Cause: A Record of the Men of Hawaii Who Died in the Second World War.* Honolulu: University of Hawaii Press, 1949.

Vine, Josephine Emmons. *Auburn: A Look Down Main Street.* Auburn, WA: City of Auburn, 1990.

Walker, Stephen. *Shockwave: Countdown to Hiroshima.* New York: Harper Perennial, 2006.

Wallach, Ruth, Dace Taube, Claude Zachary, Linda McCann, and Curtis C. Roseman. *Los Angeles in World War II.* Charleston, SC: Arcadia, 2011.

Watanabe, Miyoko, ed. *Peace Ribbon Hiroshima: Witness of A-Bomb Survivors.* Hiroshima: Peace Ribbon, 1997.

Weglyn, Michi Nishiura. *Years of Infamy: The Untold Story of America's Concentration Camps.* Seattle: University of Washington Press, 1996.

Wilson, Robert A. and Bill Hosokawa. *East to America: A History of the Japanese in the United States.* New York: William Morrow, 1980.

Yamada, Michio. *Fune ni Miru Nihonjin Imin Shi.* Tokyo: Chūōkōronshinsha, 1998.

Yamasaki, Toyoko. *Two Homelands.* Honolulu: University of Hawaii Press, 2008.

Yoshioka, Masako M. "Terry Mizutari." *Puka-Puka Parade* 34, no. 3 (1980).

INDEX

About the author

About the book

Insights,
Interviews
& More . . .

Meet Pamela Rotner Sakamoto

PAMELA ROTNER SAKAMOTO is a historian. Fluent in Japanese, she lived in Kyoto and Tokyo for seventeen years. She works offsite as an expert consultant on Japan-related projects for the United States Holocaust Memorial Museum in Washington, D.C., and has taught in the University of Hawaii system. She teaches at Punahou School in Honolulu.

~

Q&A with Pamela Rotner Sakamoto

1. Why did you write this book as narrative nonfiction?

When I finished a dissertation and an academic book on a separate topic, I realized that while I was proud of my research, I had not accessed the heart of the story—the protagonists' emotions and motivations. With that particular episode, it was not possible because of how little remained of credible records and eyewitnesses. But I privately vowed that if I ever wrote another book, I wanted to conduct rigorous research, interview my subjects at length, and capture their reactions to small and large events. I was determined to write a fully fleshed, resonant story free of academic restraint.

When I met Harry Fukuhara, he was an esteemed retired colonel in the U.S. Army's Military Intelligence Service who had been decorated by both the Japanese government and the United States for his contribution to U.S.-Japan relations. Harry had reached a point where he wanted to take stock of his life. So had his siblings. I could not get their story out of my mind. *Midnight in Broad Daylight* is the book that I dreamed of writing.

2. What surprised you?

The more I dug, the richer the soil. Japanese and American journalists had interviewed Harry and his youngest brother Frank—a private assigned to a suicide squad in the Japanese Army during the war—for feature stories. But the articles traveled the same ground. When I began to research, I learned about a host of other fascinating figures, such as their irrepressible Aunt Kiyo, the founder of a venerable traditional sweet shop in Hiroshima, and their headstrong sister Mary, who had been interned with Harry at Gila River in Arizona. Each possessed a compelling story that added layers of depth to the family's bicultural existence. I never tired of learning more about them. ▶

3. What were some memorable occasions in unearthing this story?

Frank, my travel partner, and I were walking down the street to his family's former home in Hiroshima one day when a woman came running, calling his name. Her name was Masako, and she was his former neighbor who had moved back to the area after decades away. Frank and Harry's mother Kinu had doted upon Masako, treating her like a daughter. Kinu and Masako had spent a lot of time together during the war. In fact, Masako was with Kinu on the day that the atomic bomb exploded over Hiroshima. Masako recounted their steps that fateful morning and revealed many fascinating details.

Harry suspected that his brothers were in the Japanese Army because of their ages. While he was island-hopping across the Pacific as an interrogator with the U.S. Army, a Japanese POW recognized him in New Guinea. The encounter chilled Harry and made him wonder whether he might confront his brothers in battle. Harry and the POW had been neighbors and enemies in Hiroshima. They had fought, and Harry suspected that this man—named Matsuura—disliked him because he was Japanese American. But it was precisely because they had exchanged blows that Matsuura recognized Harry at the front. "Fighting brings intimacy," Matsuura told me in an interview in Hiroshima. This comment made me pause. Perhaps Matsuura was correct. Although Harry feared that his family had perished in the bomb, meeting Matsuura made him wonder whether the unlikely was possible. He decided to go find his family in Hiroshima.

4. What would you like readers to take away?

On one level, I hope that readers simply find this an engrossing story about a family that could be any ethnicity with immigrant parents from any given nation. I hope that they connect with the story and their own heritage. Moreover, what happened during World War II could just as easily happen now between siblings with one in the United States and others in a trouble spot elsewhere.

On another level, I hope that the book is a cautionary tale about the perils and costs of wartime hysteria, racial prejudice, and unjust internment. In 2014, the late Supreme Court Justice Antonin Scalia addressed students at the University of Hawaii's law school. "In times of war, the laws fall silent," he said in Latin. He predicted that an internment could happen again in the wake of heightened tensions. After 9/11, the Japanese American community had been the first to support Muslim Americans as they faced suspicion and a rash of hate crimes. We live in tense times. Our nation has to confront its history, including its blemishes, and stay vigilant to prevent miscarriages of justice from occurring again.

At the same time, we should celebrate the occasions that we get it right. Approximately 6,000 Japanese Americans served in the Military Intelligence Service during the war and the Occupation of Japan. They made invaluable contributions to one of the strongest alliances today. Yet Japanese Americans living in Japan during the war—like Harry's brothers—had to suppress their background and blend in for fear of reprisals. Japan failed to utilize their strengths. The United States benefited. ~

How Long? That Long?

I have been researching and writing this story for approximately seventeen years. It is hard, almost embarrassing, to put that number on paper. Yet, the years haven't felt interminable. As I look back, several defined periods have comprised the journey.

The book concerns the horror of modern war and its devastating impact on one family. The first time that the Fukuhara siblings revisited the war together was the mid-1990s, half a century after the atomic bomb. When I began this project several years later, they had not discussed it further. They approached anguished events gingerly, holding back their true feelings so as not to offend one another, changing the topic, leaving sentences vague and unfinished. I had interviewed Jewish refugees who had fled the Holocaust and understood their reticence. Survivors of traumatic events need time to take stock of their lives and put their thoughts in order.

I was, after all, asking the Fukuharas to reveal their innermost feelings about war, internment, divided loyalties, and losses from the atomic bomb. People who have led private lives do not spill their thoughts on command. This applied especially to the only sister Mary, who had never recovered from what she perceived as abandonment by her mother when she was a child. As Mary neared the end of her life, her unresolved relationship with her mother consumed her. Her brother Harry and I planned to fly to Los Angeles in mid-September 2001 to meet Mary. In the uncertain days after 9/11, we delayed our trip. Postponing our interview was better, Mary's daughter assured us, as Mary was too distressed to meet a stranger.

A year and a half later, we tried again when Mary was ready to talk. She expressed more of her irrepressible spirit in two interviews than others would in multiple chats over years.

Another challenge was checking the family members' individual accounts of lives spent in two countries. Would the details come to light in Japan or the United States? I researched the story in both places and in two languages. As the narrative emerged, I needed to focus on certain events. For example, I knew that the family's passage from Seattle to Yokohama in 1938 was a physical and emotional turning point, but I couldn't find much in American shipping records about their trip. One year, on my birthday, a friend, who is a curator at the Yokohama Maritime Museum, and I unearthed a 1938 daily shipping newspaper. A small article detailed the hailstorm that prevented the ship from docking on schedule and the sunrise that followed the day after. I had the means to craft a factual, heightened scene. Writers live for these discoveries in the midst of dogged research. Other valuable tidbits appeared in Washington, D.C.; Seattle; and Hiroshima.

Then there was the overarching narrative itself. At first, everyone I interviewed assumed that the book would be a biography of Harry, the family patriarch and a legend in Japanese and American military intelligence circles. I wrestled with the concept of military history and a biography until the story that inspired me took hold. The book would not be complete if it focused solely on Harry. I had to include the lives of his brothers, particularly his inseparable youngest sibling, Frank. Constructing the dual narrative was demanding, but, in the end, I believe, absolutely essential.

My personal circumstances required time. I researched this book for eight years while living in Tokyo, but I experienced an odd sensation. I was gradually losing my native English. No one else noticed, but the more fluent my Japanese became, the more ▶

How Long? That Long? *(continued)*

I strained to summon English. When I needed a synonym for the color blue, I would grope and come up with one or two. Although I was learning firsthand what the Fukuhara siblings experienced in Japan after growing up in America, this situation wouldn't do. When I moved back to the United States in 2007 and reimmersed myself in the rhythms of my home country and read voraciously in English, I regained the confidence and language to write with more prowess.

And last but not least, there was the struggle to bring this story to publication. A new work about an unknown, minority family by a first-time trade author faces formidable obstacles in the marketplace. For me, the Fukuhara saga was a great big American story, resonating with monumental history, rich with drama and redemption. I was willing to persevere and be patient. Happily, one undaunted agent and a singular editor grasped my reasons for persistence. Yes, years have passed, but the moment has turned out to be perfect. ～

About the book

Reading Group Guide
Discussion Questions for
Midnight in Broad Daylight

1. Harry feels content and secure in Auburn, Washington, in the late 1920s and 1930s. Do you think that his youth insulates him? If so, how? If not, what other factors come into play?
2. Kinu and Katsuji Fukuhara send Victor and Mary, their two older children, to Hiroshima to learn Japanese and traditional ways. This was a trend in the 1920s and 1930s that had unimagined consequences. What do you think of their decision and its repercussions?
3. Mary feels abandoned by her parents and stranded in Japan. She would never forgive her mother. How were her feelings understandable? Could her parents and aunt have mitigated her sense of loss and subsequent bitterness?
4. Do you believe that Kinu Fukuhara had no other choice than to move back to Japan in 1933 with her five U.S.-born children? What might you have done in similar circumstances?
5. What surprised you most about Hiroshima before Pearl Harbor?
6. Mary is desperate to return to the United States, to the point of staging a clumsy suicide attempt. What do you think of her preference for the United States over Japan and her determination to return to Seattle alone?
7. Upon his own return to Auburn, Harry is rebuffed by his friends. Were you surprised by his reception in 1938, three years before Pearl Harbor?
8. How does Harry's life on the West Coast in the late 1930s and early 1940s mirror his father's immigrant experience?
9. Frank, Harry's youngest and closest brother, encounters difficulties of his own at his prestigious middle school in Hiroshima. What did you find interesting about his education and environment? ▶

10. Aunt Kiyo was an imperious, magnetic presence in the family's life. Can you conjure her elegant, dynamic world and sense its gradual crumbling?

11. When the attack on Pearl Harbor occurred, Harry was fired on the spot by an employer whom he had regarded as friendly. Can you envision a similar scenario today?

12. The ethnic Japanese population is interned under the guise of national security. How easily could a similar situation occur today?

13. Harry and Mary lose contact with their mother and brothers in Hiroshima several months after Pearl Harbor. Was this for the best?

14. What did you learn about the internment experience that you have not heard before?

15. Harry decides to enlish in the Military Intelligence Service out of Gila River and leaves his sister and niece behind. Explore Harry's reasons to leave and consider whether it might have also been courageous for him to stay and act as the head of household for Mary and Jeanie.

16. On the surface, it may seem as if Kinu's and Frank's lives do not change as much as Mary's and Harry's, but their lives too possess drama. How would you describe their living situation as the war persists?

17. What are some of the Japanese qualities, social structures, or slogans that are both strengths and weaknesses? Why?

18. Harry island-hops throughout the Southwest Pacific. What intrigued you most about his journey?

19. Frank suppresses his American identity, yet still feels American at heart. Nevertheless, he is prepared to die for Japan with a bomb strapped to his back. Consider this seeming paradox.

20. What did you learn about the atomic bomb?

21. What did you think of the family's reunion?

22. As the author, I wanted to capture Victor, but there were few people who remembered him well. How would you describe this reticent young man and his abbreviated life?

23. I was always moved by Harry and Frank's unwavering bond. What were the most meaningful moments for you?

24. Harry re-enlists in the United States Army and ends up serving almost half a century, with much of the time in Japan. Do you find it intriguing that he subsequently spent so much time there by choice?
25. How did the family come to terms with the atomic bomb?
26. Jeanie described her mother Mary as an "enigma" to the end of her life. Do you believe that Harry was also enigmatic? What are some possible reasons?
27. This book is a work of narrative nonfiction, with a careful weaving of narrative and factual research. Did this approach work for you?
28. What are the take-away messages from a single family's life?
29. Do you believe that people change the course of history or does history change people?

Discover great authors, exclusive offers, and more at hc.com.